Scarlet Autumn

Jack the Ripper

Scarlet Autumn:
The Crimes & Seasons
of
JACK THE RIPPER

GIAN J. QUASAR

BRODWYN, MOOR & DOANE
PUBLISHERS
2013

Library of Congress Cataloguing-in-Publication Data

Quasar, Gian Julius

SCARLET AUTUMN:
The Crimes and Seasons of Jack the Ripper

1. The Whitechapel Murders. 2. Jack the Ripper. 3. London 1888 -1891.
Bibliography. I. Title.

ISBN 978-0-9888505-4-5

Contents

Prologue

1	Wormwood Gutter	15
2	Darkness by Gaslight	27
3	Silence of the Wolves	39
4	Riddler at the Scene	57
5	Leather Apron	75
6	Gory Details	84
7	Uproar	114
8	Night Stalker	126
9	October Terror	155
10	From Hell	201
11	November Echo	217
12	Pall Mall	255
13	A Clockwork in Crimson	304
14	Foolscap	316
15	Hypothesis non Fingo	344
16	The Identity Game	368

Bibliography

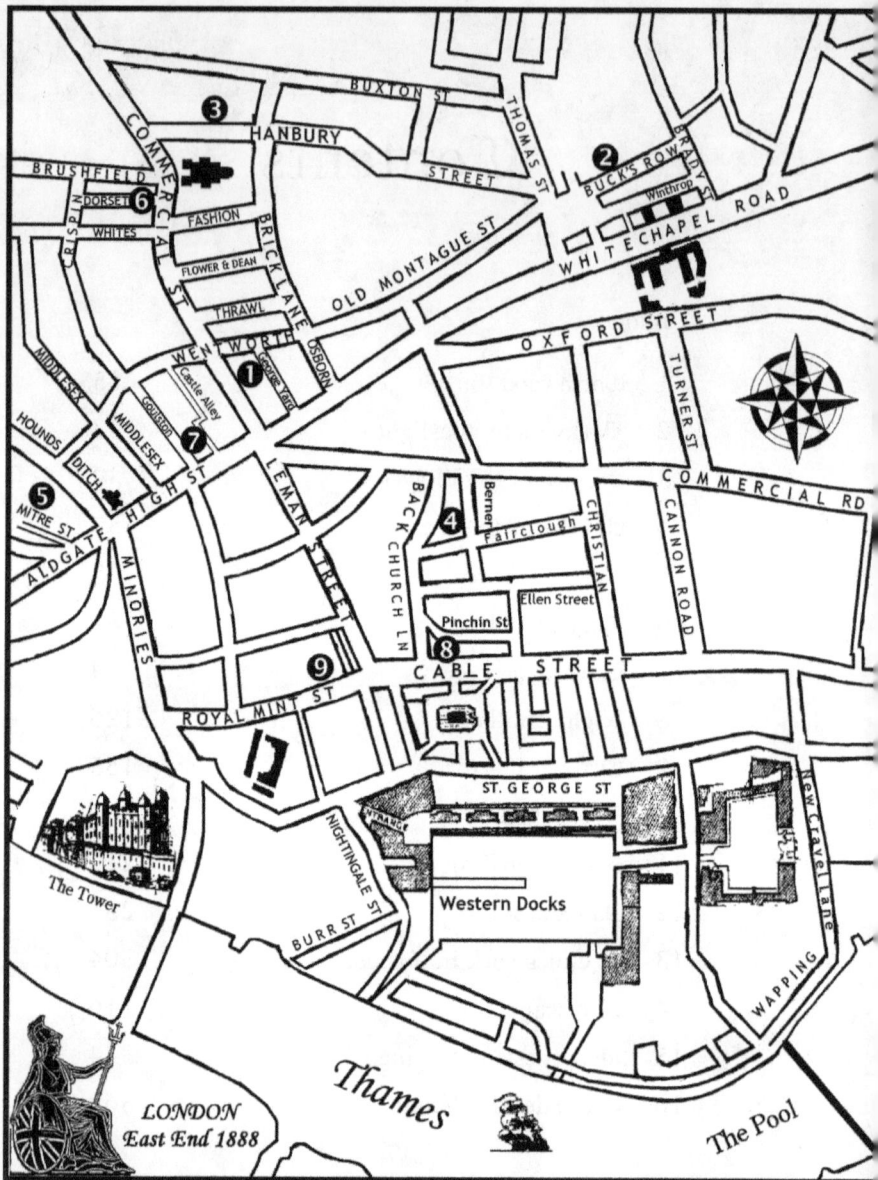

London's East End in 1888-1891— Whitechapel and Spitalfields

1 — Martha Tabram Aug. 7
2 — Polly Nichols Aug. 31
3 — Annie Chapman Sept. 8
4 — Liz Stride Sept. 30
5 — Catherine Eddowes Sept. 30
6 — Mary Kelly Nov. 9
7 — Alice M'Kenzie July 17 (1889)
8 — Pinchin St. Torso Sept. 10 (1889)
9 — Francis Coles Feb. 13 (1891)

Not graphed: Whitehall Torso; Thames Torso; Rose Mylett.

Prologue

ogic is. It is the rational expression of thought. It is the line we draw between the dots of known facts. With it we can create substance from a void, reason from abyss, cohesion from a fractured tablet. Facts are everything and yet not half enough. We need logic to use them, manipulate them, to put them in place and fill in the gaps.

Yet logic is so taken for granted that we seldom stop to define it. Natural logic is easily (and academically) defined as conclusionary statements that are supported by the reasons the person gives. Logical behavior is appropriate response to the stimulus, motive or known facts. Logic is not a fact. Nor is it moral probity or truth. It is simply a criterion.

As seemingly simple as this seems, the process of logic is also so natural that we are unaware of its complexity. Our mind works so quickly that we do not consciously define the steps it takes in coming to an hypothesis and from there to a conclusion. We first observe. Then we classify. Then we infer. Then we interpret. Not so surprisingly these are the first four skills in the Ten Process Skills of Scientific Inquiry which together constitute Scientific Method. The full monty is: Observe; Classify; Infer; Interpret; Measure; Predict; Questions; Hypotheses; Experiment; Model Building (in other words, reproducing an effect).

Somewhat surprising to many people is the fact that the first 9 of these 10 points are engaged in every day by everybody about their daily affairs. Immediately after we Interpret, we Measure or determine proportion of an object or speed. With this we immediately Predict outcome. Questions lead us onward to Hypotheses, and from there we Experiment to test their viability. Even in just the arranging of furniture, the mind consistently follows this pattern. From this unflagging sequence, we can see why Einstein referred to science as "merely the refinement of everyday thinking."

Is it somewhat encouraging or discouraging to discover that all we do is based on logic and that science is merely the tool of refinement? I say this, perhaps unforgivably tongue-in-cheek, because we have elevated the very concepts without being aware of how inscrutably they guide and temper our everyday approach to life's problems and solutions. These 10 skills are the mandatory steps of science *only* because they are the natural steps of a thinking and inquiring mind.

The criminal mind cannot be an exception to this rule. Criminals act logically, you see. It is a fallacy of thought that evil people must be stupid or demented, compulsive or impulsive. Very evil people can be very calculating. And even if they aren't, they are still logical, for their actions are always guided by their motives. If we unravel a criminal's goal, we can understand the motives and second-guess his actions. As crazed as a killer may be, there will be a "method to his madness."

For unsolved crimes logic therefore becomes a keen surgical tool by which to connect facts and extract truth. What is essential is that we have undisputed facts. We do not need the marketing lingo of hand soaps— "new and improved" facts. We need original facts. Even after over 100 years, as in the subject of this book, we are on much better ground than most think.

'The Whitechapel Murders' in London's East End in the frightening fall of 1888 are the most documented series of unsolved murders in history for a reason. They were not just gory butcheries of London prostitutes. The victims were dissected for parts. Coroner inquests laboriously tried to understand it all. Newspapers followed every clue. Thanks to the powerful information highway that exists today, the massive amount of original documentation can be resurrected and accessed relatively easily. With this we can rebuild the long-changed East End in our minds and recreate the crime scenes accurately and, logically, backwork the actions of the perpetrator more securely than ever before. The result is to restore the details of the crimes, and as Holmes said— "the devil is in the details."

Contemporarily the murders were attributed to a phantom killer given form only by the moniker "Jack the Ripper." In substance, that's about the only bit of original information that has come down to us unaltered by economic rehash, pulp vignettes, and theorizing skewed to support pet suspects. It is not even accurate to say that the Ripper murders have been chronicled let alone investigated. Many writers have been content to recite generalities as a platform before introducing their suspect, crediting to him various bloodlust, sexual, conspiracy or ritual black magic motives, but none of this has been inspired by an examination of the actual crime scenes or analysis of the disturbing sequence of events. In consequence, one of the biggest mistakes perpetuated to the present has been to promote that the Ripper was after uteri. In fact, he was not. Rehash after rehash has always begun from this premise. By this mote, the actual pattern of the killer that autumn of fear has been obscured and therewith his motives and the clues to his identity. It is a true statement that the greatest hindrance to solving the 'Whitechapel Murders' has been their own popularity.

Sensationalism began almost immediately due to the unbelievable circumstances of the crimes. But the sensationalism was of the worst kind. It wasn't of the murder scenes, or even an exaggerated flare about the mystery. The sensationalism centered on the suspect. Theories were governed by politics and social position. To the poor, the Ripper was a West End topper haughtily preying on the righteous hides of the downtrodden. To the West End, the Ripper was an East End lout with a vendetta against whores.

Yet truth, as always, seems to be in between. The killer was actually of clerkly appearance, dark, foreign, only about 5 foot 7 inches, stocky, a very calm fellow, soft spoken, of some education and even more inclination to put on airs. Upon this he hung an apropos veneer— dark, bland cut-away suit, sometimes a long overcoat, and the misplaced gentility of a country gentleman's deerstalker hat.

This last fact is remarkable, for the bloke must have

looked as though he had eloped from a bird-watching tour in the forest. Though at the pinnacle of his bloody career there must have been a bobby behind every culvert, none ever saw such a noticeable apparition strolling along. A blow on a police whistle would bring plainclothes detectives out of the woodwork within minutes after a gutted corpse was found. Still there was no sign of this uncouth villain in his gauche headgear.

One would imagine that a fiend who comically looked like some misplaced member of the Audubon Society would be an image not easily forgotten. But this was a socially tumultuous time, and it just seemed that there was no middle ground between topper and lout. And the truth is the Ripper was seen only twice in person, and this very briefly and only before the crimes. The great metropolis was sent reeling into a panic by the one sure image it had— his bold modus operandi. The very first book written on the Ripper killings captured the grisly but true mystique. It was published in December 1888 while the autumn terror and public interest was at its zenith— and leave it to an American to have been first. In *Leather Apron: The Horrors of Whitechapel*, the author Sam'l E. Hudson wrote:

> He defied the entire population of the East End, every soul of whom was detective for the time being. He paid no heed to the swarm of Scotland Yard's sleuth hounds, or the thousands of "bobbies" who patrolled the streets of London. He plied his knife right under their eye. He committed atrocities that sickened the soul. He left his dead, with bodies still warm, lying on the sidewalks, the yards of houses and in darkened alleys. People would pass certain spots and in a moment or two thereafter the corpse of a woman would be found there, with the body scientifically mutilated, and the murderer—gone.

It is not the gruesome scene of the murders— abdomens flayed wide, putrid stench of sliced bowels, the sweet/sour smell of coagulating blood, bulged eyes and throats torn open—that gave him his reputation and keeps it alive today; nor has this inspired so many to try and unravel these unsolved series of riddles. It is skillful execution at carefully planned public murder, not the number of victims or the gore that sets the Ripper apart both before and after.

Ever since then we have only contributed to the old extremes. The finesse of his crimes has given us the most interesting image— the archetypical urbane villain. He became a Simon Pure or a mad doctor. Over the last 125 years we have romanticized this image with all the trappings of a good Halloween haunted house. We framed him in the black silhouette of a Victorian gentleman, replete with top hat and elegant cape and mahogany walking stick. He is the quintessential stalker: innocent veneer hiding diabolical intent. He is the shadow against a brick wall, a hazy figure in a deep fog, his methodical footsteps punctuated by the fog horns of the Thames or the chimes of Big Ben.

Modern criminal profiling has been employed to try and draw at least a psychological profile of the Ripper. The synthesis of this process has only swung the pendulum in the extreme opposite direction and endorsed the Ripper as merely being that low class impulsive sexual killer. To quote Charlie Chan: "Any powder that kills flea is good powder." But all too often profiling has proven to be nothing but "scientific" stereotyping. And truth be known, this profile hasn't been based on the uncouth, stocky man and the context and details of his crimes. The comparatives used were 1960s and '70s sexual revolution maniacs and the dossier 100 years of folklore.

Both extremes have always done an injustice to the actual character of the Ripper. The topper image merely misleads us, but the image of the gutter villain is a false explanation. It tells us he killed for his own perverse thrills and that in his poverty he had no choice but to kill on the streets. This erases one of his quirks and eclipses his ingenuity. His quirky appearance didn't make him a toad on white rice like the topper image, but with that deerstalker he should have been readily identifiable in the lower class East End. This makes his success at anonymity all the more the product of careful planning. It is safe to say his character was eccentric and premeditative. His unrelenting drive to carry out his murders of worthless dregs even in the face of incredible odds shows how confident he was. The little fellow in the deerstalker hat hunted his game and murder for the sake of murder was not the ultimate motive.

It is the image of an unstoppable fiend which created that Gothic autumn. The Ripper started in late summer. Every day the nights fell sooner, the dread of encountering him became greater. Foggy dark nights were animated only by footsteps approaching and fading away. Incandescent orbs hovered over the cobblestones from distant gaslights, cottony and soft in the clutches of fog. Any unexpected sound sent a chill up the spine. Rushing along the streets, people stopped to wait for the solemn chimes of Big Ben to stop tolling so they could listen again for footsteps in the mist. Women secretly armed themselves. Everybody bolted their doors and windows.

The Ripper no doubt intended to baffle the police and all who read of his crimes, but his motive even for this is up to debate. Did he do so to cover his ultimate motive? He could have killed them in parks or indoors, but he chose streets, courts and backyards. When he saw that he could create chaos, he tried even harder to plunge the greatest capitol in the world into terror and intrigue. In this he succeeded. His murder scenes grew more gruesome, he more and more gave the appearance of being a maniac, but he still took the desired organ with precision. His care is seen in his success. He left the scene without trace— not a drop of a trail of blood, not a bloody shoeprint, not an accidental step into the pools of sticky blood despite the blinding darkness. He inspired debates of the supernatural and fears of an unstoppable predator who could move through locked doors. He coveted his ghost-like anonymity. . .And as far as history is concerned he walked away clean. To this day no one is sure of the identity of Jack the Ripper. Sadly, no one even remembers he's the clerkly little guy in the gauche deerstalker hat.

The purpose of this volume is to let the crimes and seasons of Jack the Ripper speak for themselves. It is to be a conduit by which we go back in time and vividly relive two years in Whitechapel and hopefully thereby catch a glimpse of the "shabby genteel" man with the pleasant albeit eccentric veneer and diabolical motive. He left many clues, most of which were not picked up on by the bland minds of Victorian detectives. He followed several risky patterns, and yet ably hid subtle mistakes, mistakes that he no doubt felt were far more revealing than his pattern. Scotland Yard had stereotypes and impressions that only a sexual maniac did these things. More than anything this caused them to innocently limit their scope of suspects and overlook evidence on the type of man that was at work and his ultimate goal. They didn't see him try to opportunistically exploit his crime spree, nor did they see the unoriginality in his attempt. I intend to fully resurrect the clerkly fellow through his crimes and bring him to the fore of theorizing yet again.

Without a doubt, the Ripper was the furthest thing from a homicidal maniac. I intend to minutely bring forward every clue at the collective crime scenes to show that he did, in fact, remain calm and unwavering from his purpose; that any variation he made was based on circumstances and the necessity to hide clues that the newspapers had picked upon from a previous murder. The newspapers rightly condemned him as a monomaniac— a person who obsesses on perfecting one thing, one object, one task.

I am very well aware that many modern scholars or "Ripperologists" have attributed only 5 victims to the Ripper during a single autumn of terror in 1888. But that was not a contemporary consensus. We must forget what we think today. We must go back and we must relive. We must walk the streets. We must examine the crime scenes. We will sit at the inquests and hear the gory details. We must forget the overlay of 125 years of theorizing and impressions. For over 2 years there were 12 murders, all prostitutes, and then they stopped. The Ripper's ominous reputation hung over Whitechapel like a gray, vapid wraith each time one was reported. To this day the aura has never died. It is not hype and hyperbole that keep it alive. The circumstances truly baffled a city and inducted police into the realities of modern barbarity. For cunning, even to this day, they have never been surpassed.

Truth lies in the body context. Therefore the reader must go back in time. Only from all the contemporary evidence can we classify this killer and begin to understand why these series of murders captured the imagination of the world and why their nameless perpetrator remains identified even to this day only as Jack the Ripper.

London — the year of Grace 1888

1

WORMWOOD GUTTER

ON THE LATE night of August 30, 1888, Whitechapel was drenched in heavy rainfall. Thunder rumbled. Then there was a slap, a crackle. A searing jagged streak of white lightening slashed the dark gray heavens. It briefly illuminated the prickly forest of chimneys and stovepipes daubing the spired skyline of old London with black puffs of smoke. The scene is worthy of an old black and white etching, bloodless, ominous and colorless. . .save for the glowing pink bloodstaining the ominous sky. It was not the beauty of dusk. Two dock fires on the nearby Thames belched up dark plumes. Flames licked about wildly as they consumed more wood. Their brimstone colors pulsed off the bloated cheeks of the swollen clouds and caused them to throb with pain. The reflections thus were not those of warmth but of hellish torment.

The smell of scorched tar and aged wood coursed through Whitechapel like a boney finger. Down each dark lane it crept. Over the dilapidated tile roofs it slithered. Past the ruckus of late night pubs it crawled. Even in the heavy rain the smell of the docks was noticeable. It didn't have to contend with the putrid smell of the squalid district. Rain had settled that. Horse urine didn't rise from the dark cobblestones. Decaying rubbish had its sour smell doused. The smell of slaughterhouses and dead fish is gone.

Whitechapel was a gangrenous wound in old London. It

was ancient and utilitarian and as such it became both the city's ghetto and, incongruously, the cusp of modernity. Where else to build the ugly new factories and workhouses? What other place then would become the destination of laborers throughout the kingdom? In this age of steam it was also the gateway of immigration and commerce from the nearby and sprawling docks. Its roots were frightfully English, but the branches were foreign— Germans, Poles, Russians, Jews, crowded the district. Hawking was exuberant and interactive. For the poorer and itinerant, it took the place of trade. The streets were lined by booths. Butchers set up in certain rows; so did weavers, importers, tailors, vegetable merchants. Thousands of sailors and dozens of foreign languages added daily to the exotic melting pot that foreign immigration had made the district. Egress and regress, the world tread Whitechapel.

Its architecture fit this incongruous mixture. Jacobean gables, Georgian galleries and Victorian utilitarian brick barracks formed an interesting mélange of neglected progress and discard. Modernity added those ghastly workhouses, sweatshops and smokestacks. During the day a cloud of coal dust hung over the place. The smoke of furnaces, stoves, open-air fires and grease pits rose up. Mixed with the coal, a black plaster was slowly forming on the buildings.

Storms could not altogether clean Whitechapel. Storms past had left their mark in the soot. The coal dust was streaked by water run-off. The bloodless white pulses of lightning revealed the buildings weeping mournfully from window sills and over ledges. The moody haunts morphed into skulls in the witching light— their windows gaunt, sunken eye sockets, their form vapid and starved. Odd and malevolent shadows grasped out from under ledges and eaves before dissolving back into the charcoal gray mist when the pulse faded.

Lightning bursts revealed a different scene on the broad streets. Stately Victorian institutions gleamed for a second as austere beacons of order, then faded to malevolent and, sadly, indifferent Gothic silhouettes. Huddled about their shoulders were middleclass businesses, clinging to the ostentation of the high streets.

Whitechapel High Street during the day. At night, even late night, there was still a carriage clopping along, people milling, and police constables walking their beats.

But all this was to some extent merely the whitewash on the tomb. Certain places the pulses of lightning shed no beam. Behind the broad streets lay a veritable maze of pestilential narrow byways and crisscrossing lanes. Alleys were chiseled out of bricks the color of old dried blood. Labyrinths snaked about between tenement houses, warehouses, the back walls of pubs, stables, slaughterhouses, factories, tobacconists, and sundry shops. Broken windows were closed and boarded with makeshift wood shutters. Lanes dead-ended at brick walls or at tall wood gates. Sometimes they opened up into small squares devoid of any light. Dank passageways went through buildings— echoing promenades that went from claustrophobic courtyards to dismal streets. The agriculture here was one of whitewashed poverty; each building stained by death, by crying, hungry babies, and crammed with laborers paying their nightly wages. It was dirty not with life-enriching soil but with the residue of the Industrial Revolution.

Tens of thousands were being born to this world. They became the seagulls that feed off the garbage of a ship's wake and they became every form of infusoria in stagnation. London was the world of Lazarus. Thousands in the East End were under the beautiful white tablecloth of the West End waiting for the scraps to fall from the table. . .or so many felt.

The East End was naturally the home of many radical ideas and "left" leaning news rags. Foreigners —usually Jews— were suspected of some radical (i.e. socialist) subversion. Irish Fenian terrorists had hideouts in the district, and Okhrana, Russia's secret police, believed the area was a hive of anti-Czarist sympathizers.

A dreary back lane in Whitechapel. . .Cold, dank, artless and poor. Brick, whitewashed brick, coal stained brick, Spartan, dark. . .London's utilitarian underbelly 1888.

The pestilential conditions and the grueling tyranny of the sweatshops were certainly the ideal breeding ground for desperate ideas and actions. But it was the grim absence of beauty that accentuated the attitude of despair and with this the stimulus for reform. The response, however, was often ill-thought and the solution a cause of greater problems. The Victorians didn't like the Georgian plaster whitewash and great varnished beams and galleries, peaked and gabled roofs and tall chimneys. Brick fit the new industrial age. In the

Examples of Dickensian rookeries razed in the 1880s. Rookeries got their name from the style of architecture, which looked off kilter and like so many birdhouses made by the rooks or ravens.

1880s they started destroying the world of Oliver Twist. The rookeries of central London had been razed, and Whitechapel soon flooded with the displaced poor.

Within this tomb behind the whitewash, even on a stormy night like this, night trade of one sort or another festered.

Smugglers crept along. Blackmail gangs and pickpocket clubs skulked about. Scraping of steal signaled knife fights in alleys. Robberies and fights abounded. It was a boiling ghetto of contention. Shouts of "Help, Murder!" were common and meant little.

By the 1880s Whitechapel also became the destination for any who wanted to cheaply experience the forbidden vices. Prostitution was the main illicit profession for women. It thrived in corners. Sidewalks and landings were cupid's dirty bed; shadows were the sheets. The blackness of alleys was a doorway. They yawned with the smell of a filthy proposal. Into them led prostitutes their lover for the hour. The furniture of their parlor of love was dust bins, rubbish cans or the back of a parked wagon. The language of love was mixed with the splatting sound of horse dung. Gutters coursed with urine, the gentle brook of this wormwood Eden. Its flora was wilted cabbage, bones, soggy bread crust, putrid fish entrails, dead birds; and its fauna was maggots.

Gaslights added little light or color except to reveal brief snapshots of forlorn melancholia. These were set few and far between on a street or bolted into a bland wall in a dismal alley. They teemed with moths and every other flying vermin: a living dust cloud deprived of its carrion in the gutter by this night's rain. In the wash of these amber cottony orbs, brick took on a rust color, dead, mottled, decaying; cobblestones: the gray paleness of death.

The gloomy netherworld behind the high streets *was* Whitechapel at night. It was a sewer, its narrow lanes the bowels into which passed the dregs of the world and in which festered the urban East End poor of the greatest city on Earth.

The rain was now a heavy curtain. Runoff gulped in down-pipes and wept over the top of buildings. The old weathered sidewalks were pelted with the heavy drops and dowsing streams. The storm had made Whitechapel a moody haunt of muffled pub sounds seguing in and out behind the loud clopping of passing horse hoofs and clumping wagon wheels.

Foot traffic was pretty slim. At 11 p.m. one of the local drabs, Polly Nichols, was walking down the main thoroughfare of Whitechapel Road. She was a dark figure, with a dark complexion, some of it grime. Upon this the bland colors of Victorian sobriety and poverty matched well. She wore a black wicker bonnet trimmed with black velvet. It was a bit nicer than most, but not flashy. Her dress was brown and over this she had a woman's ulster, with its own little cape over the shoulder. For a woman it tied around the neck and had large buttons. It was reddish brown, the same color as this rusty, corroded community.

Polly was a small woman, about 45 years old, but she had the good fortune to look about 10 years younger. That still made prostitution viable, especially in Whitechapel. . .and on a dark and stormy night. She had lost up to 5 front teeth, so that she wasn't a raving beauty. But she had another huge plus. She was more cleanly where it counted than the average drab.

She wasn't on her way home this night, for she really had none. Her lodgings were on Thrawl Street, a claustrophobic brick and stone tunnel worthy of Dickensian plaintive moans and a charcoal pencil's morbid strokes. It was a "dosshouse," where you could pay nightly and share a room with perhaps 16 others. She was, truly, a citizen of the street and a person of the night. There was nothing for her at Thrawl Street yet anyway. No money in sleep.

Polly's type of prostitute wasn't that of the professional houses, where buxom young call girls flattered generous gents. There were no madams organizing the trade of middle-aged scullery wenches winking over toothless smiles. This kind of prostitution was self-employment. They did not profit; they made a living, a very meager one. . .And this night Polly probably wasn't too successful in the heavy rains. Where indeed would a successful prostitute take a chap on a night like this? The streets were too filthy to lie down on, and it was simply too stormy. A bloke needed a few pints in him to get up the gumption on a night like this.

For Whitechapel the night was still young. The Frying Pan Pub was a jumble with folks enjoying their night indoors. It was at Brick Lane and Thrawl Street, so that Polly was familiar with all the nearby places she could take any willing and paying lad. It was a Thursday night and the cattle boats had come into the Thames from all over England and the continent. There were many potential customers waiting.

The dosshouse price for a bed was 3 pence, the price of a customer. Unfortunately, for Polly it was also the price of a good stout gin, which had proven to be mother's milk to her. Perhaps she was successful at the Frying Pan, but when she went back to her Thrawl Street lodging around 1:20 a.m., now Friday August 31, she was dead broke. She was stopped in the kitchen by the deputy-in-charge. She was told to hop it.

"Never mind," she replied in her heavy lower-class accent. "I'll soon get me doss money. See what a jolly bonnet I've got now."

Prostitution wasn't openly admitted. Thus she might have been implying she intended to pawn it. But Polly had other avenues in mind. Off she went, with a confident flourish.

At 2:30 a.m. Emily Holland, one of her former dossmates, is at the corner of Whitechapel Road and Osborn Street. She had been watching the Shadwell Dock fire. The glow on the horizon was of a dim sunset as the last embers of the fire smoldered toward the tempestuous gray heavens. The tops of what remained of old Georgian inns and modern Victorian brick warehouses only vaguely glowed in reflection now. Blood-tinted shadows crawl toward Emily. Out of one of these, Polly slowly emerged into the cottony halo of the street gaslight, her jolly bonnet no worse for wear.

She was "very drunk and staggered against the wall," said Emily later.

"I've had me doss money three times today and spent it," complained Polly.

Emily Holland paid little attention to it. Polly frequently had a snoot full.

Confidence and compulsion must have inspired Polly to forsake her doss for a gullet of booze. Even now she was certain that she could get another doss down-payment. She spoke with Emily for about 7 to 8 minutes and then staggered off to find some bonnie bloke still about. "It won't be long before I'm back."

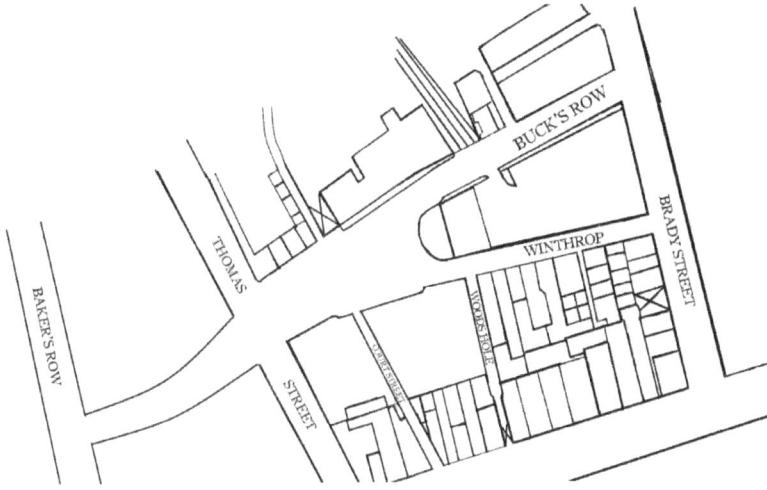

At 3:15 a.m. Constable John Neil is walking his beat in the gloomy, bleak morning. Buck's Row is one of his lanes. This part of it is narrow and dark. It is like a small appendix that funnels from a long, wide section of the street. There is a solitary sentinel, a spindly lamppost here where the narrow lane begins.

Neil passes and transposes into the charcoal darkness. The good constable's shoes echo up and down the narrow lane as he strolls on to Brady Street. The ugly brick walls of warehouses are streaked by his bright bull's eye lamp. It plays off their faded painted signs—Schneider's Cap Factory, Brown & Eagle Wool Warehouse, and the Essex Wharf. Thick wood gates are shut. Some middleclass merchant cottages stand opposite. The circle of his spotlight reveals everything is quiet and in mimic suspension.

This is not merely the subjective impression of one constable. Sgt. Henry Kirby must have missed Neil by minutes. He also walked the lane with his bull's eye lamp coasting about and noticed nothing unusual.

There was really no reason to expect anything odd here. Although Buck's Row is only 2 streets over from the hubbub of Whitechapel Road, the businesses here are shut down at night. Only the slaughterers on Winthrop, one street over, are open. There is no reason for anybody to walk through the neighborhood unless they lived here. It is so quiet that a

Looking down Buck's Row. The School Board Building in on the right. The middleclass cottages behind it.

wagon's clunking wheels can be heard a street over.

At 3:40 a.m. many begin their trek to work. Carman Charles Cross is on his way to Pickford's on City Row. (A carman is the driver of a horse-drawn tram or other business cart). He is more than halfway up Buck's Row from Brady Street when he sees a body lying on the sidewalk at the beginning of the tradesmen's cottages. It is right by the closed wood gate to Brown's Stable. He walks into the center of the narrow lane and notices it is that of a woman. He stops and does not approach closer. He hears another man coming up the lane from Brady Street. He calls him over and they walk up and stand over her.

Cross thinks this woman is dead. But because her dress has been lifted to be a bundle over her lower body and thighs, the other man thinks a bloke got too fresh with her and she fainted. They feel her face and it's cold. They feel her arms and legs. The arms are warm above the elbow but cold below. The legs are warm. The man with Cross thinks he detects a slight heartbeat. He even thinks she is slightly breathing.

What to do? By the sound of methodical steps on Winthrop, Cross is sure that a bobby is on his way anyway. They need to be off to work, so they head up Buck's Row. They see nobody until Baker's Row. It is Constable Jonas Mizzen. They stop him and tell him they found a woman in distress.

"All right," he says, and he is quickly on his way.

Minutes pass.

From the beam of a bull's eye lamp moving about on Buck's Row, Mizzen realizes another constable is standing over the body. As he approaches, the constable's lantern beam flirts with Mizzen's lantern beam and directs it to follow its path. The beams join over the body's face. The woman's eyes stare wide open. Blood oozes from a deep slash in her throat. Her left hand touches the wood gate. Her jolly bonnet lies nearby. She looks as though she was stopped dead in her tracks on the sidewalk. Up close, Mizzen now recognizes John Neil as the other constable. He tells Mizzen that he had already called to Constable John Thain, who was passing on Brady Street, and told him to fetch a local doctor, Rees Llewellyn. He tells Mizzen to hop it for an ambulance. Mizzen rushes off.

Puzzled, Neil shakes his head. Now alone again, he considers the ghastly yet confusing scene. Despite the gory appearance of the corpse's neck, there isn't much blood. This leads to the immediate thought that she might have been killed elsewhere and only dumped here. He decides to stroll up and down the street in order to see if he can uncover the killer's trail. His lamp beam streams over the dark cobblestones and worn sidewalks, but there is no sign, no blood, not even a sign of a carriage wheel having passed. He then walks across the lane and knocks on the door of Essex Wharf warehouse and asks the watchman if he heard anything. Nothing.

Sgt. Kirby now arrives. Neil tells him he cannot figure how the body got here. Such little blood. He found the body at 3:45 a.m. (on his methodical rounds, he walks Buck's Row every half hour). Kirby, too, is skeptical, especially after his lamp illuminates the grotesque scene. There is only a small puddle of blood by the neck and left shoulder. It is still liquid and mirror-like in his spotlight. She had to have been killed in the last 30 minutes since both walked the lane. Neil reiterates that the watchman heard nothing. Kirby decides to walk around and also ask the watchman again. Neil stays by the body. Two local workers from the slaughterhouse on Winthrop Street have now arrived, but Neil keeps them back.

By 4 a.m. Thain has returned with the good doctor. Llewellyn quickly checks the body. He says she has been dead for no more than 30 minutes. This places her death just after 3:30 a.m., just about 10 minutes before she was found. The doctor is also surprised by how little blood there is. He estimates that there is only about "a wine glass and a half" of blood. Nevertheless, Llewellyn was certain: she was killed where she had been found.

Initially the three constables greet this with skepticism. But a quick glance between them— Kirby, Neil and Thain— confirmed they had heard nothing. But what was the alternative? It seemed impossible that a man could have carried the body here that quickly after killing her elsewhere. It was more outrageous to consider that a cart and horse could have trotted up in the silence and not have been heard. So far, it seems the murder was committed with unusual silence, in the narrow interim between the beats of 3 constables.

Early morning questioning by Inspector John Spratling produced the same skepticism. The body, as yet unconfirmed as Nichols, was found almost under the window of the widow Emma Green. She proudly boasted of being a light sleeper. Moreover, her two sons and a daughter live with her. None of them reported hearing any sounds either. Across the street lives Walter Purkiss. He is the manager of the Essex Wharf. He lives with his wife and children and even a servant. They reported that they had been awake off and on throughout the night but had nevertheless heard nothing.

Spratling had arrived at the scene just before 5 a.m. A typical cleanup was underway. A constable had waited to throw a bucket of water on the stain of blood until Spratling had a chance to look at it. As the blood diluted and seeped into the cobblestones, he wrote down his notes. Ultimately, he too was surprised. He would come back later to get witness depositions in detail. He wanted to examine the body at the morgue first. There he would receive the biggest surprise of all. . .

2

ᴅARKNESS ʙʏ ᴳASLIGHT

Even before the inquest would bring out the startling details to the public, Scotland Yard faced the fact they were dealing with a potentially explosive case. Aside from the fact that the evidence wouldn't fit any ordinary murder, they were forced to consider the worst thing imaginable: that the Buck's Row killing was more than a single, isolated crime. Despite its apparent uniqueness, Nichols' death did not entirely stand alone. This was the second barbarous murder in the Whitechapel area that month. None of the constables or inspectors on the Nichols case were ignorant of the details. Reports and the inquest proceedings had been published in the newspapers, and the case was still being discussed by the public. Both were of women, and the first murder had set a precedent for mindless brutality. There was also one other frightening similarity in these two crimes: the incredible stealth with which they were both carried out.

On Tuesday, August 7, a middle-aged part-time prostitute, Martha Tabram, had been brutally knifed 39 times. The number of stab wounds would immediately suggest a "maniac." But there was much more to it than that. The evidence suggested a paradox— a very calm and cool maniac. Like in the Nichols case, it had been perpetrated in the quiet early morning hours but in circumstances that were even more incredible— on the first floor landing of a crowded tenement house, no less. Yet despite this no one had heard a blessed thing. The

killer had been unusually silent. But— and this is significant— Tabram's fingers were tightly clenched in death. She
had obviously been conscious and had dug them into somebody. Put together, all this made the silence of her murder
quite inexplicable. The result was that her murder became the
first of its kind to generate more public and Press interest because of the mystery surrounding the death scene rather than
the brutality inflicted on the victim.

Tabram had been stabbed 5 times in the left breast (each
time penetrating the lung) and two in the right breast (penetrating the right lung). Another single stab penetrated the
heart. Five stabs in the upper abdomen which penetrated the
liver, two in the spleen, and six in the stomach (18 wounds
had not been detailed because they were "of a nature too disgusting to mention" and they were in her lower abdomen and
groin). The wounds themselves indicated a right-handed person. The weapon appeared to have been a bayonet (which
were commonly sold in the market stalls), but some wounds
were so slight they could have been made by an ordinary pen
knife. There was yet another paradox. The killer must have
knifed her repeatedly at close quarters while she lay on the
landing. Yet no trail of blood led away from her despite the
fact she was found in a pool of blood. The killer had been remarkably clean.

The other similarity between the Tabram and Nichols case
might be found in the type of victim. Tabram, too, was not
just a part-time prostitute; she was a heavy drinker and was
also near destitute and had turned to prostitution as a result.
Her road to it was little different than Polly Nichols. Neither
Nichols nor Tabram were rosy characters. Newspapers can
build them up into the benighted and exploited lower classes,
"unfortunates" and "fallen sparrows," who had to turn from
the straight and narrow in order to survive, but that was far
from the truth. That may look good on paper and establish an
easy and profitable antagonist/protagonist formula, but the
ultimate purpose is merely to drag out the story and sell
copy. In reality, both women were dissolute, drunken harlots
who had caused every problem they ever had.

Yet they had never done anything to merit this kind of re-
prisal.

Polly Nichols was actually born Mary Ann Walker. She had married William Nichols in 1864 and had 5 children by him. They had separated many times, and finally after the last time in 1881 she went to live as a common prostitute. William took care of the children and paid Mary Ann a maintenance fee. This he stopped when he was able to prove she lived as a prostitute. She spiraled further into dissolution, but there were attempts at reform. She lived with her father for a while. He considered her dissolute but not immoral since she did not stay out late. After this, she lived in workhouses or slept as a bum on the street. In May 1888 the Lambeth Workhouse attempted to help her by finding her employment at the house of the Cowdrys. They are teetotalers and religious. She works for them for a few months and then nicks a few quid worth of clothing, and takes off. From there she was back to Whitechapel to her old drunken, dissolute ways.

Tabram was born Martha White, May 10, 1849, to a warehouseman, Charles White. Sixteen years later her parents separated. Before Martha was 20 years of age she had shacked-up with a furniture packer much older than herself, Henry Tabram. He was quite staid compared to Martha. He was neat, well-manicured with a close-cropped beard and his hair was already gray. On Christmas 1869 they were finally married. Eventually they had 3 children together. However, already by this early age Martha had developed a taste for liquor and not family life. By 1875 Henry had left her. He could no longer handle her drunkenness and hysterical fits.

For the next three years he gave her 12 shillings per week. Yet she continued to stop him in the streets and pester him for more. He finally had enough and he lowered the money to 2 shillings 6 ducats per week. The money hadn't been going to the children anyway. Martha was drinking it and the children basically are no longer in the picture. Henry had not yet learned that Martha was, in fact, living with another man, Henry Turner. When he found out he completely stopped the allowance, which legally he could get away with since she had another provider. Spitefully, Martha went behind his back and swore out testimony and said he wasn't providing for the children. A warrant was issued. In consequence, staid and true Henry Tabram was locked up.

Henry Turner was quite different from Henry Tabram. He was much younger, and he was considered a dirty little man compared who always looked like a slob. His profession was carpentry. But he frequently didn't have a job. For 12 years he and Martha lived together off and on. Martha was not an habitual drunk, and when sober they got on well-enough. She enjoyed fattening ales and ate well. She had become quite corpulent. Heavy drinking did not affect her eating habits.

But finally he too got tired of Martha's boozing. He had testified at the inquest that if he gave her any money she "generally spent it on drink." He told the police that she stayed out late into the night, seldom coming home before 11 p.m. Sometimes she was out all night. She would return in the morning and say she had hysterics and was at the police station— in other words, she had been taken in for drinking or she was merely covering up for prostituting all night. Epileptic fits was a claim many a Whitechapel drab used when taken in for drinking. This way they were discharged without charges. Turner finally left her in July 1888.

Tabram's movements the last night of her life, that Bank Holiday, Monday, August 6, were little different than Polly Nichols. She went out that evening with Pearly Poll, the professional name or nickname of Mary Ann Connelly. Throughout the evening they made the rounds of the pubs with soldiers. Finally, in the Two Brewers Pub they met two Guardsmen, a corporal and a private. They accompanied them to other pubs, most notably the White Swan on Whitechapel High Street (they may have met them separately in the other pubs but at the White Swan finally got together)[1] where they enjoyed the festivities and the soldier's free liquor. The soldiers had by now probably thought they had more than paid for enough good times to merit return payment. At 11:45 p.m. the couples left the pub and separated. Pearly went into the lane euphemistically named Angel Alley with the corporal and Martha led the private into the dark George Yard Lane.

---

[1] According to her sister-in-law, Tabram was seen entering the White Swan alone at 11. p.m. Pearly Poll says they were together inside for only 45 minutes. However, in answer to a question at the inquest, she said they had made the rounds of several pubs for an hour and three quarters. They may not have been together but just in the same bars.

The dark, narrow George Yard Lane, looking toward the tunnel to Whitechapel Road.

At 1:50 a.m. August 7, Elizabeth Mahoney entered George Yard Buildings, a cold brick tenement house with a misplaced stately Victorian Gothic entrance. Mahoney went upstairs. She noticed nothing amiss.

Ten minutes later outside on Wentworth Street, the north side of George Yard Buildings, alert Constable Thomas Barrett stopped and asked a Guardsman why he was hanging about. The Guardsman declared he was waiting for a "chum who went off with a girl."

At 3:30 a.m., one and a half hours later, Alfred Crow entered George Yard Buildings and went upstairs to his room. On the landing to the first floor (second floor in American English), he noticed a woman sleeping in the shadows and thought it a homeless person. This wasn't unusual. It was very dark and he continued on upstairs.

At 4:45 a.m. John Reeves descended the stairs to go to

work. Dawn was approaching. In the gray humorless light he noticed the body on the landing. It was a woman. She was lying on her back in a pool of blood. He rushed off and found Constable Barrett nearby.

When they returned, Barrett carefully noted the scene. Her arms were lying by her sides; her fingers tightly clenched. The legs were spread. Clothes were rumpled as if mussed in the fight; the bosom area ripped off. Barrett called for a doctor; and Dr. Timothy Killeen, who lived on nearby Brick Lane, soon arrived. He estimated she had been dead for about 3 hours or between 2 to 2:30 a.m.

Questioning all and sundry in the house revealed that none had heard a thing. This included the caretakers, the Hewitts, whose flat opened onto the landing.

Newspapers were naturally intrigued by all this. "The circumstances of this awful tragedy are not only surrounded with the deepest mystery," wrote the *East London Advertiser*, "but there is also a feeling of insecurity to think that in a great city like London, the streets of which are continually patrolled by police, a woman could be foully and horribly killed almost next to the citizens peacefully sleeping in their beds, without a trace or clue being left of the villain who did the deed."

Four different persons identified Tabram with 4 different names. Rather than delve into her sordid life, love-ins and aliases, the *Echo* cashed in on this

The dark George Yard Lane looking toward Wentworth, with the tenement George Yard Buildings at the end of it.

identity problem and the horror scene. The "woman's features are rapidly changing from post-mortem appearances. As soon as she was discovered the police had a photograph taken of her body, but the features were so distorted— possibly by an agonizing death— that some difficulty was at first experienced by her supposed friends in accurately recognizing her."

The mystery and horror were so captivating that an odd thing was happening. On the 13th, the *Echo* elaborated: "There have been many visitors to George Yard Buildings with the rather morbid purpose of seeing the place where the deceased was discovered. Here there is still a large surface of the stone flags crimson stained. It is at the spot where the blood oozed from the poor creature's heart."

It would be unforgivably cynical, not to mention grossly inaccurate, to ascribe the fame that the Tabram murder would take on to newspapery's slight-of-hand and sensational reporting. The newspapers never once fudged in describing her death scene or the conundrums contained within the crime. The newspapers capitalized on facts and circumstances, but they didn't create them. What the papers did do was clean up the victim's reputation. She was a fallen sparrow who together with the other "poorest of the poor" but honest "find protection and shelter in the miserable hovels bearing the name of houses." Without the pure image the murder of Tabram would excite little sympathy from a moral Victorian majority. It also allowed the papers to include everybody as a possible future victim and this sold more copy. This way the papers brought into the news the broader questions of the city's overcrowding, police inefficiency, and social reform. In short, this was a cash cow with lots of calves.

Political and social capitalization aside, the inquest into the death of "the unfortunate woman" would show how the Press had not overplayed the mysterious circumstances of the killing. The inquest actually provided the Press with the best fodder to hold the East End in the grip of macabre fascination.

A heavy pall had fallen over the lecture room of the Working Lad's Institute on Whitechapel Road on Thursday the 9th. Mr. George Collier, the deputy coroner for the South Eastern Division of Middlesex, "was painfully quiet" and listened to the testimony as he presided. Twenty men "good and true" sat under a giant brass placard carrying a Biblical quote.

> He hath shewed thee, O man, what is good; and what doth the LORD REQUIRE of thee, but to do JUSTLY, and to love MERCY, and to walk HUMBLY with thy GOD?
>
> MICAH 6:8

Nearby, Detective Inspector Edmund Reid watched quietly. He was H Division's — i.e. Whitechapel's — chief Criminal Investigation Division detective. He was a no-nonsense, keen sportsman and hunter who had led a varied life both before and during his career with the Metropolitan Police. This included being an actor, singer, and an expert at "sleight-of-hand." He had received a national medal for ascending higher than anybody before his time in a hot air balloon. His police work had already made him the inspiration for author Charles Gibbons' "Detective Dier" in his crime novel series. Being a legerdemain expert, he didn't take anything at face value. He was the perfect fit for this type of murder. He would notice every clue.

Collective testimony, however, made it clear that the clues could not be easily interpreted. The killing was a bloody affair at close quarters, and yet inexplicably the only blood was in a pool in which the body lay. This was quite a conundrum, for Reeves, the first key witness, described the body as appearing as having been in a struggle. Dr. Killeen's testimony underscores this enigma, since he felt that all the 39 wounds had been inflicted while she was alive. On the other hand, he rather strangely testified that "there was no sign of a struggle whatever." Reeves based his deduction on her appearance. The doctor's statement appears influenced by his impression of the landing. Yet what is there in a bland tenement house landing that could reflect a sign of a struggle? Killeen's

The Penny Illustrated *gave us a lively snapshot of the moment of finding Tabram's body.*

impression may not have been from the evidence but from the circumstantial evidence of the Hewitts, whose newspaper accounts underscored that this must have been a very silent affair.

The possibility that the murder weapon had been a bayonet implicated one of the two Guardsmen. Police testimony established how Scotland Yard dutifully had all the soldiers at Wellington Barracks parade before Pearly Poll for identification. Yet she had recognized none. As valiant as this effort was, the police had probably engaged in it out of perfunctory duty. They already knew that only a 10 minute gap existed between Elizabeth Mahoney passing the empty landing and Constable Barrett coming along the Guardsman outside waiting for his buddy. It was unlikely these were the same two Guardsmen that had gone off with Tabram and Poll over 2 hours earlier. It would not have taken the Guardsman and Tabram 2 hours to walk the couple of hundred yards to the building from where they were last seen. It seems more than likely that Tabram had found another customer afterward and brought him to the dark landing soon after Mahoney passed on her way upstairs.

Developing the testimony of the chief witnesses more or less negates the theory that one of the soldiers did it. Killeen said there had been no rape. Thus she seems to have been the object of murder. Specially, Killeen detailed that there was blood between the scalp and the bone of her skull, indicating her head had been bruised. The killer must have kept her silent with one hand clutched over her mouth, and while she struggled with her hands clenched into him he repeatedly pushed her head against the cement. Yet her hands were clenched in death, not from being unconscious. She must have been killed while she still struggled. Put together, such a stabbing at close quarters would most certainly have gotten blood on the attacker, something that would have been immediately noticed on a soldier returning to the barracks. In this light, it is hard to imagine how a Guardsman, who must account for his expensive uniform, could explain a bloodied or missing uniform.

Pursuing this in detail was not relevant to the inquest, however. After the witnesses finished, the room was silent. Mr. Collier finally spoke. "It was one of the most shocking things one could possibly imagine. The man who could have inflicted 39 wounds on a poor defenseless woman must have been a perfect savage. . ."

The inquest left London with a scenario of a baffling murder in the most impossible area of the city. As the sun did not set on the Empire, so was the crowded East End the one area of London that did not sleep.

On August 13, the *Echo* reporter set out to uncover how such a stealthy killing could have been done. "The police authorities regard as little short of marvellous the fact that no dweller in this model block heard any disturbance. Thinking this point ought to be cleared up, our reporter again visited to-day Mr. Francis Hewitt, the superintendent of the dwellings, who, with his wife, occupies a sleeping apartment at nearly right angles with the place where the dead body lay. Mr. Hewitt produced a foot-rule, and measured the distance of his sleeping place from the stone step in question; it was exactly 12 ft. 'And we never heard a cry,' remarked Mr.

Hewitt. Mrs. Hewitt remarked that early in the evening she had heard a single cry of 'Murder!' It echoed through the building, but did not emanate from there. 'But,' explained Mr. and Mrs. Hewitt in a breath, 'the district 'round here is rather rough, and cries of 'Murder!' are of frequent, if not nightly, occurrence in the district."

Because of this bizarre mystery murder, all London and indeed Britain was learning the shocking truth of what the East End was really like. Whoever those 2 Guardsmen were, they too never wanted to come forward and clarify their evening out. The Press made it evident that Scotland Yard had been lucky to even find Pearly Poll. Knowing the police wanted her, she had first vanished. Reporters had nosed around and uncovered that she had been heard to say she would "drown herself in the Thames before talking to coppers." This was just the typical world of Whitechapel. The police were hindered by the suspicious nature of its dregs, the many foreigners, and the locals' fear that the death might have been caused for other reasons.

Crime gangs abounded. "High Rip" gangs were known to blackmail prostitutes into sharing their earnings with them. If they didn't, they would "rip" them with knives, hence their names. No one wanted to be considered to know too much. It wasn't safe. The papers had already tried to link these gangs to the murder. The *Echo* had ended its 10 August article by making this look like one in a series of crimes. They offered that the first victim had been a woman, Emma Smith, who had been killed months before by having a walking cane thrust into "her body with great violence" nearby at Osborn and Wentworth. "For ferocity, the two cases are somewhat analogous, and some of the Scotland Yard experts in tracing criminals and fathoming crime incline to the opinion that one man is responsible for the two crimes."

The Tabram murder had been so shocking that on August 13 the Whitechapel District Board of Works met to discuss public lighting. One member complained: "Commercial Street had hitherto been badly lighted; indeed, it was hardly safe for women to walk along there."

Collier, the assistant coroner, a member of the Works, added with emphasis: "And men too!"

On August 18, the *East London Advertiser*, which obviously was one of the papers that had the greatest journalistic interest in the area of the crime, ended its article on the murder with: "No conclusion can be come to at present as to the ultimate success of the detective force in elucidating the truth about this terrible deed, but it is sincerely to be hoped that justice will be meted out to the inhuman villain who could so foully maltreat a fellow creature— let alone a woman— and we trust that this Whitechapel murder will not be placed upon the records of the police as one of those undiscovered crimes of which there have been far too many within the last decade."

The plea had once again been made. The subtle assignation against police competency poked its head up. But what really could they do? They were equally stumped. They had little chance of removing the enigma from the case. The darkness added to that. The little orbs of gaslight glowed meekly about 2 feet from their posts. They made the darkness around them seem deeper by contrast; the doorways black portals to death, the corners around fences a menacing cloak of accomplice. Whoever the perpetrator was, he knew Whitechapel well. . . and he knew the darkness better. He could give the appearance of maniacal brutality and yet remain oddly silent.

3

SILENCE OF THE WOLVES

VIOLENCE WAS OBVIOUSLY quite commonplace in White-chapel, but gruesome and, even more, baffling murder was not. Now, only thirteen days later, was the wrong time for another prostitute to be brutally murdered in a public place. . . and in circumstances that were proving to be just as inexplicable. By the time dawn broke and the ambulance had trotted off Polly Nichols' body, a crowd had assembled around the murder scene here too. The crowd was told to disperse. Made up of local workers, they naturally chattered amongst themselves.

Wisps and nothing more got back to the newspapers for the early editions. But the *East London Advertiser* learned enough to make the connection right away. "Another White-chapel Mystery. Horrible Murder in Buck's Row," read the headlines. "Scarcely has the horror and sensation caused by the discovery of the murdered woman in Whitechapel some short time ago had time to abate," introduced the article, "when another discovery is made which, for the brutality ex-ercised on the victim, is even more shocking and will no doubt create as great a sensation in the vicinity as its prede-cessor."

In rather vivid style, the *Advertiser* continued: "her throat cut right open from ear to ear, the instrument with which the deed was done traversing the throat from left to right. The

The Penny Illustrated *captured the scene at Buck's Row fairly accurately. This shows John Neil finding Nichols' body.*

wound was about two inches wide, and blood was flowing profusely. She was discovered to be lying in a pool of blood. She was immediately conveyed to the Whitechapel mortuary, when it was found that besides the wound in the throat the lower part of the abdomen was completely ripped open, with the bowels protruding. The wound extends nearly to her breast, and must have been affected with a large knife. As the corpse lies in the mortuary it presents a ghastly sight. . ."

The *Echo* reporter lived up to the maxim that a writer doesn't need to see anything in order to write a good story. Instead of a pool of blood, as in the *Advertiser* rendition, the actual fact of a *lack* of blood on scene inspired ghoulish theorizing: "A very general opinion is now entertained that the spot where the body was found was not the scene of the murder. Buck's Row runs through from Thomas Street to Brady Street, and in the latter street what appeared to be bloodstains were found at irregular distances on the footpaths on either side of the way. Occasionally a larger splash was visible, and from the manner in which the marks were scattered it seems as though the person carrying the mutilated body had hesitated where to deposit his ghastly burden, and had gone from one side of the road to the other until the obscurity of Buck's Row afforded the shelter sought for. . .The theory is that the woman was murdered in a house and killed whilst undressed, her clothes being then huddled on the body, which was afterwards conveyed out, to be deposited in the street. . .the body was then carried, enveloped in her large, heavy cloak, and thrown outside the gateway at Essex Wharf. Mr. Seccombe, Dr. Llewellyn's assistant, is of the same opinion, especially, he says, as there was comparatively little blood where the deceased lay."

Both papers erred greatly, but the *Echo*'s botched job is valuable because of how true it should be. The scene of Nichols' murder should only be explainable this way. Yet it was untrue. An imaginative reportorial mind was clearly excited by the snippets of facts it had picked up from police gossip. The most pondersome was that such little blood was found in contrast to the horrendous nature of the cut throat. There was such little blood, in fact, that the police didn't even know the victim had been "disemboweled."

This was only discovered at the morgue, and this gave the reporter his second snippet. There he got the sense of how surprised John Spratling had been when he checked the body and found it mutilated.

The actual details are grisly but perplexing. Spratling had pulled back the dress while the body lay on the morgue slab. Her lower abdomen was sliced open in several deep cuts. Yet there was no appreciable amount of blood on the under linen. And unlike in the newspaper report, in reality she had been fully dressed. Indeed, her stays had not even been removed. They were only loosened in order to make the cuts below the navel. Spratling had seen the bloodstain at the scene. There probably had not been 10 ounces of blood on the sidewalk. Nothing appreciable had come from the gut either.

This gave the reporter his third snippet. QED— she was killed elsewhere.

Spratling, too, must have felt this. He was soon out at the scene again and walked up and down the roads to find a trail of blood. Then he went with Sergeant Godfrey and searched the nearby East London and District Railway lines and their embankment. Then they searched the Great Eastern Railway yard. The watchman here had his box only 50 or 60 yards from the spot where the body was discovered. Yet he had heard nothing. In all this, Spratling had found only one possible bloodstain on Broad Street, which could not be tied into the killing at all.

This was a far cry from what the *Echo* had conveniently adlibbed for circulation. The *Echo* reporter filled it in all nice and logically like a good writer should. He imagined loads of blood but he spread it out along a gruesome trail from some secret murder scene elsewhere. Nice and logical, but utterly false. The reporter should have accompanied the police around their ferret-like investigation of the neighborhood. Had he done so he would have picked up the most newsworthy codicil on the bloody[less] spectacle.

The cut throat certainly set Nichols' murder apart from Tabram's, but the lack of blood complicates the case far above and beyond Tabram's murder. It is not my desire to digress from the narrative, but in order to translate the reader back to the moment, free of any mitigating theorizing, some

THE ILLUSTRATED POLICE NEWS
LAW COURTS AND WEEKLY RECORD
SATURDAY, SEPTEMBER 8, 1888. Price One Penny.

REVOLTING AND MYSTERIOUS MURDER OF A WOMAN—BUCK'S ROW, WHITECHAPEL.

FINDING THE BODY IN BUCK'S ROW

THE MURDERED WOMAN. WHITECHAPEL MORTUARY

The Police News *shows us how the body was propped up for display. It also gives us tableaux from the inquest as the main players tried to make heads or tails out of the macabre slaying.*

rather lame excuses for the lack of blood, proposed decades later by uninformed writers, must be dealt with. One, the blood *was not* there. The blood did not neatly soak down the back of her clothes, thus accounting for the lack of visible blood. It is not physically possible for a viscous liquid like blood to do that in just 10 minutes time (between 3:30 a.m. and Neil shining his light on her). A heavy rainfall could possibly take up to an hour to completely soak under a prostrate body dressed in such voluminous Victorian garb. Moreover, blood, like any liquid, will follow the path of least resistance. The shoulders would have acted as a barrier, and the rest would have flowed along the shoulders and down the arm. The theory that the blood flowed neatly down her back also presupposes that the sidewalk inclined *drastically* in that direction. Inquest testimony, which will soon follow, will set in place other facts which underscore how the lack of blood surprised the police and was not explainable.

Certainly on its own the lack of blood was enough to motivate Spratling to prowl around. But if he knew all the details about Tabram's murder, he may have been more motivated by the thought the same phantom killer was afoot. Nichols' "disemboweling" was egregious Press exaggerating. Rather the cuts in her were deep and pointless and limited to the lower abdomen and groin. This draws yet another disturbing parallel with Tabram's murder and her 18 wounds "too disgusting" to detail. In addition, there were the obvious similarities of circumstances—public murder yet utter silence.

On September 1, 1888, Mr. Wynne Baxter, the district coroner, convened the inquest. He was perhaps the perfect person for the case. He was not adverse to any amount of publicity. He was himself from a newspaper family. He also felt his importance in the case, a decided prerequisite to those who cultivate publicity successfully. It was unfortunate, he no doubt also felt, that he had not been around for the Tabram Inquest. The Nichols case now revealed how important that case must have been. It was far too lightly covered by his assistant, Collier. Baxter intended this to be a searching inquiry far beyond merely establishing type and circumstances of death, the coroner's usual job.

Baxter was an officious but in some ways foppish totem. His collar was dapper, his tie almost flamboyant, but his suit was dark and formal. Together this created only an appearance of seedy grandeur. His mustache was full, hiding his stiff upper lip look; but his sideburns were fluffy and frivolous and his thin eyebrows were flourishes over eyes far too deep set to express grace. He was, however, a force to be reckoned with. He had been trained in law, and was a solicitor. He had been elected to various levels of the constabulary for his local parish of Lewes, including Senior High Constable, and he was its first mayor. He had also been an Under-Sheriff for London and Middlesex twice. He had a keen mind, and if not truly keen it did not cower at any circumstance. But it far too often was a perfunctory one that would not be ready for such oddities as this case would present.

Nevertheless, under his guiding hand the inquest placed in order contemporarily and for posterity how extraordinary the circumstances of the crime truly were.

He took his place in his rightful elevated seat in the room at the Working Lad's Institute, the same room where Collier held the Tabram Inquest, and filled it far more imposingly than his meek assistant had. The jury of common folk lined up under that huge placard with its Biblical motto about humility and duty.

The mystery in this case was felt keenly in Constable John Neil's testimony. Coupled with the fact she was murdered on the spot, his description of the darkness imposes on us that her killer must have had true eyes-in-the-night. Despite the street lamp up the lane, when he saw her body he could only call it a "figure." He energized his lamp and only then saw the blood "oozing from a wound in the throat" and that her "eyes were wide open."

After having learned that the victim had been found "disemboweled" at the morgue, Neil admitted, in an understandable tone of amazement, that none of them had even suspected that while on the spot. Naturally, Mr. Baxter and the jury were curious. Rumors had already spread about how impossible it was that she could have been killed on that spot and yet there should be such little blood.

Baxter: Did you notice any blood where she was found?

Neil: There was a pool of blood just where her neck was lying. It was running from the wound in her neck.

Baxter: Did you hear any noise that night?

Neil: No; I heard nothing. The farthest I had been that night was just through the Whitechapel Road and up Baker's Row. I was never far away from the spot.

Baxter: Whitechapel Road is busy in the early morning, I believe. Could anybody have escaped that way?

Neil: Oh yes, sir. I saw a number of women in the main road going home. At that time anyone could have got away.

Baxter: Someone searched the ground, I believe?

Neil: Yes; I examined it while the doctor was being sent for.

Inspector Spratling:
    I examined the road, sir, in daylight.

A Juryman (to witness):
    Did you see a trap in the road at all?

Wynne E. Baxter stands in all his glory by the sovereign's mace, with his charter. He was a Renaissance man. Aside from law, he dabbled in science and translated from the French a book on microscopes.

Neil: No.

A Juryman:

Knowing that the body was warm, did it not strike you that it might just have been laid there, and that the woman was killed elsewhere?

Neil: I examined the road, but did not see the mark of wheels. The first to arrive on the scene after I had discovered the body were two men who work at a slaughterhouse opposite. They said they knew nothing of the affair, and that they had not heard any screams.

Baxter had not yet formalized his feelings, but he clearly leaned toward the idea the killer must have gotten away by melding into the early morning traffic on Whitechapel Road only two blocks over from Buck's Row. Neil anticipated him correctly when he offered that anybody could get away that way.

Escape is not the greatest part of the mystery, however. Adding together the testimonies of Thain, Kirby and Neil makes the arrival of the killer and Nichols a greater conundrum. Their methodical intermeshing beat routines placed them at given points every 30 minutes. This means there was only a narrow window in which the crime could have been committed; very narrow actually when considering that the killer and Nichols would have to walk into the lane unseen by *any* of the constables. Buck's Row was off the beaten path for prostitutes, and one of the slaughterhouse men would confirm that in testimony. No one races to the place of amours. How did a couple walk, perhaps even stroll, at a normal pace to the spot of the murder and 3 vigilant policemen (4 if counting Mizzen) never saw them in such early morning solitude? Not even a glimpse from a distance. Baxter was actually the first to concentrate on the wrong end of the mystery — the escape — and this obscures a major clue we must bring up later.

Dr. Llewellyn was called and confirmed he arrived there around 4 a.m., that the body was still warm ("Her hands and wrists were cold, but the body and lower extremities were warm"), and that there "was very little blood 'round the neck." He remained factual, but his careful description of strange bruises on her face betrays his explanation for her silence— the killer had grabbed her mouth so tightly he embedded his fingers in her cheeks. He went into detail:

". . .Five of the teeth are missing, and there is a slight laceration of the tongue. On the right side of the face there is a bruise running along the lower part of the jaw. It might have been caused by a blow with the fist or pressure by the thumb. On the left side of the face there was a circular bruise, which also might have been done by the pressure of the fingers." Nichols was already missing the five teeth, so in light of the fact there was no struggle or fisticuffs the bruise marks correspond to a hand, with its boney fingers clutching the mouth so strongly that bruise marks were left. The thumb left a distinct print on one side, and the fingers on the other cheek. Llewellyn doesn't mention if the tongue laceration was recent, but if it was it meant that she bit her tongue when the brutal hand suddenly seized her mouth.

The villain not only clenched her jaw so hard to keep her from calling out, but to hold her head steady to cut her throat. Llewellyn describes the wound in detail: "On the left side of the neck, about an inch below the jaw, there was an incision about four inches long and running from a point immediately below the ear. An inch below on the same side, and commencing about an inch in front of it, was a circular incision terminating at a point about three inches below the right jaw. This incision completely severs all the tissues down to the vertebrae. The large vessels of the neck on both sides were severed. The incision is about eight inches long. These cuts must have been caused with a long-bladed knife, moderately sharp, and used with great violence. No blood at all was found on the breast either of the body or clothes"— meaning she was laying down when her throat was cut. He also testified that "There were no marks of any struggle or of blood, as if the body had been dragged."

The lack of blood becomes more astounding as he continues with his postmortem. "About an hour later I was sent for by the Inspector to see the injuries he had discovered on the body. I went, and saw that the abdomen was cut very extensively. . .There were no injuries about the body till just about the lower part of the abdomen. Two or three inches from the left side was a wound running in a jagged manner. It was a very deep wound, and the tissues were cut through. There were several incisions running across the abdomen. On the right side there were also three or four similar cuts running downwards. All these had been caused by a knife, which had been used violently and been used downwards. The wounds were from left to right, and might have been done by a left-handed person. All the injuries had been done by the same instrument."

After the doctor testified, Baxter adjourned for the day so he and the jury could consider the testimony. The number of witnesses called at the next sitting (September 3) and the amount of questions put forward by the coroner and the jury shows to what extent they digested and puzzled over the two most astounding facts— the stealth of the crime and the lack of blood.

The police were well-represented. Not only were Inspectors Spratling and Joseph Helson and a Scotland Yard detective, Sargent Enright, sitting in, Inspector Frederick Abberline, now placed in overall charge of the case, commanded attention merely by his presence in the room.

Abberline was a stodgy, un-dynamic appearing man, with mustache that grew into his sideburns, leaving his portly chin bare. His dark suit was buttoned up to the highest button,

News sketches brought the inquest members to life.

revealing only a little of his tie. For all the world, he didn't look like an inspector at all but some kind of rumpled clerk or musty records keeper.

But Abberline's presence in itself said something, and Baxter knew it. Abberline had been a staple of ranking Division H's C.I.D. inspectors and then finally its head. Then just a year ago he was kicked up to A Division— Whitehall itself. He was now in an administrative office in the actual Scotland Yard at Whitehall from which the Metropolitan Police got their nickname. He was now essentially part of the general staff. The very fact he had been sent temporarily back out onto the streets and back to Whitechapel testified to how seriously the case was being taken at headquarters. Abberline also probably wanted a crack at it. After 14 years in the district, he had dozens of underworld contacts he could tap again. These had proven helpful, especially for his involvement in breaking up Irish Fenian terrorists in 1885 and their plot to blow up the Tower of London. He wasn't a man to shirk. He had been threatened with assassination many times in the above caper. His presence here at the inquest indeed spoke volumes.

Baxter signaled his assistant, Banks, to call Spratling. After his bellow died down, the room quietly listened to Spratling confirm all the particulars.

Unfortunately, this is where the first controversy about competence comes in. Now the jury and coroner discovered that when Spratling returned to the morgue with Llewellyn to carefully examine the body they found it already stripped.

Enright immediately stood up and clarified that this had been done by the workhouse officials.

Baxter was not happy. "Had they any authority to strip the body?"

Spratling replied: "No, sir; I gave them no instructions to strip it. In fact, I told them to leave it as it was."

"I don't object to their stripping the body," replied Baxter, "but we ought to have evidence about the clothes."

Enright stood again and clarified that the clothes were lying in "a heap in the yard." He then itemized them and noted that the flannel petticoat was marked "Lambeth Workhouse" and another bore markings "P.R." for Princes Road, which they cut out in hopes they could trace any clues. Then he offhand introduced something significant: there was also a pair of stays.

In light of the abdominal mutilations, the stays became of immediate interest. Fortunately, Baxter pushed the point. He explicitly wanted to know the "exact state in which the stays were found." Because of this we have a valuable clue. We know that the stays, surprisingly, had not been removed from Nichols' body. Nor were they cut. Rather the killer had loosened them by pulling them and then made the deep slices and mutilations in her lower abdomen.[2]

Lack of blood had been the sensitive issue, of course. Spratling didn't have to be explicit to reveal how it had surprised him. Instead the extent to which he searched the neighborhood conveys it all. After he detailed this, he confirmed how no person in the vicinity had heard a thing.

Altogether this must have struck an ominous chord with the jury. In the short amount of time the murder must have been committed, how did the killer cut the throat, leave little blood, yank at the stays enough to loosen them and then start "disemboweling"?

Possibly the most significant witness was Charles Cross. He detailed hesitating to approach the body until the other man, whom he heard approaching from 40 yards away through the darkness, had arrived. Cross touched her hands, then face, and the other man (whose name he never learnt) put his hand on her heart. "Witness suggested that they should give her a prop, but his companion refused to touch her. Just then they heard a policeman coming. Witness did not notice that her throat was cut, the night being very dark.

[2] Inspector Helson would qualify that he had seen the body in the mortuary at about 7 a.m. It was still dressed. There was no blood on the back part of the dress. It was on the back of the hair, the collar of the ulster and bodice. The stays were still fastened. There were no cuts in the clothes.

He and the other man left the deceased. . .In his opinion deceased looked as if she had been outraged and gone off in a swoon; but he had no idea that there were any serious injuries."

Cross and the other man where obviously stepping about the body. Thus his testimony mutely bears witness not only to the darkness but to the lack of blood. Quite obviously, they did not step close enough to the shoulders to touch the small pool of blood.

More than anything, Cross' testimony underscores what a soulful promenade the area was at this time of night. Neil must have been a street over on Winthrop. Cross and the other man (who would testify later and be identified as Robert Paul) did not see Neil at all. Yet as they walked away they heard his methodical footsteps. The stillness is also underscored by the fact that Cross heard the other man (Paul) approaching from 40 yards away (120 feet), which must have placed him not far up Buck's Row from Brady Street.

Few walk a wet street briskly on a dark morning. Therefore Cross must have waited a while until Paul arrived. This is significant. During this period of silent waiting, Cross heard nobody else. But, as he had testified, he must have later heard Neil from quite a distance on the street over. I do not list these conundrums to no purpose. Twenty men sat on the jury and were quite aware of what Whitechapel was like. Indeed, the Working Lads Institute overlooked Winthrop right by the horse slaughterers. They could step out and see the row of cottages. They undoubtedly puzzled over how Cross must have literally been on the heels of the killer and yet heard nothing. He must have waited a bit for Paul, yet only heard Paul's shoes clacking on the cobblestones.

The darkness of the spot is well testified too. Thus the killer had murdered and mutilated in pitch blackness, something not easy to do and still did it adroitly enough as to not make a sound from his victim, and to make two incisions in her neck, one a careful 4 inch slice. He left little blood. No less mysterious is the fact that the killer himself must have performed all this without leaving a drop of blood from the scene.

These mysteries are confirmed in Robert Paul's testimony.

Baxter had adjourned the inquest that day to give Scotland Yard enough time to continue the investigation and come up with more witnesses and evidence. It was a long adjournment. The inquest was not reconvened until September 17. Scotland Yard had found Paul by this time and he confirmed the details, adding that he pulled her dress down to preserve her modesty.

But more significant for this current inquest now was the fact another murder had been committed, that of another prostitute, this one named Annie Chapman. Her throat had been cut in the same way, except this time the abdomen was flayed open and organs were missing. There was no one who didn't suspect the same killer was at work. Coroner Baxter and the jury entered the large room, faces grim at their duty. All must have also entered certain Cross had interrupted the killer in the Nichols case before he had time to eviscerate her.

The inquest was reconvened amidst the hype of a city and its newspapers going berserk.

Due to the reports about Annie Chapman being gutted, Baxter recalled Llewellyn and made him the first witness. Only one pointed question was asked, that of missing organs. Llewellyn immediately confirmed that no organs had been missing from the victim. The other witnesses that day were those who were living or working in the area, and they merely confirmed that they had heard nothing. This included Purkiss across the street, and Emma Green, under whose window the body had been found.

On the 22nd September, Baxter made his summation. For those of the readers who are familiar with how a British coroner or judge summarizes a case, the dialogue below takes on a very vivid nature. It is a large, quiet room at the Working Lads Institute. Baxter was so eloquent that most is quoted by the *Daily Telegraph*, which follows verbatim.

Having reviewed the career of the deceased from the time she left her husband, and reminded the jury of the irregular life she had led for the last two years, Mr. Baxter proceeded to point out that the unfortunate woman was last seen alive at half-past two o'clock on Saturday morning, September 1, by Mrs. Holland, who knew her well. Deceased was at that time much the worse for drink, and was endeavouring to walk eastward down Whitechapel. What her exact movements were after this it was impossible to say; but in less than an hour and a quarter her dead body was discovered at a spot rather under three-quarters of a mile distant. The time at which the body was found cannot have been far from 3.45 a.m., as it is fixed by so many independent data. The condition of the body appeared to prove conclusively that the deceased was killed on the exact spot in which she was found. There was not a trace of blood anywhere, except at the spot where her neck was lying, this circumstance being sufficient to justify the assumption that the injuries to the throat were committed when the woman was on the ground, whilst the state of her clothing and the absence of any blood about her legs suggested that the abdominal injuries were inflicted whilst she was still in the same position.

Coming to a consideration of the perpetrator of the murder, the Coroner said: "It seems astonishing at first thought that the culprit should have escaped detection, for there must surely have been marks of blood about his person. If, however, blood was principally on his hands, the presence of so many slaughter-houses in the neighbourhood would make the frequenters of this spot familiar with blood-stained clothes and hands, and his appearance might in that way have failed to attract attention while he passed from Buck's Row in the twilight into Whitechapel Road, and was lost sight of in the morning's market traffic.

"We cannot altogether leave unnoticed the fact that the death that you have been investigating is one of four presenting many points of similarity, all of which have occurred within the space of about five months, and all within a very short distance of the place where we are sitting. All four victims were women of middle age, all were married, and had lived apart from their husbands in consequence of intemperate habits, and were at the time of their death leading an irregular life, and eking out a miserable and precarious existence in common lodging-houses. In each case there were abdominal as well as other injuries. In each case the injuries were inflicted after midnight, and in places of public resort, where it would appear impossible but that almost immediate detection should follow the crime, and in each case the inhuman and dastardly criminals are at large in society.

"Emma Elizabeth Smith, who received her injuries in Osborn Street on the early morning of Easter Tuesday, April 3, survived in the London Hospital for upwards of twenty-four hours, and was able to state that she had been followed by some men, robbed and mutilated, and even to describe imperfectly one of them. Martha Tabram was found at three a.m. on Tuesday, August 7, on the first floor landing of George Yard Buildings, Wentworth Street, with thirty-nine puncture wounds on her body. In addition to these, and the case under your consideration, there is the case of Annie Chapman, still in the hands of another jury.

"The instruments used in the two earlier cases are dissimilar. In the first it was a blunt instrument, such as a walking-stick; in the second, some of the wounds were thought to have been made by a dagger; but in the two recent cases the instruments suggested by the medical witnesses are not so different. Dr. Llewellyn says the injuries on Nicholls [sic] could have been produced by a strong bladed instrument, moderately sharp. Dr. Phillips is of opinion that those on Chapman were by a very sharp knife, probably with a thin, narrow blade, at least six to eight inches in length, probably longer. The similarity of the injuries in the two cases is considerable. There are bruises about the face in both cases; the head is nearly severed from the body in both cases; there are other dreadful injuries in both cases; and those injuries, again, have in each case been performed with anatomical knowledge. Dr. Llewellyn seems to incline to the opinion that the abdominal injuries were first, and caused instantaneous death; but, if so, it seems difficult to understand the object of such desperate injuries to the throat, or how it comes about that there was so little bleeding from the several arteries, that the clothing on the upper surface was not stained, and, indeed, very much less bleeding from the abdomen than from the neck. Surely it may well be that, as in the case of Chapman, the dreadful wounds to the throat were inflicted first and the others afterwards.

"This is a matter of some importance when we come to consider what possible motive there can be for all this ferocity. Robbery is out of the question; and there is nothing to suggest jealousy; there could not have been any quarrel, or it would have been heard. I suggest to you as a possibility that these two women may have been murdered by the same man with the same object, and that in the case of Nicholls [sic] the wretch was disturbed before he had accomplished his object, and having failed in the open street he tries again, within a week of his failure, in a more secluded place. If this should be correct, the audacity and daring is equal to its maniacal fanaticism and abhorrent wickedness. But this surmise may or may not be correct, the suggested motive may be the wrong one; but one thing is very clear— that a murder of a most atrocious character has been committed."

All and sundry in Great Britain read this while at the same time pages of the newspapers were full of shocking details of the gruesome murder of Annie Chapman. She had now become one in a definite string of bizarre murders. "High Rip" gangs blackmailing prostitutes was no longer a tenable theory. Emma Smith probably had indeed been killed by one. But Baxter had introduced the most piquing theory: an individual with a twisted purpose. He had been very justified to note that Chapman's and Nichols' murders seem to have been done by the same person. In fact, when put together it is undeniable that they stand alone. Chapman's death would also in retrospect reveal things for us in Nichols' slaying that had gone unnoticed, and this would telescope back to reveal things in Tabram's death. The more sublime clues will prove to be the most illuminating.

4

RIDDLER AT THE SCENE

BY SEPTEMBER 7 the nights were growing increasingly cooler
and falling sooner. Smoke curled up from thousands of chimneys and stove pipes. The sun struggled to glow through the
rusty firmament. Dusk turned the smog into a golden musty
cobweb, a hazy veil made visible at night only around the
constricted orbs of light the scrawny lampposts eked out in
this inferno of poverty.

Dorset Street was a narrow cleft of gloomy shadows.
Dusty light had little to reveal but cobblestones etched with
years of wagon wheels and strewn with rubbish. This was
London's center of vice. Not the East End's alone. It was the
worst street in all of greater London. At night it seemed as if
the street was plunged to the depths of a murky harbor.
Charcoal night, tinted by the moon's amber smog, was thick
and moved about as if with ebb and flow. Within the ripples
of dank shadows moved every culprit of the dark. Over cheap
shops were dosshouses, whorehouses, and every form of lair
for thieves' gangs plotting about dim gaslight. Inside the disease of poverty cringed in shameful voids, but the rogue and
scallywag festered around clandestine embers.

At 5 p.m. Annie Chapman was also there. At the moment
she is sober, but she doesn't seem well. She is sitting,
slouched on a crate. Dark Annie was fairly easy to recognize.
She must have been close to 50, though her hair was not yet
turning gray. She was dressed in the only sure home she

Dorset Street, a horrid, depressing center of poverty and licentiousness. It was a scar on London.

had— her bland dress and long black coat. She was a stoutish woman, about 5 feet high, but she was one to hold herself in a fight, though she had sacrificed some teeth on the altar of beer and perhaps to a fist now and again.

Another woman, Amelia Palmer, passes, stops, and asks if she's going to the place where she plies her trade. Annie says "No." Nothing else. Amelia greets this with a shrug and simply walks away. A few minutes later she returns. Annie finally sighs and says: "It's no use my giving way. I must pull myself together and go out and get some money or I shall have no lodgings." She gets up and strolls off to earn her bread amongst the hubbub of Commercial Street.

The path of Annie Chapman to this sorry point is a long and sad one. In 1869 at the age of 28 she had married John Chapman. She had by him 3 children and lived a peaceable life, or so it was thought. In 1881 they moved to Windsor. He was a coachman in private service, and Windsor was a grand place and breath of fresh air. It was in the country, and it had the honor of the Royal castle nearby.

But tragedy happened soon thereafter. John Jr., born in

1880, was too crippled for them to handle and he was sent to a "home." Their eldest daughter Emily, only 12 years old, died in 1882. The toll was no doubt heavy upon Annie and John. She had, in fact, been arrested on several occasions for drunkenness. A few years later they both agreed to a separation. A police report says that John Chapman had had enough of her drinking and "immoral ways."

Somehow Annie gravitated to the worst part of England and London — Whitechapel. She was by 1886 living on Dorset Street in a ghastly dosshouse. Living on Dorset was a statement in itself. Surviving here was an even bigger statement. When chasing a criminal, even bobbies stopped at its entrance and didn't proceed further without support. It took a tough hide and good fists to survive here and earn a reputation.

Yet as tough as she was, Annie cried when John's brother was able to let her know that her estranged husband had died in Windsor of cirrhosis. By this time she was living with a sieve maker nicknamed Sivvey. Until that time John Chapman had been paying her 10 shillings per week. When this now stopped, coincidently Sivvey left her.

"The Pensioner" took her up. He was Edward Stanley, a mountebank who dubiously claimed the distinction of being a military pensioner when he was not. He was an odd one, even amongst the dirty dregs of Whitechapel. How he made his money was a bit of a mystery. He was gone for weeks and then returned. He and Annie spent weekends together at her lodging house (Crossingham's). He was apparently jealous enough or extravagant enough that he also paid for her bed (8 pence for a double bed). He instructed the caretaker of the house, a one Tim Donovan, not to admit her if she ever came in with other men. It seemed "The Pensioner" was concerned that Annie might have a bloke on his bob. He, however, was broadminded and hypocritical enough to pay for another woman's bed during the week, a tough scarecrow named Eliza Cooper.

Although there is evidence that Annie was on the weekends being kept by "The Pensioner," she was also certainly making a living by prostitution. She had first turned to it after John died and again when Spivvey ran out. She apparently only augmented her income with it when needed. Otherwise she did some crocheting and sold flowers.

In May 1888 she accidently stumbled into her brother, Fountain Smith, while on Commercial Road. She explained her appearance by saying she was hard up. Her work with crocheting, etc., hadn't been paying off. She hesitated at first and then avoided telling him where she was living. He gave her 2 shillings.

Soon Annie would be in a more precarious position. Stanley's support, as awkward as it was, at least gave her a week-end bed once in a while. But that sinewy magpie Eliza was apparently tiring of the mutual relationship. Stanley had been away for a month, and the acrimony between Annie and Eliza was no doubt building. Now on September 1 he had returned. While all three were together at the Britannia public house, a brawl breaks out. The blows miss Harry the Hawker, a local scamp who is talking with Stanley, but nobody else. Amidst the squawking cat fight Eliza belts Annie a good black eye and gives her a bruise on her breast.

Supposedly, Annie saw this as a good time to do in Eliza's reputation before same could be done to her. Some heard that she saw Cooper pinch a florin from Stanley and replace it with a penny. Annie sounds off to Harry about it, but before it's completely out of her mouth Eliza cocks her snoot. There is yet another story, as told by Amelia Palmer. She says that Annie said the contretemps happened at the pub but the knock-down-drag-out took place at the Crossingham lodging house on lovely Dorset Street.

Eliza's version is far more entertaining and punctuated by the lower East End accent and sense of cockney irony and wordplay. "The quarrel arose in this way, see: On the previous Saturday she brought Mr. Stanley into the house where I lodged in Dorset Street, and coming into the kitchen asked the people to give her some soap. They told her to ask 'Liza'— meaning me. She came to me, and I opened the locker and gave her some. She gave it to Stanley, who went outside and washed himself in the lavatory. When she came back I asked for the soap, but she did not return it. She said, 'I will see you by, and bye.' Mr. Stanley gave her two shillings, and paid for her bed for two nights. I saw no more of her that night. On the following Tuesday I saw her in the kitchen of the lodging-house. I said, 'Perhaps you will return my soap.' She threw a halfpenny on the table, and said, 'Go and get a halfpennyworth of soap.' We got quarrelling over this piece of soap, and we went out to the Ringers Public-house and continued the quarrel. She slapped my face, and said, 'Think yourself lucky I don't do more.' I struck her in the left eye, I believe, and then in the chest. I afterwards saw that the blow I gave her had marked her face."

Stout Annie, presumptuous that she had the upper hand in any brawl, had apparently met her match. When the black eye became a beauty, she said to Tim Donovan, the lodging house deputy (when he saw it): "Tim, this is lovely, ain't it?" Stanley himself didn't know what to say when he saw it a couple days later.

On September 3, Annie bumps into Amelia on Dorset. "How did you get that?" cried Palmer. As though the black eye was nothing, Annie pulled her dress back to reveal the bruise. "Yes, look at my chest." The bruises are bad enough that she doesn't feel well, but Annie's not one to whine. She says she has a chance to make some money during the yearly hop harvest where all itinerant workers are desperately needed. "If I can get a pair of boots from my sister," she said, "I may go hop picking."

The damage was bad enough that after Annie goes inside she tells Tim she may have to go to the infirmary. Instead Amelia sees her the next day before Christ Church. Annie repeats she isn't feeling well and that now she may go and spend a couple of days at the infirmary. Amelia gives her 2 ducats and warns her stiffly not to spend it on rum.

To the workhouse infirmary Annie goes, but she wasn't bad enough for them to keep her. She is given some pills and sent away.

By Friday, September 7, at 5 p.m., when Amelia saw her languishing on Dorset, Annie was better but not tip-top. She still wasn't, and had not been, eating well. Although she didn't tell Amelia, she had been spending the money on booze.

In this condition she got up and prepared herself. Without a real scarf she tied a gay handkerchief around her neck and sashayed onto Commercial Street.

Christchurch, Spitalfields, at Commercial and Brushfield.

Commercial Street was a vein that grafted from the artery that was Whitechapel Road. Victorian tenements, shops, tobacco manufactories, breweries, receiving yards and lodgings were more modern and adorned here. Brick fronts sported tall gabled pediments and roofs. There was a certain weekend hubbub in the air this night. Classes were easy to spot. Working lads had their drab jackets and white scarfs tied in an unfashionable knot about their necks under their open collar. The middleclass blokes perhaps had a waistcoat and tie. West End gents had their cravats with large frivolous bows, their hair wavy and flamboyant. Checkered or plaid pants added a gaudy touch, and pointed high steps shoes seemed a rigid contrast. Bowlers, top hats, John Bulls, wideawakes and, of course, cheesecutter (newsboy) caps, bobbed along the streets, a jaunty tilt to some. Pavilions and music halls clamored with delight. Hackneys jammed up in front, picking up and dropping their clients.

Frankly, this wide spectrum was clientele too far above a soiled gutter flower like Annie. But further from the weekend merriment, the gay lights dimmed to the gray-green of charcoal dirty streets. Such a street was Hanbury Street. A clock

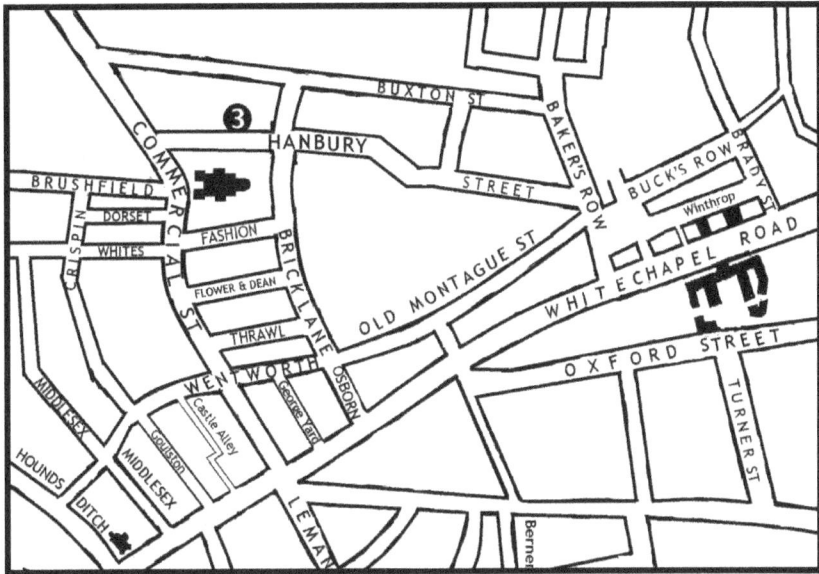

Hanbury Street in relation to Dorset and other main Whitechapel streets.

outside a shop might strike from the shadows. Big Ben chimed in the distance. Fog horns sounded. People ambled along only sporadically. Barrows were still hauling goods. Horse hoofs clopped along in the darkness.

It is here that Annie was in her environment. Though she had dressed up, she was a stocky mess. Her hat was tied snugly under her chin, but it could not hide her bruised face and black eye. Many layers of flannel petticoats stank, but they kept her warm. Two bodices increased her stout figure. That black bonnet made her look shorter, but her boots compensated and gave her a little height. Her stained apron flounced around as she sashayed about. It kept the grime of the street from her black dress. Not much white showed. Her black jacket came to her knees, and this evening she had it buttoned. The brightest thing on her was her neckerchief. It had a jaunty tie in it, with a flashy red border. She couldn't appear too respectable and just be one of the poor of the poor. She was now at 47 a pathetic sight, her left lower jaw gaunt from the absence of teeth, her winking black eye not so inviting. She was a very middle-aged catch for the night. . . and she wasn't too successful.

At 11:30 p.m. she staggered into the kitchen of the lodging house and asked to remain a while. The kitchen in any lodging house was the center of late night entertainment and utilitarian chores. Clay pipes puff from the mouth of gossipy lodgers. Other members wash their clothes or cook what dinner they got at the corner stall. Light from the fireplace, clandestine and moody, flickers in the dull eyes and warms the gray faces before it. Others just sit and booze. At 12:10 a.m., Saturday morning now, another lodger, Frederick Stevens, has a pint of beer with Annie.

Even more the worse-for-the-wear now she tells another lodger, William Stevens, that she has been to her sister and got 5 pence. No doubt she was lying. She either made the money prostituting or, more likely, not at all. But saying that she had 5 pence on her would make them think she was a sure lodger for the night and they would let her enjoy the warm kitchen.

While downing the ale, Annie takes a broken pill box from her pocket and it breaks completely. She takes a worn piece of envelope from the mantelpiece and wraps the pills in it. She leaves the kitchen but says nothing.

However, it wasn't to bed. She returns to the lodging house at 1:35 a.m. eating a late night baked potato she bought in one of the pubs or stalls. The night watchman, John Evans, approaches her about her bed money.

She goes upstairs and talks to Donovan. "I haven't sufficient money for my bed," she tells him, "but don't let it. I shall not be long before I'm in."

Donovan is amazed. "You can find money for your beer and you can't find money for your bed!"

She stands in the doorway for a while, considering what to do. She turns back. "Never mind, Tim," she says confidently. "I'll soon be back." Evans is standing by. "I won't be long, Brummy," she says to him. "See that Tim keeps the bed for me."

Evans watches her leave and head down Little Paternoster Row going toward Brushfield Street. There she turns toward the Spitalfields Market.

Back to Hanbury she must have gone, for at 5:30 a.m. Elizabeth Long is passing by 29 Hanbury, going west to

Hanbury Street. Arrow marks the spot of 29 Hanbury.

Commercial, when she notices Chapman leaning against the shutters, still trying to score. She is facing and speaking to a man whose back is toward Long. He wears a deerstalker hat (Sherlock Holmes' hat) and a long overcoat. He is dark, a bit foreign looking. Together with his manner it creates an interesting hybrid: "shabby genteel." Long takes no more notice than this as she passes, except she hears Chapman finally have success. The man says "Will you?" to which Chapman replies "Yes." At that moment, the clock on the Black Eagle Brewery on Brick Lane strikes the half hour. Long continues on her way.

No. 29 is a former weaver's shop now converted into a small lodging house. The ground floor street-side is a cat's meat shop. There is a long passageway next to it that passes through to the small backyard. The doors are always left unlocked front and back for the residents coming and going. The man, whoever he was, must have led Annie Chapman back here. The backyard is three steep steps down from the back door. Standing up here gives one a vista over the short fences of all the adjoining yards. Loos and woodsheds line the back fences in each. They step down and sink into the gray mist of the yard.

Although the last word she said to him out front was "Yes," the last word Annie says back here is "No!" The man clutches her neck until her tongue swells and little pin pricks of blood erupt in her eyes. Her hands clutch on him so firmly that her fingernails bruise. Her hands finally let go and arms fall limp. He lets her down to the ground. She is still breathing but unconscious. He turns her face to the right to reveal the left of her neck more. He clutches her jaw. He takes out a long, sharp knife and jabs it into her left carotid artery. He angles the blade to direct the gushing of blood to the ground. Moments pass. Starting on the left under the ear, he slices deep and quick across and back over. More blood oozes out over her right shoulder. He unbuttons the coat quickly, pulls down the dress and under-linen to reveal her bare abdomen. He notices a little sack tied around her held by strings. He has time to wait while the body drains completely of blood. He tears it and empties the contents by her feet along the fence. The body has drained enough now and the skin is pale.

He jabs into the abdomen his knife blade and cuts down from the sternum to the groin. Loops of intestines budge out and no doubt there is a release of steam in the cold morning. He cuts more and removes skin in flaps and flays the abdomen open. He throws up the small intestines over the right shoulder; loose folds of skin and part of the stomach over the left. It splashes into the pool of blood. Splatters hit as far as the back wall by the door. With a sure slice of his knife he removes her uterus. He takes what he wants and quietly goes.

It is not even 6 a.m. yet. John Davis comes out the back door. He lives on the third floor with his family. He is a carman and he is preparing to go to work. He is stunned to find a woman's body laying out the back door, her head just inches from the bottom of the steps. It is a grisly sight.

Davis stumbles through the passageway to the front door on Hanbury Street where he alerts 2 other men. Together they dash off to find a constable. Fortunately, his frantic appearance attracts the attention of a plainclothesman at Commercial and Hanbury. It is Inspector Joseph Chandler. Davis tells him about the dead body.

They rush back.

There Chandler descends the steps and peers over the brutally gutted body. Chapman lies along the fence, just a foot or so from it, her feet pointing to the woodshed at the back of the yard. Her face is to the right and her grotesquely bulged eyes stare into the yard. The left arm is folded and the hand rests on the left breast. The right hand, with arm extended, is on the ground by her side. Her throat was slit just under her tied gay handkerchief, and there was a pool of blood under the neck and *smears* of it on the wood palings of the fence. Her legs are propped up, the feet on the ground, still wearing the boots. There was no blood on the stockings. Her black coat was unbuttoned and opened, her clothes parted out of the way. But *none* of the clothes were cut.

Chandler immediately sent for Dr. Bagster Phillips and more constables. A crowd was beginning to form in the passageway, and people were rushing to the spot all along Hanbury Street. Chandler had the body covered with a sack as they waited for the good doctor.

George Bagster Phillips was no ordinary local sawbones.

The backyard of 29 Hanbury. Along the fence at the bottom of the steps the body lay.

He was the actual district surgeon for the police. But he wasn't a hardened, crude slum doctor. He struck many as a gentleman who had eloped from an old portrait of some 50 years before. He should have been in an early Dickens novel, walking along with long tails on his coat, a handkerchief up his wrist, and boasting about the grand days of Regency England. His manner was old style, nothing "modern" about him.

His horses clopped his comfortable brougham up to the street crowd. He stepped out and squeezed his way through the tumult and down the passageway.

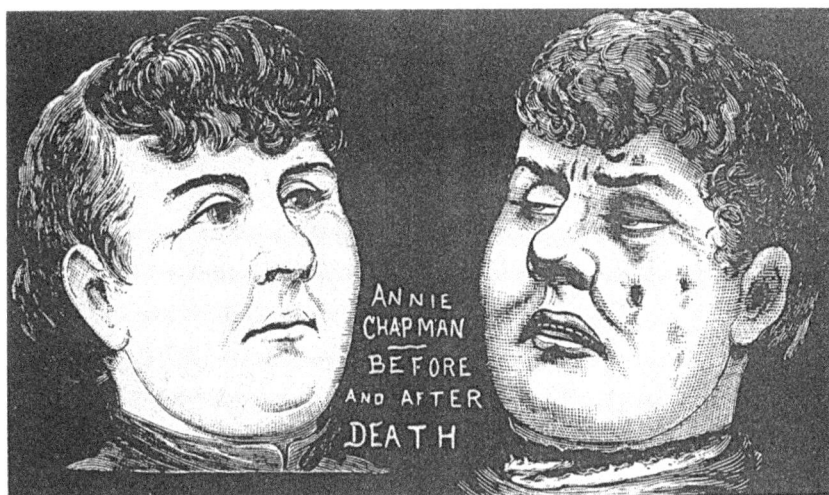

ANNIE
CHAPMAN
BEFORE
AND AFTER
DEATH

Illustrations spared the public nothing. But they made many mistakes. Chapman already had the black eye, and the bruise marks on her face are in the wrong locations. Bagster Phillips would stress their correct location at the inquest.

Little escaped his contemplative eyes. The victim's face was swollen. The tongue protruded between the teeth but not beyond the lips— signs of strangulation. The tongue was also swollen. Her shoulders were a mess with slimy intestines and cut stomach. The large bowel was not disturbed, but remained in the open cavity of the abdomen. Horrid bruises had purpled her cheeks and jaw. His eyes wandered past her hideous pose. He noted that items apparently belonging to the victim ("a piece of coarse muslin, a small tooth comb, and a pocket hair comb in a case"), which must have come from the torn purse, were lying near the feet and "apparently arranged" there.

Bagster Phillips must have called this idea to Chandler, for after the body was taken away (Phillips replaced the sections of skin and muscle and closed up the body) Chandler searched the entire yard. He found nothing more than the piece of the envelop Chapman had taken from the fireplace mantel at the lodging house. It had been by her head. In it remained two pills. Chandler makes no mention that the articles were "arranged." Thus he might have disagreed with Phillips' interpretation. But of all that was found, one article overshadowed them all. Chandler found a long leather apron on the stone slabs under the yard's dripping tap. Such a garment was ominous. It was often used by slaughterers or anybody whose profession required they use a sharp knife.

The newspapers went wild. The *Echo* was naturally first, putting out copy that very morning. "Another ghastly murder has been committed in the Whitechapel district this morning, the circumstances of the crime being almost identical with those which horrified London last week. . .The murder was affected precisely the same way as that of Mary Ann Nicholls [sic], the throat being cut and the lower part of the body horribly mutilated."

Then, as before, the *Echo* sharpened its own axe, bringing up how dissatisfied the community was with the police not apprehending the criminal already. "The dissatisfaction arises from the fact that the police, as they have become militarised, seem to have lost the art of detecting murders."

Two years prior, Sir Charles Warren's appointment as Commissioner of Police had been greeted favorably. But that view was now long in the tooth. General Warren had set about early to unintentionally create a controversy in Trafalgar Square on November 13, 1886, by ordering the police in like a military troop to clean out peaceful demonstrators and squatters. His methods had been viewed as crude and militaristic, and the day was condemned as "Bloody Sunday" after the police had to put down a riot that they had needlessly provoked. The papers were likewise beginning to view this as the police approach to detective work. The shotgun effect may work in battle, but detective work required a subtle knack at odds with the method of military bulls in china shops. Warren was now being blamed for making the police good for nothing but anti-insurgency at the sacrifice of the art of criminal detection.

Animosity against the police and the entire system was fomenting. It had no real core before. But now these bizarre murders highlighted what detractors of militarization wanted to exploit. Instead of seeing within the killer's modus operandi an exceptional talent (and greater purpose), the liberal press seized the opportunity to attribute the killer's success to official indifference and militarized incompetence.

This agenda did an injustice to the cunning that was inherent in the crimes. The scene here was especially hard to fathom. The yard of 29 Hanbury was essentially like the stage of an amphitheater. Windows looked down all around it. Yet nobody had seen anything. The police questioned all and sundry in the buildings. But there wasn't the slightest clue.

Moreover, the killer was not only incredibly quiet but unbelievably phantom-like. Chandler checked and checked again. No one jumped the fences. There was no blood in the passageway. Not a trail. Not a drop of blood anywhere. Not a clue. The killing and butchering was done in dawn light in a fishbowl of a yard, separated by only a rickety 5'6" fence from a line of other yards, and the killing was done as many were getting up, going to work, and heading to Spitalfields Market. It was an incredibly bold crime, and the killer left no trace from the scene. He must have walked casually away on the street and drew no attention to himself in the foot traffic of laborers going to work.

The *Echo* actually made many mistakes in order to rationalize the mystery because no one at first could believe the above scenario. The murder must have happened hours earlier under the cloak of darkness, the rag suggested. John Richardson, a tenant, had passed through the yard at 4:50 a.m. and saw nothing, but the *Echo* explained it away: "This, however, can be accounted for by the fact that the body lay in a corner, and might not have been observed by the young man." In quoting Davis' wife, they have her say that the body was "just in such a spot that no one could see from the outside, and thus the dead creature might have been lying there for some time."

The truth was quite the opposite. The body was at the foot of the stairs, and upon these Richardson had even sat and cut a piece of protruding leather off his shoes. It would have been impossible for him not to see the body.

So many excited rumors had already been spreading in the neighborhood that the *Echo* reporter merely repeated nonsense or wanted to help ease the local fears about a bizarre predator. There was so much excitement, in fact, that the police were becoming worried.

Crowds on Commercial Street, for example, were thrown

A close up of Hanbury Street.

into a tizzy by a 19 year old pickpocket. While he was being chased by a citizen shouting "stop thief," someone shouted he was the murderer. He straightaway plowed into a bobby in an alley and was in the process of being carted off when a crowd assembled. Hundreds of angry citizens followed the bobby and lad to the police station. Then it happened. At the mouth of Hanbury Street someone raised a shout that the murderer had been caught. "This was the signal for a general stampede in the direction of Commercial Street," wrote the *Echo*. Hundreds came from all the cross-streets, alleys, and from out of the shops. Someone then made it worse by shouting 'The murderer is caught!' This naturally was passed through the crowd. They soon found out their mistake when it was revealed the little weasel was but a pickpocket. Yet Hanbury was now so congested that traffic couldn't go through it. The people remained idling before the residence and discussing the incident. Then it got worse. Nearby a small group of police were escorting an ambulance to the mortuary. The crowd immediately gathered around, and a woman jumped on top and looked in. She swore to all those around that a dead body of a woman was inside, her head almost taken off. This incited the crowd to believe another murder had happened. The mortuary gates were then besieged, as people wanted to see what was going on.

The *Echo* brought up the rumor that on Hanbury Street a graffito was found and "the following paragraph, written in chalk, was seen upon the wall of one of the back gardens there, and four persons distinctly stated they had actually seen the writing. The words are, 'I have now done three, and intend to do nine more and give myself up, and at the same time give my reasons for doing the murders.' Whether there is any truth in the matter remains to be seen."

This was not the first time that newspapers reported graffiti. After Nichols' murder someone rudely scrawled on the horse slaughterer's gates that "this is where the murder was done," which caused the entire company and its workers to be outraged. The papers even allowed them an equal time to respond. After the inquest revealed how it was impossible that Nichols' murder could have been committed anywhere other than where she lay, the furor of accusation against the slaughterers died down.

But this Hanbury graffito was different. It was reported to be from the killer himself and was not an accusation. It was a challenge and a warning. Interestingly, the writer of the graffito does not consider the first death, Emma Smith, to be one of his, a conclusion only the police and not the papers had come to as well.

The excitement was intensified after the *Echo* and other papers rushed their articles into the September 8th editions. The murderer was quickly called a "monster" by the Press, but they had little understanding of how efficiently and cold-bloodedly he worked, how slyly he made his escape, and how discriminatingly he selected his middle-aged victims.

In the September 10 edition the *Echo* declared: "The mystery surrounding the crime serves, of course, to aggravate the interest." This in itself inspired them to report something very logical: the killer must fit in rather well in his environment. "Who may be the next victim? is a question to which is attached a terrible importance. 'For all we can tell,' said an agitated woman in the crowd yesterday assembled before the house at which the body had been found, 'the murderer may be one of the mob listening to the speechifying about it.' It was anything but improbable. That the assassin should have been there would have been quite in keeping with the cool audacity which must of necessity be characteristic of the man who, in all probability, has perpetrated all four of the murders which have so shocked this locality."

As far as it goes, this was indeed logical. But the Press did not have Elizabeth Long's description. In essence, the killer *had* stood out. A deerstalker hat? That's an odd bit of headgear to wear in an urban environment. Despite our false impressions from Sherlock Holmes movies, a deerstalker hat was not worn in the urban environment but rather worn when stalking deer or other game in the rural areas. It was a rather thin veneer of misplaced gentility on behalf of the man seen with Chapman that should have made him easily recognizable in the East End. But, strangely, the image never took hold on the public.Only the *Police Gazette* would offer a penny dreadful illustration of the killer in his deerstalker hat.

A different image was being formed in the public mind. In addition to the articles found at her feet, Annie's three cheap brass rings had vanished. From the abrasions apparent on her finger, clearly described by the meticulous Bagster Phillips, it was obvious they had been yanked off. Without being aware of Elizabeth Long's eyewitness descriptions of the man, newspapers were putting together their own mug shot of the killer. Facts were: silence with which he came and went, his obvious hatred for prostitutes, the petty theft of cheap rings, then, finally, that hideous leather apron, the mantel of a common, knife-toting working man. That leather apron was the worst possible coincidence. One denizen of Whitechapel nights had already earned a place in the Press. Surprisingly, he was known as "Leather Apron."

5

ℒEATHER APRON

IN THE WAKE of Polly Nichols' death "High Rip Gangs" had been the favored theory. At this time there had been no pattern but the type of victim. Tabram had been stabbed repeatedly. Nichols' throat had been slit and then her abdomen ripped up. Adding Emma Smith to the equation, whose deathbed testimony implicated a gang of cutthroats, and "High Rip Gangs" seemed a logical deduction. It was essentially the English theory. Most British newspapers carried some mention of Rip Gangs and the systematic blackmailing of prostitutes as a working theory. Ironically, the idea the killer was a single low-class demented bully stemmed from an American, and it first appeared in detail in the *New York Times* just days before the Chapman murder. This nemesis of "unfortunate women" was given the moniker "Leather Apron."

The journalist responsible was an American reporter on the London paper the *Star*, Harry Dam by name, who was also the stringer for the *New York Times*. Through Dam, this nebulous character, some nefarious tanner or slipper maker, crept quietly in custom made slippers about Whitechapel's dingy nights and into newspaper sensationalism. Only the *Star* ran detailed stories in England and evolved the character of Leather Apron in Dam's not-so-discriminating hands.

But the *Star*'s endorsement of the whole idea was no small

bagatelle. It boasted the largest evening circulation in the kingdom, and each night Victorian Britain rather favored sitting down before dark and getting a good dose of the willies.

According to Dam this Leather Apron was long known to "ill-use" prostitutes. Taking his leads from such a popular tome as *Murders on the Rue Morgue*, Dam's inspired *New York Times* article described him almost like a human gorilla. "A character halfway between Dickens' Quilp and Poe's baboon," declared the *Times* on September 4. "He is short, stunted and thickset. He has small, wicked black eyes and is half crazy."

On the 5th of September the *Star* introduced this hideous slipper-wearing villain in detail to London: "LEATHER APRON. A NOISELESS MIDNIGHT TERROR." Amidst the froth and spin of the article, Dam described the ghoulish assailant.

'Leather Apron' by himself is quite an unpleasant character. If, as many of the people suspect, he is the real author of the three murders which, in everybody's judgement were done by the same person, he is a more ghoulish and devilish brute than can be found in all the pages of shocking fiction. He has ranged Whitechapel for a long time. He exercises over the unfortunates who ply their trade after twelve o'clock at night, a sway that is based on universal terror.

He has kicked, injured, bruised, and terrified a hundred of them who are ready to testify to the outrages. He has made a certain threat, his favorite threat, to any number of them, and each of the three dead bodies represents that threat carried out. He carries a razor-like knife, and two weeks ago drew it on a woman called 'Widow Annie' as she was crossing the square near London Hospital, threatening at the same time, with his ugly grin and his malignant eyes, to 'rip her up.' He is a character so much like the invention of a story writer that the accounts of him given by all the street-walkers of the Whitechapel district seem like romances. The remarkable thing is, however, that they all agree in every particular.

Dam went on to elaborate how "about 50 of the unfortunates" in the district have furnished a consistent description to a *Star* reporter. "From all accounts he is five feet four or five inches in height and wears a dark, close-fitting cap. He is thickset, and has an unusually thick neck. His hair is black, and closely clipped, his age being about 38 or 40. He has a small, black moustache. The distinguishing feature of his costume is a leather apron, which he always wears, and from which he gets his nickname. . .His expression is sinister, and seems to be full of terror for the women who describe it. His eyes are small and glittering. His lips are usually parted in a grin which is not only not reassuring, but excessively repellant. He is a slipper maker by trade, but does not work. His business is blackmailing women late at night. A number of men in Whitechapel follow this interesting profession. He has never cut anybody so far as known, but always carries a leather knife, presumably as sharp as leather knives are wont to be. This knife a number of the women have seen. His name nobody knows, but all are united in the belief that he is a Jew or of Jewish parentage, his face being of a marked Hebrew type. But the most singular characteristic of the man, and one which tends to identify him closely with last Friday night's work, is the universal statement that in moving about he never makes any noise."

The success was such that next day, September 6, Dam and the *Star* elaborated. "The man is unquestionably mad, and that anybody who met him face to face would know it. That his eyes are never still, but are always shifting uneasily, and he never looks anybody in the eye."

The *Star*'s continuing coverage of Leather Apron was in the mold of the current stage success of *Dr. Jekyll and Mr. Hyde*. It told of a police hunt to find the man and bring him to book and then, out of nowhere, called him a "crazy Jew." They "went through lodging-houses, into 'pubs,' down side streets, threw their bull's-eyes into every shadow, and searched the quarter thoroughly, but without result."

The *Star*'s ever vigilant reporter, Dam's minion sent to the East End (probably reporter Fred Best), visited one of the lodging houses on Thrawl Street, describing it as "one of the darkest and most terrible-looking spots in Whitechapel." Scores of women huddled in this lodging like so many doves frightened of this "terror of the East-end." The owner of the establishment was interviewed. "Night after night, he said,

GHASTLY MURDER

IN THE EAST-END.
DREADFUL MUTILATION OF A WOMAN.

Capture : Leather Apron

Another murder of a character even more diabolical than that perpetrated in Back's Row, on Friday week, was discovered in the same neighbourhood, on Saturday morning. At about six o'clock a woman was found lying in a back yard at the foot of a passage leading to a lodging-house in a Old Brown's Lane, Spitalfields. The house is occupied by a Mrs. Richardson, who lets it out to lodgers, and the door which admits to this passage, at the foot of which lies the yard where the body was found, is always open for the convenience of lodgers. A lodger named Davis was going down to work at the time mentioned and found the woman lying on her back close to the flight of steps leading into the yard. Her throat was cut in a fearful manner. The woman's body had been completely ripped open and the heart and other organs laying about the place, and portions of the entrails round the victim's neck. An excited crowd gathered in front of Mrs. Richardson's house and also round the mortuary in old Montague Street, whither the body was quickly conveyed. As the body lies in the rough coffin in which it has been placed in the mortuary · the same coffin in which the unfortunate Mrs. Nicholls was first placed · it presents a fearful sight. The body is that of a woman about 45 years of age. The height is exactly five feet. The complexion is fair, with wavy brown hair; the eyes are blue, and two lower teeth have been knocked out. The nose is rather large and prominent.

The menace that was "Leather Apron" grew so large that it went hand-in-hand with the broadcast of the Chapman murder.

had women come in in a fainting condition after being knocked about by 'Leather-Apron.' He himself would never be out in the neighborhood after twelve o'clock at night except with a loaded revolver. The 'terror,' he said, would go to a public-house or coffee-room, and peep in through the window to see if a particular woman was there. He would then vanish, lying in wait for his victim at some convenient corner, hidden from the view of everybody . . .One of them said she saw him crossing London Bridge as stealthily as usual, with head bent, his skimpy coat turned up about his ears, and looking as if he were in a desperate hurry."

The villainous menace that was "Leather Apron" leapt from the *Star*'s evening pages and careened through the streets. Its placards at stands carried daily headlines of the fiendish haunt silently stalking the shadows of Whitechapel and, thanks to Dam, the West End and the promenades of the rich, idle and aristo.

The *Star*'s editors may have nightly added the fangs and wings and then laughed at their paper's creation, but Dam's minion reporter in the East End had unwittingly fleshed out something amongst the pots of Whitechapel. There was indeed a man nicknamed "Leather Apron." Amidst the flurry of people set into a panic by Dam's articles, a woman had mentioned a man named Jack Pizer to the police. This was no surprise to Police Constable William Thick. His beat was along Pizer's home street. When he was first told about the *Star* stories, he knew right away that "Leather Apron" always meant Pizer. The police started looking for him, but it was soon obvious that he had vanished.

There seems little doubt that Dam's creation was thinly based on the real life Jack Pizer, thanks to the reporter who carried back snippets of tales from Whitechapel's gossipy dregs. Pizer was indeed Jewish and was a cobbler. However, thanks to Dam's imaginative writing, something not-so-pleasant began after Chapman was murdered. The East End was so excited by the grotesque murder and the phantom form Dam had created that Anti-Semitism broke out.

On September 9, *Lloyd's Weekly*, which boasted the largest circulation in the kingdom, ran a special Sunday Edition, speaking about "Yesterday's Tragedy" which described Chapman's body as "shockingly mutilated." Number 29 Hanbury Street was so congested with sightseers that the occupants were charging a penny per peek at the bloody scene of the crime. Several hundred pence were made by that afternoon. Then it began to happen. "As the day advanced and the Jewish East End crowds congregated around the scene of the murder, and its neighbourhood became more leavened with English working men, the excitement grew; and, unfortunately, owing to the rumours about the individual 'Leather

Apron,' took a rather nasty turn. Bodies of young roughs raised cries against the Jews, and many of the disreputable and jabbering women sided with them. This state of things caused several stand-up fights, thus putting a further and serious strain on the police, many of whom began to express their fears of rioting."

This was no longer Press exaggeration. Tensions were increasing. Extra police were already on hand to direct traffic and keep it moving from gawking at the Hanbury residence, but despite this the crowds had started to stagnate. "Just as our correspondent was writing, a gang of young vagabonds marched down Hanbury Street," read the *Lloyd's* article, "shouting 'Down with the Jews!' 'It was a Jew who did it!' 'No Englishman did it!' After these the police were prompt, and whenever there was a stand they quickly, and without ceremony, dispersed them. There have been many fights, but the police are equal to it, as men are held in reserve under cover, and when there is a row they rush out and soon establish order."

Then as dusk was approaching, it got worse. Laborers just off work joined in. They swelled the crowds to such an alarming extent that the bobbies called for extra men from Scotland Yard.

Early the next morning Thick trumped them all. He appeared at the door of 22 Mulberry Street, the residence of Jack Pizer's family. Pizer himself answered the door and Thick said "Just the man I'm looking for."

Pizer's family was clearly expecting this. Aside from his mother and sister-in-law, a patroness of his, Mrs. Nathan, was also there to give comfort and bear favorable witness. After searching the house for any weapons, Thick took Pizer into custody. Due to the undercurrents in Whitechapel, Pizer was taken as quietly as possible to Leman Street police station to be questioned regarding his whereabouts during the crimes.

But Pizer's capture was not secret for long. Leman Street station was soon surrounded by a crowd. They were more curious than aggressive, but from yesterday's experience the police prepared themselves. A cordon of bobbies held their staves drawn to keep back the crowd.

Inside, Pizer was giving his story. He was a nervous but simple fellow. He was a boot finisher by trade and had been living at 22 Mulberry for quite a while with his stepmother and a married brother, a cabinet maker. He had been scared of all that was going on and therefore had stayed inside. While he continued, the police waited for certain members of the Wilmot's lodging house to come by. The police told him that they would or would not identify him as this "Leather Apron." This very term upset him and he insisted he never knew that he had been referred to as that before. He also insisted he had never worn a leather apron on the streets before either. For the last 6 weeks he had been working for his step-brother in cabinet making.

As time wore on, the crowds outside grew and made it difficult to bring the witnesses here. The police warned him that they would feel better taking him to the main police station in the district at Commercial Street. Pizer, too, was beginning to suffer. His mother and sister had confirmed that prior to his recent work he had been sick with a carbuncle on his neck and had been in the hospital. After two hours at the police station, Pizer was fatigued and fading gray with nervousness about whether the thin police cordon would hold the crowd back.

One hour later he was finally led into the main station. Enough reporters and people were there to make a small to-do, but 6 bobbies were sufficient to guard the steps.

No sooner had he sat down "on the seat next the outside wall. . .pale and rather dejected" when a woman waiting by predesign was nudged and told to have a look at him. "Then Piser [sic] was taken into the inner office, the doors were closed, and the further ceremonies were known only to the detectives," reported the *Star*.

This was that newspaper's baby, and the *Star* hung on Pizer like a leech. Unfortunately for Dam and the gang the police were quite satisfied with Pizer's account of himself. They were also influenced by his weak appearance and poor health. What was most disastrous for the *Star* was that the witnesses confirmed this was the only man known as Leather Apron. The paper glossed over this. "The man arrested by the police this morning and erroneously described as 'Leather

Apron' was able to satisfy the authorities of Bethnal Green Station of his identity and of his absolute innocence of anything connected with the Spitalfields tragedy. Consequently he was immediately discharged."

Not so surprisingly, the *Star* quickly went on to the other arrests. "The police, however, attach far more importance to the arrest which has been made at Gravesend, but will not express an opinion until witnesses who have been sent for have seen him." The Gravesend arrest amounted to nothing. He was a 52 year old man who had stopped to help a woman having a fit and she bit his hand and he punched her a couple of times for it. Inspector Abberline himself escorted him to the station for identification. He barely stood 5 feet tall, was nervous, and smoked a clay pipe while he waited patiently. He was quickly released. None of the crowd around the police station had even noticed him.

Seven other suspects were also in custody in the East End, each an unlikely fit for being the night assassin. By the end of the day several of them had been released. None had amounted to much, least of all Leather Apron.

On Tuesday September 11, there was a minor attempt by the *Daily Telegraph* to salvage the idea that Pizer was not the actual Leather Apron to which all in Whitechapel had made onus reference. Was there indeed another? Well, by the end of the article it became clear that the answer was no. Pizer alone had been it. The paper had to print that all those who knew of him "were careful to add that in no case of annoyance to women had he been detected in offering violence to them such as had been attributed to the perpetrator of the Whitechapel murders. Further, those who were more or less familiar with his ways of life inclined to the opinion that he was of too weak a frame, and too cowardly a nature, to commit such aggravated assaults as those which had been perpetrated upon the bodies of Mary Nicholls [sic] and Annie Chapman."

Leather Apron as a story died quickly, and finally the *Star*'s Dam was inferred by other papers to have done nothing but listen to an "idiot" reporter (Fred Best) sent to the East End.

Without Pizer as a central figure, the mystery of who actually was stalking the rusty nights returned. "The scene of the latest murder was yesterday still visited by large numbers of people, while groups of men and women hung about the street corners discussing the details of the tragedy. As for the police, they have been inconveniently worried by inquiries, while they have also received a good deal of gratuitous information, which has, unhappily, proved of little value. Last night, at a late hour, there were still a few idlers around the police-stations, but there are signs that the excitement of the last three days is gradually waning."

Whitechapel's more prosperous tradesmen were getting worried and mad. A committee was formed on the 10th consisting of 16 of the chief tradesmen. Since it was against the policy of Scotland Yard to issue any reward for a criminal, the Committee issued a formal statement that they would give a reward for any information leading to the arrest of the villain. This was greeted by the locals as the right thing to do. They were sure that with a fat reward hanging over the killer's head someone would turn magpie and tip off the police. After all, these were gory murders. The killer must be conspicuous at one point, even if only when returning to his lodgings. That evening the papers reported that "The proposal to form district vigilance committees also meets with great popular favour, and is assuming practical form. Meetings were held at the various working men's clubs and other organisations, political and social, in the district, at most of which the proposed scheme was approved and volunteers enrolled."

Whitechapel was bracing itself. Details had been coming out at the inquest, and these suggested something far more sinister was afoot than some poor odd fellow like John Pizer.

6

GORY DETAILS

AMIDST THIS FUROR the Working Lad's Institute once again saw a gathering of concerned citizens, newspapermen, news couriers, a twenty man jury, a line of police, witnesses, and several Press artists to sketch the proceedings and give form to the event for an eager Britain and world. Now on Tuesday, September 10, it was the time for the actual facts to come out.

The jury filed in looking very frustrated and angry already. The police sitting about waiting to testify were also frustrated, but for a different reason. The inquest gave Wynne Baxter the greatest soap box upon which to set his topper suit, dapper cravat, and narrow gaze. He had drawn out the Nichols inquest, so that as this one now began hers was still only on a recess, the Press still salivating for more dreadful revelations. He was, it seemed, milking this for all it was worth. With all this attention, Baxter could use center stage for whatever he wanted. And he had so far shown with Nichols' inquest that his inquests were in essence to be trials *in absentia* of the miscreant. This in itself could project to the people that he shared in the Press' subtle indictment of police competency — the militarization the papers had already complained about.

Wynne Baxter could not help but look better by comparison. He presented the appearance of authority, but that of the Queen's coroner and not a lackey of the Metropolitan Police.

Police News *brought us the details in graphic and dramatic tableaux— suspects fleeing, women arming themselves, the tumult, and, of course, the inquest details.*

His deep, dark eyes recessed in the shadow of his hard brow. His frightfully voluminous mustache took away any benevolence a relaxed mouth can give one. It added to his cold, immovable visage. His collar was starched and rigid, and perhaps this caused people not to notice that by comparison he was actually a flabby totem.

Baxter wasn't above snide inference to the police or escalating the issues to make them acquiesce. His jab at them was evident in the very first witness called. John Davis was the man who found the body. He detailed his movements from 8 p.m. the previous night and then described the yard. Here Baxter interrupted and asked the police if he could get a plan of the yard.

"In the country, in cases of importance, I always have one," he said.

Inspector Helson spoke out. "We shall have one at the adjourned hearing."

Baxter clipped him. "Yes; by that time we shall hardly require it."

This same attitude is seen in Baxter's regard for Davis not knowing who the 2 men were whom he had first fetched to assist him.

"They must be found," insisted Baxter.

"They work at Bailey's," offered Davis, "but I could not find them on Saturday, as I had my work to do."

Baxter was incredibly crude in response. "Your work is of no consequence compared with this inquiry."

Clearly Davis was taken aback. "I am giving all the information I can," he replied.

But Baxter merely stressed: "You must find these men out, either with the assistance of the police or of my officer."

The need was pressing, of course, since either of these men may have seen the killer fleeing the scene. But it was really pressing only for a police investigation, not for an inquest. Yet this was Baxter at a typical moment. It was pressing for *him* to know and for *him* to present them to the world Press first.

Many witnesses to the life of Annie Chapman testified that day, including Donovan, Palmer, and Evans. This merely set in order her miserable decline to the slums of the East End.

It was the next day that the first witness, James Kent (one of the men who worked at Bailey's and who had been found in the interim), was able to add to the grisly scene that Davis had already painted.

"Deceased's clothes were disarranged," he said, "and her apron was thrown over them . . .She appeared to have been on her back and fought with her hands to free herself. The hands were turned toward her throat. The legs were wide apart, and there were marks of blood upon them. The entrails were protruding, and were lying across her left side. I got a piece of canvass from the shop to throw over the body, and by that time a mob had assembled, and Inspector Chandler was in possession of the yard."

When asked to describe the position of the victim, he was able to point out her position on a plan that the police had quickly prepared by this morning in order to appease Baxter.

Kent contradicted Davis by about 10 minutes. He said it was 6:10 a.m. when Davis came bursting out. Otherwise he confirmed Davis' testimony. James Green was the other packer. He agreed with Davis that the time was 6 a.m. He had nothing else to add save that he too saw nobody touch the body. Neither Kent nor he were before Bailey's until 6 a.m. and neither saw anybody leave No. 29.

Mrs. Amelia Richardson's testimony is particularly interesting due to her knowledge of the house. She managed it for the owner and knew everybody in it. She made this plain enough by describing them and where each lived. Widow Richardson's rooms gave her a unique position, no doubt by design, to know all that went on in her house. The doors front and back were always left unlocked since people were coming and going to work at all hours of the night. With her rooms situated above the passage on the first floor (second floor in American parlance) she could hear anybody walking in the passage or in the yard, and oversee the street out front when she wanted. Going up or down, into the yard or out, her floor was a bulwark that had to be passed. She underscored that she was a light sleeper that night. She had had a bible study in the front room upstairs and went to bed late. At 3 a.m. she finally fell asleep but only dozed off and on thereafter. She had heard no noise whatsoever.

Baxter was naturally curious. Her response to his question "Did you ever see anyone in the passage?" is so specific that it reflects to what extent she was aware of intruders.

"Yes, about a month ago I heard a man on the stairs. I called Thompson [a lodger], and the man said he was waiting for market."

"At what time was this?"

"Between half-past three and four o'clock. I could hear anyone going through the passage. I did not hear anyone going through on Saturday morning."

"You heard no cries?" asked Baxter.

"None."

"Supposing a person had gone through at half-past three, would that have attracted your attention?"

"Yes."

"You always hear people going to the back-yard?"

"Yes; people frequently do go through."

Baxter clarified: "People go there who have no business to do so?"

"Yes; I dare say they do."

"On Saturday morning you feel confident no one did go through?"

"Yes; I should have heard the sound."

"They must have walked purposely quietly?"

"Yes; or I should have heard them."

The apparent silence of the couple was underscored by the cats' meat woman, Harriet Hardiman, who occupied the ground floor. She had heard nothing that night until 6 a.m. when there was stampeding in the hallway. She had her son go look as she thought there was a fire.

John Richardson was then called. He provided some curious testimony about why he came to the house at the lonely hour of 4:50 a.m. He said he came back from Spitalfield's Market (where he worked) to check the padlock on the cellar, for he had had things stolen before and wanted to make sure it was secure. This proved to be a bit of a surprise to his mother, since only a saw and hammer had been nicked but that had been a long time before.

Son John was plain about how the premises were used by couples.

Baxter: "You have been there at all hours of the night?"

"Yes."

Baxter: "Have you ever seen any strangers there?"

"Yes, plenty, at all hours— both men and women. I have often turned them out. We have had them on our first floor as well, on the landing."

Baxter: "Do you mean to say that they go there for an immoral purpose?"

"Yes, they do."

Richardson was told to go home and fetch the knife he used to cut the loose leather off his shoe.

When Baxter recalled Mrs. Richardson, she was horrified at the question: "Had you an idea at any time that a part of the house or yard was used for an immoral purpose?"

The bible believing Mrs. Richardson emphatically replied: "No, sir!"

Baxter didn't pursue it right away. The leather apron that had ignited so much interest had belonged to her son. He asked rather for her to clarify why she was cleaning it under the tap. It had been moldy, she said. After she finished, he came back to his original point. "Did you ever know of strange women being found on the first-floor landing?"

"No."

"Your son had never spoken to you about it?" said Baxter with some skepticism.

"No."

The devout bible studier was probably not keen on the idea that the premises of the local chapter of the ladies home bible study was being used for immoral purposes at late night. It would not be something she would want to face or broadcast to a roomful of newshounds. As for devout Son Richardson, we might have to face that he was not so pious as his mother. His excuse for having come home was pathetic, especially since it had been so long since something had been pinched from the cellar. Rather he might have come home at this dismal hour to find a bit of companionship himself, and when none was around decided to mend his shoe and go back to work. After a gutted corpse was found in the backyard, he had to think up some excuse, and the theft in the cellar a month before was the best thing he could come up with.

Contemporary sketch of the proceedings. Baxter sits rigid at center, flanked by the jury, Press and Dr. Phillips. Insets highlight key witnesses.

Smirks, if there were any on the newsmen's faces, were quickly wiped away. Leather Apron himself was now finally called. As the echo of Pizer's name faded, the room was quiet in anticipation. He confirmed he lived at 22 Mulberry Street off Commercial Road East.

"I am a shoemaker."

Baxter asked the big question. "Are you known by the nickname of Leather Apron?"

"Yes, sir."

"Where were you on Friday night last?"

"I was at 22, Mulberry Street. On Thursday, the 6th instant, I arrived there."

"From where?"

"From the west end of town."

Baxter: "I am afraid we shall have to have a better address than that presently."

There was no response. Baxter may not have given him time, and by his inflection he may have indicated it would be coming up at a more significant moment to follow, as indeed it does.

"What time did you reach 22, Mulberry Street?" asked Baxter.

"Shortly before eleven p.m."

"Who lives at 22, Mulberry Street?"

"My brother and sister-in-law and my stepmother. I remained indoors there."

"Until when?"

"Until I was arrested by Sergeant Thicke [sic], on Monday last at nine a.m."

"You say you never left the house during that time?"

"I never left the house."

"Why were you remaining indoors?"

"Because my brother advised me."

"You were the subject of suspicion?"

"I was the object of a false suspicion."

"You remained on the advice of your friends?"

"Yes; I am telling you what I did."

"It was not the best advice that you could have had," said Baxter. "You have been released, and are not now in custody?"

"I am not. . .I wish to vindicate my character to the world at large."

Clumsy. And no doubt Baxter restrained a sigh. "I have called you in your own interests, partly with the object of giving you an opportunity of doing so," he declared. He now asked formally: "Can you tell us where you were on Thursday, August 30?"

This was Pizer's big moment. . .and he used it to think. "In the Holloway Road," he finally said.

"You had better say exactly where you were," said Baxter sternly. "It is important to account for your time from that Thursday to the Friday morning."

Pizer was cagey. "What time, may I ask?"

"It was the week before you came to Mulberry Street."

It must have been painful to hear this slow-witted man grumble out these responses. But eventually Baxter was able to milk him enough so that Pizer got to the gist of his whereabouts. He was even in the presence of a constable talking about the Albert Dock fires at the relevant times of Nichols' murder.

"It is only fair to say," finally declared Baxter, "that the witness's statements can be corroborated."

Indeed, it was only fair for Baxter to reveal he already had much of this information. Calling Pizer to testify was done to help assuage the trouble in the East End. Otherwise how was Pizer truly relevant to the inquest? The purpose here was to determine how the body died and then return a verdict. Baxter was playing politics to a certain extent. He cared less about Pizer's reputation than he did about avoiding the public mania over the murderer. More than anybody, he knew Pizer could not have so deftly committed these crimes. He was a dullard, probably petty crook, and thoroughly too blunt and witless to carry out these crimes. From what Baxter knew of the Nichols' killing, and now having thrashed this case out in his chambers, he was impressed by the killer's style and swiftness. Pizer *never* could have done it.

Pizer cleared himself of Nichols' killing and in doing so by effect cleared himself of Chapman's, for it was undeniable the same hand had done both. Constable Thick soon confirmed the details of Pizer's arrest and release. More importantly he made it clear that when locals spoke of Leather Apron they spoke of Pizer. Thick himself had known him by that nickname for years.

The controversy was settled. The newshounds scribbled. News boys carried the messages back to the papers.

On September 13, 1888, the third day of the inquest was convened amidst the Leather Apron stories decidedly dying; slowly with the *Star*. One simply can't curse their own dog for not making the finish line.

Today, Inspector Chandler was the first witness called. He spoke of the gruesome sight. He noted that the palings of the fence were not that secure, but that they would no doubt support a man. However, an investigation was carried out in the adjoining yards and the fences did not appear as if they had been jumped at any time. Nor was there any sign of bloodstains.

"Did you search the body?"

"I searched the clothing at the mortuary. The outside jacket— a long black one, which came down to the knees— had bloodstains round the neck, both upon the inside and out, and two or three spots on the left arm. The jacket was hooked at the top, and buttoned down the front. By the appearance of the garment there did not seem to have been any struggle. A large pocket was worn under the skirt (attached by strings), which I produce. It was torn down the front and also at the side, and it was empty. Deceased wore a black skirt. There was a little blood on the outside. The two petticoats were stained very little; the two bodices were stained with blood round the neck, but they had not been damaged. There was no cut in the clothing at all. The boots were on the feet of deceased. They were old. No part of the clothing was torn. The stockings were not bloodstained."

It was the Nichols case all over— care taken with the clothes, but great mutilation to the body. Baxter couldn't help but cock his eyebrows as he scribbled his notes.

Yet one would expect Baxter to inquire further here and ask about the empty pocket and to what extent its articles indicated they were arranged by the fence by design. But he did not. Did Baxter intend to rely more on the astute Bagster Phillips who was waiting in the wings to testify? It is hard to say how Chandler affected Baxter. At present his career was secure, but in three years' time Chandler would be broken and reduced in rank for drunkenness on duty.

As it stood already, Baxter did not seem to care for him. This is seen when Chandler was later recalled to confirm that the body was taken to the mortuary on Old Montague Lane at 7 a.m. and the "shack" (the mortuary) was thereafter locked. It came out in his testimony that there were more problems at the "shack." Two nurses came in afterward to strip the body. At this time they apparently removed the handkerchief that Chapman had worn about her neck. When Dr. Phillips was doing the autopsy, Chandler found it in the corner on the pile of clothes. He showed Phillips, who asked him to put it in some water.

This handling of evidence was considered very disturbing to Baxter. He went into a dissertation about how the "shack" was no mortuary at all but a shed attached to a workhouse. The inmates had no business handling a body from such an important case like this.

Now, to make matters worse, Chandler had left a constable in charge but had given him no instructions. Thus when the nurses came, without instructions to the contrary, he apparently just let them in.

"Did you see the handkerchief taken off the body?"

"I did not. The nurses must have taken it off the throat."

"How do you know?"

"I don't know."

"Then you are guessing?"

"I am guessing."

"That is all wrong, you know," said Baxter with a shake of his head. He turned to the jury. "He is really not the proper man to have been left in charge."

In truth, Chandler should have given direct orders for the body not to have been touched, as Spratling had given in the Nichols case. It didn't help much there because of how things were done at the "shack," but apparently Chandler hadn't even made the effort.

Dr. Bagster Phillips' testimony was the one for which all were waiting. It would prove to be the longest and most controversial. He, too, complained about the "shack" and that he should have to work under those conditions; then he got into the meat of his testimony. He described the conditions of where the body lay, which has been gone-into enough already. But relevant details are: the largest amount of blood was to the left of the head and shoulders. "The face was swollen and turned on the right side, and the tongue protruded between the front teeth, but not beyond the lips; it was much swollen." It was clear that the throat had been cut from left to right. The bloodstains on the back wall were 18 inches from the ground and six in number. The blood smears on the wood palings were above where the neck of the body lay.

Examination of the brain indicated suffocation had taken place, which corroborated the swollen tongue and face. The fingernails were "turgid," and the fingers were partly bent, which means she must have really clutched on to the assailant to such an extent as he choked her that her fingernails bruised. "There was an abrasion over the bend of the first joint of the ring finger, and there were distinct markings of a ring or rings— probably the latter." (Eliza Cooper would later confirm that Chapman wore 3 brass rings of no value on the middle finger of the left hand.)

Phillips continued with the initial wound at the throat. "The throat was dissevered deeply. I noticed that the incision of the skin was jagged, and reached right round the neck." The throat had been slit below the neckerchief. "The incisions of the skin indicated that they had been made from the left side of the neck on a line with the angle of the jaw, carried entirely round and again in front of the neck, and ending at a point about midway between the jaw and the sternum or breast bone on the right hand. There were two distinct clean cuts on the body of the vertebrae on the left side of the spine. They were parallel to each other, and separated by about half an inch. The muscular structures between the side processes of bone of the vertebrae had an appearance as if an attempt had been made to separate the bones of the neck. There are various other mutilations of the body, but I am of opinion that they occurred subsequently to the death of the woman and to the large escape of blood from the neck." Phillips paused for a moment. "I am entirely in your hands, sir, but is it necessary that I should describe the further mutilations? From what I have said I can state the cause of death."

"The object of the inquiry is not only to ascertain the cause of death," responded Baxter, "but the means by which it occurred. Any mutilation which took place afterwards may suggest the character of the man who did it. Possibly you can give us the conclusions to which you have come respecting the instrument used."

Phillips received the compromise with relief. "You don't wish for details? I think if it is possible to escape the details it would be advisable. The cause of death is visible from injuries I have described."

Baxter treated a professional man far differently than a juror or laborer, but he remained hesitant. "Supposing anyone is charged with the offence, they would have to come out then, and it might be a matter of comment that the same evidence was not given at the inquest."

Phillips responded: "From these appearances I am of opinion that the breathing was interfered with previous to death, and that death arose from syncope, or failure of the heart's action, in consequence of the loss of blood caused by the severance of the throat."

In answer to Baxter's question whether the knife was the same one used on the abdomen as the one that cut the throat, Phillips agreed. "Very probably. It must have been a very sharp knife, probably with a thin, narrow blade, and at least six to eight inches in length, and perhaps longer."

Baxter brought the inquest back to the Tabram killing in an interesting way. He asked if a bayonet could have inflicted the wounds.

Phillips was quick to negate that.

Baxter had already been suspicious that expert knowledge was used in the killing and mutilations. He asked if it could have been "an instrument as a medical man uses for post-mortem examinations?"

Phillips didn't seem to like that. He was careful. "The ordinary post-mortem case perhaps does not contain such a weapon."

Baxter: "Would any instrument that slaughterers employ have caused the injuries?"

Phillips was more enthusiastic. "Yes; well ground down."

"Would the knife of a cobbler or of any person in the leather trades have done?"

"I think the knife used in those trades would not be long enough in the blade."

The big question followed. "Was there any anatomical knowledge displayed?"

"I think there was," Phillips replied confidently. "There were indications of it. My own impression is that anatomical knowledge was only less displayed or indicated in consequence of haste. The person evidently was hindered from making a more complete dissection in consequence of the haste." (Reference no doubt to Phillips' belief that the killer tried to behead the victim.)

Dancing around the mutilations issues, Baxter asked carefully: "Was the whole of the body there?"

Phillips was reserved. "No; the absent portions being from the abdomen."

"Are those portions such as would require anatomical knowledge to extract?"

"I think the mode in which they were extracted did show

some anatomical knowledge."

"You do not think they could have been lost accidentally in the transit of the body to the mortuary?"

"I was not present at the transit. I carefully closed up the clothes of the woman. Some portions had been excised."

"How long had the deceased been dead when you saw her?"

"I should say at least two hours, and probably more; but it is right to say that it was a fairly cold morning, and that the body would be more apt to cool rapidly from its having lost the greater portion of its blood."

"Was there any evidence of any struggle?"

"No; not about the body of the woman. You do not forget the smearing of blood about the palings."

This is the one clear indication that we get from Phillips, a keen observer, that the *smears* were indeed smears and not spurts of blood. This is not a small point. From a living person, blood from a cut jugular can spurt out up to 3 feet. But there is no overt statement that blood spurted from Chapman's neck. We know that no blood spurted from Nichols' throat. There was only as small puddle by the neck. So far, the only acceptable description we have is that these appeared to Phillips as *smears*, and he reminds us of them in the context of a struggle.

Aggravatingly, Baxter does not follow through to help clarify the matter. All he asks is a perfunctory: "In your opinion did she enter the yard alive?"

"I am positive of it," replied Phillips. "I made a thorough search of the passage, and I saw no trace of blood, which must have been visible had she been taken into the yard."

Baxter: "Was the bruising you mentioned recent?"

"The marks on the face were recent, especially about the chin and sides of the jaw. The bruise upon the temple and the bruises in front of the chest [received in the fight with Cooper] were of longer standing, probably of days. I am of opinion that the person who cut the deceased's throat took hold of her by the chin, and then commenced the incision from left to right—"

Had Phillips' testimony not been stepped on at this moment but left there it could have proceeded better. He was asked questions about suffocation and strangling, which only caused redundant answers. This caused the entire proceedings to overlook the significance of the chain of events he was trying to propose. This is the first time he actually mentioned the recent bruises. Those he had mentioned before were the older ones Chapman had got in the fight with Cooper. But these facial bruises were made by the killer and as such constitute a significant clue. The thumb of the villain left a bruise on the right cheek, and under the left earlobe there were three distinct scratches, corresponding to the 3 longest fingers of the hand.

When Baxter recalled him and pressured him to speak of the mutilations in detail, Phillips hummed and hawed again. But it is evident from how he slipped in the exact location of the bruises on the face that this was far more important to him as a clue. Then, after squirming under Baxter's steely gaze, he addressed his issue with the mutilations. "When I come to speak of the wounds on the lower part of the body," continued Phillips, "I must again repeat my opinion that it is highly injudicious to make the results of my examination public. These details are fit only for yourself, sir, and the jury, but to make them public would simply be disgusting."

But this is what Baxter was bent on hearing.

"We are here in the interests of justice," patiently reminded Baxter, "and must have all the evidence before us. I see, however, that there are several ladies and boys in the room, and I think they might retire."

(Two ladies and a number of newspaper messenger boys accordingly left the court.)

The room quieted.

"In giving these details to the public," objected Phillips, "I believe you are thwarting the ends of justice."

"We are bound to take all the evidence in the case," replied Baxter, "and whether it be made public or not is a matter for the responsibility of the Press."

"We are of opinion that the evidence," injected the Foreman, "the doctor on the last occasion wished to keep back should be heard."

"Hear, hear," murmured several of the jurymen.

"I have carefully considered the matter," Baxter declared

firmly, "and have never before heard of any evidence requested being kept back."

"I have not kept it back," clarified Phillips defensively. "I have only suggested whether it should be given or not."

"We have delayed taking this evidence as long as possible," officiously replied Baxter, "because you said the interests of justice might be served by keeping it back; but it is now a fortnight since this occurred, and I do not see why it should be kept back from the jury any longer."

Amazingly, Phillips still drug his heels. "I am of opinion that what I am about to describe took place after death, so that it could not affect the cause of death, which you are inquiring into."

Baxter was brusque. "That is only your opinion, and might be repudiated by other medical opinion."

"Very well," Phillips conceded. "I will give you the results of my post-mortem examination."

Unfortunately, the actual words of Dr. Phillips were redacted by the majority of newspapers. It would not be until days later that a detailed account of the evisceration would be had. The following is a composite taken from the *Morning Advertiser* (Sept. 20), *The Lancet* (Sept. 29), and the *Times*.

The abdomen had been entirely laid open. There was a greater portion of skin removed on the right side than on the left. On adjusting these three flaps it was evident that a portion surrounding and constituting the navel was wanting. The intestines, severed from their mesenteric attachments, had been lifted out of the body and placed on the shoulder of the corpse; whilst from the pelvis, the uterus and its appendages with the upper portion of the vagina and the posterior two thirds of the bladder, had been entirely removed. No trace of these parts could be found and the incisions were cleanly cut, avoiding the rectum, and dividing the vagina low enough to avoid injury to the cervix uteri. It was apparent that these absent portions, together with the division of the large intestine, were the result of the same incising cut. I am of opinion that the length of the weapon with which the incisions were inflicted was at least five to six inches in length— probably more— and must have been very sharp. Obviously the work was that of an expert— of one, at least, who had such knowledge of anatomical or pathological examinations as to be enabled to secure the pelvic organs with one sweep of the knife. The removal of the abdominal wall indicated certain anatomical knowledge, as did the cutting in three portions of the abdominal wall, and the non cutting of the intestine. Also the way in which the womb was removed showed this in a more marked degree.

Baxter came straight to the key point now. "Can you give any idea how long it would take to perform the incisions found on the body?"

"I think I can guide you by saying that I myself could not have performed all the injuries I saw on that woman, and affect them, even without a struggle, under a quarter of an hour. If I had done it in a deliberate way, such as would fall to the duties of a surgeon, it would probably have taken me the best part of an hour. The whole inference seems to me that the operation was performed to enable the perpetrator to obtain possession of these parts of the body."

Phillips' comment was loaded. It made the skill of the killer as undeniable as the existence of an ulterior motive. The murders were but a means to an end.

What kind of person could do this? Mrs. Elizabeth Long's testimony was crucial for more than merely establishing a time frame. She is perhaps the first person to see this unspeakable "monster of the East End." Now her name bellowed through the room as she was called. In addition to what we already know of her statement about going to work, she describes what she saw:

> . . .I saw a man and a woman standing on the pavement talking. The man's back was turned towards Brick Lane, and the woman's was towards the market. They were standing only a few yards nearer Brick Lane from 29, Hanbury Street. I saw the woman's face. Have seen the deceased in the mortuary, and I am sure the woman that I saw in Hanbury Street was the deceased. I did not see the man's face, but I noticed that he was dark. He was wearing a brown low-crowned felt hat. I think he had on a dark coat, though I am not certain. By the look of him he seemed to me a man over forty years of age. He appeared to me to be a little taller than the deceased.

Baxter asked: "Did he look like a working man, or what?"

"He looked like a foreigner," Mrs. Long replied in her English way.

Baxter stressed his actual point. "Did he look like a dock labourer, or a workman, or what?"

"I should say he looked like what I should call shabby-genteel."

"Were they talking loudly?"

"They were talking pretty loudly. I overheard him say to her 'Will you?' and she replied, 'Yes.' That is all I heard, and I heard this as I passed. I left them standing there, and I did not look back, so I cannot say where they went to."

"Did they appear to be sober?" asked Baxter.

"I saw nothing to indicate that either of them was the worse for drink."

"Was it not an unusual thing to see a man and a woman standing there talking?"

"Oh no," she replied frankly. "I see lots of them standing there in the morning."

"At that hour of the day?" he asked with some surprise.

"Yes; that is why I did not take much notice of them."

"You are certain about the time?"

"Quite."

"What time did you leave home?"

"I got out about five o'clock, and I reached the Spitalfields Market a few minutes after half-past five."

"What brewer's clock did you hear strike half-past five?" asked the Foreman.

"The brewer's in Brick Lane."

Moments after Chapman said yes, and agreed, they must have entered the passageway of 29 Hanbury to the backyard. This is confirmed by the last genuinely significant witness the inquest called. Albert Cadosch (or Cadoche) was one of the lodgers next door at 27 Hanbury.

"On Saturday, September 8, I got up about a quarter past five in the morning, and went into the yard. It was then about twenty minutes past five, I should think. As I returned towards the back door I heard a voice say 'No' just as I was going through the door. It was not in our yard, but I should think it came from the yard of No. 29. I, however, cannot say on which side it came from. I went indoors, but returned to the yard about three or four minutes afterwards. While coming back I heard a sort of a fall against the fence which divides my yard from that of 29. It seemed as if something touched the fence suddenly."

Baxter asked perfunctorily: "Did you look to see what it was?"

"No."

"Had you heard any noise while you were at the end of your yard?"

"No."

"Any rustling of clothes?"

"No. I then went into the house, and from there into the street to go to my work. It was about two minutes after half-past five as I passed Spitalfields Church."

"Do you ever hear people in these yards?"

"Now and then, but not often."

"What height are the palings?" asked the Foreman.

"About 5 feet 6 inches to 6 feet high."

"And you had not the curiosity to look over?"

"No, I had not."

"It is not usual to hear thumps against the palings?"

"They are packing-case makers, and now and then there is a great case goes up against the palings. I was thinking about my work, and not that there was anything the matter, otherwise most likely I would have been curious enough to look over."

"It's a pity you did not," said the Foreman.

After Baxter asked him what the street looked like, he replied: "I did not see any man and woman in the street when I went out."

Cadosch's testimony threw a bit of a kink in the chronology. Long was sure it was 5:30 a.m. that she passed the front of Hanbury. But Cadosch exits the building close to that time, and by the time he's at Spitalfields Church it is 5:32 a.m. Is it possible that the clocks were that far out of sync?

Britain was numb. It had days to digest this information, thanks in part to the number of papers that reproduced the inquest proceedings. Unlike the *Daily Telegraph*, the *Lancet* and the *Times* did not censor Dr. Phillips' details, so that the gruesomeness and professional expertise of the crime was apparent to all.

On September 26, four days after he rendered his conclusion on the Nichols case, Baxter gave his summation. Remarkably he believed that the yard was not picked by predesign by the killer. He believed that Chapman had led him there. "There is little doubt that the deceased knew the place," he declared, "for it was only 300 or 400 yards from where she lodged. If so, it is quite unnecessary to assume that her companion had any knowledge— in fact, it is easier to believe that he was ignorant both of the nest of living beings by whom he was surrounded, and of their occupations and habits."

From the evidence which the condition of the yard affords and the medical examination discloses, it appears that after the two had passed through the passage and opened the swing-door at the end, they descended the three steps into the yard. On their left hand side there was a recess between those steps and the palings. Here a few feet from the house and a less distance from the palings they must have stood. The wretch must have then seized the deceased, perhaps with Judas-like approaches. He seized her by the chin. He pressed her throat, and while thus preventing the slightest cry, he at the same time produced insensibility and suffocation. There is no evidence of any struggle. The clothes are not torn. Even in these preliminaries, the wretch seems to have known how to carry out efficiently his nefarious work. The deceased was then lowered to the ground, and laid on her back; and although in doing so she may have fallen slightly against the fence, this movement was probably effected with care. Her throat was then cut in two places with savage determination, and the injuries to the abdomen commenced. All was done with cool impudence and reckless daring; but, perhaps, nothing is more noticeable than the emptying of her pockets, and the arrangement of their contents with business-like precision in order near her feet.

The murder seems, like the Buck's Row case, to have been carried out without any cry. Sixteen people were in the house. The partitions of the different rooms are of wood. Davis was not asleep after three a.m., except for three-quarters of an hour, or less, between five and 5:45 a.m. Mrs. Richardson only dosed after three a.m., and heard no noise during the night. Mrs. Hardiman, who occupies the front ground-floor room, did not awake until the noise succeeding the finding of the body had commenced, and none of the occupants of the houses by which the yard is surrounded heard anything suspicious.

The brute who committed the offence did not even take the trouble to cover up his ghastly work, but left the body exposed to the view of the first comer. This accords but little with the trouble taken with the rings, and suggests either that he had at length been disturbed, or that as the daylight broke a sudden fear suggested the danger of detection that he was running.

There are two things missing. Her rings had been wrenched from her fingers and have not been found, and the uterus has been removed. The body has not been dissected, but the injuries have been made by someone who had considerable anatomical skill and knowledge. There are no meaningless cuts. It was done by one who knew where to find what he wanted, what difficulties he would have to contend against, and how he should use his knife, so as to abstract the organ without injury to it. No unskilled person could have known where to find it, or have recognised it when it was found. For instance, no mere slaughterer of animals could have carried out these operations. It must have been someone accustomed to the post-mortem room.

The conclusion that the desire was to possess the missing part seems overwhelming. If the object were robbery, these injuries were meaningless, for death had previously resulted from the loss of blood at the neck. Moreover, when we find an easily accomplished theft of some paltry brass rings and such an operation, after, at least, a quarter of an hour's work, and by a skilled person, we are driven to the deduction that the mutilation was the object, and the theft of the rings was only a thin-veiled blind, an attempt to prevent the real intention being discovered. Had not the medical examination been of a thorough and searching character, it might easily have been left unnoticed.

The difficulty in believing that this was the real purpose of the murderer is natural. It is abhorrent to our feelings to conclude that a life should be taken for so slight an object; but, when rightly considered, the reasons for most murders are altogether out of proportion to the guilt. It has been suggested that the criminal is a lunatic with morbid feelings. This may or may not be the case; but the object of the murderer appears palpably shown by the facts, and it is not necessary to assume lunacy, for it is clear that there is a market for the object of the murder.

To show you this, I must mention a fact which at the same time proves the assistance which publicity and the newspaper press afford in the detection of crime. Within a few hours of the issue of the morning papers containing a report of the medical evidence given at the last sitting of the Court, I received a communication from an officer of one of our great medical schools, that they had information which might or might not have a distinct bearing on our inquiry. I attended at the first opportunity, and was told by the sub-curator of the Pathological Museum that some months ago an American had called on him, and asked him to procure a number of specimens of the organ that was missing in the deceased. He stated his willingness to give 20 pounds for each, and explained that his object was to issue an actual specimen with each copy of a publication on which he was then engaged. Although he was told that his wish was impossible to be complied with, he still urged his request. He desired them preserved, not in spirits of wine, the usual medium, but in glycerine, in order to preserve them in a flaccid condition, and he wished them sent to America direct. It is known that this request was repeated to another institution of a similar character.

Now, is it not possible that the knowledge of this demand may have incited some abandoned wretch to possess himself of a specimen? It seems beyond belief that such inhuman wickedness could enter into the mind of any man, but unfortunately our criminal annals prove that every crime is possible. I need hardly say that I at once communicated my information to the Detective Department at Scotland Yard. Of course I do not know what use has been made of it, but I believe that publicity may possibly further elucidate this fact, and, therefore, I have not withheld from you my knowledge. By means of the press some further explanation may be forthcoming from America if not from here.

I have endeavoured to suggest to you the object with which this offence was committed, and the class of person who must have perpetrated it. The greatest deterrent from crime is the conviction that detection and punishment will follow with rapidity and certainty, and it may be that the impunity with which Mary Ann Smith [sic] and Anne Tabram [sic] were murdered suggested the possibility of such horrid crimes as those which you and another jury have been recently considering.

It is, therefore, a great misfortune that nearly three weeks have elapsed without the chief actor in this awful tragedy having been discovered. Surely, it is not too much even yet to hope that the ingenuity of our detective force will succeed in unearthing this monster. It is not as if there were no clue to the character of the criminal or the cause of his crime. His object is clearly divulged. His anatomical skill carries him out of the category of a common criminal, for his knowledge could only have been obtained by assisting at post-mortems, or by frequenting the post-mortem room. Thus the class in which search must be made, although a large one, is limited. Moreover it must have been a man who was from home, if not all night, at least during the early hours of September 8. His hands were undoubtedly blood-stained, for he did not stop to use the tap in the yard as the pan of clean water under it shows. If the theory of lunacy be correct— which I very much doubt— the class is still further limited; while, if Mrs. Long's memory does not fail, and the assumption be correct that the man who was talking to the deceased at half-past five was the culprit, he is even more clearly defined.

In addition to his former description, we should know that he was a foreigner of dark complexion, over forty years of age, a little taller than the deceased, of shabby-genteel appearance, with a brown deer-stalker hat on his head, and a dark coat on his back.

If your views accord with mine, you will be of opinion that we are confronted with a murder of no ordinary character, committed not from jealousy, revenge, or robbery, but from motives less adequate than the many which still disgrace our civilisation, mar our progress, and blot the pages of our Christianity. I cannot conclude my remarks without thanking you for the attention you have given to the case, and the assistance you have rendered me in our efforts to elucidate the truth of this horrible tragedy.

The Foreman stood up. "We can only find one verdict— that of willful murder against some person or persons unknown. We were about to add a rider with respect to the condition of the mortuary, but that having been done by a previous jury it is unnecessary."

Well, Baxter was profound. Phillips had impressed him with his certainty that there was surgical skill involved. But neither Phillips nor Baxter could believe that a doctor did this. Baxter narrowed it down to the most logical compromise. Yet his personal theory for the killer's ulterior motive no doubt blinded him to some facts. Principally, his theory cannot explain Tabram's and Nichols' murders. Taking their lead from Phillips' testimony, all the papers at one point or another made it clear there were no pointless cuts or mutilations in Chapman. This, however, is a far cry from Nichols' murder. Her abdomen had been ripped up with a number of cuts. This does not indicate a scientific evisceration commencing that had been interrupted. This is closer to the 18 wounds in Tabram that were "too disgusting to mention."

In contrast to this, Chapman's murderer was brisk for business. He sliced her up and took what he wanted. Somewhere in that first week of September our man made great progress in his operations or he always had the skill and simply acquired a new motive. But Baxter couldn't see this. He accepted skill was displayed in Nichols' murder because he believed the same objective applied, the difference being that the killer was interrupted from completing the removal of the uterus. In actuality, skill was displayed in Nichols' murder by how she appears to have been neatly bled. The slices to her lower abdomen therefore must have another motive. It is safe to say that Baxter's personal theory had already blind-sighted him by the time he made his closing statements in that inquest. He had conceded that little blood came from both gut and neck in that case, but then overshadowed that significance by asserting that the killer had been interrupted from taking Nichols' uterus. In actuality, in Chapman and Nichols' murders we see a similar modus operandi but two different objectives — blood and uterus with navel.

While there wasn't enough combined evidence in the Chapman and Nichols cases to definitely pinpoint the killer's level of skill or his ultimate reason for wanting what he took, there was enough evidence to give us an accurate appearance of the killer. Elizabeth Long's description is mutely contained in Polly Nichols' murder. She was found far off the turf for prostitutes, right at the beginning of a line of middleclass tradesmen's homes. This may have been the enticement. The police and, indeed, the inquest concentrated too much on the escape of the killer from Buck's Row. But the greater mystery is found in how the killer led his victim to the spot and she continued to tag along. The only logical answer is that he must have told her they were going to a cottage. On such a stormy night, this would have been perfect. To be believable the killer must have looked as if he could have afforded one of the cottages, and this fits with Elizabeth Long's descriptive of "shabby genteel"— some middleclass clerk attempting some airs, not some toff, not some lout.

Both inquests also gave us enough evidence to build a partial character profile. The killer was certainly cool, manipulative, and premeditative. Despite Baxter's belief, the killer carefully selected the murder locations. This is evident in that not only were both victims laid down before their throats were cut, both victims were also laid on a section of the street or yard that sloped slightly, with their heads in the direction of the incline so that the blood gushing from the neck would flow *away* from the direction of the abdomen. The killer thus had no worry of blood flowing around his shoes while he knelt by or straddled the midriff and dissected the corpse.

This not only requires forethought, but it implies he knew the murder sites well enough to know how to lay the victim down so as to prevent stepping in any blood and therewith leaving a trail from the scene. This is not a man being led anywhere. This is a man leading his victims to the slaughter.

At Buck's Row, we know that he and Nichols came silently, that she died silently, and that he, too, then left without any detection. The only real explanation for all this is that *he* knew the general neighborhood and the times of the constables' beats. We can even surmise that he took Woods Hole Buildings. It's a narrow brick lane that is connected with Whitechapel High Street via a narrow walking tunnel over which are built 3 story dwellings. Woods Hole terminates on Winthrop, just west of the slaughterers. Turning left here one must only walk just a bit and around the old School Board building and down the narrow part of Buck's Row.

It seems certain that the killer did this with Nichols, for her body was found on the cottage side of the road. It was found before the gate of horse stables that probably served the cottages, the first of which, widow Green's, overlooked

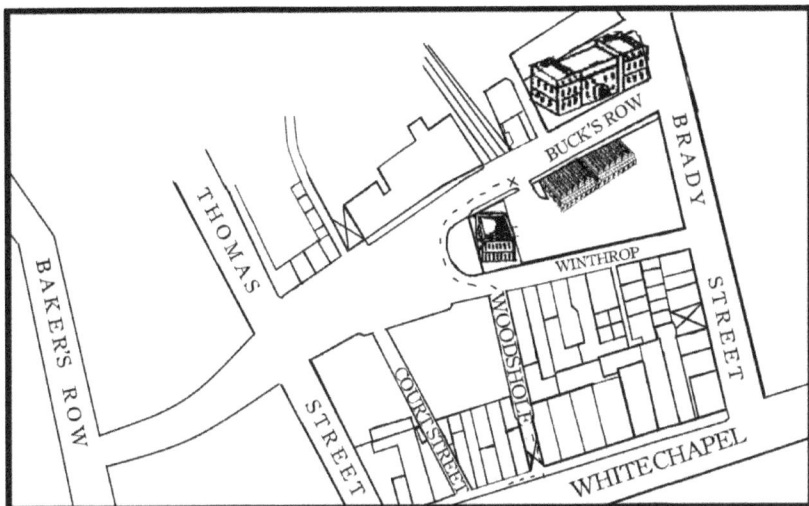

Close up of the Buck's Row area, showing Woods Hole in relation to Winthrop, Buck's Row, and the murder location.

the gate. The killer couldn't have afforded to walk along the row of cottages and risk detection. The killer would strike at this moment before they walked along the cottages. It is at this moment that a poor, desperate middle-age woman is most unsuspecting.

It also seems certain he reenacted this same general scenario on Hanbury Street. Number 29 was not off the beaten path. It was quite the opposite. It was an area where such a soliciting couple would not be given much notice. Instead of transposing into darkness, they transposed into the licentious trade of the area. There should be no question that he led her here or waited and took advantage of an appropriate prostitute heading along the street. This is underscored by how he asks her "Will you?" to which she agrees. She hardly would have led him here and then waited for the advance and acted coy.

In light of this the man reported by Mrs. Richardson as having been on the first floor steps one month before the murder becomes of interest. This was just around the time that Martha Tabram would soon be found murdered, coincidently also on a first floor landing. The man had a feeble excuse for being caught there. He was not a tenant. Nor did he say he was going to meet someone. He was merely on his way

Wood's Hole at night. It is partially intact today. Beyond the narrow tunnel is Whitechapel Road.

to market. Was he the killer scouting for a possibly convenient murder spot? The first floor landing here was also known to be used for prostitution.

There was much debate whether the killer was right handed or left handed or even an ambidexter. However, thanks to Bagster Phillips' able description, which the redoubtable surgeon obviously felt was important, we can determine the killer was right handed and even reconstruct his exact method of killing Chapman.

Bagster Phillips had made sure to introduce into the inquest minutes the exact locations of those hideous bruises on Chapman's face. "On the last occasion, just before I left the court, I mentioned to you that there were reasons why I thought the perpetrator of the act upon the woman's throat had caught hold of her chin. These reasons were that just below the lobe of the left ear were three scratches, and there was also a bruise on the right cheek" — i.e. the marks of 3 fingernails and a thumb.

It would be impossible when facing Chapman to have held her jaw with the right hand (with the nails of the 3 longest fingers leaving abrasions under the left ear) and cut her throat with the left hand, with the cut commencing on the left side of the neck. The right arm would be in the way. However, after laying her down, if the killer shifted and stood over her head, he could easily grab her chin with his left hand and cut her throat with his right hand. Fingernail marks— those telltale 3 scratches— and thumb mark would be left in the exact same locations, and his left hand would not have been in the way of his right hand and knife.

The marks on Nichols' face bear out the deduction that the killer was *right* handed. The unique bruises were not identical to those on Chapman, but similar. The bruises were limited to Nichols' *cheeks*. They never extended to under her ear. This can be explained by the killer grabbing her mouth from *behind* with his left hand and pulling her to the ground before cutting her throat with his right hand. The circumstances before the cottages bear this out. He could obviously not ask her to lie down all of a sudden after a tempting offer to go within. He had to strike now by the gate. Taken by surprise, Nichols also might have bitten her tongue at this moment, thus accounting for the laceration Llewellyn discovered. Something went wrong with Chapman. She suspected something. "No!" He had to choke her insensible and then let her drop. Now he has time to grab her jaw firmly, his long fingers reaching to under her ear where the fingernails left marks.

Baxter may have proposed a medical man because of the sleekness of Chapman's dissection, but there are other subtleties that Baxter missed that nevertheless support his profile. The lack of blood spurting from the severed carotid arteries is seen clearly in Polly Nichols' death scene; but the method of preventing it suggested in Chapman's postmortem. There were two notches in the left side of her vertebrae, though the cutting edge of the knife had not been brought back that far over the neck. Phillips had also thought that there was an attempt to wedge apart the muscles on Chapman's neck. This can be explained by the knife being jabbed in to cut the carotid artery and then angled to direct the blood flow to the ground. The man seen with Chapman before she was found mutilated was not in a position to ever remove and abscond with a head. It seems therefore that the scoring of the neck and the wedging of the muscles must be explained in another way. Since there was no blood spurting, it is logical to deduce the killer used this method to kill and bleed the victim sufficiently to make cutting the throat afterward a less messy affair to himself.

The blood smears on the fence palings were not those of spurts of blood. They were *smeared* blood. Splashes of blood may have been thrust upon the palings when the killer threw her stomach into the pool of blood by her shoulder. Blood certainly splattered as far as the back wall of the residence. But this could not smear the blood. When working on her afterward, the killer could have brushed against the fence, thus causing it to quake, and smeared the blood. Or, more likely, when he yanked her rings off the fingers of the left hand, he smeared the blood. Phillips doesn't mention Chapman's hands were bloodied, but James Kent said they were. The only explanation seems to be that when he wrenched the rings off, his bloody hands smeared blood all over hers. At the very least, the left one must have been smeared.

Baxter also didn't seem to notice a very obvious kink — the killer never cut clothes. Even Chapman's purse was not slit but manually torn. This may actually tell us he used gloves. Phillips underscored the killer's brutal grasp on the face. It wasn't to keep her quiet as Baxter believed. He had, in fact, grabbed her jaw with such force just to hold the head steady to cut the throat. The fingernail marks extended as far as under her left earlobe. Obviously, he didn't wear gloves. But he was not going to dig through her guts in his bare hands. He must have put them on while the body drained of blood. Then removing her clothes he came across the purse. With the cumbersome gloves he was not in a position to work the drawstring. He tore it open and emptied the contents. Now with Chapman fully drained of blood, he went to work. I repeat this here because it will become even more significant later, and it also highlights how Baxter, despite being eager to pry further, passed over significant evidence

There is little reason to believe the killer walked away

with bloodied hands. The streets are incredibly narrow. Amidst workers going to work, he would have been spotted. Had he removed his gloves, he would look naturally enough. Had he bloodied his jacket by knocking against the bloody fence, he would merely have folded it over his forearm, thus hiding the bloodied sleeve, and looked equally casual . . . except for that gauche deerstalker.

London may have been agog now with the idea of a rampant, fiendish doctor or medical man of sorts on the loose, but there is also much in Baxter's mug shot that does not fit the evidence and circumstances. It overlooks the blatant evidence that there was no attempt to eviscerate Nichols. Her death is linked to Chapman's in that a separate 4 inch slice was in her neck distinct from the slitting of her throat, indicating she was bled first. A medical man is capable of this, but why kill in such obvious places in order to obtain the organ/substance desired?

Baxter liked the media attention, and at points his summation almost seems a defense for how he exaggerated the length of the inquest, allowing both the Nichols and the Chapman inquests to overlap. But his conclusion was legally questionable. He made himself a witness and introduced the very notion that a medical man was behind it all. Not just this alone, but that someone was also butchering amongst the lower class East Enders for mere filthy lucre. That made the citizens of Whitechapel indignant. In a socially tumultuous time like this, this was the wrong image to form and broadcast to London and all Britain.

The citizens of the East End were ready to take matters into their own hands.

7

꙰PROAR

SIR CHARLES WARREN must have sighed with agitated relief over the morning paper. The relief came from Wynne Baxter finally concluding the inquest; the agitation from that long and inciting summation. The city, especially the East End, was now suspecting a "topper" from the West End preying ruthlessly upon their expendable hides. This is all the Commissioner of Police needed. On top of riots against Jews, he didn't need a social riot.

General Warren was by demeanor qualified to take some of this stoically. And if it wasn't stoicism, which implies a state of reaction that is the byproduct of careful, self-denying thought, then he at least had the thick skin to endure it. He was already enduring the dislike held for him by many members of his own Criminal Investigation Department. C.I.D. was lorded over by James Monro, whom Warren finally ousted after two years of petty inter-departmental squabbles. Although Monro was his subordinate, he had enjoyed a great independence when previously in charge of the Secrets Department (prior to Warren's commissionership). After being appointed head of the C.I.D. he continued as usual reporting to the Home Secretary, Henry Matthews, completely independent of going through Warren.

Sir Charles naturally didn't care for this. He was a military man. It was unfathomable to him that a subordinate could act independent of his superior as a matter of daily operation and routinely go over his head and officially include him out of the goings-on of his own department. Monro was head of the most important investigative branch of the Metropolitan Police and yet had no supervision. Matthews, however, was letting him do it, and Warren, apparently, was making little headway with Matthews. Matthews was a man, unfortunately, who had little rapport with anybody, and contact with him was only through his secretary. Matthews was also the least liked of all men in government. In addition to his aloofness, he was vacillating and apathetic, and as such easily manipulated by those who knew how.

By this time, Warren already had some eye-opening experiences with government. He accepted his appointment as Commissioner of Police following a major fiasco involving protestors in Trafalgar Square. On 8 February 1886 his predecessor Sir Edmund Henderson bungled the job and full scale riots broke out. He resigned. In March, Warren was appointed. Mr. Gladstone's government was in charge then, and his Home Secretary, Hugh Childers, guaranteed Warren a free hand at his new post. But Gladstone wasn't to last. By June the government had changed hands, and the new Home Secretary, Matthews, had no such open-minded notions as Childers.

This was a volatile time. Warren was appointed in case of mass insurgencies of "radicals." He was a man of action. But his new boss was not. Matthews had always felt safe playing politics' most rewarding pastime: don't climb the fence if you can sit on it. Warren was a man of action, but he was a man of action along tried and true military lines. This may have worried Matthews. He knew that Henderson had gone down the pipe after the first Trafalgar Square riots. Gladstone's government was surfing down the Thames. Perhaps he was right about removing Warren's free hand. He began to do so in the Summer of 1886, and this proved prescient after November 13, 1886, when Warren proved himself "twice the child of hell," to use a Biblical phrase. A peaceful demonstration was broken up in Trafalgar Square by police organized in military style. Violence ensued, and it became known as Bloody Sunday.

After that Warren had no chance of a free hand from Matthews, and little hope of bringing into the barn his hardnosed subordinate James Monro and the C.I.D. It would be near two years of contention before Monro was ousted in August 1888. Warren was glad.

Sir Charles could look at the newspaper articles this morning and take them with a grain of salt. After all, his appointment had been greeted in the *Times* in 1886 as "the right man for the job." But the newspapers were now complaining about the militarization of the police by this "martinet." No connection about Warren's friendship with the lamented and heroic maverick "Chinese" Gordon was raised. Warren was portrayed as merely a mindless military administrator appointed by a system of unqualified chums.

Personally, Warren didn't believe that rubbish. He fancied himself anything but a political appointee of chums. It was his lost independence which had soured him. He had survived the Gladstone Government and was now under a new Home Secretary. It was Childers' guarantee which had tempted him to take a job for which he truly had never been trained. It was his fights with Monro that had demoralized the C.I.D. and mired his reputation with many there. On top of his demand for autonomy, *Monro* had wanted friends appointed to ranking administrative positions. One of them was Melville Macnaghten. He was one of the sons of the last head of the famed East India Company. They were new money, and Macnaghten was only educated at Eton before going to India to merely manage his father's personal estates there. Land tenant riots struck the nation, and Macnaghten found himself badly beaten and left lying senseless on the fertile plain. Monro, of all people, wanted him appointed Assistant Chief Constable. "I saw his way of handling men when I was in India," declared Monro to Warren, "and I was struck by it, for he had a most turbulent set of natives to deal with, and he dealt with them firmly and justly." Warren disagreed after he engaged in a little research. He discovered that Macnaghten was the *only* one of the landlords upon whom the "Hindoos" had taken revenge. Warren saw no use in him and refused to have a chum system used by Monro. Even Matthews agreed to reject Macnaghten's appointment. It was then that Monro resigned.

Warren was no doubt justified. How was Macnaghten's management of "turbulent Hindoos" relevant to administrative and investigative police matters? But Warren's fault lay perhaps in that he was not the maverick of his friend Gordon. Gordon would never have tolerated Monro for two years. He would have sacked him outright. Warren's tolerance shows to what an extent he was a team player and to what extent Mathews hindered him. But in the end his supposed disgraceful treatment of Monro left a C.I.D. in a very counterproductive position and embittered. Yet to what extent was this really Warren's doing? Monro stepped out when he didn't get his way over a chum's appointment. There was nothing wrong in Warren refusing a man with no real qualifications.

By a perverse trick of fate, the fame of the Whitechapel Murders exploded on the heels of Monro's resignation. On top of internal problems in the wake of his stormy exit, Warren had to deal with a Press biased in favor of Monro, partially if not totally because of their disfavor of a military man. Instead of any blame for not having found the killer being hurled at Monro, the Press was blaming Warren for having demoralized the entire C.I.D. by how he allegedly was degrading Monro during the last months of his sovereignty over the detective branch. The way in which Warren had brought it about was basically declared cowardly. Yet, ironically, it was Monro who had failed to stem the murders in Whitechapel early-on. Not Warren. Yet the Press perceived Warren as in charge. Thus the Press could lambaste Warren for his militarism and praise Monro for Scotland Yard's detective branch, despite its inability so far to apprehend this bizarre killer.

Robert Anderson had been appointed in Monro's place. He was a former Secrets Department man as well. Ardently protestant Irish, he was also a religious philosopher. Anderson had actually been one of Monro's appointees in a junior position in the most secret work of C.I.D's political investigations. He had been a former spy chief (sometimes against the Fenian League). Because he was not a former military man his appointment was not credited to Warren but in spite of Warren.

But Anderson was, amazingly, told by his doctor to wait 4

months to take up his post due to his health and exhaustion. Anderson compromised and said he'd take a month off in Switzerland before he began. In essence, the Press had nobody *but* Warren to blame right now.

While both inquests were ongoing, recessing and awaiting reconvening at Baxter's goading pleasure, on September 15 the *East London Advertiser* took the opportunity to itemize Warren's faults. Warren's goal to modernize was mocked. It was rather declared centralization. The paper extolled the virtue of the "old parish constable." Instead Warren's revolutionary and high-handed management of the Met caused him to oust these old guardians and replace them with the type of man who had no more than "a few years of military service behind him, but with no other qualification for serving the public as a policeman." The result, said the columnist, was to destroy the "most valuable characteristic" of the old force. "That is to say, the old idea of the policeman was that he was a man appointed by the neighbours to look after their lives and property. He was a hired servant, of course, but still he was a member of the community whose interests he looked after, and had some sort of an acquaintance with every one of the black sheep who were the special objects of his attention. Now this is as far removed from the idea of a centralised bureaucratic police as can well be imagined. Moreover, it is obvious that the guarantee of public safety offered under the old plan is infinitely stronger than that which our new organization is able to supply."

The op-ed adroitly overlooked that these murders weren't happening anywhere but in Whitechapel. It also carefully overlooked the unique crowded conditions of this particular district in order to beat the tambourine against an organized police that it painted as more capable than anything of putting down insurrection. "We are militarising our police, but we do not seem to be able to make either good detectives of them or good local guardians of our lives and property. That is, at all events, the case in London, where Sir Charles Warren, a martinet of apparently a somewhat inefficient type, has, according to the *Daily News*, committed the double folly of weakening his detective force, and strengthening his ordinary police force from the ranks of reserve men and others of a military or semi-military type. Now, it is obvious that a policy of this kind destroys the two safeguards of a community, so far as the detection of crime is concerned. In the first place it deprives it of a specially trained force, consisting of men of superior intellect and specially adapted powers, for detective purposes."

Cropping an image always concentrates the viewers' eyes on the area at which you want them to look. The papers were succeeding. The *Advertiser* ascribed all four killings to the mysterious Whitechapel Murderer, whom it declared was a "man monster" and a "madman." This put the police ineffectiveness back to Spring when Emma Smith was attacked by what seemed to be an actual "High Rip Gang." This meant months of incompetence, but the slinging stuck nothing onto Monro. In fact, more and more the paper looked like it had been coached by Monro or some of his adherents. "You cannot have a good detective service unless you place it in a position of supreme authority, as it is placed in Paris, and give it precedence over all other branches of the police force. If a detective has to delay acting until he has orders from a superior officer he may lose the one chance he has of following up a likely scent, when it is hot and fresh.

"Nothing, indeed, has been more characteristic of the hunt after the Whitechapel murderer than the want of local knowledge displayed by the police. They seem to know little of the bad haunts of the neighbourhood, and still less of the bad characters who infest them. The chances are that if Whitechapel had had a properly organised local force it would long ago have been rid of the ghoul whose midnight murders have roused all London and frightened decent citizens in their beds."

Nothing more out of context than this agendized muck can be imagined. The reporter's radical views merely used the Whitechapel slayings in order to hound against authority. Locating Pizer was actually a triumph of the very system that the reporter was trying to convince his readers Warren had destroyed.

What the Press was overlooking, and dare I say of what it could not have been unaware, was that Warren wanted numbers. There were too few bobbies and far too many people in the East End. It was impossible for the police to know who all was coming and going. There were streets in Whitechapel and Spitalfields where police didn't even tread, and in this modern era people came and went so much that no bobby could remember them all. Dorset Street had a reputation for doing whatever it liked, and police were known to stop and not pursue a miscreant into the street unless backed up by several other bobbies. Flower and Dean Street was a center of depravity, and the locals were never accustomed to helping the police. From whom locally, pray, could Warren enlist into the ranks of bobbies?

The docks, too, were nearby, and thousands of sailors came into Whitechapel after their cargo ships or cattle boats docked from the continent. How would local bobbies get to know sailors that came and went in such numbers?

Despite the newspaper denouncements, the C.I.D. had already picked up on a pattern. The last 3 murders had happened on holidays or weekends. Tabram was killed on a Bank Holiday, and Nichols and Chapman on Friday and Saturday morning respectively. This pattern would not soon escape the Queen either. Victoria would conclude that the killer was coming from the continent on a cattle boat.

Blinded by their desire to lambaste Warren, the papers also overlooked the significance of Baxter's summation on the 26th. Both his theory and the growing popularity of the idea the killer came from the continent removed the very idea that the killer was some wretch from the East End. Baxter's culprit was a man with some professional qualifications and not some dreg in an old tavern. There was, in fact, no reason to lambaste Warren or decry the police in general because the constables supposedly were no longer the parish locals. The evidence was not pointing to any common crook with whom the police should have been familiar.

The signs of the times overshadowed so much of the evidence that the papers could heap together incongruity and seem profound. They could help Monro stick another hole in the bucket of bad blood between he and Warren. They could denounce Warren and the police for not being locals, then play with the idea the killer was a foreigner. They could salivate to Baxter's grandstanding ideas and then gloss over that if he was right the hands-on knowledge of the bobby on the beat was inapplicable.

None of what Baxter independently offered was in a coroner's position to do so, but Baxter, too, was a symptom of the problems in London. He was now using unnecessarily long inquests, installments of which were adjourned and reconvened weeks apart, to highlight several problems: the lack of a mortuary in the very heart of London's cesspool; crowded living conditions; inefficient police methods; and most of all, as he dragged this out, it highlighted how Warren's sleuths weren't catching their man.

The *Star*, Harry Dam's paper— the very one that brought us a tabloid look at the greatest incongruity "Leather Apron"— was Britain's most liberal newspaper. Already on August 31, in the wake of Monro's departure, it had taken up the *Daily News'* attitude toward Warren. The opinion piece was entitled "What We Think." It concluded in scathing rhythm:

It is not a case of Trafalgar Square only. That would be bad enough; but what the Square did wholesale, Sir Charles's men, under the brutal initiative from Scotland Yard, have done in detail. During the last few weeks hardly a day has passed when some constable has not been convicted of gross insult and harshness to some peaceful inhabitant, supported by still grosser perjury. The London magistrates have for the most part given up the police and rejected their evidence as worthless. The Moral Miracle has become a Miracle of Lying, thanks to the knowledge that whatever a policeman said would be accepted as gospel in the Star Chamber where our Prefect of Police holds absolute sway. Now there is only one moral about the Warren business, and we enforced it long ago. Sir Charles must go. From the beginning he misconceived his mission.

Major-General Sir Charles Warren, K.C.B., G.C.M.G., was far too lofty a personage to look after petty larcenies and street inebriates. His mission was to put down the Social Revolution. His first Pyrrhic victory in bludgeoning the people out of the Square intoxicated him, and henceforth we have had nothing but a carnival of perjury, violence, and discontent. If a vote of the people of London could be held in a matter in which they ought to have the determining voice, Sir Charles would not remain another week in the position he has so grossly abused. But what is still more satisfactory is the fact— now clear as the sun at noon— that if a similar *plebiscite* of the force were taken to-morrow, his dismissal would be decreed by a majority of twenty to one.

Naturally, this was horrendous publicity for Sir Charles. But not all the papers trounced him so utterly. In fact, too much was being hurled at him. Too much had been hitting the news that sounded like Monro or his friends were behind it. Too obvious was it that political opportunists were using Warren as a print pariah. The result was some Press caution and even support from unexpected places.

One source was the *Echo*. It got into specifics about the battle between Warren and Monro. The latter's complaints had been duly outlined by most of the London newspapers, including Monro's worry about the "numerical weakness" of his C.I.D. staff. But the *Echo*, in its way, seemed disturbed by the "last straw." This was the failure on Monro's part to achieve the appointment of Macnaghten, who, of course, was not mentioned by name. According to the *Echo*, this initiated a "crisis" in which both Warren and Monro had to go to the Home Office and have a meeting with the Secretary of State. The upshot we know, of course, was not good for Monro. He was to "immediately take leave of absence, with a view to his subsequent resignation." Monro was then to come work for Matthews as the head of the Secret Inquiry Department.

This raised some brows. Matthews was the most disliked of government officials, and the Press knew this. Monro got along with this man? On September 6, the *Echo* reported: "Mr. Monro's transmigration to the Home Office has occasioned considerable surprise. It is still a matter of comment in many quarters. According to the London correspondent of the *Manchester Guardian*, we have not yet heard the whole story about it. When Parliament assembles, the full particulars may be expected to be made public, and it is thought Sir C. Warren will not then look so black as he is now painted. It will turn out, there is good reason to believe (so the Correspondent mentioned above says), that the late Assistant-Commissioner was the direct representative of the Home Secretary at Scotland Yard, with a very special object in view. Sir Charles Warren has always objected to the transformation of the detective department into a political police, and was at loggerheads with Mr. Monro over the latter's espionage of Irish Members of Parliament and the further attempt to connect some of them with convicted dynamitards. Mr. Monro's evidence on the subject before the Select Committee on the regulations for the admission of strangers to the Houses of Parliament will be remembered."

Warren was so fatigued by his tarnished victory at ousting Monro that he went on a short vacation to the south of France. When he returned he perhaps received some relief to see within the stack of newspapers that awaited him that some in his absence had begun to vindicate him.

Any relief, however, was short lived. Chapman's murder had the papers screaming again. He now had to prove there was something behind the redemption he had received after Monro's stormy departure. He had to show without Monro they'd catch the villain quickly. He began to take a direct hand.

It was not a hand that Whitechapel openly saw. Rather, all London saw, and Whitechapel took comfort in, the new high profiled Vigilance Committee begun by key members of Whitechapel's tradesmen. On September 16, newspapers in the East End accentuated that no arrests had yet been made by the police. This set the stage for the papers to highlight "The Duty of Government," and they used the newly formed Committee as an example. The very existence now of the Vigilance Committee by effect made the government look negligent.

On that previous Saturday, the Vigilance Committee had met at the Crown Tavern. Amidst the rhubarb, the whole idea of how to help the police was thrashed out. Unlike the government, the Vigilance Committee saw nothing wrong with offering a reward for information that would lead to the criminal's capture. Warren had made it clear in the newspapers that rewards simply were not given. It was a citizen's duty to give any pertinent information. The Vigilance Committee knew, however, that the Whitechapel Murders were far different than anything London had seen before. They were now taking up the slack of what they saw, and what the Press was glad to angle, as the government's negligence.

Mr. Joseph Aarons, presiding at the meeting, read a letter from the owner of Anchor Brewery, Spencer Charrington, in which he started the ball rolling by inclosing a cheque for 5 pounds. Aarons then announced that both he and a George Lusk, a builder in the area, had both donated 5 pounds each. Others contributed what they could, including guineas. Cheers rang out. After it fell silent, Aarons introduced Mr. Rogers. He had gone cap-in-hand to the merchants of White-chapel in order to raise a reward. He now declared to all and sundry that he had been "forcibly reminded" during his pursuit that it was the duty of government to offer the reward and not of the citizens. He was amazed that some merchants had pontificated that they were ready to "lay down 100 pounds toward any charitable endeavor" but flatly refused to give a bob for a reward. It was, frankly, the duty of government! He made it clear that, notwithstanding this sentiment, the police reiterated they would lay down no reward, and the Home Office was not going to budge. This caused some rumbles, but Aarons was quick to mediate the mood. He ventured that the police's hardened stance was probably because they knew much more about the killer right now. Therefore the audience should deduce a capture was no doubt pending. He was certain, nevertheless, that in a few days they would have a tempting sum raised.

"Hear, hear," rang out the audience.

"Time, of course, might show how the matter stood," reported the *Echo* on the 17th, "and he trusted that the police were right in what they were doing. The proceedings were eventually adjourned until today, when a definite programme will be arrived at as to the amount to be offered as a reward for information."

The uproar was not merely amongst the native English community. Jews, like the English, are certain God is on their side. The difference is that Jews have held that opinion much longer; in fact, even before England existed. Even more so, Jews are certain, like their English counterparts, that no Jew is capable of such uncivilized acts. History was even more on the Jewish side. Hasn't history shown how everything bad happens to us and not to others!?

Saturday, the Day of Atonement services were held. Rabbi Dr. Herman Adler spoke from the pulpit at the Baywater Synagogue. In his sermon he denounced the "grinding tyranny and physical and social debasement known as the sweating system." From there it was a short step to the Whitechapel murders. The papers carried his emphatic statement that no "Hebrew, native or alien, could have been guilty of such atrocious and inhuman crimes. He said he felt sure he uttered the sentiments of the Jewish community generally, and especially of their East End brethren, in expressing a hope that the mystery would soon be cleared up, and that the spread of true religious and secular education, the culture of the mind and heart, would stay the commission of such abominable and revolting deeds."

By the time Baxter concluded the Chapman Inquest on the 26nd there had been no murder for over two weeks. The idea that the spree was concluded without solution prompted the *East London Advertiser* to declare that the police were still at fault. There it might remain. No one was sure. Perhaps it was a mad mortician or medical assistant who had enough of the risks of getting a uterus. Twenty quid just wasn't worth it. London now waited, horrified, bewildered, and yet intrigued. Was it over?

8

ℕIGHT 𝕊TALKER

FLOWER AND DEAN Street was only a couple blocks from that rotten canker of Dorset Street. Toughs and gangs controlled the neighborhood. Few crimes were reported. Revenge was the order of justice, not the Thames Magistrate.

Only a certain type could get on here. "Long" Liz Stride was the kind. At 45 now, she was at the bottom of a descending spiral of iniquity. Already be middle-aged she looked like a vapid scarecrow. All the teeth from her lower left jaw were gone. The cause? Perhaps it was one too many drunken brawls? She said otherwise. But with her foul mouth perhaps she had incited too many punches her way. She was the female version of Dr. Jekyll and Mr. Hyde. Booze was her demon. It turned a rough and tumble but obliging neighbor into an angry, obscene guttersnipe.

Her journey to Whitechapel began far away in her native Sweden. She was born in 1843, and in 1865 police records there already list her as a prostitute. She had also given birth to a stillborn baby and was later treated for venereal disease. In mid-July she had moved to a Swedish parish in London. She supposedly came in the equipage of a gentleman. If so, she was on her own by 1869.

This year brought a respectable change. She married John Stride. Together they operated a coffee shop on Crisp Street in Poplar near the East India Docks. They seemed to do all right. They moved the business twice and kept it until 1875 when another owner, John Dale, took it over.

In the early 1880s John was no longer in her life, but she could not gainsay him. She had been a respectable enough proprietress and there was no hint from her that John was bad or that he had left her. On the contrary, she had declared he had died in the very famous Thames ferry accident in 1878. It was a national disaster when the *Princess Alice* collided with the *Bywell Castle*. Over 600 people died. She said they had been sailing together and when the ship sank John went down with it. She was climbing a mast to survive and got her face kicked in. This explained her lack of teeth on the lower left jaw. She had not been cast off. She was merely a poor widow now who wasn't doing well. Those who remembered the coffee shop perhaps felt sorry for her. She had at least a respectable excuse for her new poverty and ignoble time spent in workhouses. Others perhaps knew her husband was alive and only in 1884 would he die. No one pushed the point, I suppose, as to who left who.

By this time, Liz had sunken to a common lodging house on Flower and Dean Street. She was still respectable, she said. She made money by charring. In an odd job sort of way she did, but she also augmented her meager and precarious income by a method she had taken up early in Sweden. She could survive the dregs of Whitechapel nights. She didn't run from a fight, especially with a gullet full of good ale.

By 1885 she had a new man in her life. She had shacked-up with a dock laborer named Michael Kidney. The relationship is a strange one. He seems to have sincerely cared for her, but he grows accustom to her periodically leaving him to prowl the streets at night.

Liz had been prostituting herself for quite some time it seems, even though she had a man to help with her room and board. It is perhaps this tendency to roam and booze nights which broke apart her marriage with John Stride. At first, Kidney had locked her in to keep her from going out, but she always managed to get out. In April 1887 she even charged Kidney with assault. Yet it is certain that Stride herself was an aggressive drunk. She had been before the Thames Magistrate for drunken and disorderly conduct many times.

Flower and Dean Street, another pestilential narrow street.

By spring 1888 Kidney has had enough. He had moved her out of Flower and Dean to 36 Devonshire Street off Commercial Road. But nevertheless she continued to go out and prowl the old center of vice.

Liz Stride obviously had several problems. She was lucky enough to have caught Kidney, since he was 7 years younger than her, but her dissolute ways couldn't hold him. Without him she was registered in workhouses or received alms from the Swedish parish. She was last seen there on September 20, 1888, and described as "very poor."

Yet she always came back to Kidney. He had gotten used to her binges. When she left him on September 25, he didn't think anything of it when she didn't return yet again. She was on the town, he was sure. She was, in fact, back on Flower and Dean Street at a dosshouse.

Back amongst her old cronies, she told some more stories to justify her presence amongst them again. She tells them that she and Kidney had "words" and she walked out on him. All those that remember Liz Stride and her dangling-tongue brawls at the taverns can easily believe it.

In a dramatic tableau of the times, the famous Dr. Thomas Barnardo comes into the kitchen to solicit opinions on his plan to save children from the depravity and filth of the doss-houses. There is a group of women huddled in the kitchen warming themselves and talking about the fiend of White-chapel. One drunken brewmeister stands up: "We're all up to no good. No one cares what becomes of us! Perhaps some of us will be killed next!" Liz, ironically, is a part of the group. Huddled together they gossip and gripe after Barnardo leaves.

It is a stormy fall afternoon this Saturday the 29th of September. The wind skips dried leaves through Whitechapel from the grounds about Christ Church. The smell of horse dung swirls from the chilly main avenues down the narrow and vacant side streets. It is a day of faded ambers and brown dried leaves. It is a day of cold gray cobblestones and dark coated humorless men and women rushing along before the old brick buildings.

There is little reason for Liz to be out. Mrs. Elizabeth Tanner, the lodging house deputy, wisely employs her to clean two rooms. She pays her 6 ducats.

With money in her hand, the young night is reaching out to embrace Liz Stride. The pubs will be a clutter. Hundreds will be warming themselves from the wind with soothing ales and toasted cheddar and a good slice of bread. At 6:30 p.m. she is still at the Queen's Head Pub. Even Mrs. Tanner comes in. They share a pint.

By 7 p.m. Stride has returned and primped herself at the dosshouse and is ready to sashay out on the town. She has a bright striped silk scarf around her neck and a long dark coat on. She gives a nice piece of green velvet to Catherine Lane and asks her to keep it for her until she returns. Of another lodger, Charles Preston, she asks for to borrow his clothes brush. Alas, she is out of luck. He has mislaid it, he says.

No mind. Cheerfully she glides along, passing Thomas Bates, the watchman.

She is next seen on Settles Street, leaving the Bricklayer's Arms with a respectably dressed man. He was wearing a mourning suit, a dark coat and billycock hat. He was about 5'6". Due to the rain, they waited in the wings of the entry way for it to stop. He put the time to good use, and she cooperated. He kissed and hugged and fondled her. It was such a stirring scene it drove two dock laborers, John Best and John

The Bricklayer's Arms, at Settles and Fordham, looking south toward Commercial Road.

Gardner, to smirk as they passed by into the pub. They suggested that he tear himself from her and come inside for a pint. But the lovebirds really made no positive reply. They just continued to fawn each other. In fact, both men were quite surprised by how this respectable dressed man was "going at her." One of them decides to really get a response.

"That's Leather Apron getting 'round you," he declared to Stride.

This got the response the two ornery dock workers wanted, but even they were surprised by how the two then shot off down the street toward Commercial Road.

By 11:45 p.m. she must have finished her job with the indiscrete bloke in the billycock hat. She is now seen by William Marshall on Berner Street. The rain has let up and he is standing a few doors down from his residence, taking a deep breath of fresh air. Stride is across the street kissing and cuddling with a man. They are about 20 feet from the only lighted gas lamp, so they are dark effigies moving in the gray netherworld that hangs over the late night sidewalks. But Marshall was able to make out that he is wearing a black cut-away coat and a low crown hat; she was wearing a black bonnet, dress and coat.

There is some billing and cooing, and then the shadowy man said: "You would say anything but your prayers."

To this, Stride laughed.

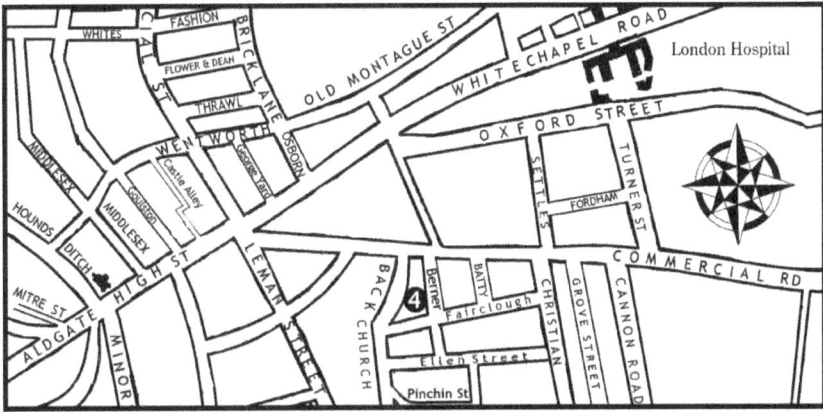

The area of Whitechapel where Stride was seen off and on that night.

At 12 a.m. Marshall goes back into his home.

At 12:35 a.m. Liz Stride is not far away on Berner Street. She is now across the street from the International Working Men's Educational Club. She is seen by police constable William Smith as he is making his rounds. Liz Stride is with yet another man (possibly). Smith thought this man was around 28 years old. He was wearing a long dark coat and, interestingly, a deerstalker hat. He has a parcel under his arm. It is approximately 6 inches high and 18 inches long.

Smith continues on his rounds.

At 12:45 a.m. James Brown is on his way home with his supper. He sees a couple leaning against a wall near the curb of Fairclough Street and Berner. The woman is speaking to a man of average build, about 5'7". He stands with his arm against the wall. She leans backward against the wall and is leaning toward him. It is hard to make anything out. Both are dressed in black. The man wears a long black coat down to his heels. He hears the woman say "No, not tonight. Some other night."

Only 15 minutes later at 1 a.m. Louis Diemshutz turns down Berner Street from Fairclough, driving his trap at a steady pace. He had been hawking jewelry south of the Thames and is now returning to the Educational Club, where he and his wife are stewards. The Club is in the throes of closing down. The faint sound of singing comes from the windows as the last of the revelers remain in the twinkling amber gaslights to sing a European song. Club members were mostly (if not entirely) eastern European Jews, who fled to England because of persecution. It is a socialist club, and adherence to the principles of socialism is required.

Dutfield's Yard services the backdoor of the Club, the back of cigar and tailor shops next to it, the cottages opposite it in the yard, and at that very end of the yard the old rickety stable turned into Hindley's Sack Manufactory. It is an enclosed, artless, narrow space of depressing mottled brick, coal stained whitewash and gray cobblestones. The slender entrance is the worst part about the yard. It is only 9 feet wide and guarded by double gates. When open, as now, the gates are flush against both brick walls, eclipsed in the lee of two tall building's gaunt shadows. Indeed, the entrance is a black ribbon at night.

Diemshutz transposes into the pitch darkness of the chasm before him. It was a tight squeeze, but the horse clopped along surely. Suddenly it rears. It shies nervously, whinnies and ruffles. Diemshutz was taken by surprise. His horse, strangely, would not calm down, nor would it proceed. He leaned over to his right and saw something dark, even blacker than the shrouded cobblestones. He poked about with his whip. It was soft and pliable. Levering the whip, he tried to lift it but couldn't. It wasn't just an old coat. He jumped down and rummaged in his pockets for a match.

The wind moaned about the gate and softly howled through the dripping downspouts. It played about him as he struck the match. It flickered light for the barest moment. He gasped. In the kaleidoscope of dancing ambers, a woman's

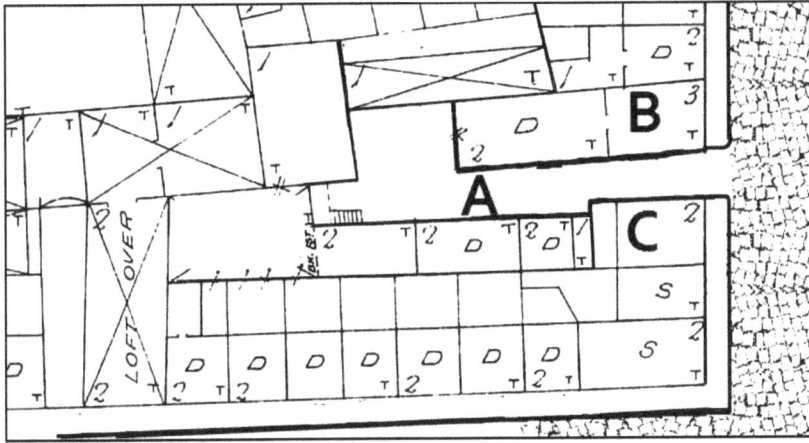

A 19th century plan of Dutfield's Yard (A). Diemshutz passed through the narrow entryway between the Socialist Club (B) and the tailor shops (C). Stride was found in the entry passage just under the B.

body lay next to the wall of the Club, her feet just shy of the swing of the open right gate. The match quickly snipped out.

He rushed to the backdoor and found his wife. He told her that a woman was lying in the yard. He wasn't sure if she was drunk or dead. A few members milling about were intrigued and followed behind him, for he now had a candle and was going to go back outside and check.

As soon as he stepped outside, he raised the candle. In the wind the wick danced violently about, and the light dimly pulsed off the sour bricks of the cottages opposite and throbbed off the gray cobblestones. His horse had finally trotted into the yard and stood quietly. A river of blood ran down from the body to the drain right here in the gutter by the door.

A collective gasp seized them.

Diemshutz and another man bolted out of the gates and ran for the police. Moments afterwards, Morris Eagle, another member of the Club, stepped outside to join the growing huddle of horrified people by the body. He struck a match and in the dancing flickers noticed the blood oozing down the gutter came from her neck. Diemshutz had not noticed that. The cut throat now meant that the Whitechapel fiend was responsible. He, too, now rushed off to find the police.

Meanwhile Edward Spooner is standing with his girlfriend in front of the Beehive Pub at the corner of Christian Street when Diemshutz and the other man come running by yelling "Police"; "Murder." They run past to Grove Street, continuing to shout, but see no constable. They then run back, still shouting. Naturally curious, Spooner now stops them and asks what has happened. They tell him and rush off to find a policeman. He bolts down to Dutfield's Yard.

When Spooner arrived the crowd around the body had grown to between 15 to 20 people. But most, if not all, being Jewish, none wanted to touch a dead body. Spooner wanted to check if she was indeed dead. A man struck a match and this brought to light the grisly scene. The body was lying slightly on its left, with the upper body resting on the left arm and the lower body almost facing up. Legs were drawn up; only the soles of the shoes were visible under the dress. The face was looking at the wall, only 5 or 6 inches away. She had a rather peaceful expression. Her left hand held a crumpled paper. There was a flower pinned to her dress. Her black hat was a few feet away. Most disturbingly, her neck was positioned perfectly over the rut in the alley. Here her throat had been cut and the blood flowed neatly in the rut to the drain by the backdoor. Spooner felt her chin to see if it was still warm. It was.

Running footsteps echoed in the narrow entryway to the yard. More people had heard Diemshutz's distant cries and came running. Coming with them were constables Harry Lamb and Albert Collins. Their bull's eye lamps energized and streaked about the yard. Morris Eagle came in gasping after them. He had found them up at Commercial Road.

About 30 people were now around the body. Lamb asked them to stand back so they wouldn't soil their clothes with blood. Collins was immediately dispatched to get the nearest doctor. Lamb knelt down and felt her face. It was still warm. But when trying to take a pulse, he found her wrist to be cold. He could not feel any pulse. Due to her position it was hard to say whether the blood was still oozing from her throat or not. Only the left side of her throat appeared to be deeply cut, and it was that side she was laying on. The blood nearest the body was congealing.

He blew his whistle.

One of the first constables to arrive was William Smith. He immediately recognized the dead body as the woman he had seen talking to the man with the deerstalker hat. He rushed out to go get the ambulance. After more constables arrived, Lamb posted one on the gate and told him to close it and await Collins and the doctor.

Dr. Frederick Blackwell was a top hat wearing, fastidious man. He was also a stickler for time. He noted it was 1:10 p.m. when Collins came to the door. He wasn't fully dressed so he sent his assistant, Johnson, back with Collins. It was but a moment though and, bag in hand, he rushed out. He noted the time at his arrival at Dutfield's Yard. It was 1:16 a.m. He estimated the victim had been dead from 20 minutes to half an hour. But it was hard to say. She had slowly bled to death. Although the entire throat was cut, only the carotid on the left side was cut and that not clean through. The windpipe, however, had been completely severed.

DR BLACKWELL

Blackwell had barely knelt down to examine the body when the constable on guard admitted Inspector Charles Pinhorn through the gates. He quickly discovered that Lamb had already done a thorough job of looking for clues. (He had shined his light on the hands of each person standing around and checked for blood. Then he had gone inside the Club and examined the hands of members who were still there.) As Pinhorn ordered statements taken down, Lamb continued his door-to-door questioning at the cottages. The terrified owners, usually the man of the house, stood in their nightshirts with candle in hand, and all confessed they had heard nothing. After talking to each one, he came back to find the heavyweights had arrived — Edmund Reid, Bagster Phillips and Chief Inspector John West.

West was only recently back on the street now. With the

Phillips examines Stride carefully—another Penny *dreadful.*

Superintendent of H Division, Thomas Arnold, on leave he had acted in his place. It was his request and recommendation which got Scotland Yard to assign Abberline back to his old division to be in charge of these cases. Pinhorn would brief him as Reid took over inside.

Meanwhile Bagster Phillips had made a brief examination of the body. But as Lamb approached he looked eager to put his sleuth hound's nose immediately to work. Seeing a certain clue, Phillips might have been skeptical to ride the tide of suspicion that was taking hold of all in the yard: that Diemshutz had disturbed the fiend in the act before the mutilations could be performed. Stride's blood, Phillips could see, had flowed close to 18 feet. It was remarkable that blood should flow that far to begin with, and it would have taken some time to do so. Phillips, however, said nothing. The attention was on Diemshutz. Still shaky, he was saying how his horse would not calm down even while he was rushing to the backdoor. He thought the killer might have been hiding in the yard.

Though a narrow yard, there were places to hide. An old gate behind the tailors' opened to a narrow alley to the back-yards of cottages. There was a recess by the dustbin, two loos behind a wood partition, and Messrs. Hindley Sack Manufactory. Lamb confirmed that he had checked that and found nothing. But now Phillips wanted to check out the wood partition by the loos, the recess, and any other culvert in the gloomy yard. There could be signs someone had hidden or, possibly, even blood.

The people were in an understandably nervous shudder now. They were becoming more certain that Diemshutz had indeed disturbed what must be an unusually evil person, one so possessed that the horse could sense him lurking in the shadows. While people continued to wait to have their names taken down (before being allowed out the gate), there was some wonder if the horse hadn't shied from the body but from the killer nearby, in doing so perhaps saving Diemshutz's life. One fact had supported this notion. Diemshutz had been able to lean over while still on his trap to try and lift the body with his whip. This meant that the horse was actually past the body but would not proceed into the yard. The horse, it seemed, was not afraid to pass the body, but it would not go into the abysmally dark yard.

The fretting, gasping and exaggerating continued on in the background as Phillips and Lamb ferreted about. Then faintly, in the distance, the shrill of a police whistle animated the black cutout silhouette of Whitechapel's skyline. Then another, and another. It was far away, but something was happening.

As the shrieking whistle of George Morris faded away, Constable Edward Watkins remained gaping at the horrifying sight. There in the round beam of his bull's eye lamp was a mutilated woman, flayed open, throat cut, part of her bowel neatly severed and lying between her partially extended left arm and her gutted body. Her face was cut up, one gash particularly deep. Her intestines were thrown over her right shoulder, a pool of blood rippling out from the corpse's neck; the retching stench of torn guts rose up.

Watkins was white. He looked about and couldn't believe the circumstances. He stood in the darkest corner of Mitre Square, a small dark, box-like piazza between warehouses and a couple of attached homes. He passes through every 12 to 14 minutes on his methodical beat. When last he moseyed through at 1:30 a.m. there was no body here and nobody loitering about. When he passed through at 1:44 a.m. it seemed unbelievable all this had happened in 14 minutes — considerably less actually since he had heard nobody fleeing the scene. And Mitre Square, with its tall brick and stone buildings rising on all sides, and its narrow tunnel-like passageways, was a place for reverberations, especially at this vacant time of the night.

As Morris receded, still frantically blowing his whistle to get more police, Watkins looked about. His bull's eye traced the path from the mutilated body to Church Passage opposite. No trail of blood on the gray stones. He lifted the beam's angle, but it proved powerless to penetrate the black void into which the long, narrow walking passage transposed to Duke Street. The circle of bloodless white light zoomed across a building. Arched and deep set windows winked as the light skimmed past. It stopped at the slanting angle of darkness that marked the oblique narrow portal of Mitre Passage. Aside from the Mitre Street entrance by which he had come, these were the only two other ways to get into and out of the dismal square. The only sign of life was the open door at Kearley & Tonge's tea warehouse where he had fetched Morris, the night watchman, moments ago.

There is little that would not make an echo in this court. Indeed, Watkins' survey only underscored the swiftness and silence of the predator. While he was sweeping out the entryway, Morris had had the door slightly ajar to the warehouse. He had heard no disturbance until the door burst open and Watkins declared "For God's sake, mate, come to my assistance!" Morris had told him to keep his cool, got his police whistle, and went with Watkins. He remained calm until he saw the gruesome scene. He then fled, blowing and blowing

138

FINDING THE MUTILATED BODY IN MITRE SQARE

Contemporary illustration showing Watkins finding the body.

The murder location in Mitre Square—contemporary illustration drawn from the perspective of Kearley and Tonge's warehouse.

the whistle as he ran down Mitre Street.

Watkins streaked his light beam back to the body. The buildings slunk back into morose shadows as careless, uninterested sentinels. Now alone, he tried to figure it out. The beam of his lamp streamed over the sidewalk and cobblestones all around. Not a drop of blood, not even a heel or half a shoe print outlined in crimson. Yet the pool of blood encircled the shoulders and rippled out beyond the head and down along the arms. The killer would have had to kneel or straddle the body somehow to have performed the gross operation. It was as if a wild animal had got at her. Buttons from the many layers of clothes she was wearing were scattered about. The fiend had ripped them apart furiously to reveal her bare stomach; the buttons had shot forth and peppered the ground. Then he carved at her wildly. . .yet left no trace, no step in the blood or other fluids, and had made no sound coming or going. Such a horrid sight and yet without a clue.

Watkins waited.

The victim would prove to be Catherine Eddowes. Like with the other victims, it would take some time for the police to discover this, for she too was known by aliases or had taken a live-in beau's name. Eddowes road to this fate was also like the others, a long one paved with liquor and occasional prostitution.

Catherine Eddowes was born in 1842. Thus like the others she was middle-aged in 1888. So far, she was probably the most promising of the victims to go bad. She had been born to respectable enough people. Her mother had been a cook; her father, George, a tin plate worker in Wolverhampton. They moved to London to make their way to the big time, but unfortunately her mother died when she was 9. No great success came of George Eddowes' stay in London, and with 12 kids he was strapped. After her mother died, George sent her back to Wolverhampton to live with her aunt.

This relationship seems to be a good one, but perhaps the aunt was domineering or, more likely, Catherine was a bit feckless and flighty. At 21 she is still living with her aunt when she becomes infatuated with a pensioner from the Royal Irish 18th. His name is Tom Conway alias Tom Quinn. They elope or simply run off together to Birmingham.

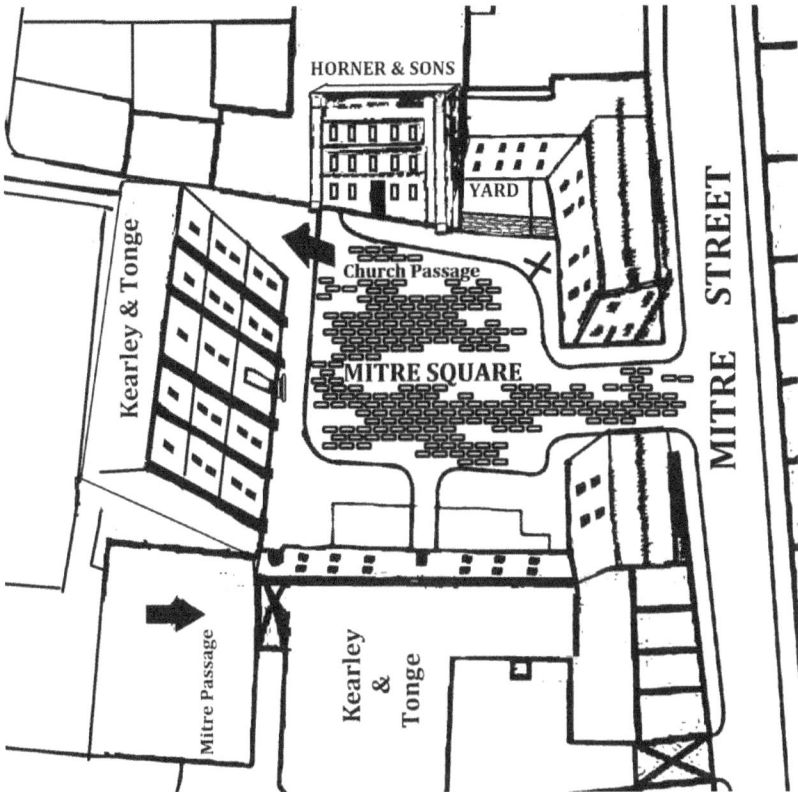

Overhead of Mitre Square. X, of course, marks the spot.

Conway has a knack, self-perceived or real, of writing pamphlets about the lives of people. These they hawk to help pay their way. Gallows ballads seem particularly popular. These are barked and sold to those interested in the lives of criminals facing execution. They mix truth and fiction and are often quite dramatic pieces. Tastelessly, Catherine and Tom hawk one at the execution of her cousin in 1866.

She had thus rather spiraled into a bit of a sordid and base life. All for love it seemed. Catherine even got a tattoo on her arm: TC. Maybe he's a mountebank, but she loved him and they must do what they can to survive. Their first child had come in 1865, a second in 1868, and then the last in 1873.

But there were problems. For the birth of one of the children she had returned to Wolverhampton. She wasn't back in London long ere she tried to go back to Wolverhampton and get away from Conway. Yet her aunt would not have her back. Reluctantly, she returned to London.

In 1881 it was finally over. She and Conway split up. She took the girl, he the boys. The daughter (Annie), however, decided to marry young. A man named Louis Philips had caught her arm and charms and they moved to Southwark to avoid her mother's not-so-motherly touch on her purse. It seems that Catherine was quite a pest for handouts.

This isn't surprising since she really didn't have much background for employment. Conway had only taught her to be well-read, to the standards of Whitechapel at any rate. On her own now, what did this leave her? Nothing. She was too old to be a flower in the gutter.

She attracted instead a man named John Kelly. This didn't help much financially, but he was a kindly man and they loved each other. He's a bit of a hard one to define. He's a sedentary itinerant, if there is such a thing. He often worked for a fruit salesman named Lander. But he also bummed odd jobs. Perhaps he and Eddowes are made for each other. She seems a happy person to others, often singing, and his relationship with her is a rather free one.

She indeed seemed rather carefree at this time. Sometimes she did drink to excess, but she was not known to walk the streets. More often than not she was in at Cooney's boarding house, Flower and Dean Street, between 9 and 10 p.m. Her life with John follows this routine. Despite boarding in the heart of Whitechapel's worst area, she was an easy lark, and John and her got along.

Every year they'd go hop picking out to the country. This month, September 1888, it had not gone so well for the two. They had made little or no money. They made the trek back to London near destitute. Yet they must have been an endearing couple to others. They are walking back to London with a couple going to Cheltenham. At the crossroads they split. As they part, the other woman insists that Catherine takes a pawn ticket from her. It is a ticket to a coat. It's only pawned for 2 ducats, and the coat may fit John. They won't be going back to London. They'd have no need of it, she assures Catherine. Please take it. This Catherine does. She really didn't have to urge Catherine. She was quite the bit the sticky hand scrounger.

On Friday, September 28, they reach London dead broke and tired. John and her part to earn some quick cash. He makes 6 ducats. It is not enough for both to room at Cooney's. She insists he take 4 of the ducats and she'll take 2. This way he can sleep at Flower and Dean and she will sleep at the casual ward at Shoe Lane. He's the bread winner, and needs his sleep to keep his fruit handler side-job. He finally agrees.

Eddowes spends the night at the casual ward. She hadn't been there for a long time, but she was well known there.

On Saturday morning she turns up at Flower and Dean early. She was tossed from the casual ward for some reason. Kelly decides that he'll pawn his pair of boots. Eddowes does this on his behalf under the name Jane Kelly. Getting 2 and six for the boots, they buy some necessary food, tea and sugar. They eat breakfast back at the lodging house between 10 and 11 a.m.

Things are truly bad. She herself is wearing a pair of man's boots already, and John has no shoes. She decides she'll head to her daughter and bum some money. Eddowes, however, did not know that her daughter had moved since last she had tried to tap her. If she did make the trek, perhaps when there she was told by neighbors where her daughter had moved and she went to the new abode in Bermondsey. Whichever is the case, she did not make it back by 4 p.m. as she had promised John.

Whatever happened, whether she had some row or not with her daughter over what a disgrace of a mother she is, Eddowes had enough money and enough reason to do a tankard Aldgate way. She was next seen sprawled on a heap at 29 Aldgate High Street surrounded by a bemused crowed. She was so drunk she couldn't move. This condition was from far more than a bloke buying her a drink or a few ducats worth of brew.

Constable Louis Robinson tries to make heads or tails of it, but none standing by know her. He struggles to get her up and lean her against the shutters. But she is so drunk she slides off sideways. Another bobby (George Simmons) has come to help. Together they haul her to Bishopsgate Police Station.

There she stands, arms over each bobby's shoulders, before sergeant James Byfield. From his elevated position, he asks her her name. She replies: "Nothing" in a drunken slobber. At 8:50 p.m. she is locked into a cell in order to dry out. Every 30 minutes the gaoler, George Hutt, supervises the prisoners. Eddowes is sleeping it off.

At 12:15 a.m., September 30, Eddowes has long stirred. She starts singing. Fifteen minutes later she calls out: "When will you let me out?"

Hutt calls back: "When you are able to take care of yourself."

"I can do that now," she replies.

He ignores her and goes about his work. But it is Sunday early morning now, and more Saturday drunks are being picked up. At 12:55 a.m. he sees if any are fit to go so space can be made. Eddowes seems capable enough. She is released after she gives her name. She says she is Mary Ann Kelly. She says she lives on Fashion Street.

Whatever her reason for lying, she knows she is in trouble at home. She asks: "What time is it?"

Hutt: "Too late for you to get anything to drink."

"I shall get a damn fine hiding when I get home," she says as she faces the door.

"And serve you right," he chided. "You had no right to get drunk." He pushes open the door. "This way missus. Please pull it to."

"Ohll right," she accepts. "Goodnight, old cock."

Unknown to Hutt, Eddowes is not going home. She turns left at the station and that keeps her in the City of London proper, where she had been picked up. Whitechapel was a part of greater London. As such it was the jurisdiction of the Metropolitan Police or "Scotland Yard." But due to the fact that London grew from the actual City of London, wherein or nearby were such ancient edifices and institutions as the Tower, Royal Mint, and the Bank of England, the City maintained its own autonomous police force. Scotland Yard answered to the Home Office whereas the City of London police, which were responsible for no more than a square mile, answered to the Corporation of London and the Lord Mayor.

Eddowes is next seen at 1:35 a.m. outside Mitre Square. It is a small business square right at the border of the City of London and Whitechapel. Therefore it almost straddles the two police jurisdictions. There is only one major entrance to the square, and that is on Mitre Street. She should have made it here in only 10 minutes. She either was so hung over still she could not walk quickly, she huddled in a doorway to stay out of the brief rain shower, or she was idling about hoping to get some doss money. She had no money anymore. Whatever she might have had, from wherever it had mysteriously materialized, she had drunk it. What would she say to Kelly?

This we shall never know, for when she was last seen she was with her murderer on Duke Street outside Church Passage, the long walking passage to Mitre Square. She is up close to the man, with one hand on his chest, but she is not pushing him back. It seems very friendly, actually cozy. He is a few inches taller than her, stout, dressed in a loosely fitting salt and pepper jacket. He wears a gray peak cap. He has a red handkerchief tied jauntily around his neck. He has a fair complexion, with a small fair mustache.

The witnesses, casually walking past, think little of it.

And this brings us back to the shocked look on Watkins' face. Eddowes was now, minutes later, brutally butchered. Watkins waited what seemed a lifetime. Finally, Constable Frederick Holland came rushing in and stopped at the gruesome scene in Watkins' bull's eye beam. Soon other constables arrived and gaped. After Watkins gave some background, he started checking around the buildings and down the other two passages.

It was about 5 minutes to 2 a.m. at Bishopsgate police station when Inspector Edward Collard heard that a

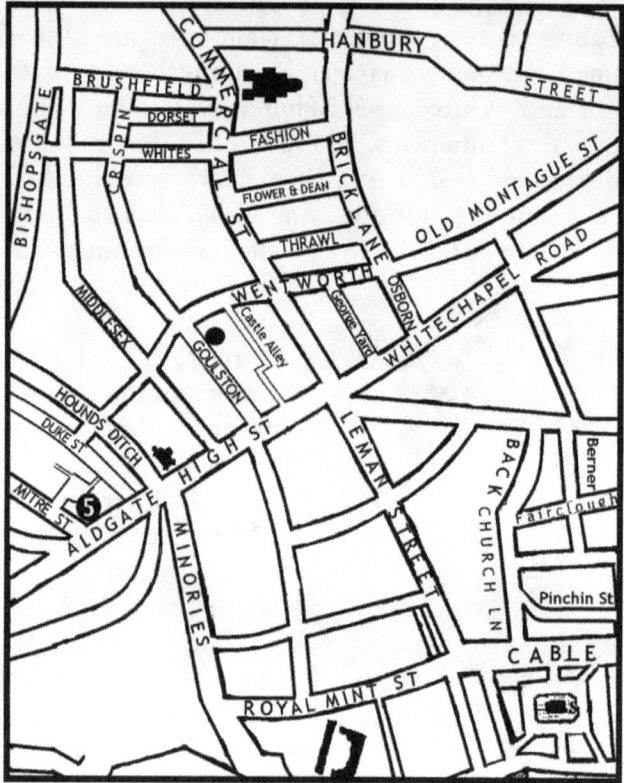

Mitre Square (5) in relation to other streets in nearby Whitechapel.

murdered woman was found in the square. He immediately telegraphed the main office and had a constable go fetch the City of London's surgeon, Dr. Frederick Gordon Brown. Collard then bolted out the door and arrived at Mitre Square about a few minutes after 2 a.m. He recoiled at the scene.

Dr. George Sequeira, a local surgeon, was already bent over the body, logistically considering how the murder was done. It was a gross, clumsy sight to him. He thought a maniac had torn at her. He saw no professionalism in it at all. Although this was the darkest corner of the square, he thought there had been enough light for the fiend to have been able to at least have a gray image of what he was doing.

Collard had Sergeant Jones pick up those loose items about that weren't soaked in blood. They were "three small black buttons, such as are generally used for boots, a small metal button, a common metal thimble, and a small penny mustard tin containing two pawn-tickets." Collard put them in his pocket.

Then just before Collard could set the men about, there arrived Chief of the City Detectives, James McWilliam, a lean man with gaunt cheeks, a Quaker beard, and a tweed suit under his dewy ulster. This was an horrendous scene. Obviously, it was the maniac from Whitechapel. Finally, he had struck in their jurisdiction. From what that Sequeira chap was telling him, the body must be dead now only 15 minutes. McWilliam checked his watch. It was only shortly after 2 a.m. He immediately ordered the men to fan out and head across into the Met's jurisdiction in Whitechapel and Spitalfields as far as they could. Stop all people and check them. Any signs the fiend went into a house, check it. The men saluted and bolted off.

Major Henry Smith was Assistant Commissioner of the City of London Police. With the Commissioner on leave, he was a "hands on" Acting Commissioner. More than any policeman of rank, he was fascinated with these series of crimes. He had been so anxious to have a crack at the fiend, he had long made preparations. In anticipation of a strike in their jurisdiction, he had already set police about covertly. For days constables were in plainclothes, enjoying themselves *incognito* at the pubs and lounging about the city benches.

When Collard's telegram came in, men set about trying to find him to tell him. At that time he was at the Cloak Lane Police station, trying to sleep. At 2:10 a.m. a man walked in and gave him the news. Smith dressed and dashed downstairs. He had ordered his hansom ready, a small covered two man carriage on tall bowed metal shock absorbers. He plopped in. Cramping him was a 210 pound inspector. He barked at three detectives, and they jumped on the back, setting the hansom to bob and jounce around. The whip cracked and they were bounding down the road. Around each corner they rolled to wide angles, the whip cracking, and Smith grousing about being crushed by the heavy inspector. At last they rolled into Mitre Square. A group of constables still surrounded the body, and Dr. Sequeira had been joined by Dr. Gordon Brown.

Smith left the examination to the medical men and now personally partook in the blood hunt for the fox. He headed northeast with some men and they melded into Whitechapel.

Smith was certainly in good company in his willful intrusion into the Met's jurisdiction. Before those that McWilliam had ordered in, City detective constables Daniel Halse, Robert Outram and Edward Marriot were rushing along the dark, narrow streets. They had been near Aldgate Church at 1:58 a.m. when police bustling past on the hunt had told them of the carnage in Mitre Square. They ran to the square, got their bearings, and then rushed off into Whitechapel. Halse went down Middlesex Street and as far into Wentworth where the murders of Tabram and Smith had occurred. He stopped two men, searched them, but they gave a good account of themselves. Then he came back through Goulston Street around 2:20 a.m. heading back to Mitre Square.

By this time, the body had been removed by ambulance. He headed to the morgue where Major Smith was already trying to get an account of things. There they noticed that a rather large portion of her apron was missing. It had been recently torn (not cut!), and the tear went across a patch on it. He and Smith went back to Mitre Square to thrash out exactly what the chain of events must have been, and to get the most recent information from all the scouring detectives returning. It had become a rather impromptu command base, and there was also the need to protect the scene of the crime, especially before the people would start to crowd around at daylight.

When they arrived the latest news greeted them immediately: a piece of apron had been found on Goulston Street by as Met constable on patrol. From there Halse went to the Met station at Leman Street. Smith's liaison, City Det. Robert Sagar, was already there. In the hands of the redoubtable Bagster Phillips, they were shown the apron. It was filthy, streaked with blood and smelled of fecal matter. Met detectives confirmed that Constable Alfred Long had found it.

It had happened about 2:55 a.m. when Long was casually making his way down Goulston Street on his regular beat. Met constables had naturally come across the City of London police streaming through their territory. He had, like the other bobbies, heard there had been another ghastly murder, this one in the City. But there was also a rumor that another had been committed south of Whitechapel at Dutfield's Yard. The details of that one remained unconfirmed. Goulston Street was far enough from Mitre Square that there was little need to be overly on the alert. However, in shining his bull's eye about he saw a crumpled swath of cloth in the entrance to a model dwelling, as the purpose-built tenements were called — London's attempt to build habitable apartments for the poorer of the city. Long saw that a corner of the apron was stained with blood. But above it, on the door jamb of the deep entrance about at shoulder height, was a graffito. He panned his light over it:

> The Juwes are
> The men that
> Will not
> be Blamed
> for nothing.

Long scanned about looking for more blood. He then went inside and searched all 7 staircases to the top of the stairs. Finding no blood or evidence of recent footprints he informed another constable nearby of what happened and told him to take charge. He went to the Leman Street Station with the evidence.

Having this information, Halse was back at the scene at Goulston Street. He looked at the writing carefully. It was white chalk on the black dado of the door jamb. There was no fresh chalk dust underneath it, but it seemed recent. Had it been there awhile, in a neighborhood heavily Jewish, he was sure it would have been rubbed out already.

Whitechapel was slowly coming to life in this early morning. The trickle of people on Whitechapel Road increased to a slow river, signaling the fruit markets were now open. Goulston Street, however, was still in the shadows of dim morning undercurrents. Therefore it was a bit of a surprise to hear and see a brougham and its two horses turn from the traffic of Whitechapel Road and clop surely on to the residence. Halse was even more surprised when it stopped and out stepped Sir Charles Warren himself accompanied by the Superintendent of Police for H Division, Thomas Arnold.

Their road to Goulston had begun at Leman Street Station, where Warren had popped up for a briefing. Phillips was still in possession of the apron at the station and examining it. It was the one thing the City C.I.D. did not have: the clue to the killer's residence. The apron was proof that the killer fled back into the Met's territory. Long had already confirmed he had not seen it when he last strolled through the street at 2:20 a.m. This meant that the killer hung about in the shadows some place, perhaps as much as 45 minutes after the killing, and came back out and staged the apron. This time lapse meant the killer had a hideout in the area.

There should be no question that the apron was considered vital evidence. Yet to what killer did this apron point? From the descriptions of the mutilated corpse the first instinct should be to suspect the Whitechapel fiend. However, that may not be what Phillips told Warren. We know Bagster Phillips was to an extent the Dr. Watson of the Met. He was meticulous and logical. Gordon Brown had him called before the body was even removed from the square, and it appears by early morning Phillips had already seen it at the mortuary. Out of professional courtesy he would be allowed to attend the postmortem on Sunday afternoon. After this he would feel that the same killer who had murdered Stride had *not* killed Eddowes. Whether he had any doubts yet, we do not know. But we know he had also examined Stride just before. This may have predisposed him to believe that a second murder the same night by the same killer was unlikely. He may now have expressed his doubts about the Mitre Square killing.

In addition to this, there was the graffito. It obviously incriminated Jews. But even more obvious, it was opportunistically contrived to dovetail on the unexpected anti-Semitic protests that started fuming due to Harry Dam's "Leather Apron" articles. This certainly must have made the graffito suspicious to Warren and all those about. There had been no hint of anti-Semitism in the previous murders. All that rot had pollinated only *after* Dam and the *Star* played a yellow hand.

Put together, Warren may have felt that any evidence involving the killing, *including* the graffito, was not important to the apprehension of the actual maniac of Whitechapel. However, all that we do know for certain is that Superintendent Arnold expressed his worry about the graffito. In light of what happened over the stupid "Leather Apron" debacle, Warren no doubt agreed. Tomorrow would bring a nightmare from the papers and possible riots from the locals. Arnold now wanted to send an inspector with a sponge to rub it out, but Warren wanted to go see it first.

Unbeknownst to the Met at Leman Street Station the tenement house was being searched by City Police. Thus when Warren arrived he was probably equally surprised by Halse standing by and the stairwells clamoring with flat feet City detectives. This may have shortened Warren's already-fatigued fuse. He quickly made it plain that the graffito had to be rubbed out. Halse objected. He had sent a message to McWilliam telling him he'd wait by the graffito until it was light enough to take a picture. This McWilliam agreed with. It was 5:30 a.m. now. In an hour it would be light enough to take a photo. That didn't satisfy Warren. He said he didn't need a bloody riot. It had to go. Arnold suggested a compromise. Rub out "Juwes." No, Warren wanted it all out and quick. Halse was out of his jurisdiction. When Warren demanded, there was little he could do.

There were reasons for Warren's precipitous attitude. Goulston Street was also known as Petticoat Lane because all the tailors and clothier wholesalers set up their stalls in the road. Already down the street, merchants were setting up. Many lived nearby and would be ushering out of the buildings any time now. This would be a veritable river of customers, merchants and wholesalers shortly.

Halse still rightly objected. Obviously, the newspapers were already getting snippets of the night's events, but how much would the local people know in an hour? As far as anybody might see there was a misspelt and slightly convoluted assignation against Jews in the doorway. After all, the capital letters were only three quarters of an inch high, and the other letters smaller in proportion to the capitals. It could be shielded easy enough.

In a huff, Warren stopped the argument. Halse was to write down the message in a notebook. When done Warren seized the sponge from Arnold and rubbed out the message himself. It was his call, his territory. He would inform Henry Smith himself. That was that.

Warren's coach and two clopped off down Goulston Street. City policemen were exiting the building. Everybody going to work now wanted to know what happened.

Warren's coach rocked to a stop at City Police headquarters, but Smith was not there. He was still roaming his precinct stations or had gone to sleep. Warren told McWilliam bluntly what he had done. McWilliam was just as earnest in his reply. He told Warren that he had made a huge, costly mistake. Evidence should not have been destroyed.

But it was too late. The damage had been done.

London went berserk yet again that Sunday. News had so far only spread by rumor. But it was certain two murders had been committed in unbelievable circumstances. This was no longer a killer on the loose, but an adroit madman running amok. The newspapers, as indeed all London, regarded the same killer to be responsible for both killings and for those of the earlier victims.

When, on October 1, the details hit the newsstands there was enormous blame hurled at the police. The *Daily News* declared: "His proceedings of Sunday morning seem to confound every possible speculation as to the manner of the crimes. To reach Mitre Square from Berner Street he must have hurried, dripping with blood, through streets still not entirely deserted, in spite of the hour. He must have been literally drenched with blood, after the completion of the second crime, yet he passed on unchallenged and unmolested, until he reached his lair. To add to these risks of detection he had to accost the second woman, and to win her confidence while he was still fresh from the butchery of the first. Never was there a greater mystery of crime. Yet, in this state, he was observed by no one, and especially by no member of that Force which is supposed to have eyes for a sleeping world. It is impossible to avoid the depressing conviction that the Police are about to fail once more, as they have failed with Chapman, as they have failed with Nicholls [sic], as they have failed with Tabram, as they have failed with Smith. . ."

The early accounts, as usual, were horribly inaccurate when it came to details. But the *Daily News* set the tempo for many other East End papers. It was, of course, as Sir Charles Warren had feared: the police were being blamed for everything. The trail of blood, macabre, Poe, and picturesque, was false. Even the Goulston Street bloody apron rag popped up without a trail. The only thing the *Daily News* got right was when it declared: "Never was there a greater mystery of crime. . ." but then it overshadowed the significance of this by blaming the police for not solving the greatest mystery instantly.

Without real knowledge, the news quills were dipped in venom. "The Police have done nothing," continued the *Daily News* in scathing tempo, "they have thought of nothing, and in their detective capacity they have shown themselves distinctly inferior to the bloodhounds which a few years ago, in the provinces, tracked the mysterious murderer of a little girl to his doom. The trail must run true and clear from Berner Street to Mitre Square, and beyond, for those who have the true instinct of the detective calling. None of the accepted apologies for the shortcomings of the Force will cover their repeated failure in these extraordinary cases."

The *Echo* echoed the *Daily News*' sentiments that bloodhounds should be set onto the killer's trail. The reporter went into a long dissertation about how he was able to witness the efficiency of the animals while in Southern California recently. Then he told of another American story. Kansas City was a tough place, but even people there were shocked by a brutal stabbing. They were sure only a stranger could do this. They called for a bloodhound from nearby Albuquerque (New Mexico!) and before the body was even removed, the dog had arrived and straightaway got the scent and ran to a dive at the end of town to corner the culprit.

Doubtless no Brit knew the impossibility of this scenario. But neither did anyone know the inaccuracy of the London news reports over the crimes. The comparative was just another knife in the back of Warren and the Met's competency. The journalists may have expiated their need to trounce "Cock Warren" and his handling of the Met, but the effect was to cause people to believe that they were completely unprotected. The result was to put a city in fear for all the wrong reasons.

9

OCTOBER TERROR

PADDY WAGON BELLS jingled frantically as the horses sped it through the intersections. The driver snapped the reins; the man riding beside him clanged the bell. Bobbies hung on the back. An American was being whisked into custody. The day after the crime this Yank had come into the lodging house known as Albert Chambers. His manner "riveted" all the lodgers, and he stayed and conversed all the day about the murders. His knowledge of them, however, began to arouse their suspicions. Then at a later dissertation, the deputy keeper of the lodging house was afraid that this man was the killer. He called the police. The papers knew nothing on October 1 except that a man wearing an American hat was in the clink.

There is a reason why Scotland Yard took any American as a suspect seriously. The Central News Agency had received an unusual letter on the 27th of September claiming to be from the murderer. They dismissed it as the work of a crank until news from the Eddowes murder leaked out. When her clothes were removed at the mortuary a piece of her ear fell out. There was a reference in the letter to clipping the next victim's ears. Central News dutifully took it to the police.

Scotland Yard immediately noticed the same thing the newsmen had noticed. The letter began with "Dear Boss." This was an American expression. The British expression would have been "Dear Gov'". A clue at last. When a constable reported that the Albert Chambers lodging house residents were excited over a Yank who seemed to know too much, no time was wasted.

The news of an arrest, however, did not assuage the rancor of the newspapers' denouncements of the Met's failures. There had been arrests before, including Leather Apron, that hadn't amounted to much but red faces all around. On the other hand, the letter was of interest. It was printed for the first time, October 1, and placed amidst the columns of gore, theory, and denouncements.

25 Sept. 1888.

Dear Boss,

I keep on hearing the police have caught me but they wont fix me just yet. I have laughed when they look so clever and talk about being on the <u>right</u> track. That joke about Leather Apron gave me real fits. I am down on whores and I shant quit ripping them till I do get buckled. Grand work the last job was. I gave the lady no time to squeal. How can they catch me now. I love my work and want to start again. You will soon hear of me with my funny little games. I saved some of the proper <u>red</u> stuff in a ginger beer bottle over the last job to write with but it went thick like glue and I cant use it. Red ink is fit enough I hope <u>ha. ha.</u> The next job I do I shall clip the ladys ears off and send to the police officers just for jolly wouldn't you. Keep this letter back till I do a bit more work, then give it out straight. My knife's so nice and sharp I want to get to work right away if I get a chance. Good Luck.

Yours truly

JACK THE RIPPER

Dont mind me giving the trade name

PS Wasnt good enough to post this before I got all the red ink off my hands curse it No luck yet. They say I'm a doctor now. <u>ha ha</u>

The *Daily News* drew the parallel between Eddowes' face mutilations, the clipped ear and the warning in the letter. It also noted that the penmanship in "this extraordinary epistle" was that of a fine "clerkly hand." We can certainly follow their thinking. This fit the description of the man who was with Stride before she died. This would also match the "shabby genteel" chap seen with Chapman. In short, it seemed real. On top of this there was the letter writer's eagerness to get started "ripping" again; and in a few days this had come to pass with the "Double Event."

Most significantly, the murderer at last had a name. Putting a name on an item or a person somehow helps to crystalize certain attributes. There was something about the name Jack the Ripper that now held the city in its power. The newspapers were no longer exaggerating when they spoke of the "Terror in the East End."

Under "Universal Fear of the Murderer," the *Echo* introduced Watkins' vivid account ". . .I saw the body in front of me. The clothes were pushed right up to her breast, and the stomach was laid bare with a dreadful gash from the pit of the stomach to the breast. On examining the body I found the entrails cut out and laid round the throat, which had an awful gash in it, extending from ear to ear. In fact, the head was nearly severed from the body. Blood was everywhere to be seen. . .The murderer had inserted the knife just under the left eye, and, drawing it under the nose, cut the nose completely from the face, at the same time indicating a dreadful gash down the right cheek to the angle of the jawbone. The nose was laid over on the cheek. A more dreadful sight I never saw; it quite knocked me over." Morris added much to the mystique by insisting the murder could not have taken place there because he had heard no sound at all. This conveyed the typical amazement that overwhelmed both public and Press in the wake of such a brutal slaughter. The almost-supernatural abilities of this new Jack the Ripper were ever-growing.

By the morning of October 1, the police were having trouble controlling the crowd at Mitre Square. Thousands came to gawk and chat amongst themselves about the murder. At Berner Street it was little different. The carriage gates to Dutfield's Yard were kept closed, but Hindley's was still in

THE PENNY ILLUSTRATED PAPER
AND ILLUSTRATED TIMES

THE DISCOVERY IN BERNER STREET

THE DISCOVERY IN MITRE SQUARE

LONDON'S REIGN OF TERROR: SCENES OF SUNDAY MORNING'S MURDERS IN THE EAST-END.

Popular rags like The Penny Illustrated *animated the scenes of the "Double Event" while the inquests brought us the shocking details.*

operation. Two police constables watched the gate and opened only the walking gate fixed therein when the employees came and went. It was then that the crowd, grasped by curiosity, lunged forward to try and steal a peek inside to see where the woman Stride had been found murdered.

The socialist club got remarkably capitalistic. Anybody who was a member was admitted for free, but they held a special meeting and decided not to admit any stranger without charging them a fee. The secretary suggested 5 shillings. The *Echo* couldn't help but call this "extortionate considering there is nothing to see."

There was at least one thing on this gloomy morning from which Sir Charles could garner some relief: only one of the murders occurred in Wynne Baxter's jurisdiction. Fortunately, this one was also by far not the most macabre of the two. Over his breakfast this fact may have affected Baxter in just the opposite way. Nevertheless, he wasted no time. On that very day, October 1, he convened Stride's inquest.

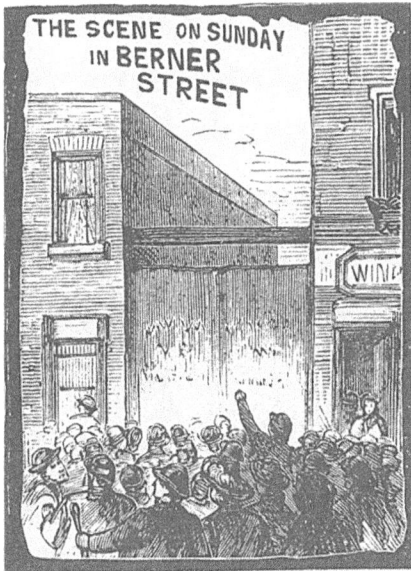

The autumn fogs were very light right now, but they nevertheless cast a gloomy mantel over Whitechapel. Damp fall leaves did not move from the ground. They did not even ebb with a passing carriage or hansom. The horses trotted slowly. Bells jingled with reserve. Foghorns were distant and hoarse. Lights from within buildings cast amber pools upon the wet cobblestones and curbs, but they added no feeling of warmth. Buildings sweated dew, the streets glistened with moisture. Autumn repose and the heavy feelings in the wake of the double murder gave Whitechapel the tempo and feel of a graveyard: neglected, forbidden, monumental, cold.

All this helped create a perfect theatrical backdrop for the heavy meeting at the Vestry Hall in Cable Street. Twenty four jurors had been picked. They had observed the body at the "mortuary," and now sat in file. Despite the enormous publicity, Vestry Hall had only a handful of spectators. This perhaps did not bode well for Baxter. This was a large enough hall to accommodate more than the Working Lads Institute, and he must have been expecting more interest. No mind, the Press packed the house; their little errand boys ready to run with the latest details to the managing editor.

Illustrators walked us through the steps that must have led to Liz Stride's brutal murder.

The only ones who testified this day were William West, the overseer of the printing office (which overlooked Dutfield's Yard from the back and side of the Educational Club), Morris Eagle, and Louis Diemshutz. Amazingly, Baxter let it hang there. In order to attend to other business, ostensibly, he adjourned after only these three testified. The inquest would sit again tomorrow, he said.

Perhaps it was the lack of a crowd. More likely, Baxter had simply jumped the gun and didn't have enough yet to probe too deeply. Baxter rightly wanted more time for more information to eke out from the gutters of Whitechapel. But the taste he gave us in these three witnesses was actually very valuable, both then and from our vantage today.

The combined testimony of Diemshutz, West and Eagle, dashed to pieces the idea that Stride's death was the result of some impromptu argument. West confirmed that couples never used the area. The last time he had seen a pair was a year before. Together they also confirmed how dark the gateway area was. Eagle had passed through at 1:40 a.m. and couldn't swear that the body wasn't there already. Clearly, Stride's murderer had unusually good eyesight. Adding what we know about how Stride was neatly positioned with her neck over the rut, we know the killer knew the area and pre-planned to cut her throat here.

The whole idea of a heated, impromptu squabble had begun with a rather dramatic police witness named Israel Schwartz. The night of the murder he had gone into the Leman Street police station and insisted that he saw Stride in a contretemps with another man, who was slightly tipsy, not long before she was found dead. In the very gateway where her body had later been found this tipsy brute had thrown her to the ground and she screamed three times, though conveniently not loudly. When the brute saw Schwartz he called to a chum standing in the shadows across the street. He called "Lipski!" which was the name of a famous murderer about those parts, now long dangled at the end of a hangman's rope. It was at this point that "Lipski" seemed to follow Schwartz. Schwartz fled. Now, after the murder, believing he had seen too much and might be a marked man, he went to the police and told his story.

Before Schwartz's claim became doubted even by the very paper that promoted it the most, there was enough evidence gathered by the police to frankly contradict the whole scenario. For starters, there were many more witnesses to the street. Mrs. Mortimer was one, and the *Daily News* carried her report October 1 in which she made it plain that she was outside her door almost all the time between 12:30 and 1 a.m. She only went indoors to bed just before 1 a.m., and when she soon heard the row she went outside and over to the yard. She personally saw Ed Spooner touch Stride's face and heard him say it was warm. "There was certainly no noise made, and I did not observe anyone enter the gates. . .If a man had come out of the yard before one o'clock I must have seen him. . . A young man and his sweetheart were standing at the corner of the street, about 20 yards away, before and after the time the woman must have been murdered, but they told me they did not hear a sound."

Well dressed and combed, Schwartz is described by the Press as "a theatrical," which might be taken as a grandstander trying to opportunistically get his name in the papers. He probably was an actor by trade, but not a very distinguished one. The *Star*, the paper that comically brought us "Leather Apron," was the only rag to carry Schwartz's claims in detail. In an unusual contradiction, in the very same issue on another page, the *Star* dismissed Schwartz's story as "*a prior* incredible." Baxter, too, had no intent to call him.

Aside from Mrs. Mortimer (and other witnesses) negating some impromptu squabble, there are the "intangibles" in this case that match those in the earlier murders that suggest the location was carefully picked in advance and the murder not some impromptu affair by a clumsy, tipsy bully. Together they prove too sublime to be a coincidence. More than this evidence will be brought out shortly at the inquest, and it explains why Baxter never called Schwartz to testify.

Bagster Phillips' testimony is what everybody awaited. This would reveal the details and even perhaps how the Stride death scene could be linked to the others. Surprisingly, Baxter would not call him the next day, October 2. Instead he called Constable Harry Lamb in order to get a blow-by-blow of what went on after the body was found. After Lamb, he called Edward Spooner. The purpose, following a coroner's sense of chronology, is to help determine time of death, since he touched her first and was reputed to have disturbed her head. He denied he lifted her head. He said he only touched her chin and it was still warm.

All the witnesses were overshadowed by the only significant medical witness called this day: Dr. Frederick Blackwell. He describes the scene of death in clear detail, which has already been gone over in the narrative. However, he noted what had caught the attention of so many. "Her head was resting beyond the carriage-wheel rut, the neck lying over the rut." She was, in fact, positioned perfectly to be bled over the rut so the blood would flow down it toward the drain. This, coupled with Eagle's earlier testimony about the darkness is another intangible. Once again, the Ripper always showed he had extremely good night vision.

Continuing, Blackwell described the wound:

The deceased had round her neck a check silk scarf, the bow of which was turned to the left and pulled very tight. In the neck there was a long incision which exactly corresponded with the lower border of the scarf. The border was slightly frayed, as if by a sharp knife. The incision in the neck commenced on the left side, 2 inches below the angle of the jaw, and almost in a direct line with it, nearly severing the vessels on that side, cutting the windpipe completely in two, and terminating on the opposite side 1 inch below the angle of the right jaw, but without severing the vessels on that side. . .The blood was running down the gutter into the drain in the opposite direction from the feet. There was about one pound of clotted blood close by the body, and a stream all the way from there to the back door of the club.

As in earlier Ripper killings, the slit of the jugular commenced on the left side of the neck. In this case, however, the circumstances more than clearly accentuated that extra touch of mystery in Ripper killings that I have mentioned earlier. Specifically, Stride's face and neck were only inches away from the brick wall— yet *no* blood had spurted onto the wall indicating Stride was alive when her throat was slit. Baxter asked this distinctly. Blackwell admitted it was very dark and he was aided in his examination only by a policeman's lantern, but he didn't see any blood on the wall.

The inexplicable nature of this mystery, integral to the Ripper killings, is reflected in how it jumbled the opinions of an otherwise meticulous physician. Blackwell was asked by a juror:

"Can you say whether the throat was cut before or after the deceased fell to the ground?"

"I formed the opinion that the murderer probably caught hold of the silk scarf, which was tight and knotted, and pulled the deceased backwards, cutting her throat in that way. The throat might have been cut as she was falling, or when she was on the ground. The blood would have spurted about if the act had been committed while she was standing up."

Baxter became curious. "Was the silk scarf tight enough to prevent her calling out?"

"I could not say that," replied Blackwell.

"A hand might have been put on her nose and mouth?" ventured Baxter.

"Yes, and the cut on the throat was probably instantaneous."

This guesswork shows how incongruous Blackwell's thoughts were as a result of this mystery. First, it must assume she was attacked from behind. If not, there was no way her mouth could have been held tight. If the killer was facing her, one hand clutching his knife handle and the other on her mouth, she could easily recoil. Also, if one hand is over her mouth and the other grasping the knife, how can another hand pull the neckerchief tight into a knot?

Perhaps from the cachous clutched in her dead left hand we should suspect she was rendered unconscious by some other means?

Bagster Phillips was the doctor to ask. He was also the one who would have written the detailed report of the autopsy. But Baxter adjourned again.

However, he did not wait a week or so as in the last inquests. He sat again the next day, October 3. Many more witnesses were called, the bulk of which were those who knew Stride at the lodging house and had been the last to see her. All confirmed she had not been wearing the flower with which she was found when dead. Michael Kidney was called, and despite their rows he still seemed to mourn her loss.

Yet the Press this day was aware that Bagster Phillips was to be called. He was sitting somewhat patiently awaiting his turn.

Nevertheless, so far Baxter dragged it out.

Before Phillips would be called, the audience had to sit through the testimony of Thomas Coram. He had found a bloodied knife far from the scene a full day after the incident. Baxter, thinking he might have found the murder weapon, considered him significant.

This is how it happened. While going to work in the early morning hours of October 1, a full 24 hours after the murders, he saw a deadly looking knife on the first step of Mr. Christmas' Laundry at 253 Whitechapel Road. The knife was about close to a foot long, and it was the kind that baker's use. It was bloodstained. Its handle was riveted to the stock in three places and a handkerchief was folded and then wrapped around it.

The knife had not been in such a conspicuous place long. It was well-lighted there, and he had passed about a dozen people coming his way as he walked up Whitechapel from Brady Street near where he lived. None could have missed it. Three of them were also policemen. One constable was now approaching (Constable Drage) to whom he drew his attention to the knife. Drage took charge of it and took him to Leman Street Station to fill out a report. There, more or less, Coram's testimony ends.

The most value in Drage's testimony is in retrospect. He gives us a splendid snapshot of how "modern" they thought their era was. In describing Coram, he said: "The boy was sober, and his manner natural. He said that the knife made his blood run cold, adding, 'We hear of such funny things nowadays.' I had passed the step a quarter of an hour before. I could not be positive, but I do not think the knife was there then. About an hour earlier I stood near the door, and saw the landlady let out a woman. The knife was not there then. I handed the knife and handkerchief to Dr. Phillips on Monday afternoon."

Finally, George Bagster Phillips was called. The Press and the audience, plus the news artists sketching faces, perked up. The room became silent as he sat in the witness chair. He described what Blackwell had described, yet giving us some extra and significant details. Blackwell had said Stride's right hand was smeared in and out with blood. Not true. The back of the wrist and hand had oblong drops of clotted blood. He describes the body lying much as Chapman's body was discovered, with the right hand lying on the breast and the legs drawn up, close to the wall. The body was "still warm, face warm, hands cold, legs quite warm, silk handkerchief 'round throat, slightly torn (so is my note, but I since find it is cut). I produce the handkerchief."[3]

He illustrated for Baxter and the audience by pointing at certain areas on it. "This corresponded to the right angle of the jaw. The throat was deeply gashed, and there was an abrasion of the skin, about an inch and a quarter in diameter, un-

---

[3] Blackwell's assistant, Edward Johnson, had earlier undone the collar to feel how warm the chest was.

der the right clavicle." He pulled out his notebook. Among the details he read aloud, he noted that they found peculiar bluish discoloration "Over both shoulders, especially the right, from the front aspect under collar bones and in front of chest . . ."

After more minutiae, he finished and closed his book. His testimony took up a much more free flow. Essentially, his testimony agrees with Blackwell on the major points of the throat being cut with a *dull* knife. Despite the fact there were no mutilations, Phillips was certain that the killer had anatomical knowledge, which was clearly displayed in how he knew the location of the carotid artery and cleanly cut the throat.

Baxter scribbled and then asked: "What was the cause of death?"

"Undoubtedly the loss of blood from the left carotid artery and the division of the windpipe."

"Did you examine the blood at Berner Street carefully, as to its direction and so forth?"

"Yes. The blood near to the neck and a few inches to the left side was well clotted, and it had run down the waterway to within a few inches of the side entrance to the club-house."

Desiring to have clarified Blackwell's claim there was no blood on the wall, Baxter asked: "Were there any spots of blood anywhere else?"

"I could trace none," replied Phillips, "except that which I considered had been transplanted— if I may use the term— from the original flow from the neck. Roughly estimating it, I should say there was an unusual flow of blood, considering the stature and the nourishment of the body."

Amazingly, on that note, Baxter said he would adjourn. One can imagine the Press grumble upon heading out the door.

Much indeed still needed to be clarified. The excessive flow of blood was an enormous clue. It takes quite a while for blood to flow that far. It casts serious doubt on the notion that Diemshutz interrupted the killer. If that's so, why were there no mutilations? The blood was already clotted by her neck. This takes a while too. How long before Diemshutz came upon her had she been attacked?

Other things needed clarification. Phillips had given us details about Stride's clothes, which were just as valuable as clues as the blood flow. "Examining her jacket I found that although there was a slight amount of mud on the right side, the left was well plastered with mud." The inference was obvious. This was obviously not a location where Stride was going to willfully lie down for a customer. She must have collapsed or been thrown down. Considering that her neck was conveniently situated over the waterway or rut, the killer obviously premeditated the attack and the location in order to bleed her properly. This means he would have to force her down here. Why no screams? Why did the blood not spurt? Also, Israel Schwartz's claims in the *Star* needed more formal clarification or dismissal. Phillips had described injuries to the shoulders which were recent, but didn't proceed with it. Without more clarification these could be interpreted as being caused when Stride was thrown down by the "tipsy" brute. Phillips was the wrong one to call last and then cut off and all made to wait until the next sitting.

Politically, and for publicity, perhaps it was the best move. Samuel Langham, the corner of the City of London, had decided to call the inquest on Catherine Eddowes the next day, October 4. Baxter had rushed 3 days of inquest on Stride back-to-back and now adjourned on the most interesting witness. He had decided to skip tomorrow and call the next meeting on October 5, coincidently on the day he would have no competition from Langham's inquest. London had to wait to hear Phillips continue. They now anticipated Langham and the first inquest outside of Baxter's direct control.

By October 4, the terror had seized London. All the eerie props associated with haunted nights were truly there. Thames fogs were coming in thicker. The foghorns moaned. Big Ben chimed in the distance. Cottony orbs hovered over the cobblestones from the gaslights.

Bobbies abounded on the street. Some walked in pairs. Dozens were in plainclothes. Some really ugly women walked around who looked remarkably like bobbies under wigs and behind makeup. Under their cloaks their hands flexed over truncheons. In addition, there were the members of the new Vigilance Committee, whose ranks now swelled.

Women screamed at any bloke off which something had sparkled. Watch fobs became daggers. Bobbies jumped out of nowhere and seized them. For a wrong word or too great a curiosity in the sordid murders a man was trotted to the station. One stout man of 5 and half foot, the height at which the Mitre Square suspect was judged, was walking near the square when he was stopped and asked to give account of himself. He said he had walked from Southampton and was a member of the Royal Sussex Regiment. His boots weren't the right kind and didn't look worn enough. This was enough to get him carted off to the Leman Street Station. A Maltese sailor embarking on a Scandinavian ship for America also couldn't give a good account of himself. That was enough to yank him in. Once again, he seemed to be just a sailor passing to the docks.

Paddy wagon bells chimed wildly yet again as another suspicious man near the Commercial Road was hauled through intersections to the police station. He was determined to be "dotty," and along with another man pulled in at 3:15 a.m. was scheduled to be released.

A paddy wagon would have been preferable for one man who spoke with a "slight American accent." On October 5, a young woman cried aloud outside the Three Nuns Pub near to Mitre Square that this man had accosted her and when she refused he threatened her. Dozens came rolling out of the pub. The man fled in terror. He jumped into a cab and growled for the cabbie to hop it as fast as he could. The crowd gave chase, growing and growing like the proverbial snowball. Finally a bobby jumped in and took control. The man was taken to Leman Street Station and the crowd soon surrounded the building waiting to hear if the Ripper had been caught. Supposedly, the fellow had the unfortunate habit of walking his cell, grumbling and using the word "Boss" frequently. Once again, it seemed they had the wrong man, and the woman wouldn't press charges.

Sir Charles Warren wrote a letter to the Whitechapel

Board of Works. They had requested that he boost the police force in their area. His response, published in all the papers, basically said there was nothing the police could do to prevent these "atrocious crimes." Statistics showed that London was the safest city in the world. What would help the most, basically, would be if women would not lie down in the dark with a strange man, to paraphrase him liberally.

There should have been little reason to think that a network of vigilance could accomplish anything more than the gossip it had so far yielded. Walking the streets is preventive but not investigative action. What the Vigilance Committee had hoped for was that a reward would roust out a witness, and this would direct the police to the suspect. This obviously wasn't happening, and the sum the Committee had so far raised wasn't tempting.

On September 29, before the double murder, George Lusk and Joseph Aarons, Chairman and Treasurer respectively, had written the newspapers. On October 1 it was reprinted and strategically placed in the columns and columns of reports and commentary on the horrific events of September 30. Lusk pulled some punches by revealing they had been snubbed by Home Secretary Matthews. In part, the letter read:

> If he would, however, consider that in the case of the Phœnix Park murders the man Carey, who was surrounded by, we may say, a whole society steeped in crime, the money tempted him to betray his associates. In our opinion, if Mr. Matthews could see his way clear to coincide with our views, the Government offer would be successful. The reward should be ample for securing the informer from revenge, which would be a very great inducement in the matter, in addition to which such offer would convince the poor and humble residents of our East End that the Government authorities are as much anxious to avenge the blood of these unfortunate victims as they were the assassination of Lord F. Cavendish and Mr. Burke—

Despite the social card that was played, Scotland Yard and Matthews remarkably both remained slightly obscure publicly as to why they would not budge on a reward. But behind the scenes Warren remained adamant that such a reward would not help. It might only lead to far more worthless information coming in than now was, and this would only clog the investigative channels more.

Readers of the *Financial News* had no problems making their views clear and public, however. They had created their own fund. Harry H. Marks was instructed to send a 300 pound cheque to Matthews. This money, the Home Secretary was told, he could use for the reward. Matthews was obliged to send it back. Under Marks' published letter in the newspapers was Matthews' oblique response from his secretary. *The Daily Telegraph*: "If Mr. Matthews had been of opinion that the offer of a reward in these cases would have been attended by any useful result he would himself have at once made such an offer, but he is not of that opinion."

The City of London police, however, never reticent to show their difference from the Met, offered a reward of 500 pounds. This was augmented by the officers of the Tower of London. On their behalf their commander, Colonel Sir Alfred Kirby, offered 100 pounds. He also offered 50 men to Whitechapel to be used as Scotland Yard saw fit "for the protection of the public or the detection of the criminals." From there it escalated. "Mr. Phillips, a member of the City Corporation, representing the ward of Aldgate, has given notice of his intention to move at the next council meeting that the Corporation do offer a reward of 250 pounds for the detection of the murderer of the woman found in Mitre Square, which is within the City precincts." The *Daily News* summed up: "The action of the City authorities in offering a reward is regarded with satisfaction in Whitechapel itself. The sum offered, together with 400£ which the directorate of two newspapers express their willingness to supply, the 100£ offered by Mr. Montagu, M.P., and the 200£ collected by the Vigilance Committee, make an aggregate sum of 1,200£. It is, however, more than probable that the reward will be increased to 2,000£, as the Lord Mayor has been urged to open a subscription list, and the members of the Stock Exchange seem disposed to take the matter up."

Perhaps in order to incite more contributions the newspapers each placed strategically within the news story an added inducement— a glove thrown down by the killer. On October 1 a postcard had been mailed to and received at the Central News Agency again, "the address and subject-matter being written in red, and undoubtedly by the same person from whom the sensational letter already published was received on Thursday last." On October 3 the papers first printed it.

> I was not coddling, dear old Boss, when I gave you the tip. You'll hear about Saucy Jacky's work to-morrow. Double event this time. Number One squealed a bit; couldn't finish straight off. Had not time to get ears for police. Thanks for keeping last letter back till I got to work again.

> —JACK THE RIPPER.

"The card was smeared on both sides with blood, which has evidently been impressed thereon by the thumb or finger of the writer, the corrugated surface of the skin being plainly shown. Upon the back of the card some words are nearly obliterated by a smear."

The postcard was more alarming than the original letter, for by its postmark it seemed it genuineness could not be doubted. It arrived on October 1, the very day the details of the murder had come out in the Press. Thus it seemed that the writer knew the details of the "double event" before they were announced in the papers. This is assuming, of course, that the writer was not a hoaxer who rushed the postcard off late September 30 after picking up local unpublished news or even early October 1. In that instance it could have traveled inner-city and arrived at the Central News the same day. At no other time was the foolhardiness of Warren's overreaction of that early morning felt. Had the police a photograph of the Goulston Street graffito they might have been able to compare it with the writing on the letters.

On October 3 both a facsimile of this postcard and the original Jack the Ripper "Dear Boss" letter was printed. Without having received any believable clue, the Met was putting up posters with the facsimile, hoping against hope that somebody might recognize the handwriting and inform. It is the publication of these, both on posters and in the papers, more than the original transcription in the papers,

Plastered over London, these became a magnet for crowds. Each and every citizen checked to see what the villain's bloody handwriting really looked like.

that now cemented the villain's name as Jack the Ripper.

The word "Boss" in the postcard and letter was to some extent a cause for relief to Scotland Yard. Britain knew that no Englishman could do these heinous crimes. It had proven too controversial to suggest a Jew was responsible. But now with "Boss" in the letters the police were given a wonderful compromise. It was acceptable for all to blame a Yank.

Various newspapers collectively announced there had been similar murders in Texas. Coincidentally they had mysteriously stopped not long before the murders in London commenced. London's *Daily News* proposed a link. "The fact that he is no longer at work in Texas argues his presence somewhere else. His peculiar line of work was executed in precisely the same manner as is now going on in London. Why should he not be there? The more one thinks of it the more irresistible becomes the conviction that it is the man from Texas. In these days of steam and cheap travel distance is nothing. The man who would kill a dozen women in Texas would not mind the inconvenience of a trip across the water, and once there he would not have any scruples about killing more women."

The "Texas Axe Murders" of 1884 and 85 actually bear no resemblance at all to what was overwhelming the East End. In Texas, the women had been drug from their homes or beds and raped and then hacked up with an axe in their backyards. On the surface, there was little mystery, no ulterior motive, only dreadful and pointless brutality. Five of the women had been "negro maids" and then the two last known victims were white. Only one man had been bludgeoned to death.

The *Daily News* only touched on the fact that the women killed in Texas were "mostly negroes." But one could read between the lines what kind of parallel the paper was drawing: a people considered expendable by southern bigots and the expendable dregs of the East End.

A theory came from Paris that politely skirted the issue but was nevertheless the product of reading between the same lines. It must be prefaced here that at this time many were enchanted at the ramifications of Darwin's theory. For Darwin, his theory had been largely of historical interest, and his own bulldog Thomas Huxley made it plain that there can be no link with an English gentleman and anything else. But for many others, some of them very fringe, evolution was a guiding light for all modern philosophy. In short, they wanted to prove Darwin's theory from contemporary evidence. Now the French suggested the Ripper's surgery had this "radical" motive behind it. The perpetrator was a "fanatical vivisectionist and disciple of Hoeckel, the German naturalist, who followed in the steps of Darwin in studying the origins of species and who advanced some startling ideas that have not yet been established. A naturalist's aim is visible in the way in which the knife was applied to the two unfortunate beings at Whitechapel."

To some haughty bigot, to some ghastly superior clerk, the dregs of Whitechapel and Texas negroes had this in common: they were the low life, the lesser people, and perhaps Darwin's theory explained why some people just didn't have what it took to be decent upstanding citizens. A clerkly "shabby genteel" abuser of Darwin's principles might be the type who could perform such gross mutilations. He alone, with his misshapen, disproportionate theories, could look at these women as expendable. One thing was certain so far: he took great pains never to be observed. Never was there a witness to the butchery. Never was there a disappearance or murder that might suggest he killed a decent person to maintain the anonymity he so craved. He killed only the expendable. He planned things to this end meticulously.

However well a callous vivisectionist might fit some of the evidence, namely only the skill of dissecting and the drabs he exclusively attacked, it did not fit the one glaring pattern that made these killings seize the senses: the seemingly supernatural, bold stealth with which they were done. Surely, none of this was necessary to carry out the aim of dissecting "lower humans" to prove some radical theory. Moreover, with the details of the Eddowes murder still waiting official airing at the inquest, a new addition to the Ripper's signature seen in both Stride's and Eddowes' murders hadn't really grasped the public. The attempt to incite anti-Semitic upheaval showed the Ripper followed the Press, at least the *Star*, and wanted to create more, much more sensation than merely tantalizing London with mystery. Why would a vivisectionist, or anybody with a similar narrow motive, go this far?

Several factors no doubt contributed to suppressing commentary on the Ripper's obvious attempt to incite race riots. Fear of escalating it could be one, but far more innocently it was probably Press and public fascination at the mystery of the killings. Nevertheless, the upshot was still the same. Theorizing went down pointless and blind alleys.

Another grisly murder no doubt also helped obscure the Ripper's new attempt at race upheaval. The Press announced it on October 3, days before the details about "Juwes" would come out at the City of London inquest. Race was conspicuously absent here, but mystery took on such an audacious air it captivated the public even more.

This new villain would eventually be dubbed The Torso Killer. He would never achieve the fame of Jack the Ripper because there was no mystery in how he killed. His victims— women who were either "unfortunates," poor serving girls, or just plain unidentified— would be found in pieces about London or in the Thames. The victims must have been killed and dissected in some remote place, parceled up, and then trotted about London and scattered or deposited where he saw fit. There was encrypted in this pattern alone his desire to project his gory audacity to taunt both public and police. But there was little ingenuity in how he must have killed women in secret places.

This is not to belittle the mystery that The Torso Killer sought to cultivate. Nor to disregard the part of his signature that undeniably was intended to draw startling parallels between himself and Jack the Ripper. This is seen in this his first victim. Her torso was found on October 2, 1888, and in a remarkable place. The killer took the trouble to secrete the victim's torso into the basement of the New Scotland Yard building while it was under construction. There can be no greater or flamboyant desecration of the new central police station than by christening it with a ghoulish parcel of a woman's rotting torso. Somehow The Torso Killer got into the locked compound and got into the lower vaults and placed the torso therein.

Like Jack the Ripper he must have had genuine eyes in the night. Retrieving their tools (which were stored here overnight), the workers were attracted to the parcel by its stench. They had to strike a match to even see it. The Torso Killer assured that his grotesque murder would associate him with the Ripper. He removed the uterus from this victim's torso, the very same organ that the papers, following Wynne Baxter's theory, had promoted as the Ripper's ultimate object. In an unintentional, and far more disturbing, way he also drew a parallel between himself and Jack the Ripper. It appears he was seen. After-hours, on the weekend before the body was found, a man had been seen jumping over the construction compound fence on Cannon Row and walking away. He wasn't a thief. He had nothing in his hands. But he was, amazingly, a well-dressed man, about mid-30s, just like the Ripper was thought to be.

A discussion of this and the continuing Torso Killings is reserved for later, but suffice it to say here that The Torso Killer made double sure that his "first" victim attracted attention. Removing the uterus, the pains he went to locate the basement's location, his ability to see in pitch darkness, plus, as the inquest would confirm, his anatomical knowledge, made him and this murder part of the October angst.

The inquest into this macabre mystery — known as the Whitehall Mystery Torso — would play on in the background as the Ripper inquests continued.

On this day, October 4, Samuel Langham, the coroner of the City of London, convened the inquest at his official administration, the Coroner's Court, Golden Lane. This was a much different atmosphere than the often itinerant inquests conducted by Wynne Baxter. Also, unlike Baxter's inquest into Stride's death, the court was crowded. "Many people were standing outside the building for the whole of the day," the papers reported. In attendance were Major Henry Smith and the Superintendent of Police, Alfred Foster. Also, unlike Wynne Baxter, Langham had a rumpled grace about him rather than that of a gallant, showy undertaker. At 64, he was much older than Baxter. His gray hair could give him a distinction that offset the predatory appearance presented by his beak nose. Also present was Mr. Henry Crawford, the Solicitor of the City of London, representing the City and the police. He was a slender rake, a bit in the mold of Disraeli or some Dickensian attorney. Receding hair was combed down all around and ended in one long undercurl. Long bushy sideburns frizzled down to his stork's neck to rest upon his high white collar.

The residence was austere, as one might expect for any court adjoining a mortuary. The jury only need examine the re-sewn corpse next door and then file in and take their position amidst the dour tokens that ornament any room by a death house.

Crawford declared his presence. "I appear here as representing the City Police in this matter, for the purpose of rendering you every possible assistance, and if I should consider it desirable, in the course of the inquiry, to put any questions to witnesses, probably I shall have your permission when you have finished with them."

"Oh, certainly," replied Langham.

Perhaps Langham was too far the opposite of Baxter. Perhaps the City and Lord Mayor worried he wasn't going to probe into this enough beyond determining death. To make up for the slack, perceived, feared or real, Crawford intended to act like a district attorney with witnesses on the stand.

The first witness called was Eddowes' sister, Eliza Gold. She broke down several times. The room remained unforgivably quiet while she blubbered. The Press dutifully noted every time she buried her face in her hands and wept.

The testimony of Kelly was that of a devoted partner. From him we get a sorry picture of how poor they were. He admitted that he stood in his bare feet after they pawned the boots in order to get some food. He also cleared her name at every chance. She was not a prostitute, he said. Some of his testimony must be taken as genuine. Eddowes does not appear to have been a streetwalker by trade. Wilkinson, the lodging house keeper, was quite familiar with Kelly and Eddowes and affirmed that Eddowes was frequently in before 10 o'clock. We should rather deduce that Eddowes turned to it this night in a desperate moment. She was also, he said, not one given to drink. Therefore two oddities occurred that day.

So far, Langham had significant witnesses called the first day. Acquaintances gave her background, Watkins gave his testimony of finding her, Forster, architect and surveyor, gave a detailed plan of Mitre Square and declared that it would have taken 12 minutes to have walked there from Dutfield's Yard; and now Collard spoke of his arrival and the pursuit northeast into Whitechapel. Langham was following a perfect chronological sequence: life, biography, the crime, its context and its aftermath. Now came the witness all had waited— the details of death. Langham was wasting no time. He called Dr. Frederick Gordon Brown, surgeon of the City of London Police. He was Bagster Phillips' counterpart.

"My attention was directed to the body of the deceased. It was lying in the position described by Watkins, on its back, the head turned to the left shoulder, the arms by the side of the body, as if they had fallen there. Both palms were upwards, the fingers slightly bent. A thimble was lying near. The clothes were thrown up. The bonnet was at the back of the head. There was great disfigurement of the face. The throat was cut across. Below the cut was a neckerchief. The upper part of the dress had been torn open. The body had been mutilated, and was quite warm— no rigor mortis. The crime must have been committed within half an hour, or certainly within forty minutes from the time when I saw the body. There were no stains of blood on the bricks or pavement around."

Crawford asked that the blood be clarified.

"There was no blood on the front of the clothes. There was not a speck of blood on the front of the jacket."

"Before we removed the body," he continued, "Dr. Phillips was sent for, as I wished him to see the wounds, he having been engaged in a case of a similar kind previously. He saw the body at the mortuary. The clothes were removed from the deceased carefully. I made a post-mortem examination on Sunday afternoon. There was a bruise on the back of the left hand, and one on the right shin, but this had nothing to do with the crime. There were no bruises on the elbows or the back of the head. The face was very much mutilated, the eyelids, the nose, the jaw, the cheeks, the lips, and the mouth

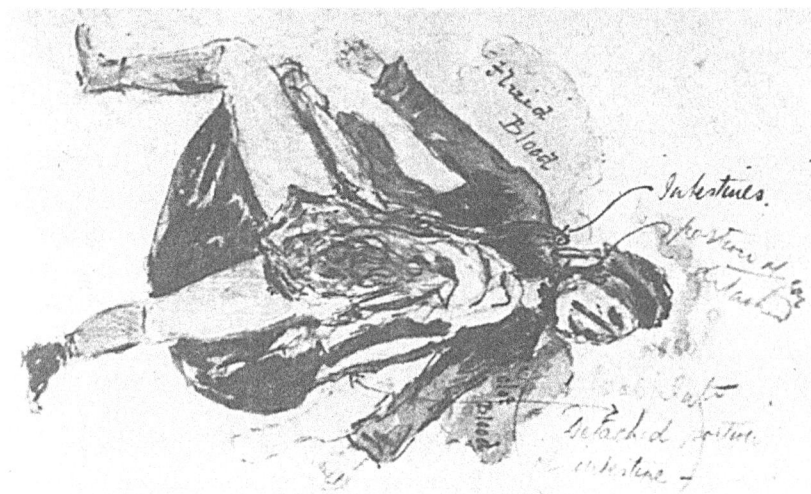

*What is perhaps the first crime scene sketch. City of London po-
lice were far ahead of the Met in their idea of details.*

all bore cuts. There were abrasions under the left ear. The
throat was cut across to the extent of six or seven inches."

Langham: "Can you tell us what was the cause of death?"

Brown: "The cause of death was haemorrhage from the
throat. Death must have been immediate."

Langham: "There were other wounds on the lower part of
the body?"

Brown: "Yes; deep wounds, which were inflicted after
death."

The newspapers redacted his detailed information, but it
is here inserted from his official autopsy report. It is several
pages long, and all of it need not be reproduced. But there
are significant observations. The most striking is how there
had been no "spurting of blood on the bricks or pavement
around. No marks of blood below the middle of the body."
The blood, though quite a quantity, had remained "on the
pavement on the left side of the neck round the shoulder and
upper part of arm, and fluid blood-coloured serum which
had flowed under the neck to the right shoulder. . .There was
no blood on the front of the clothes." This is identical with
the earlier victims and with Stride. None of the victims' arteries spurted blood.

Gordon Brown had said that there were "No bruises on

the scalp, the back of the body, or the elbows." Thus it is impossible she was thrown down. She was merely lying down. The Ripper must have grabbed her mouth and chin, leaving those telltale fingernail abrasions under the left ear once again before stabbing in, directed the blood flow to the shoulder by angling the knife, and *then* sliced.

Another similarity is found in how the intestines were "drawn out to a large extent and placed over the right shoulder." However, the killer had not been as careful. His knife sliced the bowels this time unlike in Chapman's sleek dissection.

There were other differences, of course. Folds of skin were not removed. The Ripper had sliced straight down from the sternum, around the navel, and continued on, opening the gut this way and folding back the skin and muscle. He cut many organs in doing so. The intestines were "smeared over with some feculent matter. A piece of about two feet was quite detached from the body and placed between the body and the left arm, apparently by design. . ."

This placing of the bowel by the body was not the only apparently intentional mutilation. The facial mutilations, though most of them were random, did contain intentional downward slices to the eyelids. Where the knife continued downward, it ripped into the cheek leaving "a cut which peeled up the skin, forming a triangular flap about an inch and a half."

Some 3 pages cover Brown's descriptions of how crudely the dissection was made. He was very meticulous, to say the least. He detailed the stabs and slices in the surrounding abdominal organs created inadvertently by the Ripper as he hurriedly carved up the viscera to get at the organs he wanted. Suffice it to say that this recital would have taken sometime in court. In the end all clichés come true, and in this instance most certainly the dropping of a pin could have been heard in the room.

It took a moment for the heavy silence to finally yield to a collective sigh.

Crawford asked somberly if organs were removed from the body. Brown confirmed that both organs — the uterus and a kidney — were never found. He added: "The way in which the kidney was cut out showed that it was done by somebody who knew what he was about."

Langham: "Does the nature of the wounds lead you to any conclusion as to the instrument that was used?"

"It must have been a sharp-pointed knife, and I should say at least six inches long."

Langham: "Would you consider that the person who inflicted the wounds possessed anatomical skill?"

Brown: "He must have had a good deal of knowledge as to the position of the abdominal organs, and the way to remove them."

Langham: "Would the parts removed be of any use for professional purposes?"

Brown: "None whatever."

(That was rather a jab at Baxter's theory.)

Langham: "Would the removal of the kidney, for example, require special knowledge?"

Brown: "It would require a good deal of knowledge as to its position, because it is apt to be overlooked, being covered by a membrane."

Langham: "Would such a knowledge be likely to be possessed by someone accustomed to cutting up animals?"

"Yes," Brown replied.

Langham: "Have you been able to form any opinion as to whether the perpetrator of this act was disturbed?"

"I think he had sufficient time, but it was in all probability done in a hurry."

Langham: "How long would it take to make the wounds?"

"It might be done in five minutes," Brown replied. "It might take him longer; but that is the least time it could be done in."

Langham: "Can you, as a professional man, ascribe any reason for the taking away of the parts you have mentioned?"

Brown: "I cannot give any reason whatever."

Langham: "Have you any doubt in your own mind whether there was a struggle?"

Brown: "I feel sure there was no struggle. I see no reason to doubt that it was the work of one man."

Langham: "Would any noise be heard, do you think?"

Brown: "I presume the throat was instantly severed, in

which case there would not be time to emit any sound."

Langham: "Does it surprise you that no sound was heard?"

Brown: "No."

Langham: "Would you expect to find much blood on the person inflicting these wounds?"

"No, I should not. I should say that the abdominal wounds were inflicted by a person kneeling at the right side of the body. The wounds could not possibly have been self-inflicted."

Langham: "Was your attention called to the portion of the apron that was found in Goulston Street?"

"Yes. I fitted that portion which was spotted with blood to the remaining portion, which was still attached by the strings to the body."

Langham: "Have you formed any opinion as to the motive for the mutilation of the face?"

Brown: "It was to disfigure the corpse, I should imagine."

A Juror: "Was there any evidence of a drug having been used?"

"I have not examined the stomach as to that. The contents of the stomach have been preserved for analysis."

At that Langham checked the time and it was getting late. He, too, as Baxter, called an end to the inquest in the midst of the most anticipated witness. But unlike in Baxter's case there was a triumphant epilogue provided by Mr. Crawford. He rose and grandly announced that the Corporation of London has "unanimously approved the offer by the Lord Mayor of a reward of £500 for the discovery of the murderer."

The jury rang out with "hear, hear!"

Langham recessed the inquest to that upbeat epilogue. He said they would sit again on Thursday the 8th.

It was in Wynne Baxter's corner now. The next day (Friday the 5th) he stole thunder. Bagster Phillips was recalled as the first witness of the day. Britain was already gasping over the Eddowes details in the morning edition of British dailies.

Now, Baxter's inquest played on to appropriate enthusiasm and crowds.

Phillips needed to clarify a few things before getting into the meat of his testimony. He had, as asked by Baxter, checked Stride's mouth; and there was no indication of a problem with the palate. The missing teeth were on her lower left jaw, not on top as was rumored. There was also the rumor that Stride had stopped and bought grapes from a man. Mrs. Mortimer had even said they were in her hand when dead (she probably meant the cachous). "Neither on the hands nor about the body of the deceased did I find grapes, or connection with them. I am convinced that the deceased had not swallowed either the skin or seed of a grape within many hours of her death." She had two handkerchiefs, but the stain on one appeared to be fruit and nothing else.

Then he got specific on actual details of the crime. He reasserted that Stride's neckerchief was cut, not torn. Quite significantly, the abrasion on her neck was just that. "The abrasion which I spoke of on the right side of the neck was only apparently an abrasion, for on washing it it was removed, and the skin found to be uninjured."

Stride had, in fact, not been choked. Nor had her mouth been held in a vise-like grip to keep her silent. In Eddowes' case we know her mouth was held tight enough so that fingernail marks were present under her left ear, but there was no real bruising. Nevertheless, this was still congruous with the earlier victims. The details in Stride's case were surprisingly at odds with that.

One thing Baxter had which Langham didn't— the possible murder weapon. Phillips discussed the knife which Coram had found on Whitechapel Road near Brady Street. Though it appeared to have human blood on it, Philips seemed dubious that this was genuine. It was a chandler's or slicing knife and had a rounded point.

"Such a knife could have produced the incision and injuries to the neck, but it is not such a weapon as I should have fixed upon as having caused the injuries in this case; and if my opinion as regards the position of the body is correct, the knife in question would become an improbable instrument as having caused the incision."

There may have been some skepticism in Baxter's tone when he asked Phillips to explain his idea. "What is your idea as to the position the body was in when the crime was committed?"

"I have come to a conclusion as to the position of both the murderer and the victim," declared Phillips, "and I opine that the latter was seized by the shoulders and placed on the ground, and that the murderer was on her right side when he inflicted the cut. I am of opinion that the cut was made from the left to the right side of the deceased, and taking into account the position of the incision it is unlikely that such a long knife inflicted the wound in the neck."

In essence, Phillips thought that with the brick wall so close there was no room for the killer to have brought the blade to bear over her left shoulder without hitting the wall first before drawing it back to cut the throat. In believing that Stride was pushed down, it also sounds like he actually believed the Israel Schwartz story about Stride being in a fight with a tipsy bully. The astute and capable Bagster Phillips seems to let us down here, and Baxter may have remained skeptical.

"The knife produced on the last occasion was not sharp pointed, was it?"

"No," replied Phillips, "it was rounded at the tip, which was about an inch across. The blade was wider at the base."

"Was there anything to indicate that the cut on the neck of the deceased was made with a pointed knife?"

Baxter's question subtly challenged Phillips' entire scenario. It is at moments like this that Baxter's hunting dog personality is refreshing.

"Nothing," Phillips conceded.

Baxter continued: "Have you formed any opinion as to the manner in which the deceased's right hand became stained with blood?"

"It is a mystery," Phillips naturally responded. "There were small oblong clots on the back of the hand. I may say that I am taking it as a fact that after death the hand always remained in the position in which I found it— across the body."

(Oblong clots indicate blood drops striking at an angle or

the back of the hand touched upon blood spots elsewhere. We have to recall that Diemshutz believed his wagon actually had disturbed the position of the body, so perhaps Stride's hand had hit against her throat. Also, Lamb took her pulse. Phillips' assumption is specious.)

Baxter openly showed his skepticism of Phillips' general scenario. Phillips was relying on those strange bruise marks on Stride's shoulders to infer Stride had been forced to the ground. "Does the presence of the cachous in the left hand," he asked, "indicate that the murder was committed very suddenly and without any struggle?"

"Some of the cachous were scattered about the yard."

Actually, the "scattered" cachous were only by her head. But this subtly supported his theory that she was forcibly pushed to the ground.

The Foreman pushed the question: "Do you not think that the woman would have dropped the packet of cachous altogether if she had been thrown to the ground before the injuries were inflicted?"

"That is an inference which the jury would be perfectly entitled to draw."

Baxter asked the big question: "Is there any similarity between this case and Annie Chapman's case?"

"There is very great dissimilarity between the two," said Phillips. "In Chapman's case the neck was severed all round down to the vertebral column, the vertebral bones being marked with two sharp cuts, and there had been an evident attempt to separate the bones."

"From the position you assume the perpetrator to have been in, would he have been likely to get bloodstained?"

"Not necessarily, for the commencement of the wound and the injury to the vessels would be away from him, and the stream of blood— for stream it was— would be directed away from him, and towards the gutter in the yard."

"Was there any appearance of an opiate or any smell of chloroform?"

"There was no perceptible trace of any anesthetic or narcotic. The absence of noise is a difficult question under the circumstances of this case to account for, but it must not be taken for granted that there was not any noise. If there was an absence of noise I cannot account for it."

The Foreman asked: "That means that the woman might cry out after the cut?"

"Not after the cut."

"But why did she not cry out while she was being put on the ground?" asked Baxter quite skeptically.

"She was in a yard," explained Phillips, "and in a locality where she might cry out very loudly and no notice be taken of her. It was possible for the woman to draw up her legs after the wound, but she could not have turned over. The wound was inflicted by drawing the knife across the throat. A short knife, such as a shoemaker's well-ground knife, would do the same thing. My reason for believing that deceased was injured when on the ground was partly on account of the absence of blood anywhere on the left side of the body and between it and the wall."

Phillips is basically saying that she was knocked down, collapsed to her right, was rolled to her left, then killed while on her left side. From what Phillips knew of the scene of the yard, we can understand his theory. With mud on both sides of her, Stride obviously didn't lay down willingly. Then there were those confusing bruises on the top of her shoulders. He also saw the extent of blood flow and probably seriously doubted Diemshutz interrupted the killer. This would indicate that Stride's killer intended no mutilations. Also, the dull knife used wasn't indicative of the Ripper's style.

There was already a growing schism as to which murder that night was really the work of Jack the Ripper. After having seen Eddowes' ripped up body, Phillips was straddling the fence. He had not felt that Eddowes was killed by the Ripper. But he didn't seem sure about Stride either. Baxter held similar views about Eddowes. He thought that her death was the work of a butchering imitator. But due to the finesse of Stride's silent death, he thought that the Ripper was at work here. It is the evidence of how the throat was cut that was so at odds with the Ripper's previous style.

Phillips' testimony wasn't underscoring the finesse Baxter felt was present. Baxter let Phillips continue without interrupting him. He always showed respect for professional men. But Baxter's lack of satisfaction was evident in that he recalled Dr. Blackwell, who had been the first medical man on the scene. This was fortunate. Some of his clarifications nullified Phillips' theory. He explained that he is the one who removed the cachous from her hand and had spilled them in the process, thus negating the evidence for Phillips' theory of a struggle. When he removed the packet it was only held between her forefinger and thumb. "My impression is that the hand gradually relaxed while the woman was dying, she dying in a fainting condition from the loss of blood." Thus it seems impossible that Stride was ever pushed to the ground in any struggle.

The Foreman asked about the bruises on the shoulders. Blackwell called them pressure marks. "At first they were very obscure, but subsequently they became very evident. They were not what are ordinarily called bruises; neither is there any abrasion. Each shoulder was about equally marked."

Blackwell wasn't sure how recent they were, but how does one get black and blue marks on the shoulders in the course of any normal endeavor?

The day's proceedings continued with a number of witnesses that set in order what the last events were in Stride's life. But the most significant are those who were able to describe what the men looked like with whom she was last seen. William Marshall's testimony excited the most interest, since he had observed her and a man for the longest while standing outside No. 64 Berner Street.

"Can you describe the man at all?" asked Baxter.

"There was no gas-lamp near. The nearest was at the corner, about twenty feet off. I did not see the face of the man distinctly."

"Did you notice how he was dressed?"

"In a black cut-away coat and dark trousers."

"Was he young or old?"

"Middle-aged he seemed to be."

"Was he wearing a hat?"

"No, a cap."

"What sort of a cap?"

"A round cap, with a small peak. It was something like what a sailor would wear."

Based on newspaper reports, illustrated magazines drew a picture of Marshall's suspect, giving him a Greek sailor's hat. However, at the inquest Marshall said it was rounded.

"What height was he?"

"About 5 foot 6 inches."

"Was he thin or stout?"

"Rather stout."

"Did he look well dressed?"

"Decently dressed."

"What class of man did he appear to be?"

"I should say he was in business, and did nothing like hard work."

"Not like a dock labourer?"

"No."

"Nor a sailor?"

"No."

"Nor a butcher?"

"No."

"A clerk?"

"He had more the appearance of a clerk."

"Is that the best suggestion you can make?"

"It is."

"You did not see his face. Had he any whiskers?"

"I cannot say. I do not think he had."

"Was he wearing gloves?"

"No."

"Was he carrying a stick or umbrella in his hands?"

"He had nothing in his hands that I am aware of."

"You are quite sure that the deceased is the woman you saw?"

"Quite. I did not take much notice whether she was carrying anything in her hands."

"What first attracted your attention to the couple?"

"By their standing there for some time, and he was kissing her."

"Did you overhear anything they said?"

"I heard him say, 'You would say anything but your prayers.'"

"Different people talk in a different tone and in a different way. Did his voice give you the idea of a clerk?"

"Yes, he was mild speaking."

"Did he speak like an educated man?"

"I thought so. I did not hear them say anything more. They went away after that. I did not hear the woman say anything, but after the man made that observation she laughed. They went away down the street, towards Ellen Street. They would not then pass No. 40 (the club)."

Baxter tried to qualify some of the testimony of James Brown, the last witness to supposedly see them. It is here where we can genuinely doubt whether he actually saw Stride and her killer. He described the man as wearing a dark coat all the way down to his ankles, a type of coat which essentially did not exist for men. It was reasonable to question this. Only a priest's black cassock comes down to the ankles. In the dark it is more probable that the blackness of the man's suit melded with Stride's dress, and from Brown's angle it looked like the man wore a long coat as well.

Baxter suspected this. "You are sure it was not her dress that you chiefly noticed?"

"Yes. I saw nothing light in colour about either of them."

But Brown also couldn't recall whether the man wore a hat or if he spoke with a foreign accent. He was 5 foot 7 inches about and of average build. Beyond that Brown couldn't remember.

The most reliable witness to see the pair together was Constable William Smith. He testified as to the man's appearance. It is much closer to Marshall's description, except Smith thought him much younger.

"What did you notice about him?" asked Baxter.

"He had a parcel wrapped in a newspaper in his hand. The

parcel was about 18 inches long and 6 inches to 8 inches broad."

"Did you notice his height?"

"He was about 5 foot, 7 inches."

"His hat?"

"He wore a dark felt deerstalker's hat."

"Clothes?"

"His clothes were dark. The coat was a cutaway coat."

Except for age and a couple of finer points, Smith's description matches Marshall's description. From the latter's angle earlier, he might have mistaken the deerstalker for a round cap with a single peak, not noticing the peak on the back. In any case, Constable Smith's description is crucial. When one hard clue from the crime scene is soon added to it, we can undoubtedly identify this man as Jack the Ripper, not the man who was seen 10 minutes later by Brown with a woman at the intersection.

The ball was back in Langham's formal Coroner's Court.

Day 2 of The Eddowes Inquest was convened on October 11. Crowds once again gathered at Coroner's Court to hear more of the gory details. The first witness was Dr. Sequeira. Like Blackwell in the Berner Street case, Sequeira was the local sawbones in Aldgate. On the virtue of his one treasured experience with the now-famed Ripper, he decided to add his own opinions on the skill of the killer. "I am well acquainted with the locality and the position of the lamps in the square. Where the murder was committed was probably the darkest part of the square, but there was sufficient light to enable the miscreant to perpetrate the deed. I think that the murderer had no design on any particular organ of the body. He was not possessed of any great anatomical skill."

Langham kept him on the stand for only two more routine questions (Crawford had asked him his opinion above) and then he was gone.

There was little reason to keep him a long time. Crawford, like Langham, had followed the Baxter inquests keenly. Sequeira was isolating the Eddowes case too much from the body of evidence that suggested the killer had some sort of anatomical knowledge. The urgency with which he must have killed Eddowes and mutilated her is another factor Sequeira did not take into consideration, nor the fact that the killer hovering over her would have blocked out any light. He worked in near complete darkness. The fact he got both the uterus and kidney argues that he knew what he was looking for.

The speed with which the killer worked would now be underscored by the testimony of the key witnesses of the day. Three men had passed by Eddowes and some unidentified man at 1:35 a.m. Two of them were Joseph Lawende and Joseph Hyam Levy. Lawende was certain that they had passed the entrance to Church Passage at 1:35 a.m. They had been sitting in the Imperial Club on Duke Street until 1:30 a.m. due to the rain. Then they left to walk home. At the entrance to the long, dismal Church Passage he saw a man and woman standing there close to each other. He testified that they were only 9 or 10 feet away, but he didn't get a good look at them. Eddowes was facing the man, with hand to his breast. It was very cozy. She wasn't pushing him away.

Langham would not take a description of the suspect in public, but he made sure that Lawende had given a detailed report to the police.

Lawende proved slightly disappointing. He didn't elucidate much. But the description he furnished the police, Crawford and Langham knew to be valuable. His description of the man was: about 5'7" tall, about 30 years old, fair complexion with a fair mustache. He wore a loose fitting salt and pepper jacket, a reddish neckerchief and a grey single peak cloth hat. He seemed "rough and shabby" — quite a contrast to the genteel Ripper. The shabbiness suggested a sort of sailor.

Joseph Levy was little better than Lawende in offering information, except he was remarkably specific about the man's height, saying he was 3 inches taller than Eddowes, whom he had estimated was only 5 feet tall. More than that, he couldn't say. All he would add is that he thought they were up to no good at that time of night, and that that part of the street and passage was not well-lighted. "Nothing in what I saw excited my suspicion as to the intentions of the man. I did not hear a word that he uttered to the woman."

Levy must have presented the sight of a jittery mouse. The Press already reported that he was nervous, gave the indications that he knew more than he would say, and that he had been afraid to be called to the inquest.

Levy seemed to live up to that now. He must have been reliving it as he testified, and this must have proved a comical sight, for Levy's appearance provoked Langham to ask:

"Your fear was rather about yourself?"

"Not exactly," replied Levy.

The audience laughed.

Constable Long was expected to be a controversial witness. He would have to confirm in public detail the graffito he found on Goulston Street. Nobody wanted anti-Semitic riots, but there was no way to avoid the details.

He testified that the exact wording was: 'The Jews are the men that will not be blamed for nothing.'

"Had you been past that spot previously to your discovering the apron?" asked Langham officiously.

"I passed about twenty minutes past two o'clock," confirmed Long.

"Are you able to say whether the apron was there then?"

"It was not," he said with certainty.

"As to the writing on the wall," began Crawford in a business tone, "have you not put a 'not' in the wrong place? Were not the words, 'The Jews are not the men that will be blamed for nothing'?"

"I believe the words were as I have stated."

"Was not the word 'Jews' spelt 'Juwes'?"

"It may have been."

That was a remarkably dull response.

"Yet you did not tell us that in the first place," said Langham. "Did you make an entry of the words at the time?"

"Yes, in my pocket-book."

"Is it possible that you have put the 'not' in the wrong place?"

"It is possible, but I do not think that I have."

"Which did you notice first— the piece of apron or the writing on the wall?"

"The piece of apron, one corner of which was wet with blood."

"How came you to observe the writing on the wall?"

"I saw it while trying to discover whether there were any marks of blood about."

"Did the writing appear to have been recently done?"

"I could not form an opinion."

"Do I understand that you made a search in the model dwelling-house?"

"I went into the staircases."

"Did you not make inquiries in the house itself?"

"No."

"Where is the pocket-book in which you made the entry of the writing?" asked the Foreman.

"At Westminster."

"Is it possible to get it at once?" asked Langham.

"I dare say."

Mr. Crawford: "I will ask the coroner to direct that the book be fetched."

Langham: "Let that be done."

Long was dismissed and hotfooted it out of the building to get his notebook.

Daniel Halse was called in the interim and gave his information on what he did. It was all *sans* the controversy that Sir Charles had personally come out to Goulston Street. However, it was hard to avoid the "writing on the wall," both figuratively and literally.

"As to the writing on the wall," began Langham, "did you hear anybody suggest that the word 'Jews' should be rubbed out and the other words left?"

"I did. The fear on the part of the Metropolitan police that the writing might cause riot was the sole reason why it was rubbed out. I took a copy of it, and what I wrote down was as follows: 'The Juwes are not the men who will be blamed for nothing.'"

"Did the writing have the appearance of having been recently done?"

"Yes. It was written with white chalk on a black fascia."

"Why was the writing really rubbed out?" asked a suspicious Foreman.

Halse repeated: "The Metropolitan police said it might create a riot, and it was their ground."

"I am obliged to ask this question," declared Crawford. "Did you protest against the writing being rubbed out?"

"I did. I asked that it might, at all events, be allowed to remain until Major Smith had seen it."

"Why do you say that it seemed to have been recently written?"

"It looked fresh, and if it had been done long before it would have been rubbed out by the people passing. I did not notice whether there was any powdered chalk on the ground, though I did look about to see if a knife could be found. There were three lines of writing in a good schoolboy's round hand. The size of the capital letters would be about three quarter inches, and the other letters were in proportion. The writing was on the black bricks, which formed a kind of dado, the bricks above being white."

There followed some complaining by a juror about Long not having searched the building, an attitude which is understandable given the circumstances. Mitre Square was only minutes from Goulston Street. The Ripper had obviously skulked about the street somewhere for at least 45 minutes and then chanced the manhunt to drop the apron in public. Somewhere within the area, presumably, he had a hideout. Yet Long had made no real effort to search the model dwelling. Halse no doubt added to the frustration when he testified that he too had passed Goulston on his first return to Mitre Square and had not seen any apron (although he thought he might have missed it). On top of this, the assignation had been rubbed out pointlessly. It was obviously very small writing, and the fact it was rubbed out had set bad with the City people at every level. Suspicion had already inspired the Foreman to ask why the writing was "really" rubbed out.

The complaining was about to continue, but Long's return stepped on it. The controversy over the exact wording would now supposedly be put to rest.

"What is the entry?" asked Crawford officiously.

Long read it aloud: "The Jews are the men that will not be blamed for nothing."

Langham looked at the book. "Both here and in your inspector's report the word 'Jews' is spelt correctly?"

"Yes; but the inspector remarked that the word was spelt 'Juwes.'"

"Why did you write 'Jews' then?"

"I made my entry before the inspector made the remark."

"But why did the inspector write 'Jews'?"

"I cannot say."

It was as confusing for them as it is for investigators to-day. Langham sighed. "At all events, there is a discrepancy?"

"It would seem so."

Long's reply made no sense. He had seen the writing on the wall. He would not need to have heard Halse's remark in order to have spelled "Juwes" correctly.

After the jury sweated Long a bit about not searching the building thoroughly, he was dismissed.

Langham had enough information already to say how Eddowes died. He established the time— a narrow window between 1:35 a.m. and 1:44 a.m. There was no need to probe into the Goulston Street graffito. His closing speech was short. It was summed up in the papers thusly:

> The coroner said he considered a further adjournment unnecessary, and the better plan would be for the jury to return their verdict and then leave the matter in the hands of the police.
>
> In summing up it would not be at all necessary for him to go through the testimony of the various witnesses, but if the jury wanted their memories refreshed on any particular point he would assist them by referring to the evidence on that point. That the crime was a most fiendish one could not for a moment be doubted, for the miscreant, not satisfied with taking a defenseless woman's life, endeavoured so to mutilate the body as to render it unrecognisable. He [Coroner] presumed that the jury would return a verdict of willful murder against some person or persons unknown, and then the police could freely pursue their inquiries and follow up any clue they might obtain. A magnificent reward had been offered, and that might be the means of setting people on the track and bringing to speedy justice the creature who had committed this atrocious crime.

On reflection, perhaps it would be sufficient to return a verdict of willful murder against some person unknown, inasmuch as the medical evidence conclusively demonstrated that only one person could be implicated.

The jury at once returned a verdict accordingly.

The coroner, for himself and the jury, thanked Mr. Crawford and the police for the assistance they had rendered in the inquiry.

Mr. Crawford: The police have simply done their duty.

The Coroner: I am quite sure of that.

Eddowes' inquiry was finished. The Press rushed out the doors to get the lurid details to print. The jury then hit her daughter, Annie Phillips, with their bill. The poor woman was strapped again because of her scrounger mother.

One does not appreciate Baxter so much as when around Langham, and Langham so much as when around the verbose Baxter. Perhaps Baxter's style of inquest would have elucidated much more for us today, especially about "Juwes." He certainly would have roasted the police for inconsistent spelling.

In any case, the most gruesome inquest was over. But Langham had been wrong, at least publicly. Eddowes' face had not been entirely mutilated so as to render her not identifiable. Her eyes had been carefully nicked, each nick creating on the cheek underneath "a cut which peeled up the skin, forming a triangular flap about an inch and a half." This was something new. This was writing in the language of horror.

There was a frightful lull as London awaited Baxter's inquest to resume. Would some new information be found? Would only he be bold enough to broach it to the public? No one knew. But London waited.

Over the period of these grisly inquests London continued to recede into terror. Things that rightly belong in moody haunts played on in the background. Fog swirled with the ebb and flow of people walking along the streets. It frequently parted for a perspective shop patron to reveal not the goods they sought but a handbill in the window for Jack the Ripper.

Each weekend night before the bobbies went on patrol they stood military style and listened to the commander read the latest letter purported to be from the Ripper. They marched off on their beats, truncheons at the ready. It was quite obvious by now that weekends is when Jack the Ripper struck.

Every day there was some despairing news or rumor coming from within Whitechapel. Some were even humorous. For instance, on October 9 a group of men were walking along near Phoenix Place. A woman was following close with them. A cab washer, William Jarvis, didn't seem to care for the woman, apparently thinking her in hopes of plying her trade with these gentlemen. He took her by the arm and growled: "What are you messing about here for?" The woman immediately ripped off her wig. It was Detective Sergeant John Robinson of Scotland Yard!

The men to whom Robinson had been close turned out to be Detective Sgt. Mather and a civilian Henry Doncaster, there to help give "her" cover.

Jarvis was enraged. "Oh, you are cats and frogs, are you?" he denounced.

He struck Robinson, then pulled a knife and stabbed him in the face. Robinson clobbered him with his truncheon. Another cab washer, a scurvy knave named James Phillips, joined in. He stabbed Doncaster and kicked Robinson.

Paddy wagon bells jingled frantically as the four were sped, bandaged and bruised, to stand before the Thames Magistrate.

Jack Pizer was also beaten by a woman in these days. While walking along the street she called him "Old Leather Apron" and went at his pate. He was advised he could seek a warrant against her.

Another letter had come into Central News and was forwarded to Scotland Yard. It was written in red ink and now, amidst its misspellings, threatened to go after the nobility. These letters were becoming a nuisance, and they were getting a little suspicious. They were coming into the Central News the most, and some were clearly from cranks. But although an average "High Rip" gang theory had been long discarded, the idea of a "West End Ripper" wasn't something this crank letter writer pulled out of the blue. Whitehall was in the West End, and the inquest into the Whitehall Torso Mystery was still ongoing. People were shocked by the testimony, all of which indicated that the killer must have had some unusual night vision in order to have found the vault, navigated his way down there and then left the parcel. Was this also Jack the Ripper?

The *East London Advertiser* laid it on thick. As fogs swirled outside windows, people read under the dim light of their gas lanterns:

> The two fresh murders which have been committed in Whitechapel have aroused the indignation and excited the imagination of London to a degree without parallel. Men feel that they are face to face with some awful and extraordinary freak of nature. So inexplicable and ghastly are the circumstances surrounding the crimes that people are affected by them in the same way as children are by the recital of a weird and terrible story of the supernatural. It is so impossible to account, on any ordinary hypothesis, for these revolting acts of blood that the mind turns as it were instinctively to some theory of occult force, and the myths of the Dark Ages rise before the imagination. Ghouls, vampires, bloodsuckers, and all the ghastly array of fables which have been accumulated throughout the course of centuries take form, and seize hold of the excited fancy. Yet the most morbid imagination can conceive nothing worse than this terrible reality; for what can be more appalling than the thought that there is a being in human shape stealthily moving about a great city, burning with the thirst for human blood, and endowed with such diabolical astuteness, as to enable him to gratify his fiendish lust with absolute impunity?

As in many other papers, the *Advertiser* was looking upon Wynne Baxter's theory as false, or perhaps only partly true. No one could believe that for only 20 quid anybody would take the risk a second time to try and get a uterus for the "American doctor." In another column, the *Advertiser* even called the theory "absurd."

What Stride's death lacked in sensational gruesomeness it

made up for in speculation. The *Advertiser* pondered whether or not the experience of her sister was not proof of the supernatural. She had said: "About twenty minutes past one on Sunday morning I felt a pressure on my breast and heard three distinct kisses." The *Advertiser*'s interest was not merely idle academic wonder. If her vision was true, the *Advertiser* wondered if it told us how Stride was killed. The paper believed these were the "Judas-like" kisses with which the killer entrapped her and then the pressure on her chest was when he knelt on it to cut her throat. "But it could easily be ascertained whether she spoke of her presentiment to any of her neighbours prior to the news of the murder having reached her. If it could be satisfactorily proved that she did a very interesting case would be ready for the investigation of the Psychical Research Society."

A London medium, Robert James Lees, even visited Dutfield's Yard to try and pick up an image of the assailant. He went to the police (probably Leman Street Station) and offered his services in tracking down the marauder. (According to his diary this was the Berner Street killing, so it seems likely he went to the Met). He was promptly called a "fool" and a "lunatic." He tried his hand with the City Police the next day. Here he was called "fool" and "madman." He was so sure of his vibes that he went to Scotland Yard itself. "Same result," he wrote in his diary, "but promised to write to me."

The famous Dr. Savage wrote in the *Fortnightly Review* to anticipate the next generation of murderers when you see children kicking cats and dogs to death or setting them on fire. The article was entitled "Homicidal Mania." It might begin with something as mildly fiendish as plucking the wings off a fly.

One of the most hard to describe displays happened on the 8th when thousands lined the streets, crowded open windows, and stood atop the buildings to watch the black hearse with Catherine Eddowes' coffin trot somberly to the cemetery. It was followed by a mourning coach with her 4 sisters in it. Another coach followed with newsmen, no doubt quite cynical at the display. The coffin was beautifully polished elm with oak moldings. The plate bore in letters of gold: "Catherine Eddowes died September 30, 1888, age 43." A beautiful wreath was upon it, visible to all as they walked along. It became so congested that the hearse could barely make headway. At her graveside her four sisters and two nieces, plus John Kelly, wept and placed flowers.

Fame paid for this funeral. The mortician coughed it up, and the investment no doubt paid off from the publicity. This poor temper-ridden drab was given a royal sendoff.

Amidst all this, where was the author, Jack the Ripper? The shouting of his name caused any man accused to be surrounded by a crowd and taken to the police station. Any man being taken to a police station was surrounded by a crowd who condemned him as Jack the Ripper. But the police had yet to offer up the real culprit.

In fact, they had no clues whatsoever. Even the newshawks finally accepted there was no trail from the scenes of the crimes, and therefore the police weren't being derelict. But Sir Charles Warren made the promise that next time a murder happened— if it did— Scotland Yard would use bloodhounds.

If.

London still waited and braced itself on the weekends. So far, by mid-October nothing else had happened.

10

꬗ROM ꬓELL

HITHERTO THE DATE of October 16 the name of George Lusk had been in the paper only a couple of times. He had offered up 5 pounds to the reward and he had also been named Chairman of the Vigilance Committee. His name had also been affixed to the letter asking the aloof Home Secretary Matthews to offer a reward. But most significantly his name was mentioned on the handbill posted in hundreds of shop windows throughout the East End, in which the reward by said Committee was offered to all takers. By effect he became a celebrity name of Whitechapel, City of London, and Spitalfields, and was referred to in the Press accounts as a prominent businessman of those parts.

But at 8 o'clock that night Lusk became directly involved in the evidence. A small parcel arrived at his house on Alderly Road with the evening post. It was but 3 inches square, wrapped in brown paper. He opened it and was greeted by a gross dark burgundy colored internal organ. There was only half of it there. It appeared to be from the entrails of some animal. There was, however, a note that accompanied it. It was written in red ink and not very elegantly. He read the accompanying letter and was squarely amazed:

From hell:

Mr Lusk

Sor,

I send you half the Kidne I took from one woman and prasarved it for you tother piece I fried and ate it was very nise. I may send you the bloody knif that took it out if you only wate a whil longer

Catch me when
you can
Mishter Lusk

It must be some ghastly prank, he thought. He quickly checked the postmark, but there was nothing to help trace it. Only the letters "ond" on the postmark were clear, meaning it was mailed in London.

He quickly turned it over to the police. They actually did an impressive job of interpreting just that blurred postmark. When packages travel between districts in the city they bear the mark of each district. That was not the case here. The ink may have been smeared on the parcel, but there was only one stamp. This meant it was mailed from the East End or Central East End. The parcel was too large to fit into the usual mail receptacles. This meant it was mailed at one of two places where the receptacles are much larger: Gracechurch Street or Lombard Street. It was not sent parcel post, because there would have been a separate stamp. There was a two penny stamp and a clerk would have to affix this. Obviously, the sender didn't want to run the risk of any clerk seeing him.

The kidney went to Dr. Thomas Openshaw of the Pathological Museum of the London Hospital and then it was turned over to Gordon Brown. Brown noticed something right away. He told the *Daily Telegraph* on the 20th— "only a small portion of the renal artery adheres to the kidney, while in the case of the Mitre Square victim a large portion of this artery adhered to the body."

In a roundabout way, Openshaw also gave more support to the idea the kidney could be from Eddowes. The papers reported: "It may be mentioned that Dr. Openshaw confirms the statement that in his view the article enclosed in the parcel addressed to Mr. Lusk is a portion of a human organ, and not of any animal, as has been suggested by those who regard the whole affair as a hoax."

The initial news announcement of the ghoulish parcel had come on the 19th, and it amounted to no more than a filler. This, however, was enough to excite the interest of Emily Marsh. On Monday the 15th a tall, slim man, about 45 years old, came into her father's leather shop at 218 Jubilee Street. He had a sallow, pale complexion behind a dark beard and mustache. He was dressed in dark clothes, which she described as clerical. The overcoat was long and single-breasted. The collar was turned up. The hat was of soft felt and pulled down over his eyes. In their window they had a reward sign prominently placed in which, of course, Lusk was named as the Chairman of the Vigilance Committee. He asked for Lusk's address and spoke with what she thought was an Irish accent. She told him to ask Joseph Aarons, the Treasurer of the Committee, whose establishment was only 30 yards away. But, for some unknown reason, he shook it off. She retrieved the newspaper and told him to get it from the article, since Lusk's address had been placed therein with his letter to Matthews.

The eerie man shook his head. "Read it out," he said.

As she did, he wrote it down in his pocket book, still keeping his head down. Emily Marsh was quite unnerved by his manner and had called the shop boy, John Cormack, to stand by. After the strange man left, she watched him pass Aarons' shop without even bothering to stop.

Naturally, she quickly dismissed it until the evening edition of the newspapers Friday night. Then it came back to nag at her. She immediately told the police.

What is interesting about Emily Marsh's statement is that ostensibly she did not know the exact spelling of the "from hell" letter that had come with the kidney. The news blurbs on the 19th had cleaned up some of the Irish accent, replacing "Sor" with "Sir." (The Irish accent often replaces the "ur" sound in English with "or." Examples include Chorch'l for

Churchill.) The letter addressed to Lusk was spelled phoneti-cally. It began "Sor," not Sir. Preserved was "prasarved."

Emily Marsh uncovered another coincidence between the stranger in the shop and the parcel. She was unable to give the strange man a street number because it had not been in the paper. She learned the address on the box did not have a street number. This seemed a relevant coincidence that indicated the strange man in the shop had a hand in the kidney parcel.

Street numbers or no, Ripper related hoaxes had been coming to Lusk's home, probably inspired from the same newspaper article with his incomplete address. He had received a postcard a day or so before the parcel and it too had no number on it (at least according to the Press). This postcard was another one of those "Boss" messages. These were becoming not only a nuisance but a bloody joke. British hoaxers didn't know that boss was not a casual address employed by Americans; it wasn't used in place of the common English address of Gov'. In the letters to the Central News it meant the actual editor-in-chief. Boss was being used indiscriminately in the crank letters, as in the postcard to Lusk. "Say Boss," the postcard read, "You seem rare frightened. Guess I'd like to give you fits, but can't stop time enough to let you box of toys play copper games with me, but hope to see you when I don't hurry too much. — Goodbye, Boss."

There was little reason for Lusk to worry about the "Boss postcard." It reeks of crankery — cockney phrases and American "Boss." But after Openshaw confirmed the kidney was human, there was reason to worry about the eerie Irishman and the parcel. It all comes down to the kidney. If it was human and from Eddowes, this man was an associate of the Ripper's, and Lusk was targeted for specific terrorizing.

Investigations only clouded the issue. Openshaw supposedly said the kidney belonged to a woman of about 45 years and that it was "ginny" — in other words, belonging to someone given to drinking. He also said it had been taken from the body in the last 3 weeks. The next day Openshaw said these earlier statements were erroneous. He stated plainly now that it was the anterior of the left human kidney, divided longitudinally, and it had been preserved in spirits for about 10 days.

Sedgwick Saunders, the City pathologist, was asked by an *Echo* reporter about only the first erroneous report attributed to Openshaw. "It is a pity some people have not the courage to say they don't know," Saunders replied. "You may take it there is no difference whatever between the male and female kidney. As for those in animals, they are similar. The cortical substance is the same, and the structure differs in shape. I think it would be quite possible to mistake it for a pig's. You may take it that the right kidney of the woman Eddowes was perfectly normal in its structure and healthy, and, by parity of reasoning, you would not get much disease in the left. The liver was healthy, and gave no indications that the woman drank. Taking the discovery of the half of the kidney, and supposing it to be human, my opinion is that it was a student's hoax. It is quite possible for any student to obtain a kidney for the purpose."

In the long run it becomes hard to figure out the facts here. Saunders said that Eddowes' right kidney was perfectly healthy. Openshaw said the Lusk Kidney was "ginny," suggesting disease. However, by Openshaw's own admittance that statement was erroneous. If Openshaw's retraction was correct, then the Lusk Kidney must have been a healthy kidney and not "ginny." Saunders' comments thus do not dispel the possibility the Lusk Kidney could have come from Eddowes.

This obviously becomes very confusing. Lusk preferred to agree with Saunders that it was a student's hoax.

The Press wrote-off the whole incident and went on with more exploits associated with Jack the Ripper, both solid and not so solid. The frivolous included the drunken confession of a man named Benjamin Graham, who said "I did kill the woman in Whitechapel and I shall have to suffer for it with a bit of rope." He was released as drunk and possibly insane. A comical sight was instigated by one man writing on a wall "I am Jack the Ripper." When police saw him, he took off running and they chased like the hounds after the fox.

Robert Anderson had long returned from his continental sabbatical. There had been so many complaints that he was in Switzerland at the time of the "Double Event" that he had to return. He was soon in Paris, in touch with Scotland Yard through cablegram and being briefed about what was happening. Now firmly at the helm vacated by Monro, he quickly set the Yard to organize a detailed search of the most suspected areas where the Ripper might live. By the 20th, the mission had been completed. "The force of police in private clothes," reported the newspapers, "specially selected to make the house-to-house search in the neighbourhoods of Hanbury Street, Commercial Street, Dorset Street, Goulston Street, Buck's Row, Brick Lane, Osborn Street, &c., completed their labours yesterday. They have distributed many thousands of handbills, leaving them in every room in the lodging-houses. The greatest good feeling prevails towards the police, and noticeably in the most squalid dwellings the police had no difficulty in getting information; but not the slightest clue to the murderer has been obtained."

On the surface, the Ripper's weekend pattern favored the idea of someone coming on the cattle boats. He was speculated to be some wild Malay or crazed Portuguese. But the detailed chain of events indicated someone extremely familiar with Whitechapel. Anderson and C.I.D. were on the right track when they started rousting about their own jurisdictions. The graffito and bloody apron were indeed valuable clues. It meant the Ripper had places to hide in the neighborhood.

The dates also revealed that the Ripper struck at no moon or low moon, when the streets were at their darkest save for the meager bubbles of light from the street lamps. Altogether this was suggestive of someone very clever, premeditative, and knowledgeable of his terrain. Except in Chapman's case, he also struck between rain showers, which would naturally help cover any trail he might leave from the scene of the gruesome crime. Such attributes make him rather more sinister to consider. And there is still much room to wonder who he really was. Was he low class or middle-class, medical man, mortician, butcher, baker, candlestick maker? He was by the end of October quite an amorphous villain.

But one thing is certain. The pattern of his diabolical exploits made him a type of character at an opposite to all those childish "Dear Boss" letters. It is fortunate that by this time they were beginning to be disbelieved at the Yard, including the very first one that had come into the Central News in which the moniker Jack the Ripper had been coined. In fact, suspicion had fallen on two journalists. One was Tom Bulling, of the Central News Agency itself, and the other appeared to be Fred Best, Harry Dam's apparent "idiot" who covered the East End.

Suspicion is a bit more shadowy when it comes to Fred Best, but one of the Met detectives, John Littlechild, was already surprised at how far Bulling was admitted up the chain of information. No doubt turning in those letters to Scotland Yard had made Central News and Bulling *person grata*. But Bulling's high profile in the Met was a two edged sword. It made it rather easy to finger him when the suspicion began.

It is not hard to figure out what led Scotland Yard his way. In the second "Boss" communique (that October 1 postcard talking about the "double event") there was a revealing mistake. The "Ripper" had written that the first victim— i.e. Stride— had squealed a bit. This was not the case, as the inquest would prove. Israel Schwartz alone spoke about a "to do" not long before Stride was found dead, in which she had screamed mildly three times. Only a journalist who had access to police information as soon as it came in to the Leman Street Station, where Fred Best camped out, would have made this mistake. For the postcard to have popped up on October 1 with this revealing error, the person would have had to post it September 30 or even with the morning mail October 1 (if it arrived in the evening post). Bulling and Best were the only ones around who could have heard about and capitalized on the dubious Israel Schwartz statement as soon as it was taken down but not yet evaluated. Best's shadowy part, if he had one, may have been that he was writing the letters and Bulling was his accomplice who quickly presented them to Scotland Yard as soon as they came into Central News. (Graphologist Elaine Quigley later identified Best as the author of the "Dear Boss" letters from samples of his handwriting).

Best's culpability in some scandal was alluded to by one of the *Star*'s major shareholders. Two years later, John Brunner would write a confidential letter to the Editor-in-Chief. Brunner complained that Frederick Best should have been discharged years ago for his actions then which had almost gotten the paper close to potential litigation. In one reference, Brunner mentioned that Best's "attempt to mislead Central News during the Whitechapel Murders should have led to an earlier termination of his association with the newspaper." This may have applied to Dam's creation of "Leather Apron," but the fact Central News is mentioned could also indicate that Best started the Ripper letters to keep publicity going after Leather Apron petered out. Bulling may have been a dupe or a willing accomplice. He was certainly a quick "in" to relate any letter to the Met. . .And it is certain that the "Dear Boss" postcard on October 1 made its way to the Met awfully quick from the burgeoning mailbags at the Central News.

The actual killer drew attention to his acts only by a pattern of sophisticated timing and daring, not by cockney bragging. He was, in short, a manifold mystery. Despite the hoaxed Lusk letter, Scotland Yard only knew he was from hell— H Division, Whitechapel.

October 23 finally came. . .and went with a fizzle. The Press gathered to hear anything that might have been uncovered in the two weeks since Baxter brought down the gavel (symbolically). But there was very little. Inspector Reid confirmed very briefly that he proved that Elizabeth Stride's husband had died on 24 October 1884. Constable Walter Stride confirmed that John Stride was his uncle and by photographs he confirmed that Liz Stride was his aunt by marriage. This was basically it.

But Baxter had been busy in that fortnight of suspense. He had prepared a massive closing speech and, unlike with Langham's impromptu final declarations, the Press quoted Baxter almost exact. He gave them what they wanted, and he gave London the most chilling scenario possible. Only a part of the long summation follows:

In this case, as in other similar cases which had occurred in this neighbourhood, no call for assistance was noticed. Although there might have been some noise in the club, it seemed very unlikely that any cry could have been raised without its being heard by some one of those near. The editor of a Socialist paper was quietly at work in a shed down the yard, which was used as a printing office. There were several families in the cottages in the court only a few yards distant, and there were 20 persons in the different rooms of the club.

But if there was no cry, how did the deceased meet with her death? The appearance of the injury to her throat was not in itself inconsistent with that of a self-inflicted wound. Both Dr. Phillips and Dr. Blackwell have seen self-inflicted wounds more extensive and severe, but those have not usually involved the carotid artery. Had some sharp instrument been found near the right hand of the deceased this case might have had very much the appearance of a determined suicide. But no such instrument was found, and its absence made suicide an impossibility. The death was, therefore, one by homicide, and it seemed impossible to imagine circumstances which would fit in with the known facts of the case, and which would reduce the crime to manslaughter.

There were no signs of any struggle; the clothes were neither torn nor disturbed. It was true that there were marks over both shoulders, produced by pressure of two hands, but the position of the body suggested either that she was willingly placed or placed herself where she was found. Only the soles of her boots were visible. She was still holding in her left hand a packet of cachous, and there was a bunch of flowers still pinned to her dress front. If she had been forcibly placed on the ground, as Dr. Phillips opines, it is difficult to understand how she failed to attract attention, as it was clear from the appearance of the blood on the ground that the throat was not cut until after she was actually on her back. There were no marks of gagging, no bruises on the face, and no trace of any anaesthetic or narcotic in the stomach; while the presence of the cachous in her hand showed that she did not make use of it in self-defense. Possibly the pressure marks may have had a less tragical origin, as Dr. Blackwell says it was difficult to say how recently they were produced.

There was one particularity which was not easy to explain. When seen by Dr. Blackwell her right hand was lying on the chest, smeared inside and out with blood. Dr. Phillips was unable to make any suggestion how the hand became soiled. There was no injury to the hand, such as they would expect if it had been raised in self-defense while her throat was being cut. Was it done intentionally by her assassin, or accidentally by those who were early on the spot? The evidence affords no clue.[4]

Unfortunately the murderer had disappeared without leaving the slightest trace. Even the cachous were wrapped up in unmarked paper, so that there was nothing to show where they were bought. The cut in the throat might have been effected in such a manner that bloodstains on the hands and clothes of the operator were avoided, while the domestic history of the deed suggested the strong probability that her destroyer was a stranger to her. There was no one among her associates to whom any suspicion had attached. They had not heard that she had had a quarrel with any one— unless they magnified the fact that she had recently left the man with whom she generally cohabited; but this diversion was of so frequent an occurrence that neither a breach of the peace ensued, nor, so far as they knew, even hard words.

There was therefore in the evidence no clue to the murderer and no suggested motive for the murder. The deceased was not in possession of any valuables. She was only known to have had a few pence in her pocket at the beginning of the evening. Those who knew her best were unaware of any one likely to injure her. She never accused any one of having threatened her. She never expressed any fear of anyone, and, although she had outbursts of drunkenness, she was generally a quiet woman. The ordinary motives of murder— revenge, jealousy, theft, and passion— appear, therefore, to be absent from this case; while it was clear from the accounts of all who saw her that night, as well as from the postmortem examination, that she was not otherwise than sober at the time of her death.

In the absence of motive, the age and class of woman selected as victim, and the place and time of the crime, there was a similarity between this case and those mysteries which had recently occurred in that neighbourhood. There had been no skillful mutilation as in the cases of Nichols and Chapman, and no unskillful injuries as in the case in Mitre Square— possibly the work of an imitator; but there had been the same skill exhibited in the way in which the victim had been entrapped, and the injuries inflicted, so as to cause instant death and prevent blood from soiling the operator, and the

---

[4] Baxter is incorrect. There were only oblong clots of blood on the back of her hand.

same daring defiance of immediate detection, which, unfortunately for the peace of the inhabitants and trade of the neighbourhood, had hitherto been only too successful.

To some extent Baxter's conclusion shows the weakness of his own investigative abilities. His long, drawn-out inquests were as much a part of grandstanding as they were about chronicling. They are indispensable to the historian and investigator, but the amount of time he dragged them out only staggered and buried the more relevant bits of evidence amidst the convolution that was created.

This is seen most critically in that he expresses his suspicion of James Brown's observations of the couple seen at the corner of Berner Street at 12:45 a.m., but doesn't follow through to connect it with a very significant fact — the blood flow in Dutfield's Yard. Had he done so, he would have revealed the last sequence of events in Stride's life, dispelled the myth that Louis Diemshutz interrupted the killer, and with this he would also have identified the killer.

When Baxter asked how long Stride had been dead, Blackwell responded: "From twenty minutes to half an hour when I arrived. The clothes were not wet with rain. She would have bled to death comparatively slowly on account of vessels on one side only of the neck being cut and the artery not completely severed."

This places her death around 12:45-50 a.m. ten or fifteen minutes *before* Diemshutz arrived at the yard. If she bled to death comparatively slowly, she must have been attacked even earlier. Diemshutz then could not have interrupted the killer. This is corroborated by the amount of blood flow. When he came out the backdoor it was already flowing near the drain there by (18 feet from her). It takes blood quite a while to trickle that far (about 12 to 15 minutes, if it even makes it that far). Phillips, too, puzzled over the extent of the blood flow. Either the murderer was not the Ripper and no mutilations were intended or the Ripper had been interrupted earlier by something or *somebody* else than Diemshutz.

With this, it sounds very much as if the couple that James Brown saw at 12:45 a.m. was the innocent couple Mrs. Mortimer reported she saw at the street corner and even later talked to. If so, and this seems likely, the last man seen with Stride was at 12:35 a.m. Constable Smith reported he wore a deerstalker hat, that gauche bit of misplaced headgear in an urban environment; need it be added, the same type of hat Elizabeth Long saw on the man talking with Chapman just before she must have been gutted.

This now gives us a working chronology. They were just across the street from the Club. They could have crossed, faded into the shadows, and there he killed her.

This would actually make Morris Eagle the man who interrupted the killer. At 1:40 a.m., but minutes after Stride was seen with the man in the deerstalker, he passes through the gateway. He testified it was so dark he could not even say the body was there. At this time there would have been no blood flow back to the door, so he would not have walked through blood at all. By the time Diemshutz arrives 10 or 15 minutes later, she is dead and the blood is near the backdoor.

This was not an impromptu squabble. The darkness of the gateway, for one, tells us that the killer had true eyes in the night, like the Ripper. Not only was Stride's throat cut cleanly (though not finished), her neck had been placed over the rut in order to bleed her. This indeed took keen eyesight and tells us the killer's intent all the time was to cut her throat in a clean way so the blood would neatly flow to the gutter. The lack of blood spurting is another telltale signature of the Ripper, and it was accomplished in complete darkness. William West made it clear in testimony that couples did not use the gateway. The last couple he had seen there was about a year before. This was not a spot that prostitutes or their suitors would have known. All this indicates the killer alone was familiar with the gateway.

Stride *had* to go down here. This was the one area where the Ripper could perform mutilations. And this explains the bruises on her shoulders. Rather than the result of a fight, they appear to be two karate-like chops to the shoulders. This knocks her unconscious and she collapses onto her right side— thus explaining traces of mud on her right side. The Ripper picks her up and places her on her left, with her neck neatly over the rut in order to kill and bleed her. This explains why her left side was plastered in mud. The Ripper could not ask her to lie down here. It was too wet and muddy. This necessitated knocking her out.

Stride was not killed with a deep, ripping slice, as the others. But her face had also not been held as tightly as the others. There were no bruises on her jaw. This was a stark difference to the others.

Although Baxter wanted to believe that Eddowes' murderer was a bungling imitator, too many similarities exist to connect both murders to Jack the Ripper. In fact, the most disturbing but sublime link exists between them both. Stride was carefully murdered in the shadow of a Jewish establishment. After Eddowes' death there was an open attempt to embroil the Jews. We should regard the existence of the graffito as something very disturbing beyond even the writer's obvious motivation to implicate an entire ethnicity. It indicates a whole new ulterior motive. There was no hint of anti-Semitism in the previous murders: Tabram, Nichols and Chapman. Harry Dam's stupid creation of the "crazy Jew" Leather Apron had since then showed how the notion could upset the whole East End into riots. Now the Ripper decided to follow suit and use the murders to capitalize on anti-Semitism and to start insurrection. To assume that Stride and Eddowes were murdered by different people is also to assume that it was purely coincidental that these two different assailants decided to both dovetail on the racial tensions that came to the fore after Dam's yellow quill introduced the whole idea.

More than similarities, there is a certain progressive connection. Stride's death was executed with finesse, but Eddowes was done clumsily and in a hurry. This contrast suggests the killer was the same man; that the Ripper was interrupted in Stride's case and had to find another victim quickly. Why?

In addition to this there are those *triangular* cut marks on Eddowes' cheeks. They were not intentional. Those triangular flaps of skin were the result of the knife blade ripping into the cheeks after the intentional slice to the eyelid, the blade carrying over into the cheek. This does not indicate a sharp knife, but one that was relatively dull, at least at the point. It could have been blunted into the wall or curbstone in killing

Stride (detectives looked for the sign a knife had impacted with the wall) or the knife, as the weapon in Stride's murder, was not as sharp as it could be.

Eddowes' murder must have been far more impromptu than the others, and this is reflected in how hurriedly she is murdered, and how much sloppier the Ripper was here. Yet his signature, more than in Stride's case, is evident— those telltale bruises, lack of blood spurting, and the gutting of the body, and the clean getaway.

This existence of the bruise marks here could merely indicate that he could wait for Eddowes to lay down. He would then have to seize her mouth to keep her silent. In Stride's case, she had to be rendered unconscious in order for her to go down in a muddy wet place. Being unconscious, there was no need to grasp her mouth so tightly.

How long would the stroll into the Square from Church Street and her laying down have taken? Some time. Only if the killer knew Watkins' routine would he have realized with what speed he must perform. The fact he rips open the top of the dress— the buttons go flying hither and thither— and quickly throws up the dresses and petticoats over her chest shows he knew to rush. In his hurried carving he is quite sloppy. He basically by Braille had to find the kidney and cut it out. This argues for anatomical knowledge. The operation was clumsily done. He didn't get the entire uterus. But considering the conditions under which he worked, it doesn't mean he had no anatomical knowledge.

The fact he did not cut any clothes is another link. The Ripper never cut clothes.

The killer then had to be out of the square by 1:43/1:44 a.m. This chain of events, plus a plan of Mitre Square, should impress upon anybody that the murderer knew Watkins' beat. He knew he couldn't flee into Mitre Street. It is from that direction that Watkins would enter.

It is implicit in Baxter's summation on Stride's killing that it would be deft indeed to not only imitate style of killing but more so the style of entrapment, the still-unknown method by which the killer rendered himself so invisible both to eyes and ears during and after, and his adroitness with time. Baxter is quite right. It might be easy to copycat the Ripper's signature of using the knife, but it would be hard to imitate the rest and pull it off without a hitch. This in itself should demand that both Stride and the Mitre Square murder be regarded as Jack the Ripper's respectively coolest and bloodiest work to date.

Perhaps the reason Wynne Baxter, Thomas Arnold, and eventually even Bagster Phillips, were reticent to accept Eddowes as the Ripper's victim is the description of the man seen with her just before she must have been murdered. He is not the dark "shabby genteel" fellow with the foreign appearance. He is perhaps slightly shorter, younger, with a sandy mustache. There is nothing shabby genteel here either. He is just shabby.

It could be, of course, that the Ripper changed. The outfit worn by this "sailor" appeared loose fitting to the witnesses. Could this indicate it was a disguise? Both at the time and by those today who believe the Ripper killed both women, it was and must be postulated that he had some domicile nearby where he could hide himself and even change. If the Ripper did kill both, then it is unquestionable that this has to be the case.

In any case, the circumstances and the chronicity draw undeniable links. They reveal a cold-blooded killer, with eyes in the night, who had anatomical knowledge, and apparently *had* to butcher a woman that night. Not just kill one. He had to take an organ. I'm not a fan of occult theories, but the circumstances of the "Double Event" seem to suggest some ulterior motive than the thrill killing of drabs and the taking of an organ. It is even more disturbing when seeing the Ripper's alarming shift toward trying to capitalize on racial tensions to start insurrection. This last addition to his crime spree seems all the more to suggest someone cleverly covering his actual motive. The clumsy taking of the uterus suggests that too. It seems to be fawning to Baxter's popularized theory. The actual object appears to have been the kidney, and taking the uterus was merely a feint to draw attention away from what he really wanted. The only time, so far, that he seemed to want solely a uterus was in Chapman's case.

Anyway, October finally came to an end. There had been no more murders. Much fog and dim street lamps give us a moody, black and white haunting feel. It hung over Whitechapel. Horses clopped their carriages along pensively. Echoes approached and tapped away. Footsteps methodically came and then faded away. Life went on cautiously. Police were everywhere. Muffled jocularity hummed out from pubs. Handbills littered the area. Reward posters were on mail boxes and in store windows reading "Wanted: The Whitechapel Murderer." Where was the Ripper? Why not one clue this whole time? Yet though he never made himself known the whole frightening month, he nevertheless was omnipresent and he commanded a city in terror.

Surely, the Ripper followed all this. The addition of attempting to cause anti-Semitic upheaval shows he followed the news and took inspiration from the *Star*'s burlesque image of "Leather Apron." Yet now at the end of October it must have been obvious to him his attempt to cause race upheaval in the East End had failed. What else could be done to widen the scope and embroil all London? The *Spectator* suggested that if the Ripper wanted to show himself the boss criminal of the century he would strike next on November 9, the day of the Lord Mayor's parade, a solemn and ancient celebration in the City of London. The existence of this *Spectator* article has been called into question by later writers. Tom Cullen mentions it in his *Autumn of Terror* (1965), but other researchers have not been able to find the actual article. Whether this was literary license or not, history has shown the Ripper thought along these same lines.

11

November Echo

AFTER THE FIRST week of November the echo from the October terror began to fade. But, of course, it could not altogether segue into the routine sounds of holiday life. The Ripper could strike again, all knew, upsetting the delicate balance. That he did not in October was little surprising. The fog was thick, even blinding. Police were everywhere, stopping everyone on their way about the district. But how long could that last? By now everyone knew that Jack the Ripper was clever and daring. This had been proved time and time again; so daring, in fact, that he openly displayed a pattern of striking on weekends. Yet despite this, everyone also knew, he did not have to stick to his pattern of weekends, whores, and open street slaughtering. He could move on to the West End, on up to countesses, or just select the average honest housewife as his next target. In short, his menacing reputation hung over the city.

Yet autumn repose slowly fell over London. Michaelmas was a special time of year and festivities were on the agenda for the near future. Guy Fawkes Day was one of them, but even this time-honored celebration was tainted by the current political turmoil. The *Star* reported that on this raucous day there was a rumor that an unemployed crowd at Clerkenwell Green was going to burn an effigy of Warren in place of Fawkes. In response, the "tyrannical" jackbooted Warren was reported to have ordered troops to the area. "I'll allow no bonfire to-night," supposedly declared an inspector, "and, if you try it, we shall go for you." There was near rioting among the people and lunges to and fro between the ranks and the crowd. . . so reported the *Star* of Harry Dam anyway.

Warren had come out strong in November. Baxter was not alone is using his strategic fortnight to writing and preparing. Warren, too, had been busy with writing a long article for the November edition of *Murray's Magazine*. To put it bluntly, it was dynamite! It was entitled nothing but "The Police of the Metropolis." The first sentence was a knockout. "London has for many years past been subject to the sinister influence of a mob stirred up into spasmodic action by restless demagogues." He continued for several pages decrying the practice of certain powers within the city. "It is to be deplored that successive Governments have not had the courage to make a stand against the more noisy section of the people representing a small minority, and have given way before tumultuous proceedings which have exercised a terrorism over peaceful and law-abiding citizens, and it is still to be more regretted that ex-Ministers, while in opposition, have not hesitated to embarrass those in power by smiling on the insurgent mob."

There must not have been one member of government who did not set the article aside, fully 17 and a half pages, who did not then say 'this will get him the sack.' There is a problem with writing a general polemic in politics. Everybody in government has a guilty conscious about something. The upshot is that they will all take general accusations of misdeeds, incompetence and corruption as meaning them. Philosophy is a place for generalizations. Politics is where you get down and dirty and get specific. Warren was too general. He succeeded in offending everybody!

On the 8th of November the papers briefly alluded to the fact, more of a gloss, that Warren had taken up the pen again and said something about past Governments.

Mr. Atherley-Jones rose in Parliament this day and queried Mr. Matthews about "whether it was in accordance with the usage and discipline of the Civil Service that a salaried official should be permitted to publicly discuss matters relating to his department, and disparage the conduct of ex-Ministers of the Crown." If it was not, did Mr. Matthews decide whether to take action?

"My attention has been called to the article in question," responded Matthews. "I am assured by the Commissioner that his statements are made without reference to party, and he points out that one of the passages referred to by the honourable member applies on the face of it to successive Governments, and not to any one Government in particular. With regard to the usages of the Civil Service as to the public discussion by salaried officials of matters which touch upon politics, I cannot do better than refer the honourable member to an answer given by the First Lord of the Treasury in this House on the 15th of March of this year, where he will find the subject fully dealt with. In 1879 the then Home Secretary issued a rule by which officers attached to the Department were precluded from publishing works relating to the Department without permission, and a copy was sent to the then Commissioner of Police. The present Commissioner, however, informs me that he was not aware of the existence of this rule. I have accordingly drawn his attention to it, and have requested him to comply with it in future."

This was all very polite and formal, but behind-the-scenes Warren had had enough. He never knew such a rule applied to him. He had tendered his resignation last spring over his difficulties with Matthews, and now did so again. He knew it would be accepted. Matthews received it, and sat on it for a while, ever vacilating.

Meanwhile things went on as usual in the metropolis. Political polemic could be *sans* recital of the Ripper's cases yet again. It had been too long since a murder to harp on it effectively. Insults to Warren were the old kind. Mandalay had a habit of having its police mounted and on standby. Some suggested "that was the place for Warren." Warren wasn't joking in his article about insurgency. He issued a proclamation that there would be no processions allowed on the 9th of November except the traditional parade of the Lord Mayor. Yet some tacky blighter had come along and doctored the proclamations about the street to read "no other procession but that of the Socialists." The *Star* reported: "Printed slips with the latter word upon them had been gummed over the 'Lord

Mayor.' The police were busy yesterday restoring the originals."

Things went on as before in Whitechapel, too. But even if the mysterious Ripper was still at the height of wielding his bloody knife, Mary Jane Kelly should have had little to worry about. She wasn't a hedge drab. She was very different from the women who plied their amateur trade for thrupence a stand. She was in her prime at 25 — quite obviously the wrong age as Ripper victims go — and she was tall, though stout in proportion, and had all her teeth. She was, in fact, quite pretty. Street and curbside was not her professional parlor. She had her own room, too; not so grand but her own room. It was quite a come-down from what she had been used to, but still she was head and shoulders above the others.

In her heyday she was never seen without an equipage of a few friends. She walked around in a nice dress with a spotless clean white apron. She was a blond colleen, to hear her tell it. But there was some question whether she was Welsh or Irish. She said Irish, but when young she also said the family had moved to Wales. Her last address out of London was indeed in Cardiff, and she spoke fluent Welsh. In Whitechapel, however, you could be what you wanted to be, especially in her profession.

Her spiral down to a room off notorious Dorset Street is one hard to figure out. Upon arriving in London in 1884 she was supposedly taken under the wing by a well-to-do Frenchwoman. She was a lady's companion. . .ostensibly. She rode in carriages and went to Paris many times. Yet some said she rode in carriages not with a woman but with a gentleman. Travel to Paris was not as a lady's companion but as a man's paramour. One bloke in Whitechapel who had fallen for her charms insisted that she forsook Paris because she did not care for this rich gent.

What indeed is the truth of it? It is hard to say. One account had it that when she first arrived in London she was a member of a high-end West End bordello. Thus there may be truth — albeit tongue-in-cheek — to the French lady version of her mysterious life story.

But something happened that led her straight to the East End from the West, without any stop in between, and we may

A Penny vibe illustration showing us Mary Kelly outside the door *of her Miller's Court flat.*

guess it was one too many episodes of drink. Her precipitous drop to the Ratcliffe Highway area argues for her most assuredly having been a high-end call girl. She went straight to one of those dens on a street inappropriately named for a saint— St. George's Street. There as soon as she gathered her wherewithal, the "landlady" and her went to a woman's house in the West End and collected several expensive outfits that belonged to her.

Clean clothes, captivating, friendly manner, and beautiful looks attracted many suitors. But it appears drink got the best of her a little more frequently now, and she went from George Street to live with a Mrs. Carthy. For close to two years they got along and when she left her it was to live with a man who was ready to marry her. His name was supposedly Morganstone, possibly Anglicized for the Jewish name Morgenstern or -stein. They lived opposite the Stepney Gasworks. This apparently didn't work out. She next lived with a man near Bethnal Green named Joe Fleming. He, too, was very fond of her. She may, in fact, have been less of a prostitute than she was a courtesan of the East End, being kept by men of low degree who were nevertheless willing to spend their pittance to keep a beautiful wife-in-the-making. Joe Fleming was but a stone mason, but he was true fond of her.

By 1886 she is living at a lodging house on Thrawl Street — Spitalfields. The very name invokes the unspeakable.

Yet here she met a man named Joe Barnett. He, too, grew quickly fond of her. He is a riverside laborer, of Irish heritage. He is 28. She is 23. The relationship was quick and convenient. They had met on April 8, 1887. They had a drink, and he wanted to meet her again the next day. After they had their second drink, they decide to shack-up. They stuck together and got along. They moved a few times, all within a stone's throw of Dorset Street, the very bottom of the sink of vice. One place threw them out for being loud and drunk. From there they moved (in Spring 1888) to Dorset Street proper. The little one room flat on the ground floor sported a lucky number: #13 Miller's Court.

This is a rather grand name for the place. Miller's Court was actually nothing more than a horizontal chute in the center of where many buildings met. It is accessed by a narrow arched tunnel. There is one gaslight affixed on a wall by rusty drainpipes.

No. 13 is actually the back room of a flat off Dorset, but it was divided from the rest of the place by a wood partition built between floor and ceiling. This was economizing for

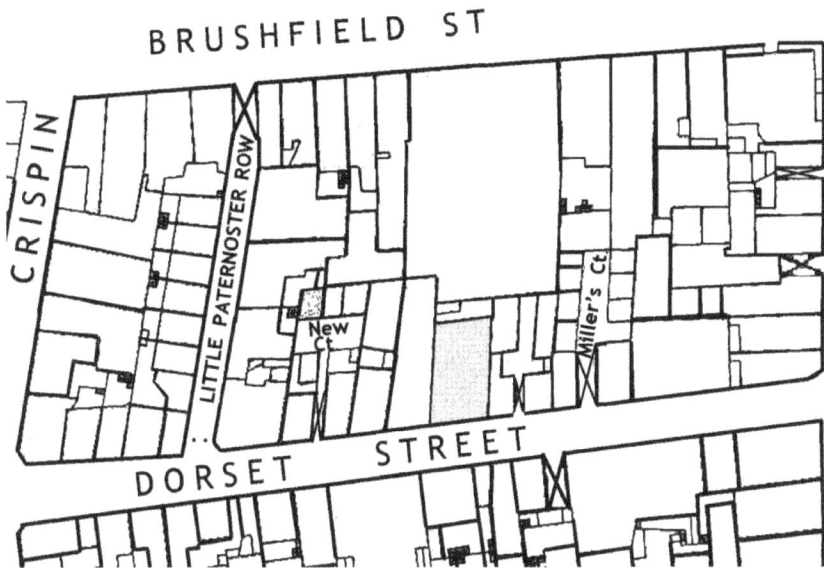

Closer view of that horrid Dorset Street, with its many dank courts, tunnels and crowded dwellings.

"McCarthy Rents," and typical economizing at that by the landlord, John McCarthy. But it wasn't a bad little 10 x 12 room as rabbit hutch's go. It had two large windows overlooking this claustrophobic court. The biggest, however, was boarded, having been long broken and too expensive to fix. The one by the door is fine. It provides the only light in the room. The door is in the narrow, claustrophobic passage to the street.

The rest of the tenants were women of a "certain class." (There were 6 two room flats that overlooked the court. McCarthy might even have been a pimp by proxy.) But it's better than where they've been. They must not lose this place. The next stop would be the dosshouses.

Yet then disaster strikes in the summer: Barnett loses his job. Apparently, Kelly goes out to ply trade to keep the room. Barnett is upset by this. Kelly was so big-hearted that she'd let a prostitute stay there to get out of the cold and rain. Joe didn't like that. However, then she allows one to move in, a Mrs. Maria Harvey. That does it for Joe Barnett. He leaves on October 30, 1888.

Yet just as so many of her past suitors, Barnett still cares for her. On November 6 he pays her a visit. It is the last night that Harvey intended to stay there. Maria decides to leave them alone. "Well, Mary Jane, I shall not see you this evening again," she said after dropping some clothes by. The entire place was hers again. . .and the rent— some 29 shillings in arrears to that shylock McCarthy. Barnett still wanted to help out where he could. But with such little money there wasn't much he could give her against the rent.

Perhaps with this cozy room she thinks she can bring in a better sort of clientele. She appears to be doing this. On November 7, she is in McCarthy's shop. She has enough money to buy a ha-penny candle. Thomas Bowyer— "Indian Harry"— then sees her talking to a chap in the courtyard later that day. He couldn't help but notice the man. He was a gent, sort of. He was dressed in a long black coat, but his collar was quite white and hung over his dark coat. His cuffs were also very white and clean. He had "peculiar eyes."

Barnett visits his ex-love, Mary Jane. On the night of November 8 he sees her between 7:45 and 8 p.m. He doesn't stay long. He confesses he's keeping company with another

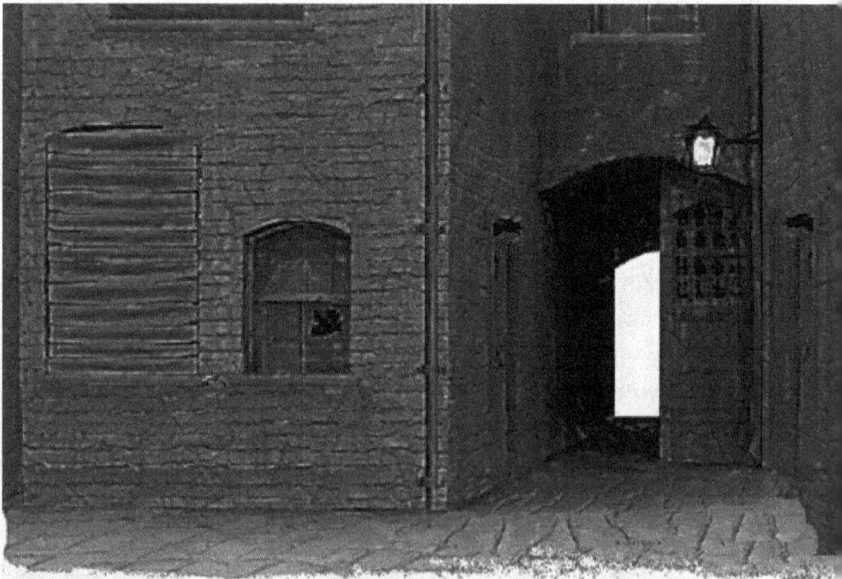

Miller's Court, a narrow, chute-like dank court. The only light was right across from the door to No. 13.

woman who lives there in Miller's Court. Barnett leaves at 8 p.m and goes to Buller's Boarding House where he plays cards until 12:30 a.m. Friday November 9.

Kelly must have suspected that Lizzie Albrook is the "other woman." There is little if any secret in Miller's Court. She sees her that evening and advises her: "Whatever you do don't you do wrong and turn out as I did."

Albrook is struck by Kelly's sincerity.

But Kelly maintains her aplomb in these dark days. Her dress is a bit shabby, but her velvet jacket is nice and her shawl is a maroon pelerine cross over. Yet from seeing all the drabs on the street she must have realized how dreadful her future was if she got evicted. She was no doubt terrified that she would soon be like those toothless dirty vagabonds winking at pawing wharf rats just to pay their doss. She wanted to go back to Ireland.

The next time at which Kelly is definitely identified is 11:45 p.m. She is entering Miller's Court with a stout man with a carroty mustache and dark bowler. He is about 35, shabbily dressed, blotchy face and fuzzy whiskers. Both are pretty tight. The man is carrying a pale of beer.

The witness who saw them is Mary Ann Cox, a widow who had to make her living "on the street" as well. She notices how drunk the man is. When she passes them at their doorway, she says:

"Goodnight."

Kelly was no doubt at her ritual of opening the door. Barnett and she had lost the key a while back. Fortunately, in some row, Kelly had thrown something and broke one of the panes in the window. This allowed them to push the coat aside (that they stuffed in the hole) and pull back the spring bolt.

Kelly turns and says "Goodnight" back to Mrs. Cox. "I am going to have a song."

It was a fair warning she was going to sing. It was then that Mrs. Cox realized how drunk Kelly was too.

The door opens. They went inside and the blotchy face man closes the door behind them.

Once inside, in the little flickers created by the ha-penny candle, Kelly sings to her guest "A violet from mother's grave."

At 12:30 a.m. Kelly is still singing. It bothers a neighbor on Dorset Street, Catherine Pickett. She is ready to stomp downstairs and tell her to muffle it, but her husband, as all husbands, seems to have pity for her. "You leave that poor woman alone," he grumbles.

At 1 a.m. Mrs. Cox, who had left to go ply trade for a while, returns yet again to Miller's Court. It is raining. It splashes from the roof, gurgles down the pipes, and splatters onto the dismal whitewashed court. Light beams reach through the slits in the boarded window and the curtains glow with the flickering light of the candle. Kelly is still singing.

Around this time Elizabeth Prater is standing at the entrance to Miller's Court. She lives in the flat right above Kelly. She is waiting for a bloke, but sees no one. At 20 minutes past the hour she goes and visits the landlady, Mrs. McCarthy. After washing her craw with a few shots, she goes to her flat. She places tables before the door as a security precaution. And she is off to a heavy gin-induced sleep.

Kelly must have entertained the bearer of beer long enough and sent him on his way. Around 2 a.m. she is back out. At Flower and Dean Street, George Hutchinson, an acquaintance, bumps into her.

"Mr. Hutchinson, can you lend me sixpence?" she asks him.

"I can't," apologizes Hutchinson. "I spent all my money going down to Romford."

She accepts stoically. "Good morning," she says. "I must go and find some money."

She walks on to Thrawl Street and Commercial Road, the direction from which Hutchinson had come. He had passed a man a bit ago and paid him no never mind. That man now advances to her, and puts his hand on her shoulder. He says something to Kelly. Whatever it is, she laughs. She then says:

"All right."

"You will be all right for what I have told you," he replied.

They walk away together toward Hutchinson. The man keeps his head down. He's a queer bird now that Hutchinson

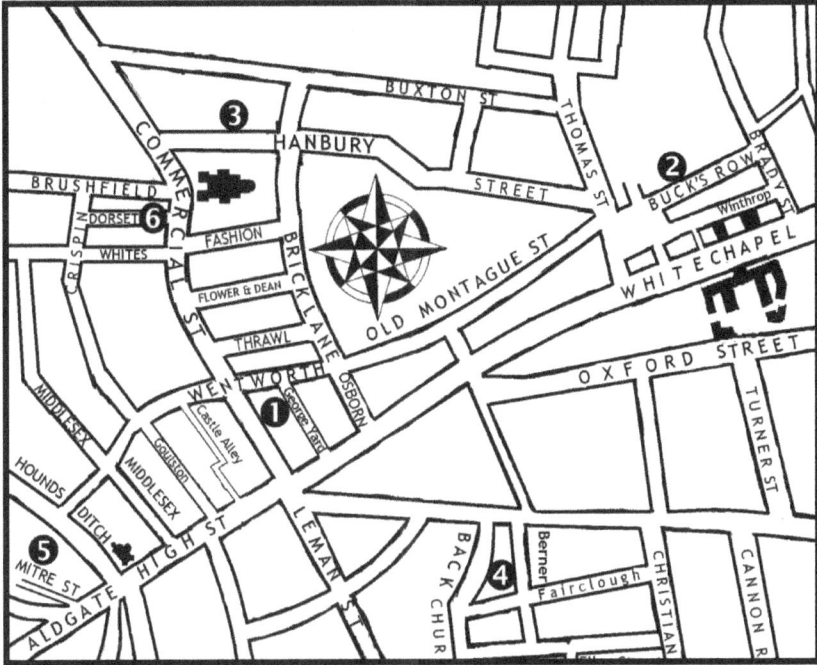

Dorset Street (6), in context to the other locations.

has a look at him. He's pale, with a small mustache turned up at the corners. His hair is dark, his eyebrows bushy. He's overdressed, rather gaudily. His long dark coat is trimmed in astrakhan. His shirt has a white collar. His necktie is black, too, stuck fancily into place with a horseshoe pin. He has dark spats over much lighter button shoes. He wears a soft felt hat, pulled down over his eyes. His coat is open. A large gold chain is in his waistcoat. It has a large fob with a red stone hanging from it. He holds his gloves in his right hand. There is a small parcel in his left. He is in his mid-30s, about 5' 6" or 5' 7" tall. To Hutchinson he looked like a Jew.

Hutchinson had incredibly good recall because he squatted a bit as they passed so he could get a better look at him. The man scowled at him for snooping.

The couple walk on, cross Commercial Street and head down Dorset. Hutchinson follows at a safe distance. They stop at the narrow tunnel to Miller's Court. Interestingly, they speak for a few minutes. Hutchison picks up more from the shadows.

"All right, my dear," says Kelly. "Come along. You will be comfortable."

They step toward the tunnel. "I've lost my handkerchief," she says.

The strange man hands her a red one. He then puts an arm around her. She kisses him and they disappear into the tunnel and into Miller's Court.

Hutchinson is curious enough to brave what looks like a heavy rainfall coming. He waits outside the entrance to the court and watches the door through the dark entrance. But by 3 a.m. it is long enough. As the chime from the local clock strikes, he leaves the entrance to Miller's Court.

This is confirmed by Sarah Lewis. At 2:30 a.m. she is visiting Mrs. Keyler at Miller's Court. She notices a man standing at the court entrance wearing a wideawake hat (Hutchinson). She didn't know who he was, but he looked like he was waiting for someone or watching something.

Further up the street she sees there is a love couple. The woman is drunk. Sarah Lewis continued into the court. Her footsteps echoed along, seguing with the heavy sound of

The narrow passage to the court.

the rain and the hurried tapping of water runoff in the down-pipes. Nobody was in the small court. She visits her friend and falls asleep there.

At 3 a.m. the roving Mrs. Cox is yet again passing through Miller's Court to her flat. There is no singing from and no light on in Kelly's flat. By this time Hutchinson is gone from the entrance.

"Diddles"— Elizabeth Prater's cat— lives up to its name at 4 a.m. and is diddling around on her neck. She jolts awake. "Oh, Murder!" she hears. It sounds like it comes from the court and not from below her in Kelly's room. But she was turning over at the time and we can assume the origin of the sound could have been obscured. Such a cry is too common in the neighborhood for anyone to give much notice to it. She goes back to sleep.

Sarah Lewis also heard it. She had awaken at half past 3 and could not go back to sleep. It sounded as though it was right out her door. She thought nothing of it since it was only one loud scream.

Mrs. Cox didn't hear it at all. She only hears routine sounds thereafter. The rain has let up and she can hear people going to work. The last before sunrise was at 6:15 a.m. when she heard a man walk along the court. She had heard no door close. It could have been a policeman walking his beat.

The day commences.

At 10:45 a.m. John McCarthy, the head skinflint of "McCarthy Rents," sent Indian Harry to hop over and get some back rent from Mary Jane. He knocks, but no answer. He tries the door. It is locked from within. It's a spring lock. It locks into place when the door slams shut. So he's not sure if she's lying doggo or not. He goes around into the court and pushes aside the coat that plugs the hole in the window pane and then pushes aside the curtain to peer in. He turns white. He rushes off to McCarthy.

"Guv'nor, I knocked at the door," he stammered, "and

THE AWFUL DISCOVERY BY McCARTHY.

Contemporary illustration . . .

could not make anyone answer; I looked through the window and saw a lot of blood."

They rush back together. McCarthy peers in and cannot believe he is even looking at a human being. He can't speak for a moment. "You better fetch the police," he hoarsely said at last.

Throughout October the Press had chided and condemned the police and, of course, Warren for not using bloodhounds as they had been used to great success in America. In response Warren had finally and openly promised to do so next time a murder happened. This was now the "next time."

Obeying his strict orders, the police havered about outside in the court waiting for the prize bloodhounds, Burgho and Barnaby, to arrive. It was quite a congested scene. As soon as murder was shouted, plainclothes policemen came out of the woodwork. The papers marveled at how many were in the court soon after the alarm was given. Two bobbies now guarded the narrow entrance and kept the crowd back. Meanwhile others were trying to close down the whole street and get these to move on. Inspector Beck was soon upon the scene and made sure Warren's standing orders were followed.

They waited. . .and they waited. . .and awaited.

At 11:15 a.m. Bagster Phillips arrived. He peered in the broken window and immediately realized the body was in no immediate need for a doctor. He, too, would now wait. At 11:30 a.m. Abberline himself arrived. Beck explained why they were still waiting. He was sure the bloodhounds were on their way per his request. Phillips just shrugged. There was no reason to force the door, he told Abberline. She was quite dead. Abberline agreed that the bloodhounds obviously had to be tested. So they would wait.

And they waited.

Fortunately, the wait was long enough for the City Police to hear about the murder. They had seen the report come over the telegraph. Despite this being Met territory, they were ready to tread. Smith was still irked at what Warren had done with the graffito, and he didn't want any of that to happen here. A camera crew headed to Miller's Court prepared to take pictures of a victim *in situ*. This is possibly the first time in history that crime scene photos were taken. The City had actually shown a far more investigative approach to the crimes under the ever-eager care of Major Smith. But now they, too, waited along with the other police in the court.

Yet where were the bloodhounds? It was now 1:30 p.m. Finally, Superintendent Arnold arrived. The bloodhounds weren't coming. The order was countermanded. Break the door in! McCarthy obliged. The door swung fast and banged against the table on the left of the bed. The police entered. The scene and the stench were overwhelming.

🕯

Flashes burst. Smoke puffs billowed up. Again and again. The City police took pictures this way and that way. The Met police stood back. Some turned away. Abberline's eyes were already prowling the room. A large fire had burnt in the fireplace, fueled by what seemed a large quantity of women's clothing. Remnants could still be sifted from the ash, which was still warm, such as the brim of a hat and a skirt. The fire had been so hot, and had been kept up for so long, that the solder on the spout of the teapot, setting on the grate, had melted off and the spout was in the ash.[5]

A carnage of pagan delight had occurred in the irreligious flickers of light that must have danced about the room as the poor woman had been slowly carved up on her bed. As before, not a trace of the fiend was had. Not a half step in blood, not a drop shaken from his drenched hands. No smears on the door handle. No drops between the bed and fireplace as he stoked the heathen embers to accompany his bloody orchestration.

Bagster Phillips had been first to study the grotesque scene on the bed. He had by now stepped aside to allow the City C.I.D. to take photographs. He, too, set his keen eye to rove

The Police *News gave us this image of Drs. Bond and Phillips examining the body. . .*

about the room. There had been a curious arrangement of Mary Jane's internal organs around her, and now he examined the room to see if there were any other irreverent innuendoes.

Both Abberline and he puzzled over how her clothes were neatly folded over a chair and yet so much other clothes apparently burned in the fire. Abberline supposed the fire was to make enough moody light for the killer to see by. Considering the horrid scene about the bed, the Ripper would have

---

[5] It is amazing that some question this and assert the pot may merely have been sans a spout. Abberline clearly testified "There were traces of a large fire having been kept up in the grate, so much so that it had melted the spout of a kettle off." He would not have said this had he not found the spout on the grate in the fireplace.

needed much light and time to do what he did.

Dr. Thomas Bond had been expected and now arrived. He was a high-end West End surgeon and budding analyst. His first encounter with the crime spree was The Whitehall Mystery Torso. Top level at Scotland Yard now got him involved in these crimes, perhaps in an attempt to see if there was a connection with The Torso Killer. Although his assistant, Dr. Charles Hebbert, had testified on significant points at The Whitehall Mystery Inquest, Bond had testified the most on the overall condition of the torso and the other remains found. He now stood over Mary Jane's remains and was flabbergasted. The scene was the most gruesome sight he had ever seen.

Mary Jane, for so the ghastly corpse was assumed to be, had had her features hacked away. Her eyes were about the only thing untouched. The Ripper had stood over her and sliced away obliquely. Nose and ears and folds of cheek were almost severed off. The abdomen was but an empty cavity, flayed open and emptied of its guts. The loose folds of skin and muscle had been cut away as well and placed on the table next to the bed. The breasts had been cut away, in a circular motion. They had been removed down to and including the muscles, so that it was possible to peak through the raw ribs and see the chest cavity. In looking inside the gut, he could see that the diaphragm had been sliced open. The heart had been cut out. The head was leaning a bit to the left shoulder. Under it he found one breast, the uterus and kidneys. The other breast was by the right foot. The legs were spread, the inside of the thighs were shaved off of flesh down to the bone. The liver was placed between the feet. The intestines were by her right side; the spleen by the left side. The folds of skin taken from the thighs were also on the table. The corpse's right hand was clenched, the arm lying by the body. The left arm was bent over the body, the lifeless hand hanging into the gutted abdominal cavity.

There is no question that this was the hand of Jack the Ripper. The throat had been cut deeply, like the others, to the point it scored the neck bones.

Politics unquestionably came to the fore. At 4 p.m. the body was scooped up and all its pieces and loaded in an

Dr. Thomas Bond.

ambulance where it was trotted off to the Northeast District of Middlesex— in other words, conspicuously *out* of Wynne Baxter's jurisdiction.

By this time London was in uproar. The people didn't need any special edition papers to ignite them into a fury. Crowds had gathered at both entrances to Dorset Street, where the police cordon had kept them. When they saw the ambulance trot up they broke the barrier to run to the entrance of Miller's Court. They now ran crazed at what they were told. The women in Dorset Street had begun it, shouting about and telling the other women, each in turn becoming angrier. From there it spread throughout Whitechapel and into the City of London. Paper boys barked the latest news like hysteric town criers of old. "Another horrible murder and mutilation in Whitechapel!"

The pageantry of the Lord Mayor's parade, in which women were adorned with garlands amidst the banners and trappings of Elizabethan England (the Lord Mayor rides in a grand coach with guards in crimson and polished armor of the 16th century), was suddenly set into a near frenzy by the news of the ghastly crime. Pomp was replaced by panic and rage. People rushed to the boys to hear the news. Slogans started being shouted. A day of traditional festivities was turned into an impromptu protest against the government's inefficiency to stop this madman.

The next day the newspapers had a field day. The *Daily News*: "The unfortunate woman had been cut and hacked by the assassin's knife in a manner which was revolting beyond all description. The fiendish assailant was not content with taking the life of his victim by severing the head from the body, but he had exercised an infernal ingenuity in despoiling the corpse of its human semblance. . .Medical assistance was immediately summoned, and a description of the discovery telegraphed to all the metropolitan police stations in the terse sentence: 'The woman is simply cut to pieces.'"

The next day the Prime Minister, Lord Salisbury, received yet another telegram from the Queen. She complained about the efficiency of the detective force, saying in part: "They are not what they should be." She insisted the courts must be better lit. She reminded him yet again: "You promised when the first murder took place to consult with your colleagues about it."

Lord Salisbury could no longer drag his heels. He summoned the Cabinet to No. 10 Downing Street. They would not agree to a reward. One can well imagine their reason. A very enticing one had been offered by both the City of London and private concerns, and any augment of it probably would not help. This left the Cabinet off the hook. Rather, they offered a full pardon:

Whereas on November 8 or 9 in Miller's Court, Dorset Street, Spitalfields, Mary Jane Kelly was murdered by some person or persons unknown, the Secretary of State will advise the grant of Her Majesty's pardon to any accomplice not being a person who contrived or actually committed the murder who shall give such information and evidence as shall lead to the discovery and conviction of the person or persons who committed the murder.

The inquest was eagerly awaited. The political shuffling was apparent to everybody in the Press and in the district of Whitechapel, and protests rather than official solemnity opened the proceedings.

After each juror answered to their names, one spoke up: "I do not see why we should have the inquest thrown upon our shoulders, when the murder did not happen in our district, but in Whitechapel."

The coroner's officer, Hammond, answered quickly: "It did not happen in Whitechapel."

The coroner, Dr. Roderick Macdonald, was an old nemesis of Wynne Baxter. Now, finally in the limelight himself, he showed he wasn't a patch on his rival. He handled the issue poorly, to put it mildly. He glowered at the juror: "Do you think that we do not know what we are doing here," he said crossly, "and that we do not know our own district? The jury are summoned in the ordinary way, and they have no business to object. If they persist in their objection I shall know how to deal with them. Does any juror persist in objecting?"

Such a reaction to one juror was enlightening. It revealed the extent that Macdonald knew the rumblings that had been going on about political shuffling.

The juror bravely responded: "We are summoned for the Shoreditch District. This affair happened in Spitalfields."

"It happened within my district," responded Macdonald brusquely.

Another juryman bravely spoke up: "This is not my district. I come from Whitechapel, and Mr. Baxter is my coroner."

Macdonald was being watched by all the Press. Yet he still overreacted. "I am not going to discuss the subject with jurymen at all. If any juryman says he distinctly objects, let him say so." He paused and glared at them. It was silent. "I may tell the jurymen that jurisdiction lies where the body lies, not where it was found, if there was doubt as to the district where the body was found."

It was a tense moment, but the jury remained silent. They were then sworn, and Inspector Abberline took them to view the body and the room. After that they reassembled, Macdonald had composed himself. He addressed the reporters and clarified that despite a "great fuss" having been made in some papers about jurisdiction, the "body was in his jurisdiction; it had been taken to his mortuary; and there was an end of it." It had also been rumored that he and Baxter had had words. "There was no foundation for the reports that had appeared." He made it clear that on a previous occasion a murder had occurred in his district and the body had been taken to the nearest mortuary, which was in Baxter's district. Macdonald stressed he had not objected to Baxter conducting the inquest at all. "The jurisdiction was where the body lay."

This ended the whole argument. Macdonald fussily began the proceedings.

Joseph Barnett was now called. "I have seen the body, and I identify it by the ear and eyes, which are all that I can recognise; but I am positive it is the same woman I knew."

He admitted that he left Mary Jane on October 30. Macdonald quickly asked why. "Because," he replied, "she had a woman of bad character there, whom she took in out of compassion, and I objected to it. That was the only reason. I left her on the Tuesday between five and six p.m. I last saw her alive between half-past seven and a quarter to eight on Thursday night last, when I called upon her. I stayed there for a quarter of an hour."

"Were you on good terms?"

"Yes, on friendly terms; but when we parted I told her I had no work, and had nothing to give her, for which I was very sorry."

Macdonald asked him outright whether they drank together. Barnett said no, but admitted that she had been drunk a few times when he was with her, but she was "quite sober" otherwise. He then admitted that at his last visit Maria Harvey was there for a while and he left shortly after she did. He goes through her life story, from Wales to a "gay house in the West End" and then from there to France for a fortnight with a "gentleman." He mentioned her suitors in the East End, Morganstone and Fleming, but admitted that he did not ever see them.

"Was that all you knew of her history when you lived with her?"

"Yes. After she lived with Morganstone or Fleming— I don't know which one was the last— she lived with me."

"Have you heard her speak of being afraid of any one?"

"Yes; several times. I bought newspapers, and I read to her everything about the murders, which she asked me about."

"Did she express fear of any particular individual?"

"No, sir. Our own quarrels were very soon over."

"You have given your evidence very well indeed," praised Macdonald. He then turned to the jury:

"The doctor has sent a note asking whether we shall want his attendance here to-day. I take it that it would be convenient that he should tell us roughly what the cause of death was, so as to enable the body to be buried. It will not be necessary to go into the details of the doctor's evidence; but he suggested that he might come to state roughly the cause of death."

An interesting way to word obligation. The doctor's presence was indeed necessary in order to establish type of death. There is a rather interesting annotation in the newspapers: "The jury acquiesced in the proposed course."

After Thomas Bowyer (Indian Harry), John McCarthy, Mary Ann Cox and Elizabeth Prater gave their sequence of events as witnesses, only two more would be called before Bagster Phillips was on the stand. These two were the most interesting. One was Caroline Maxwell, the other Sarah Lewis.

Maxwell had gained attention in the papers by insisting that she had seen Kelly at around 8:30 a.m. that Friday morning. This placed her alive long after the murder was first thought to have happened in the early morning solitudes. A pub keeper had also said he saw Kelly about 10 o'clock, but his statement was largely dismissed. Maxwell, on the other hand, was doggedly sure of her encounter with Kelly. Macdonald called her now.

Maxwell's husband was a lodging house deputy at 14 Dorset Street. "I knew the deceased for about four months. I believe she was an unfortunate. On two occasions I spoke to her."

"You must be very careful about your evidence," admonished Macdonald, "because it is different to other people's. You say you saw her standing at the corner of the entry to the court?"

"Yes, on Friday morning, from eight to half-past eight. I fix the time by my husband's finishing work. When I came out of the lodging-house she was opposite."

"Did you speak to her?"

"Yes; it was an unusual thing to see her up. She was a young woman who never associated with any one. I spoke across the street, 'What, Mary, brings you up so early?' She said, 'Oh, Carrie, I do feel so bad.'"

"And yet you say you had only spoken to her twice previously; you knew her name and she knew yours?"

"Oh, yes; by being about in the lodging-house."

"What did she say?"

"She said, 'I've had a glass of beer, and I've brought it up again;' and it was in the road. I imagined she had been in the Britannia beer-shop at the corner of the street. I left her, saying that I could pity her feelings. I went to Bishopsgate Street to get my husband's breakfast. Returning I saw her outside the Britannia public-house, talking to a man."

"This would be about what time?"

"Between eight and nine o'clock. I was absent about half-an-hour. It was about a quarter to nine."

"What description can you give of this man?"

"I could not give you any, as they were at some distance."

Abberline injected. "The distance is about sixteen yards."

"I am sure it was the deceased," insisted Maxwell. "I am willing to swear it."

"You are sworn now," replied Macdonald blandly. "Was he a tall man?"

"No; he was a little taller than me and stout."

Abberline injected again: "On consideration I should say the distance was twenty-five yards."

"What clothes had the man?" asked Macdonald.

"Dark clothes; he seemed to have a plaid coat on. I could not say what sort of hat he had."

"What sort of dress had the deceased?"

"A dark skirt, a velvet body, a maroon shawl, and no hat."

"Have you ever seen her the worse for drink?"

"I have seen her in drink, but she was not a notorious character."

When a member of the jury asked whether the man had a certain type of hat, Maxwell could not be certain. "I should have noticed if the man had had a tall silk hat, but we are accustomed to see men of all sorts with women. I should not like to pledge myself to the kind of hat."

Her caution here starkly highlights by contrast her certainty about seeing Mary Jane earlier. If she left any doubt in the coroner's and jury's mind, it was not whether she saw and spoke to Mary Jane Kelly at those times but whether she had the right day. Could it have been Thursday morning?

Sarah Lewis injected the controversy about a man seen about the crime scenes carrying a black bag. At the Berner Street affair there was such a sighting as well. There this person was explained as a local businessman Leon Goldstein. But that was not the only time a man had been seen. That very night another man, Albert Backert, had had an encounter with such a man near Mitre Square. On 13 October 1888 the *East London Advertiser* had reported: "I was in the Three Nuns Hotel, Aldgate, on Saturday night," he had told the newshawks, "when a man got into conversation with me. He asked me questions which now appear to me to have some bearing upon the recent murders. He wanted to know whether I knew what sort of loose women used the public bar at that house, when they usually left the street outside, and where they were in the habit of going. He asked further questions, and from his manner seemed up to no good purpose. He appeared to be a 'shabby genteel' sort of man, and was dressed in black clothes. He wore a black felt hat, and carried a black bag. We came out together at closing time (twelve o'clock) and I left him outside Aldgate railway station."

Backert's description had seemed a little too coached by the Press reports, but Sarah Lewis was far more detailed. When asked now if she had seen any "suspicious persons" in the area, she added to the enigma.

"On Wednesday night I was going along the Bethnal Green Road, with a woman, about eight o'clock, when a gentleman passed us. He followed us and spoke to us, and wanted us to follow him into an entry. He had a shiny leather bag with him."

"Did he want both of you?"

"No; only one. I refused. He went away and came back again, saying he would treat us. He put down his bag and picked it up again, saying, 'What are you frightened about? Do you think I've got anything in the bag?' We then ran

With Mary Kelly's murder an interesting image of Jack the Ripper took form. Because of Sarah Lewis' encounters, and the reports of a man wearing a silk hat, the Ripper became a top hat villain carrying a black surgical bag.

away, as we were frightened."

"Was he a tall man?"

"He was short, pale-faced, with a black moustache, rather small. His age was about forty."

"Was it a large bag?"

"No, about 6 inches to 9 inches long. His hat was a high round hat. He had a brownish overcoat, with a black short coat underneath. His trousers were a dark pepper-and-salt."

"After he left you, what did you do?"

"We ran away."

"Have you seen him since?"

"On Friday morning, about half-past two a.m.," she continued, "when I was going to Miller's Court, I met the same man with a woman in Commercial Street, near Mr. Ringer's public-house (the Britannia). He had no overcoat on."

"Had he the black bag?"

"Yes."

"Were the man and woman quarrelling?"

"No; they were talking. As I passed he looked at me. I don't know whether he recognised me. There was no policeman about."

Unfortunately, no one asked what type of jacket he was wearing without his coat. Therefore it is hard if not impossible to link him with the man who supposedly was speaking with Mary Jane Kelly outside the pub, if Mrs. Maxwell's testimony is to be believed. He does become a very interesting character, however. (Indeed the image of the top hat wearing Ripper with a surgical bag evolves from this). Sarah Lewis was familiar with the neighborhood, and she clearly considered him a suspicious man.

In startling contrast to Baxter's inquests, Bagster Phillips was rushed onto the stand and off again. Yet Phillips could not have been more revealing in his carefully worded statement. All he said in regard to the body was:

The mutilated remains of a woman were lying two-thirds over, towards the edge of the bedstead, nearest the door. Deceased had only an under-linen garment upon her, and by subsequent examination I am sure the body had been removed, after the injury which caused death, from that side of the bedstead which was nearest to the wooden partition previously mentioned. The large quantity of blood under the bedstead, the saturated condition of the paillasse, pillow, and sheet at the top corner of the bedstead nearest to the partition leads me to the conclusion that the severance of the right carotid artery, which was the immediate cause of death, was inflicted while the deceased was lying at the right side of the bedstead and her head and neck in the top right-hand corner.

Under the impression that "it was understood" that more medical information would be coming later, the jury asked no questions at this time. There was a short adjournment for a few minutes.

When they filed back in and sat down, Macdonald took a strong line again: "It has come to my ears that somebody has been making a statement to some of the jury as to their right and duty of being here. Has any one during the interval spoken to the jury, saying that they should not be here to-day?"

After some of the jury replied "no," Macdonald mediated his tone. "Then I must have been misinformed. I should have taken good care that he would have had a quiet life for the rest of the week if anybody had interfered with my jury."

At the very least, the politest appraisal of Macdonald is that he was unskillful. With the Press reporting every word, his manner only dredged up the controversy about the jurisdiction issue. Whether someone had spoken to the jury or not it was irrelevant now. They had been sworn and were hearing testimony. The process was speeding on, and nothing was going to stop it. Macdonald's saber rattling to send someone to jail for the rest of the week was misplaced coroner's bravado. And, in truth, it was hypocrisy; Macdonald had been interfering with his own jury by his repeated attempts at intimidation.

Maria Harvey and Jill Van Turney were next called. Van Turney could only say that she saw Kelly often drunk, and that night she slept in Miller's Court and was awake all night. She never heard any scream of "Murder." She also said she didn't hear anybody singing. Harvey had nothing to add, and confirmed that there was no individual of whom Mary Jane was afraid.

Inspectors Beck and Abberline gave very brief testimony. Abberline largely just described the room and the effects of the large fire in the grate.

"Can you give any reason why they [clothes] were burnt?"

"I can only imagine that it was to make a light for the man to see what he was doing. There was only one small candle in the room, on the top of a broken wine-glass. An impression has gone abroad that the murderer took away the key of the room. Barnett informs me that it has been missing some time, and since it has been lost they have put their hand through the broken window, and moved back the catch. It is quite easy. There was a man's clay pipe in the room, and Barnett informed me that he smoked it."

"Is there anything further the jury ought to know?"

"No; if there should be I can communicate with you, sir."

There actually was. The lock was a spring lock. It snapped into place when the door slammed. Yet the combined testimony of the witnesses shows that none had heard such a door close at all in order to set in place the lock.

At Abberline's statement above is where it was left. To this day no one knows any more details than this, for Macdonald now addressed the jury:

> The question is whether you will adjourn for further evidence. My own opinion is that it is very unnecessary for two courts to deal with these cases, and go through the same evidence time after time, which only causes expense and trouble. If the coroner's jury can come to a decision as to the cause of death, then that is all that they have to do. They have nothing to do with prosecuting a man and saying what amount of penalty he is to get. It is quite sufficient if they find out what the cause of death was. It is for the police authorities to deal with the case and satisfy themselves as to any person who may be suspected later on. I do not want to take it out of your hands. It is for you to say whether at an adjournment you will hear minutiae of the evidence, or whether you will think it is a matter to be dealt with in the police-courts later on, and that, this woman having met with her death by the carotid artery having been cut, you will be satisfied to return a verdict to that effect. From what I learn the police are content to take the future conduct of the case. It is for you to say whether you will close the

inquiry to-day; if not, we shall adjourn for a week or fortnight, to hear the evidence that you may desire.

None were expecting that. Indeed, the way Macdonald put it forward one can easily imagine the jury was taken aback. The very wording really left them only one course of action. Macdonald made it plain they were there only to determine what the circumstances of death suggested— murder or natural causes. If they balked, who would they insist be called to give more detailed testimony? Logically, it should have been Bagster Phillips and then Bond. But after consulting with themselves, they naturally agreed within the strict interpretation of their duties that they had the evidence for how Kelly died.

Macdonald formally asked: "What is the verdict?"

The Foreman rose. "Willful murder against some person or persons unknown."

That was it. Amazingly, it was over the very day. Macdonald's closing statement was a backhanded slap to Wynne Baxter for treating his inquests like trials. In retrospect, however, we can be grateful to Baxter. His inquests have provided us with much information that Macdonald's doctrinaire (or coerced) approach has failed to provide. This becomes tragic here, for the death of Mary Jane Kelly would mark a significant moment in the series of crimes attributed to Jack the Ripper. This would be the goriest of them all, but more importantly, as time would prove, some of the police would begin to suspect that this was the *last* Ripper killing. And as time has also shown to all and sundry, the Ripper was never formally identified or tried. Therefore all the details of Kelly's death, implicitly promised to come in a full trial of the suspect, have never been revealed in the light of judicial day.

As such, Kelly's killing has become the most controversial to try and explain. Tragically this leaves us with too much speculation and therewith too many implied and therefore bogus suspects. We have for starters the man that Hutchinson saw. Next, we have the man with the black bag stalking the neighborhood. Into the mix we have a bloke talking to Kelly outside the pub long after she was suspected to be dead, and

A unique perspective on Miller's Court. No. 13 was cheek by jowl with the other rooms in the court. A couple of the other female tenants seemed to room alone. Although No. 13 was the first door and therefore easiest flat from which to escape, one wonders if its unlucky number was not a factor in its occupant being chosen.

we're not even sure if she was dead by this time since we have no concrete investigative material to examine. Shadowy of them all is the man with the peculiar eyes that Indian Harry saw in the courtyard a day or so before.

The locating in 1987 of Dr. Bond's personal autopsy report was a boon of information to "Ripperologists" and criminologists, but it doesn't help answer some of the controversies: namely, when did Mary Jane truly die? It is evident in the pictures of the crime scene, which were also later rediscovered, that there was a pool of blood under the bed, but there is no comment either by Bond or Phillips how fresh or coagulated this blood was. There was that roaring fire, but to what extent would this affect rigor mortis and induce a doctor to misjudge the time of her slaying? This last point is not even raised.

Aside from being the most gruesome of the Ripper kill-ings, this murder stands out in a number of ways. Some are puzzling. Some we can understand. We can understand why this was the only known indoor killing the Ripper had thus far committed. The amount of police and Vigilance Commit-tee members on the street, plus the incentive provided by the lucrative reward, would make a public killing very dangerous. Also, the Ripper's intent seems to have been to take the heart, a protracted surgery which required more light than the street provided, plus more time and effort that couldn't afford to be interrupted. Thus he needed to work indoors. Selecting a young, pretty prostitute was also a change. But it was neces-sary since he would need an actual room in which to work. The usual drabs he had preyed upon used dosshouses in which dozens slept per room.

Despite the differences in the staging of this killing, the Ripper did not walk out of character. As the above shows, he adjusted accordingly to achieve his goals.

Everything else remains quintessentially Jack the Ripper — stealth, silence and absolutely no trail or witness. Together with the circumstances these give us the same enigma as in the other murders. For example, Mrs. Prater said she could hear Mary Kelly if she walked up and down in the room below. Nevertheless, despite awakening from her ale-induced slum-ber she heard nothing. Yet Kelly's remains look as if a maniac went at her with more than a little gusto. The silence with which all this was done argues for careful, premeditated butchery for effect.

It also suggests that Kelly never called out the words "Oh, Murder!" The Ripper would not have remained, and the noise he would have to make on the bed to immediately hush her would have been heard by Mrs. Prater. Hard-to-explain su-perficial injuries on her right hand have been argued as evi-dence of self-defense at this moment. One cut, about an inch long, was along the inside of the thumb. The other abrasions, of a similar nature, were on the back of the hand. They were very slight and only caused a little bleeding into the skin. What caused them? Self-defense can't easily explain it, for her left hand had no such abrasions. How would anybody get such abrasions on the back of one hand and inside of the thumb? The Ripper could have put his knee (or lower leg) on her left arm when he got on the bed to cut her throat. This could explain why that hand could not be used in self-defense, but still if the condition of the right hand is from self-defense. . .against what did Kelly hit or scratch her right *back* hand to account for those strange wounds? Could she already have had them? I thought perhaps she got them from repeatedly reaching through her broken window pane to un-latch her door. But given the position of the window and door, I would imagine she would use her left hand for better extension. These are yet more mysteries we cannot explain thanks to that knave Macdonald.

But though mystery is always associated with a Ripper crime scene, the mystery here of the locked door is less a mystery and more of a testimony as to how calm and cool the Ripper remained. The spring lock needed the door to audibly close in order to shoot into place. Yet no sound was heard in the early morning repose. The Ripper must have calmly left, closed the door, pulled it tight so it would lock into place, and then calmly walked down the narrow passage. Therefore he knew how it was done. He wanted Mary Kelly to be found a horrid mystery, the penny fiction thriller staging of a body in a room locked from within. It isn't difficult to figure how he did it, and it wasn't hard for the police to fathom that the door was allowed to slam shut or be silently yanked closed. But the point here is that it indicates the Ripper was calm and cool and sticking to his routine. The silence maintained dur-ing the extensive mutilations also argues not for a gorilla-like maniac but for somebody carefully mutilating and placing the pieces about the bed and table.

The Ripper's calm carefulness is seen in another bit of cu-rious evidence. Bond noted that there were several splashings of blood on the wood partition. In his craftily worded state-ment, Phillips made sure he gave us some vital clues. The first being that Kelly's throat was cut from the *right* side, not left as in the other victims. It is unquestionable that the *right* ca-rotid was cut when she was alive and blood was allowed to splash and shoot forth with each pump of her dying heart. This is the only victim to ever have the slice starting on the right side and to show that blood spurted. This evidence highlights that she was killed on the *right* side of the bed in the corner of the room. Why? This made the Ripper inconvenience himself by getting on the bed and slitting her throat from a difficult angle, something that would require some cumbersome effort. The intentionality of this act cannot be denied. It is confirmed by the fact the Ripper then pulled the body over to the left side of the bed so he could conveniently stand over it and mutilate it.

In light of his previous pattern, there can only be one explanation. To mutilate her while her body lay in a pool of blood-soaked bed sheets would simply cause blood to spray out from under the body and get on him. When murdering on the sidewalks or in a yard, the Ripper was always careful enough to place the woman down where the blood would flow *away* from the abdomen so that he never would step in the blood. The same principle is involved here. This is even more clearly evident in a telltale clue. From a picture of the murder scene, the pool of blood can be seen under the bed. It flowed under from the right side to no further than the center. Had the Ripper killed her while she lay on the left side of the bed, the blood would have soaked through the sheets, dripped onto the floor and flowed out to where he had to stand. This he never wanted. He wanted no hint of his presence in the form of shoe prints or anything. He had to kill her on the right side of the bed, let her freely bleed, then when drained pull her over to start his grim work.

The murder of Mary Jane Kelly was free of any anti-Semitic overtones. But it happened on the most important City holiday, and this shows how the murderer went one better after seeing he could not instigate race riots. This coincidence was no doubt not overlooked in officialdom. Her murder was controversial enough at the time for the body to be intentionally trotted out of Baxter's jurisdiction. What could this accomplish? It could not have been to spare details. The Press was full of macabre reports of where the portions of the viscera were found about the room. Newspaper articles even suggested parts were found hanging off nails where pictures once had hung. Thus for London at large this was hardly played down. But it was played up as the work of a wanton maniac, not the work of calm butchery for effect. Bond's autopsy report even notes how slices in the sheet indicated the Ripper covered Kelly's face before slicing it. The Ripper must not have wanted to be bespeckled by flying flesh and blood as he hacked away at her features. Much indeed was carefully done for effect.

It was an atrocious crime, and the culprit had to be none other than Jack the Ripper. Despite the carnage, and even unfinished mutilation (the calf was cut from knee to ankle but not shaved from the bone), this was a far more calculated murder than all of the previous ones. To the very end the Ripper maintained his diabolical aplomb. He had walked quietly away. In his wake he left mystery and national controversy.

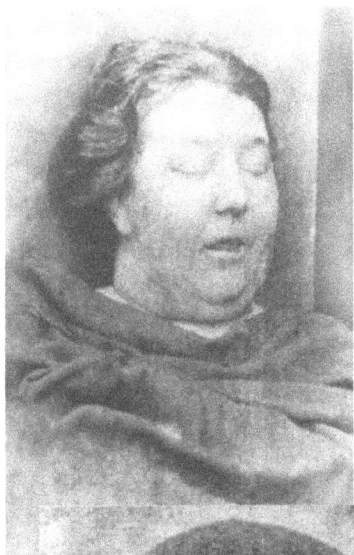

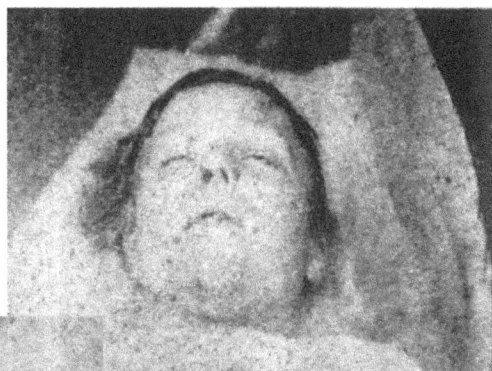

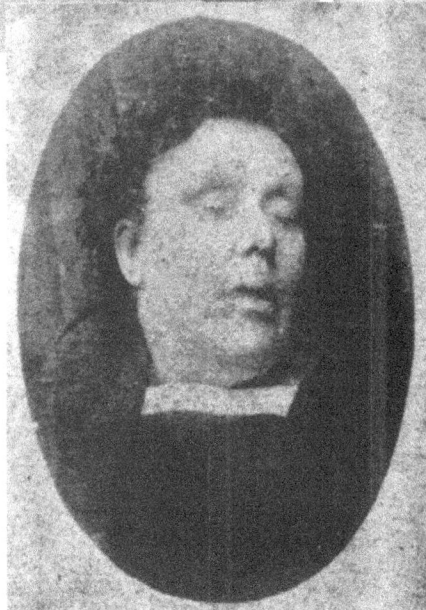

Starting top, left to right, Martha Tabram, the disputed first victim of Jack the Ripper. Polly Nichols, the first "canonical" victim. Annie Chapman, who was dissected the neatest. Liz Stride. Mortuary photos.

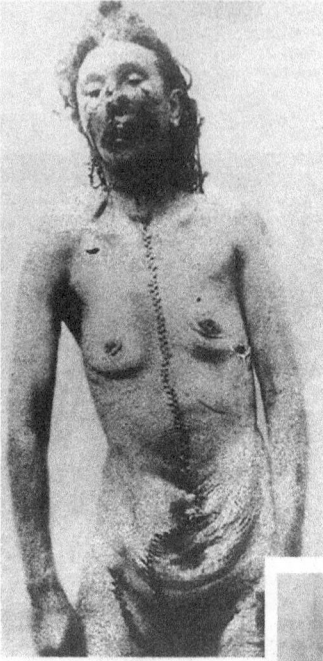

The Ripper's most gruesome work, Catherine Eddowes (left) and (below) Mary Jane Kelly.

City of London Police photograph of Kelly in situ. The thin wood partition is in the background. The pool of blood can be seen under the center of the bed. Her intestines are on the table.

General Sir Charles Warren.

Sir Robert Anderson.

Prince Albert Victor Guelf-Wettin
His reputation would later be dragged
into the enigma of the killings.

Montague John Druitt.

James Monro. He would replace Warren, but prove as ineffectual in tracking down the identity of the Ripper.

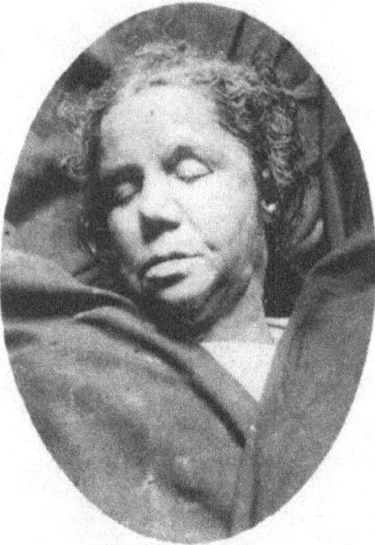

Alice McKenzie, left. Below, Frances Coles. Mortuary photographs.

12

PALL MALL

LONDON'S NOVEMBER HORRORS had been nothing but an echo of October's. Kelly's murder had hit only one ominous chord unique to itself: it meant that even indoors no one was safe.

The police did the same things after the hideous murders of the Double Event. Arrests had been made by the score, but all the suspects were eventually released. If November was any different in character it was because London was now accepting the reality of Jack the Ripper with a sigh. Sigh and wait. How long could this last? Eventually a murder would no longer cause a panic in the East End or an indignant uproar in the West.

Sir Charles Warren was quickly gone. His resignation had been debated in the House of Commons two days after the inquest closed. Matthews praised him warmly: "Sir Charles Warren was a man not only of the highest character, but of great ability. During his tenure of the office he had displayed the most indefatigable activity in every detail of the organisation and administration of the force. By his vigour and firmness he had restored that confidence in the police which had been shaken— he believed with the right hon. gentleman, unjustly shaken after the regrettable incident of 1886. . .Sir Charles Warren had shown conspicuous skill and firmness in putting an end to disorder in the metropolis, and for that he deserved the highest praise."

The *Echo* was remarkably insightful. Of his resignation, the editorial declared: "A few noisy people will lay the flattering unction to their souls that they have been the means of his removal. They are mistaken. They have had nothing to do with his removal; rather their opposition to him would, in other conditions, have strengthened him in his position. Both the Home Secretary and the Chief Commissioner have, for the last twelve months, been subject to similar hostile criticism. They have both alike been execrated. But the Home Secretary remains, whilst the Chief Commissioner has gone. Sir Charles Warren has not been undermined, nor was he weakened by outside influence. Had the Home Secretary and the Chief Commissioner pulled together, they might have smiled at the puny charges of epithets levelled against them. But they did not pull together. The Home Secretary, being the superior officer, though not the superior man, rebuked the Chief Commissioner. A house divided against itself cannot stand. Neither could the Home Office and Scotland Yard, with such men as Mr. Matthews at the head of one and Sir Charles Warren at the head of the other, work harmoniously. They, in fact, antagonised each other, and one has gone to the wall. If Sir Charles Warren had not resigned Mr. Matthews, in all probability, would have done so; and it would have been better for the Government had the Home Secretary surrendered office instead of the late Chief Commissioner. Of the two, Mr. Matthews is generally the most unpopular. But one is taken and the other is left. The essential disagreement between Sir Charles Warren and Mr. Monro, which ended in Mr. Monro's resignation, inevitably prepared the way for the other and bigger resignation of Sir Charles himself. Now the step has been taken a few fussy people will, no doubt, say, 'See what we have done,' just as the fly on the wheel may say, 'See what a dust we are making.'"

It would be so. Monro was now the new Commissioner of Police. Ironically, Monro's triumph was overshadowed by the Ripper's bloodiest slaying. Since he was new to the job, the papers could only give him an expected honeymoon when at the end of the month he had fared no better than Warren in capturing the fiend. He was not a military man, so the usual insults to Warren had no application to him anyway. He had held jobs in India in administrative and legal positions. The Press was probably also aware that it would not be necessary to harangue him about his work in order to get him to go. Sadly, he had a reputation for resigning out of "conviction" when he had not gotten his way. Ironically yet again, instead of resignations sending him down, he consistently climbed. He now found himself at the top. However, he also found himself at the highest point of scrutiny in his official life. If he failed here it would go doubly worse for him than it had ever gone for Warren.

It would not be imprudent to deduce from the collective evidence that Monro had an ability to manipulate situations and people to get his way. This was evident during the autumn while he was still nurtured under Matthews' protective wing at the Home Office. Behind Warren's back, at Matthews' urging, Abberline and Anderson still consulted with him. In this position he was, in essence, still very much on the case but insulated by secrecy against any insults for the police's failures, failures which may have arisen from his own guiding suggestions. This being said, one can wonder if he wasn't responsible for the body of Kelly being taken out of Wynne Baxter's hands. It was most obviously a political move designed to squelch evidence to the public, an attitude in-keeping with his unofficial portfolio as "head of the detective service" under Matthews.

This question becomes more justifiable to ask after examining Monro's part in the next mysterious murder of a prostitute, Rose Mylett, in the East End. He not only disparaged the idea that the Ripper was responsible, Monro apparently even influenced Dr. Bond to change his initial diagnosis of strangulation to say that this was not murder at all. This was after 4 other doctors, including Bagster Phillips, had pronounced strangulation and willful murder. If Monro had noticed the Ripper's shift toward attempts at racial riot and then political turmoil— and he would be rather dim had he not noticed— it would be natural to assume Mylett's death was not the Ripper's, for it really followed no previous pattern. Moreover, she was also killed in Poplar, about a mile from Whitechapel. But why disparage the whole idea of murder?

Despite politics smothering the issue, Rose Mylett's death

remains a strange one. The mystery began at 4:15 a.m. December 20, 1888. Constable Sergeant Robert Golding and Constable Thomas Costello found the body in the dark shadows along a brick wall in a yard between 184 and 186 Poplar High Street. It was that of a young woman, like Kelly, in her 20s. She lay on her left side, one leg drawn up and the other extended, in a scene of almost supernatural staging, for there were no footprints but hers on the soft ground. Yet blood was oozing from her nose, her hat was missing, and there were marks on her neck indicative of strangulation with a cord. There were marks of the thumb, middle and index finger on her neck. There was also an abrasion on her face.

When her body was examined at the morgue by Dr. Matthew Brownfield, the Poplar police surgeon, and his assistant, Dr. George Harris, both noticed that the line indicating strangulation went almost all around the neck, except for a few inches at the back between the spine and the left ear. "I think the murderer must have stood at the left rear of the woman, and having the ends of the string wrapped around his hands, thrown the cord around her throat, and crossing his hands so strangled her. Where the hands crossed would be just where the marks of the cord were absent." Brownfield also posited that the fingermarks were her own, made as she clenched the cord and tried to resist strangulation.

The problem with Brownfield's theory was that the police found no evidence for any footprints but hers. Although Mylett was a prostitute, she didn't seem to have led a man into the darkness of the yard to ply trade. Nor was there any evidence of a struggle. The theory that she was murdered elsewhere seemed logical. The principle clue that supported this was the discovery of a woman's hat on the railing of a fence on East India Road by Eagle Tavern. This was suspected to have been Mylett's. If this is the case, then the killer took the trouble and danger to carry her to the yard, blocks away, and deposit the body in some way that prevented him leaving prints. Why take the trouble? Was it to find a secluded place to do the mutilations? Was the killer interrupted? (A neighbor reported that a dog started barking around 3 a.m.). Except for that one common denominator— the apparent desire to make the staging baffling, almost supernatural— it wasn't the Ripper's style.

At Monro's instigation, Robert Anderson himself got personally involved. He soon believed that Mylett's death had nothing to do with homicide and certainly not with the Ripper. Whether he was cajoled to this view by Monro or not it is not certain, but it can be suspected from the chain of events. It began with Anderson summoning Dr. Thomas Bond to have a look at the body, unaware the West End doctor was out of town. Instead Bond's assistant, Charles Hebbert, examined the body and pronounced murder by strangulation. Independent of Anderson, Monro had also asked Alexander MacKellar, the chief surgeon, to examine the body. But he too returned the same verdict. When Bond first examined the body, 5 days after the killing, he pronounced the same verdict. Yet it is known that Anderson seriously objected to these pronouncements by the doctors. He wrote what is perhaps a compromising note to Monro in which he said that "After a long conference, in which I pressed my difficulties and objections, I referred them to you." Begg, Fido and Skinner write in *Jack the Ripper A to Z* that it was never ascertained if Monro saw both of them afterward. One thing, however, is certain: Bond changed his pronouncement to natural causes. He accepted that Mylett, very drunk, had staggered into the yard, perhaps after losing her hat blocks away, stumbled, fell, and choked to death on her own collar. Investigation had also revealed that Mylett was known by the nickname "Drunken Liz Davis," a sobriquet that could only help support the theory.

Being that the body was in Baxter's jurisdiction, the redoubtable Bagster Phillips of H Division was also asked to examine her. He was certain that the murderer had "studied the theory of strangulation, for he evidently knew where to place the cord so as to immediately bring his victim under control." When asked about possible Ripper comparatives, he said that of the others only Annie Chapman had been strangled first.

The inquest (December 21, 1888) guided by the snooping bulldog nose of Wynne Baxter revealed much. This was his first showing since his famous snub in November, and he gave the case his usual fine tooth comb. He obviously agreed with the 4 doctors who had examined the body and brought back a diagnosis of willful strangulation. His careful questioning elicited from Golding that Mylett's collar and a scarf were tied very loosely. This countered the idea that her collar had choked her in death. She was also still warm when found. Dr. Harris, Brownfield's assistant, describer the death scene clearly. It was on her left side that Mylett was found. The left side of her neck therefore was crinked against her collar as her head lay on her shoulder. Yet it is this side which showed *no* mark. When Bond was finally called, he clearly gave his opinion that she had died in a drunken stupor. However, he could not explain an internal injury in the throat. There were "three extravasations of blood, where incisions had been made, and found blood effused around the larynx and deep congestion of the mucous membrane of the larynx. . .Witness could find no injury to the skin where the mark had been."

At the end of the session Baxter declared that "it seemed very much as if a foul murder had been committed, and all the available evidence should be got before the jury concluded the case." He therefore adjourned so the police could make more inquiries.

When Baxter reconvened on January 2, 1889, the new year had begun and the terror of last autumn was becoming more of a mystery than a horror anymore. Yet there were still concerns that Mylett's death was caused by the Ripper. The *Star* had traced a rumor that Bagster Phillips believed the same man who had killed Annie Chapman had killed Mylett and simply had no time to do the butchering. The Press picturesquely viewed the Ripper as carrying the corpse from where he had quickly strangled her to the seclusion of the yard in order to commence the nefarious dissection. Even the Sunday *Times* noted the streets were poorly lit. The Ripper could easily have carried the body stealthily to the secluded yard.

Baxter summed up:

"After Dr. Bromfield [Brownfield] and his assistant, duly qualified men, came to the conclusion that this was a case of homicidal strangulation, someone had a suspicion that the evidence was not satisfactory. At all events, you've heard that doctor after doctor went down to view the body without my knowledge or sanction as coroner. I did not wish to make that a personal matter, but I had never received such treatment before. Of the five doctors who saw the body, Dr. Bond was the only one who considered the case was not one of murder. Dr. Bond did not see the body until five days after her death and he was, therefore, at a disadvantage. Dr. Bond stated that if this was a case of strangulation he should have expected to find the skin broken, but it was clearly shown, on reference being made to the records of the Indian doctors in the cases of Thug murders, that there were no marks whatever left. Other eminent authorities agreed with that view."

Baxter had made his point.

The jury returned a verdict of "willful murder against person or persons unknown."

The murders that would follow in Whitechapel and the East End would follow the pall mall begun by Mylett's death. In fact, they would not follow any strict pattern. Unlike those 5 autumn murders, 6 if including Tabram, there was no progression made toward a grisly crescendo of gore. Nor was there really any underlying political or race card being played. Only one thing remained consistent, however: the careful creation of baffling circumstances at the scene.

This raises the conundrum of The Torso Killer. The first body in London had been found on the 2nd of October, and in a significant way it contributed to the October Terror. There were popular and journalistic attempts to attribute the killing to the Ripper, since this torso was so conveniently missing its uterus, but the police didn't buy into it. However, on June 4, 1889, after an uneventful spring, pieces of a woman began turning up in the Thames yet again.

The discoveries began around Battersea Park. A parcel of sorts was bobbing in the eddy of the tide against the shore. This naturally attracted three boys playing nearby to go check it out. They unwrapped it and there was a human leg. They wrapped it back up and went to the police.

Scotland Yard's man in that area, Dr. Kempster, could identify it as being the thigh of a young woman, the part from the hip to the knee. It had not been in the water more than 24 hours. The white cloth was part of a woman's under-linen. The waistband had L.E. Fisher written on it. Part of a woman's ulster was also attached to the underwear to help secure the gruesome parcel.

Reports soon came in from other parts of London. Near London Bridge more boys found a parcel. The ghoulish contents were taken to Wapping police station. The importance of these remains is seen in that both Dr. Bond and none other than Melville Macnaghten came to examine them. Monro had had his way by this time, and Macnaghten was newly appointed just on June 1st to the new position of Assistant Chief Constable. Personally, Macnaghten liked this sort of thing. He turned up at most murders and loved the aura of a crime scene and the thrill of being kept abreast of the circumstances. Macnaghten had also confessed to Monro that he had a bug about the Ripper. With this in mind, we can further understand why both Bond and Macnaghten came. The part of the woman was her lower abdomen, the area from which the Ripper was known to take an organ. In this case, the uterus was present. Bond was surprised when he examined the body and blood oozed out of some of the cut arteries. The body obviously had not been dead long.

Kempster, Bond and a Mr. Braxton Hicks, the coroner for Mid-Surrey, examined the pieces together. The hip came from the same lower torso. Just as significant, the wrapping of both parcels was made of the same woman's ulster. The operation must have been brutal. The thigh carried bruises made by clutching fingers. Obviously, they were made while she was alive. Were they made by the killer clutching her while dissecting her alive?

Bond believed the young woman was the victim of an illegal abortion. The cord and placenta were still present in the uterus. But not much speaks of a botched abortion here. Over the next week several parts of the same woman would continue to be found along the Thames, carefully wrapped in parcels of her under-linen and/or ulster, something not required to merely hide the results of a bad operation. It would take time to dissect a person to this extent, and even more time to wrap each piece of the body and then stealthily toss them into the Thames, either at the same location or at a variety of locations at intervals, so they could drift intermittently. Indeed, the right thigh was found in the garden of Sir Percy Shelley's Chelsea house. (This too was wrapped in the ulster coat and pocket of a coarse apron.) Obviously, the killer was taunting the whole city. This could not merely have been the result of a botched abortion, especially with the gesture of throwing a limb over the railing of the estate of the son of Mary Shelley, the author of *Frankenstein*, the monster created by sewing together various human body parts. The killer was clearly advertising that careful human ingenuity was involved in the murder and its aftermath.

Since the head was never found the identity of the person was probably intended to remain secret. Yet everything else about her was meant to be found (except the heart was also not found).

There seems little doubt that it was the work of the same murderer who had carefully dissected the last victim and gone to the brazen lengths to place parts of her in the New Scotland Yard basement. In like manner here, each part of the body was found neatly parceled. All but one piece had been wrapped with parts of a woman's dark skirt, ulster or underlinen and tied with string, shoelaces or broom string.

Moreover, the person had been quite careful, for it turned out that the dissection had been done by someone who knew their stuff. Concerning the last piece of the body found, the autopsy declares: "The third portion of the trunk consisted of the pelvis from below the third lumbar vertebra. The thighs had been taken off opposite the hip joints by long, sweeping incisions through the skin, muscles and tissues down to the joint, the heads of the bones neatly disarticulated. . ."

As it would eventually prove, the most important piece was found on land in the shrubs of the Battersea Park, for it would help lead police to the victim's identity. It was found about 200 yards from the banks of the Thames. Like with The Whitehall Mystery, this bundle had been secreted to a part of the park not open to the public. It had been found by the gardener, Joe Davis. He was attracted to the spot by the foul stench it gave off. (The bundle contained the chest cavity, which had been emptied of its contents by being sawn in half lengthwise).

Altogether by mid-June the police had enough information to believe that The Thames Mystery body parts were not any L.E. Fisher but one Elizabeth Jackson. She was a

young woman, in her mid-20s, with red hair. She was around
5'5". She was, in fact, a destitute and homeless "unfortunate."
She had never traveled far from Chelsea where she had been
born. She lived in some common lodging houses there, then
casual wards and workhouses. Then she disappeared around
the end of May 1888.

After she had become destitute, she used to brag that she
had managed to remain in Battersea Park after the gates had
been closed at night. Homeless though she was, she could
hardly have been hacked up in the park, parceled up and removed in a cab piece-by-piece without the killer being seen.
The Torso Killer was obviously not some bum wandering the
parks. He must have been surveying Battersea Park looking
for victims. At one point he ingratiated himself or enticed her
to go somewhere or picked her up and taken her against her
will without anybody having seen them. In rather touching
ruthlessness he decided to put part of her back in her beloved
park. The police also thought that some of the lighter parts of
her body were thrown into the Thames from Battersea
Bridge.

At first, the good police doctors had a theory that the killer intermixed victims' clothing because they thought Elizabeth Jackson's hands indicated refinement but that the clothes
her body parts were wrapped in suggested a poor working
girl. Although their assessment of Jackson turned out to be
wrong, the possibility of intermixed clothes is interesting in
light of the 'L.E. Fisher' sewn on the under-linen. It makes
one wonder if The Whitehall Torso, who was never identified
by name, was indeed L.E. Fischer, and the killer had kept
some of her clothes handy.

Although the Torso Killer used an entirely different MO
than Jack the Ripper, it is not altogether devoid of connection
to those ghastly crimes. The bruises corresponding to five
fingermarks are a telltale and horrid link. They must be the
killer's as he clutched into her while torturing her or dissecting her alive. (The Ripper clutched the jaws of two of his victims so strongly that he left bruises or abrasions just before
they died.) Like the Ripper, the Torso Killer also must have
had unusually good night vision. In the case of The Whitehall
Mystery the placing of the body remains in the basement of

Wharf at *Limehouse, Poplar, on the Thames.*

New Scotland Yard was a feat in itself. At the inquest, one of the men who found the body, Fred Wildborn, stressed that in order to see the parcel he had to strike a match repeatedly. He was asked plainly if it would be difficult to find this vault, and he said "Yes, to a stranger." George Bugden, another worker, testified: "I took a lamp down; without it I should not have been able to see anything. It was as dark as the darkest night." One of the investigators, Detective Thomas Hawkes, said of the vaults: "They were very dark, so dark that it was impossible for a stranger to reach them without artificial light."

In terms of ghoulish progression, there is another link. The Torso Murders were clearly taking things far beyond Mary Jane Kelly's murder. Mutilating a young woman alive can indeed be taken as the next step in the diabolical career of Jack the Ripper.

But the biggest problem with saying this was the work of the Ripper was that this Thames Mystery, as this one became known, suggested the latest in a long line of similar killings. The Whitehall Mystery torso itself was not the first. It matched dissected body parts found at Rainham west of London in 1887. This earlier murder indicates The Torso Killer was an entirely different culprit at large and he stuck to his original MO. Unless the Ripper alternated his style, it seemed as if a worse fiend was on the loose. Some torturing maniac was traveling far and wide around London and selecting "unfortunates" for his experiments.

This brings us back to the Rose Mylett case. Was she an intended victim? Whoever The Torso Killer was he must have trotted about in a coach. Did he pick up drunken harlots and take them to a secure lodging? Did she cause trouble and did he accidently kill her? Since he obviously worked on the women while they were alive, a dead one would have given no pleasure. He would have dumped her. The result: merely an unsolved prostitute murder. (Poplar was also about a mile from where she was last seen in Whitechapel.)

Since most of the body parts had been found outside of Wynne Baxter's jurisdiction, the primary inquest into the Thames Mystery was held in Battersea by the coroner for Mid-Surrey, Braxton Hicks. Dr. Thomas Bond testified that all medical men to have examined the remains agreed that the precision used was that of someone with skill, but it was not a doctor's skill. It was that of a butcher or horse knackerer. He also noted the similarity to the Whitehall and Rainham cases.

By June 26, the Central News Agency, the agency that had given the police the dubious letters that coined the moniker Jack the Ripper, made the connection, stating in part that "various circumstances connected with the fate of this victim had led to a belief that she was really a victim of the Whitechapel fiend, Jack the Ripper." It continued: "a nameless indignity inflicted upon the corpse, which it was then considered advisable to suppress in the published reports. That indignity was of a character instinctively to suggest the handiwork of the most brutal of murderers." This indignity was that the uterus, of course, had been removed (though not taken away) and operated on after death. Another indignity, a little harder to interpret, was that a piece of linen had been inserted into the "back passage" of the victim.

As time went by little was cleared up. Jackson's paramour and possible father of her child had been found in Devon and he was cleared from having had anything to do with her death. A man was seen with her at least 24 hours before her pieces began turning up in the Thames, but a solid description of him could not be given and he was never found.

The Press finally began to doubt that Jack the Ripper was involved. There was very good reason. Another murder happened in Whitechapel that was almost a carbon copy of the earlier murders in the autumn of terror. As Hicks was winding down his inquest, London and Whitechapel were agog with worries that the Ripper had truly struck again.

It was Tuesday, July 16, 1889. A rust colored, smoggy summer evening hung over Whitechapel. At 7:10 p.m. Alice McKenzie is seen before the Royal Cambridge Music Hall. Joviality resounds from the deep entranceway. The bright venues are obscured by people coming and going through the tall Victorian Gothic archways. She has escorted a young blind man here named George Dixon. Alice had a tenderness for the blind. When she had first come to London in 1874 she had shacked-up with a blind man who played a concertina in the streets to earn his bread. When George needed to be taken to the music hall to enjoy some East End entertainment, Alice was glad to escort him.

It also fit into her schedule. Both lived at Mr. Tenpenny's Lodging House on Gun Street, Spitalfields, and Alice wanted to go out on the town. She was a woman of a lot of energy. Hardy workers usually are. And that was indeed Alice. So when her current paramour, John McCormack, gave her the rent money and a shilling extra to spend, she was brisk to go out. . .yet foolishly without paying the rent first.

The night was still young when McKenzie walked Dixon to the music hall. The hubbub of mid-summer nights' crowds provided the opposite aura of danger. She puffed away on her "nose warmer"— her clay pipe. This habit of hers earned her the nickname "Clay Pipe Alice." She even smoked away while in bed at night. She was middle-aged, about 40 now, and set in her ways.

Amidst the hubbub before the theatre, as Alice was just about to part with Dixon, she eyed her game. He hears her talking to a man. She asks him for a drink. He says "Yes." Alice liked booze and her tobacco, not in that order. She would rather smoke than drink, but she had no aversion to the latter.

Alice was by profession a charwoman or washer woman. But she was usually in at nights, and her and John had a stable relationship. She had, however, no quam to augment her income in times of want and trouble with plying trade on the streets. She was probably as much a part-time prostitute as Eddowes had been. It was something done rarely and indicated something dire had come up.

After the show ended, Alice met with Dixon and escorted him back to Mr. Tenpenny's. At 8:30 p.m. the lodging house mistress, Elizabeth Ryder, sees Alice leave the house in such a manner she assumed that McCormack and her had had heated words. Did they? Or did Alice, upon returning, realize that she had foolishly spent the rent in having a good time? Whatever the case, she rushes off toward the mishmash of Whitechapel Road.

This chain of events is partly assumption on my part. She may indeed have forgotten to escort Dixon home and was now rushing back to the music hall to get him. Whichever is the case, her whereabouts are a mystery until 11:40 p.m. when she is seen rushing along the streets again. She is passing three friends at Flower and Dean and Brick Lane. She was always easy to spot, even from a distance. She never wore a bonnet, even on a night like this where the summer clouds swelled and churned overhead with a potential rainstorm. Tonight she only wore a light shawl draped over her shoulders to keep out the cool night. Margaret Franklin asks her how she is doing. To this Alice replies quickly: "All right. I can't stop now." She continues on quickly.

It is now 12:20 a.m. July 17. Just off Whitechapel High Street a small portal through the buildings leads to a narrow lane known as Castle Alley. It is a long, bleak corridor of dark shadows. There are only two lamps in it. The dim amber orbs cast a weak wash of warmth over the dark Victorian red brick walls. They become warmer shades of brown in the halo. But the rest of the alley is black. Its skyline is that of gabled brick cottages, the unadorned back of businesses, and tall stone chimneys' black pipes reaching up to the swimming dark clouds. Barrows and carts are parked along the walls and old wood fences. Some sport the faded painted signs of their owner's business. Some are chained together. Only foot traffic can pass. This is the archetypical setting of Whitechapel at night behind the whitewash of the main road. Working Whitechapel is tucked away here, chained up and in melancholy repose amidst the dustbins and rubbish. Darkness is animated only by the sounds of rummaging cats and the squeaking chirp of foraging rats.

It is in this quiet alley that Constable Joseph Allen now strolls. He had walked through the portal and ambled along the dark cobblestones, shining his light about the parked carts and hansoms. It is under the lamp by the bathhouse that he now decides to have his lunch. Two carriages are chained by the light for safety, a scavenger's wagon and a brewer's dray. Upon one of these he sits and unwraps his meal.

Soon Constable Walter Andrews passes him, giving him a tip of his finger to his helmet, as he continues toward the portal to Whitechapel Road. After about 5 minutes Allen finishes his meal and continues his soulful promenade through the lane to its other end, which after a sharp right turn becomes Old Castle Street. This narrow street then comes out on Wentworth Street.

It was now 12:30 a.m. The Three Crowns Pub at Wentworth and Old Castle is shutting down. The proprietor is fixing shutters on his windows. Allen nods as he passes. About 100 yards down Wentworth he passes Constable Walter Andrews coming back around on his routine beat (Whitechapel Road, then Commercial Street to Wentworth here). They spoke briefly, and Andrews continued on and walked back down Old Castle Street to Castle Alley, continuing his orbit of the streets. Allen continued on to Commercial Street.

The summer heavens remain full of bloated dark clouds. They move moodily over the chimneys and spires. They suck out the vibrant colors of signs and billboards painted onto the tall brick buildings. But the summer does not lend itself to gloom. It is but a dark, peaceful night.

At 12:45 a.m. a calm, steady rain begins.

At 12:50 a.m. Andrews is back around yet again at the entrance to Old Castle Street. On the opposite side by the

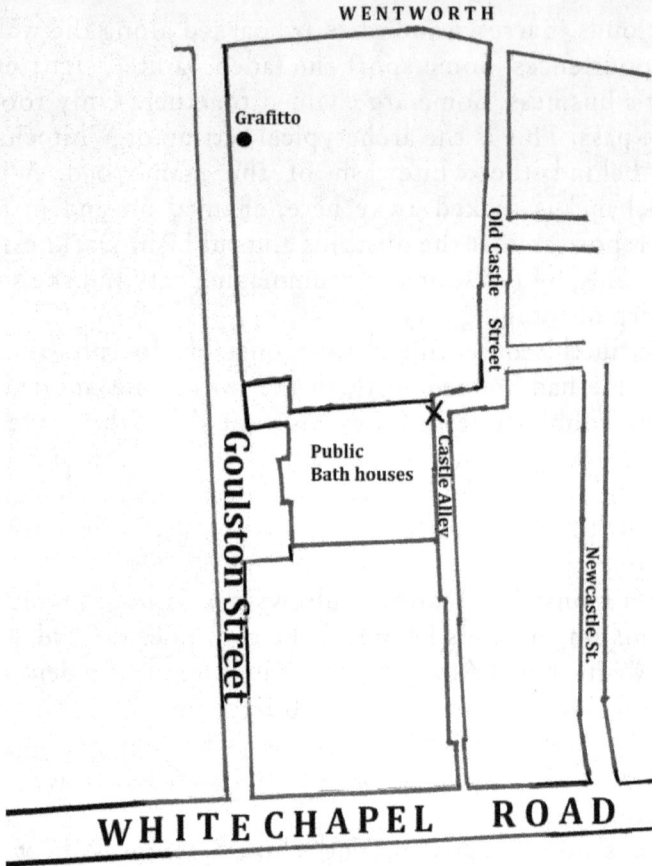

Castle Alley was right behind Goulston Street. It is along here that the Ripper had a hiding place September 30, 1888.

Three Crowns Pub is Sergeant Badham.

"All right?" asks Badham.

"All right, sergeant," responds Andrews perfunctorily.

Andrews continues walking down Old Castle Street and then turns into its little appendix of Castle Alley. His footsteps methodically clack along on the wet cobblestones. He keeps his bull's eye under his wet ulster. He begins checking the doors and windows of the back of the shops, and looking under the line of crammed hacks and barrows. Routine, routine.

At this time, Sarah Smith, the deputy of the Whitechapel Baths and Washhouses, is in bed reading under her gaslight.

She is upstairs and it is from her window that a solitary sliver of light streaks across the narrow lane to the old wood fence. She greeted the steady rainfall at 12:45 a.m. with a sigh. Now at 12:50 a.m. she is jolted from her bed by a police whistle below her in the alley.

The chain of events had happened quickly. Under the very lamp where Allen had sat to eat his lunch, Andrews now stood gaping over the body of Alice McKenzie. Her feet are angled toward the brick wall; her head toward the gutter, almost under the scavenger's wagon. The darkness was blinding. Despite the fact that her feet were touching the cone of light on the pavement, Andrews had to use his bull's eye to notice that her throat was cut. Blood oozed forth from a gash in the left side of her neck. Her dress is lifted and her bare lower abdomen is bloodied and mutilated. Andrews feels her stomach. It is still warm.

Then footsteps resound.

He dashes off. A young man with an empty plate in his hand, Lewis Jacobs, is walking in the alley.

"Where are you going?" Andrews barks.

Jacobs was on his way to skinflint McCarthy's on Dorset Street to get some dinner.

"Come with me," commanded Andrews. "There has been a murder committed."

Jacobs duly follows him back to the body. Andrews then starts blowing his whistle.

Only minutes later and sergeant Badham's shoes can be heard approaching. He is rushing up from Newcastle Street across from the alley. Andrews has stepped out and sees him. "Come on, quick!" he shouts. Badham throws his cape to the ground and runs up. Allen is soon there, too. Badham tells him to hop and get a doctor quick. Andrews was ordered to stay with the body. Badham started searching the area with another constable and local inspector who had also soon appeared. He is quickly on Commercial Street and comes across Constable George Neve. He orders him to search about. Neve actually does some of the dirtiest work. He goes down the dank narrow side passages that lead to the alley and looks over the tall wood hoardings to see if anybody is about.

All these constables are united in two things: none found a

trace and none had ever heard anything or seen anybody while going about their routine beats.

This no doubt unsettled Inspector Reid. His cab had come to a jerking stop at the Old Castle Street entrance to the alley at 1:09 a.m. The quick briefing played on behind him as he peered at an all-too familiar scene. He had barely had time to take it all in when Bagster Phillips' brougham arrived and he too rushed over. Blood was still oozing out of the left side of her neck, but now it was beginning to coagulate. The scene was, of course, dreadfully familiar to Phillips too. It was a horrifying sight for what it implied — Jack was back.

In addition to the crime scene appearance, the circumstances were remarkably similar to the Ripper murders. For one, the silence of the strike — even Sarah Smith who was reading overhead had heard nothing. The swiftness of the killer was also remarkable. Just from moving McKenzie's dress about it was easy to see that it was dry underneath. Andrews confirmed it began to rain at 12:45 a.m. Therefore she was killed sometime after he left the alley at 12:35 and before it rained at 12:45, another unbelievable narrow margin of 10 minutes. She had clearly been killed while lying down, her

Andrews discovering McKenzie's body. *Penny Illustrated*, 1889.

body placed in the way that the others had been so that the blood would flow away from the abdomen. There was no trail from the scene, no splashes of blood, no drops. The blood had not spurted from her neck, but it was oozing out and flowing underneath her head to the gutter.

Compared to the earlier victims, McKenzie's case is nearly identical with Nichols', both in staging and in appearance. Both Nichols and McKenzie had a 4 inch slice in their neck. In Nichols' case, this was in addition to the entire throat being cut. McKenzie only had another stab, as if the killer was getting ready to cut the throat all the way but didn't. Both Nichols' and McKenzie's lower abdomens were mutilated, though in McKenzie's case they were superficial compared.

McKenzie could not have been the victim of a random strike. She had no need to walk such an alley. She must have been with a customer. Her murder therefore must have been premeditated to take place between the methodical beats of bobbies. The killer, like the Ripper, had studied police beats and had strolled into the area with her without any sound or detection.

These circumstances were underscored by Inspector Reid during the inquest, led by the ever-vigilant and snooping Wynne Baxter. "There are people in High Street, Whitechapel, all night. Two constables are continually passing through the alley all night. It is hardly ever left alone for more than five minutes." The premeditated nature of selecting the location was also accentuated by Reid. "Although it is called an alley it is really a broad turning, with two narrow entrances. Any person standing at the Wentworth Street end would look upon it as a blind street. No stranger would think he could pass through it, and none but foot passengers can."

There's other disturbing evidence. When the body was lifted up into the ambulance, McKenzie's clay pipe fell out. It was broken. This would be explained by the great force the killer used when holding her down. Bagster Phillips noted that there were five marks on her abdomen; four on the left side and the fifth being on the right side, corresponding to the fingers and thumb of a hand. "The largest one was the lowest, and the smallest one was the exceptional one mentioned, and was typical of a finger-nail mark. They were coloured, and in my opinion were caused by the finger-nails and thumbnail of a hand. I have on a subsequent examination assured myself of the correctness of this conclusion." This would mean a powerful hand (left hand in this case), as in the other Ripper cases, held her bare abdomen with great force while she was still alive, which means her dress was already lifted. Yet there was no sound. He could not have held her mouth with a knife in his hand and one hand on her belly. How did she not call out?[6]

Phillips was certain that the killer had some anatomical knowledge. The wound started from the back of the neck muscle and cut the carotid artery and continued under the chin.

Despite some vagaries, there were still too many coincidences between McKenzie and with the earlier victims—age, habits, profession. In addition to all of the above, it was a rainy night. More often than not the Ripper struck on rainy nights. McKenzie was the worse for drink. Upon investigation, she was also found to have been a charwoman for Jewish families, like Stride and, on occasion, Eddowes.

This certainly did not go unnoticed. Anderson was gone from the capital yet again, and Monro investigated the crime personally. He was certain that Jack the Ripper was the culprit. If he had balked at the idea of the Ripper having gone to Poplar before, he had no qualms here in the bowels of Whitechapel again. "I need not say," he declared, "that every effort will be made by the police to discover the murderer, who, I am inclined to believe, is identical with the notorious Jack the Ripper of last year." He was good to his word. He deployed over 22 extra men in the area the next day.

Bagster Phillips was, strangely, very cautious in his opinion.

After careful and long deliberation, I cannot satisfy myself, on purely anatomical and professional grounds, that the perpetrator of all the 'Wh Ch. murders' is our man. I am on the con-

---

[6] A brass farthing was also found under her. In Annie Chapman's case, supposedly two farthings had been found. Some have speculated that the Ripper had in Chapman's case enticed her by passing off a polished farthing as a sovereign. Was that the case here too?

trary impelled to a contrary conclusion in this, noting the mode of procedure and the character of the mutilations and judging of motive in connection with the latter.

I do not here enter into the comparison of the cases neither do I take into account what I admit may be almost conclusive evidence in favour of the one man theory if all the surrounding circumstances and other evidence are considered, holding it as my duty to report on the P.M. appearances and express an opinion only on Professional grounds, based upon my own observation.

What our hitherto redoubtable Phillips is saying is that he is excluding comparative data that demands that this be considered the work of the Ripper. He is isolating the body from the others and cautiously saying that in doing so it removes the idea of Jack the Ripper from being the killer. Had he taken into "account what I admit may be almost conclusive evidence in favour of the one man theory" he would be compelled to come to the one man theory— in other words, Jack the Ripper.

Phillips' attitude is ponderous. I can appreciate his frustration. The extenuating circumstances all say Jack the Ripper, but the tangible evidence— the mutilations and the manner of slicing the carotid but not cutting the entire throat afterward— argue against it. He also explained to his own satisfaction what the motive for the mutilations must have been, the implication being that the killer was sexually motivated.

This is the one instance where Phillips agreed with Dr. Bond. . .and yet they still disagreed. Now that Monro was in charge, he wanted an analyst involved like Bond, a man used to treating government ministers and West End elite, a man who therefore knew how to be discreet. Unlike Phillips, Bond was certain the killer was the Ripper. "I see in this murder evidence of similar design to the former Whitechapel murders, viz. sudden onslaught on the prostrate woman, the throat skillfully and resolutely cut with subsequent mutilation, each mutilation indicating sexual thoughts and a desire to mutilate the abdomen and sexual organs. I am of opinion that the murder was performed by the same person who committed the former series of Whitechapel murders."

With Bond came his own trendy West End psychological ideas, and it may be the proliferation of these about the murder investigation that caused a humble but talented East End doctor like Phillips to feel outclassed and therewith to be cautious in his wording. Yet despite the professional disparity between Bond and Phillips, the latter had the edge — Chapman's postmortem had been in his province. It is her sleek dissection that impressed Phillips the killer had a ruthless ulterior goal. Phillips obviously didn't see this in McKenzie's killing. He, too, saw the "sexual maniac" profile Bond had built up. Ironically, for Phillips this negated Jack the Ripper as the suspect.

When it came time for the inquest, the disagreements, though not firmly imbedded in print from which the above quotations have been taken, must have been known to Wynne Baxter. He obviously intended a searching inquest. No murder since Kelly's had a better claim to have been done by the notorious Jack the Ripper than this one.

Baxter called the inquest the very day, July 17, 1889, at the Working Lads Institute. The scene was one of *déjà vu*. London was telescoped back to August 1888 when Tabram's inquest was called here. The 20 man jury sat under the same sterling motto of Micah. Baxter did his usual thing and drug out the inquest in installments for a month.

On August 14, 1889, he rendered his summation. It wasn't as long as the others. But it contained his plea to do something about the East End's poverty. He concluded, in part:

When the body was discovered there was no one about, and nothing suspicious had been seen. Had there been any noise, there were plenty of opportunities for it to have been heard. There is great similarity between this and the other class of cases which have happened in this neighbourhood, and if this crime has not been committed by the same person, it is clearly an imitation of the other cases. We have another similarity in the absence of motive. None of the evidence shows that the deceased was at enmity with any one. There is nothing to show why the woman is murdered or by whom.

I think you will agree with me that so far as the police are concerned every care was taken after the death to discover and capture the assailant. All the ability and discretion the police have shown in their investigations have been unavailing, as in the other cases.

The evidence tends to show that the deceased was attacked, laid on the ground and murdered. It is to be hoped that something will be done to prevent crimes of this sort and to make such crimes impossible. It must now be patent to the whole world that in Spitalfields there is a class of persons who, I think, cannot be found in such numbers, not only in any other part of this metropolis, but in any other metropolis; and the question arises, should this state of affairs continue to exist? I do not say it is for you to decide. The matter is one for a higher power than ourselves to suggest a remedy. But it certainly appears to me there are two ways in which the matter ought to be attacked.

In the first place, it ought to be attacked physically. Many of the houses in the neighbourhood are unfit for habitation. They want clearing away and fresh ones built. Those are physical alterations which, I maintain, require to be carried out there. Beyond this there is the moral question. Here we get a population of the same character, and not varied, as in a moderately-sized town or village. Here there is a population of 20,000 of the same character, not one of whom is capable of elevating the other. Of course there is an opinion among the police that it is a proper thing that this seething mass should be kept together rather than be distributed all over the metropolis.

Every effort ought to be made to elevate this class. I am constantly struck by the fact that all the efforts of charitable and religious bodies here are comparatively unavailing. It is true a great deal has been done of late years, especially to assist the moral development of the East End, but it is perfectly inadequate to meet the necessities of the case. If no other advantage comes from these mysterious murders, they will probably wake up the Church and others to the fact that it is the duty of every parish in the West to have a mission and localize work in the East End, otherwise it will be impossible to stop these awful cases of crime. Here is a parish of 21,000 persons with only one church in it. There are not only cases of murder here, but many of starvation. I hope at least these cases will open the eyes of those who are charitable to the necessity of doing their duty by trying to elevate the lower classes.

Baxter was profound yet again. But his inquests were losing their punch. How many cared anymore? The *East London Advertiser* captured the spirit that had fallen over the East End and indeed now over London and Britain. People simply weren't too interested anymore. "Painfully familiar have become the proceedings at the inquests held on the victims of the Whitechapel assassin. The same coroner presides at the table, the same number of jurymen occupy the same corner, the same police officials face them on the left, the same doctors appear with the same horrible details, the same coroner's officer acts as a lesser dignitary of the law, the same constable guards the door, and the same array of pressmen anxiously and attentively watch and listen to all that is going forward . . .It was a sharp contrast to glance out into the road, flooded with a bright sunlight and filled with the full tide of life, and then look back into the room, upon a body of men all earnestly engaged in considering the blackness of a horrible crime. In the room there was not a single individual but who had business there. At one time the public flocked to these inquiries, but now they are content to leave them in the hands of their faithful representatives, the reporters."

The most intriguing factor was gone now in these murders. People were no longer amazed and marveled at a new thing. The novelty had worn off. The murders were being accepted.

As it stood in autumn 1889 no one at the Met was sure what had become of Jack the Ripper. If McKenzie was not his victim, then he stopped after Mary Kelly for a reason.

If the dearth of victims in the span of time between Kelly's and McKenzie's murder had caused many Met detectives to have second thoughts that the Ripper, or any maniacal killer, would take months between strikes, an interesting thing now happened: The Torso Killer struck again that fall. He dumped a torso, dissected of head and legs, off at Pinchin Street in Whitechapel. This West End killer had moved to the East. It seemed irrefutable that the same killer as The Whitehall Mystery and The Thames Mystery, and possibly the much earlier Rainham Mystery, had struck again. It also seemed irrefutable that he was following the same undeniable pattern to cash-in on the mystery of a macabre and unfathomable setting.

The Pinchin Street case began at 5 a.m. on the morning of September 10, 1889. Constable William Pennet was patrolling his new beat. This required that he walk Pinchin Street about every 30 minutes. It was a typical police beat. It was also a quiet beat. This part of Whitechapel slept at night. It was not the center of vice. It was the southern, more industrial section nearer to the railroad tracks, Thames and docks. In fact, a good chunk of the south side of Pinchin was nothing but a massive brick concourse punctuated with tall, wide arched tunnels over which the railroad tracks were laid. Several of these tunnels led strait through to an open stretch of ground owned by the Whitechapel District Board of Works.

Fences closed off a couple of tunnels and appeared as teeth in grinning, sardonic mouths. But one was open. The palings were gone. Only the posts and crossbeams remained. Here they looked like jagged, rotted teeth in a dark yawning mouth. A number of the tunnels were used by bums as places to sleep. When he should find them there, Pennet had orders to chuck 'em.

Pennet was walking on the north side of the street. He crossed over and headed along the south by the archways. There was a lamppost about 9 feet from the open mouth of the archway. A foul smelled seized him. He looked over. The light daubed what looked like a bundle.

Holding his hand to his nose, he walked inside the tunnel. The bundle was not a bundle. It was actually a bloodstained, roughly folded and cut chemise. It lay over the neck and shoulders of a headless and legless body. Decomposition had begun, and it smelled horribly.

Pennet's alert eyes immediately realized the mystery inherent in the staging. A large amount of stone rubble was in the tunnel because the Works used the ground to split rock. As a result, there was a carpet of rock dust in the tunnel. Yet there were no footprints, and Pennet could tell that no coach had driven by. He was not certain if footprints, of a person walking carefully, would show. But the body certainly had not been thrown to this spot from the opening of the archway

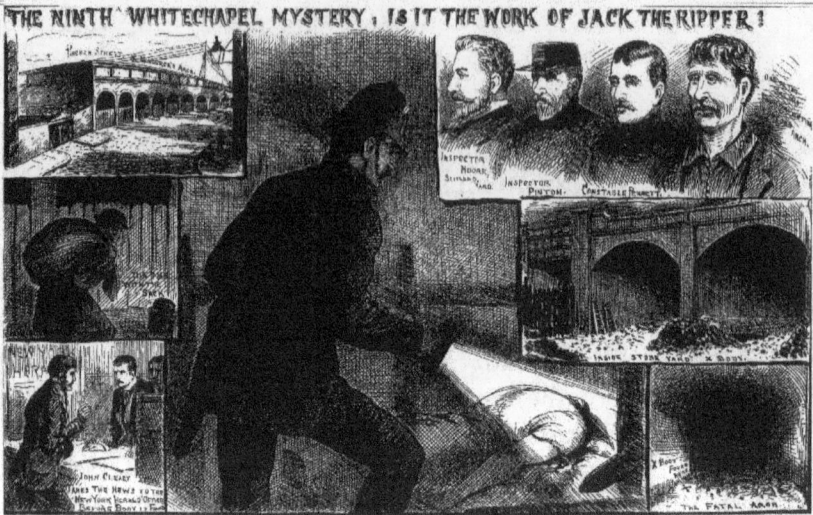

The circumstances, once again captured by British dailies.

(it was about 8 feet in), for there was no dust on the body. If the body had been thrown, it would have raised quite a cloud of dust, which would have settled on it afterward.

This macabre setting was augmented by how mysteriously the bundle had appeared. There was no way this was here last time he passed. He hadn't seen anybody and no coach had passed, and there was no way anybody could have walked along with a rotting corpse and not have attracted his attention.

Work was commencing about the city. Traps and barrows would soon be passing by. Others would soon be walking to work. Pennet didn't want to blow his whistle, so he waited a while until he heard footsteps. A man carrying a broom over his shoulder was going to work.

"You might go and fetch my mate at the corner," said Pennet to him.

"What's on, governor?" the chap replied.

"Tell him I have got a job on. Make haste."

The man bolted up Back Church Lane. Two constables were soon running up. Pennet dispatched one to get the local inspector, Inspector Pinhorn, who quickly arrived. He immediately ordered the bobbies to roust about and see what they could find.

Behind the fences in the adjacent tunnels they found 2

sailors (1 sleeping, the other smoking) and in the center arch a bootblack sleeping on the stones, smelling of liquor. None of the men had seen the bundle when they came to sleep. This was at 2 o'clock and at 4 o'clock respectively, although one admitted he was drunk and might not have recognized it. Due to the smell, however, it is unlikely that it was there until just before Pennet passed by.

Naturally, people passing by got curious, but Pinhorn quickly had the street blocked off and had it cleared of all loiterers. He also quickly gleaned information from all the constables in the area: *none* had seen any man walking with a bundle nor had they seen or heard a wagon trotting by.

Bagster Phillips was not available, so his assistant Mr. J. Clarke went down immediately. He arrived at a little before 6 a.m. He gave a vivid account at the inquest, which Baxter convened at Vestry Hall on Wednesday, September 11. On that day only Pennet and Pinhorn had been called to set the stage. In typical style, Baxter recessed and waited until the 24th of September to call the medical men. Clarke was a keenly observant and well-trained assistant and worthy protégé of the astute Bagster Phillips. According to his chilling account

Finding the torso. Penny Illustrated, September 1889.

the body was laying on its belly. The right arm was bent under the abdomen and the hand was stuck into a deep 15 inch long gash in the gut. There was no visible blood or sign of a struggle. He continues:

> On moving the body I found that there was a little blood underneath where the neck had lain. It was small in quantity and not clotted. The blood had oozed from the cut surface of the neck. Over the surface of the neck and the right shoulder were the remnants of what had been a chemise. It was of common length and such a size as would be worn by a woman of similar build to the trunk found. It had been torn down the front, and had been cut from the front of the armholes on each side. The cuts had apparently been made with a knife. The chemise was bloodstained nearly all over, from being wrapped over the back surface of the neck. There was no clotted blood on it. I could find no distinguishing mark on the chemise. Rigor mortis was not present. Decomposition was just commencing.
>
> The body was lifted, in my presence, on to the ambulance and taken to the St. George's mortuary by constables. On re-examining it there I found the body appeared to be that of a woman of stoutish build, dark complexion, about 5ft. 3in. in height, and between 30 and 40 years of age. I should think the body had been dead at least 24 hours.

Now being able to have the body under bright light, Clarke was able to see that the woman had been tortured before she died. "On the back there were four bruises, all caused before death. There was one over the spine, on a level with the lower part of the shoulder blade. It was about the size of a shilling. An inch lower down there was a similar bruise, about the middle of the back, also on the spine, and that was a bruise about the size of a half-a-crown. On the level of the top of the hip bone was a bruise 2 ½ inches in diameter. It was such a bruise as would be caused by a fall or a kick. None of the bruises were of old standing. Round the waist was a pale mark and indentation, such as would be caused by clothing during life. On the right arm there were eight distinct bruises and seven on the left, all of them caused before death and of recent date. The back of both forearms and hands were much bruised. On the outer side of the left forearm, about 3 inches above the wrist, was a cut about 2 inches in length, and half an inch lower down was another cut. These were caused after death. The bruises on the right arm were such as would be caused by the arms having been tightly grasped. The hands and nails were pallid. The hands did not exhibit any particular kind of work."

The bruises on the back of the hands and wrists suggest that this woman had been tied to bedposts or stocks, and in struggling to get out (or during torture) had repeatedly bashed her hands against them. The cuts on the left wrist after death could have been made when the killer cut the ropes that bound her. The arms had been tightly grasped by a fiercely strong hand. It would not be hard to remember that the remains of Elizabeth Jackson, the supposed Thames Mystery, had shown signs on the thighs that a powerful hand had clutched it in life and made fingermark bruises.

Bagster Phillips was next called to advance the medical report into greater details. He examined the body twice— first at 6 p.m. that day, and then the next day with Bond's assistant, Dr. Hebbert, and with the City police surgeon, Gordon Brown. It was, once again, a meeting of the doctors and their representatives most responsible for fathoming the Ripper's work. In describing the corpse, Phillips testified as to how neatly it had been dissected:

> . . .The neck had been severed by a clean incision commencing a little to the right side of the middle line of the neck behind, leaving a flap of skin at the end of the incision. It had severed the whole of the structures of the neck, dividing the cartilage of the neck in front, and separating the bone of the spine behind. The walls of the belly were divided from just below the cartilage of the ribs. The two small cuts appear on the forearm appear to me as likely to have been caused when the sweep of the knife divided the muscles covering the upper part of the thigh. Both thighs were excised by the extensive circular sweep of the knife, or some sharp instrument, penetrating the joint from below and separating the thighs from the hip joint, but the cartilages within the joint and those which deepen the joint and surround it had not been injured.

Bagster Phillips believed that death arose from loss of blood. "I believe the mutilation to have been subsequent to death, that the mutilations were effected by someone accustomed to cut up animals or to see them cut up, and that the incisions were effected by a strong knife 8 inches or more long."

"Is there anything to show where the loss of blood occurred?" asked Baxter.

"Not in the remains; but the supposition that presents itself to my mind is that there was a former incision of the neck, which had disappeared with the subsequent separation of the head."

"The draining of the blood from the body was such that it must have been a main artery that was severed?" asked Baxter for clarification.

"Undoubtedly," replied Phillips, "and was almost as thorough as it could be although not so great as I have seen in some cases of cut throats."

One juror asked pointedly if a butcher had done it.

"I cannot say whether the person who severed the head from the body was a butcher or not," said Phillips cautiously. "I merely wish to say it was a person accustomed either to see or use a knife, or some sharp instrument in cutting up animals. I have no reason for believing that he had human anatomical knowledge. In fact, it probably is known to you, and most people, that the spine is not the part to be disarticulated by a medical man."

Despite Phillips' opinion, there is much in the greater spree of The Torso Murders that argues against a mere butcher. It is evident that these women had been taken from the streets somewhere, probably peacefully. The person taking them must have had some kind of carriage, cart or brougham. They had to be taken some place where nobody would hear them. Certainly they were bound and gagged and tortured. (No wonder the heads were never found. The features of the mouth, after the gag had been removed, must have been distorted with agony.) This doesn't sound like the work of a common butcher. Given the necessity, a doctor could easily learn to separate the neck bones. Bagster Phillips may have been impressed by the neat work, but that doesn't mean a doctor didn't do it.

The room was silent in the wake of his testimony. Baxter finished his notes and had Banks, his ever-loyal assistant, call Inspector Moore, who was overall in charge of the investigation. He provided a plan of the whole area for Baxter, who loved to have a detailed plan of the premises where bodies were found. With this in hand it was indeed hard to make out how the killer could have so silently deposited the torso where it was found.

When it came to the chemise, he merely described it as 37 inches, plus the cuts, etc., and that was it. Sadly, the jury didn't pursue it. But the cuts follow a pattern. They confirm that the killer had the woman's hands tied to bedposts or stocks, her hands stretched back over her head. In order to pull the chemise off he would have to cut the sleeves in the precise way the chemise was cut — from armhole to neck — so he could pull it down. Her legs must have been tied to posts too. So he would have to cut or rip the chemise right down the front and then pull it out from under her. Can you imagine the victim wondering what is happening as the killer does this just before beginning his work?

The victim was clearly not on some padded mattress. The bruises along her back were where spine bones would hit hard material (such as a board) as she struggled. This trussed position would also facilitate handling the body when dissecting it.

Was this suspected by Baxter? It might have been. Interestingly, he now turned his attention to the audience and brought into play Mary Jane Kelly's case, the only known Ripper victim to be killed in a bed. "I should like to ask Dr. Phillips whether there is any similarity in the cutting off of the legs in this case and the one that was severed from the woman in Dorset Street?"

Thanks to that knave Macdonald we have very little information on how Mary Jane Kelly was killed and carved up in bed. But here Bagster Phillips gives an idea. "I have not noticed any sufficient similarity to convince me it was the person who committed both mutilations," Phillips replied, "but the division of the neck and attempt to disarticulate the bones of the spine are very similar to that which was effected in this case. The savagery shown by the mutilated remains in the Dorset Street case far exceeded that shown in this case. The mutilations in the Dorset Street case were most wanton, whereas in this case it strikes me that they were made for the purpose of disposing of the body. I wish to say that these are mere points that strike me without any comparative study of the other case, except those afforded by partial notes that I have with me. I think in this case there has been greater knowledge shown in regard to the construction of the parts composing the spine, and on the whole there has been a greater knowledge shown of how to separate a joint."

Unless Phillips is confusing his case, with this bit of belated information we learn that there was an attempt to take off Mary Jane Kelly's head.

There is so much that is overlooked in the Pinchin Street Case. Was the body indeed cut up to dispose of it? That's rather one dimensional thinking on the otherwise astute Bagster Phillips' part. I don't think he was as interested in these cases as much anymore, just as London was now yawning at another "Whitechapel horror." Mystery murders were getting old. When papers had declared that Jack the Ripper was responsible there was little reaction compared to a year ago.

Cutting up the body might facilitate disposing of it, but why go to the trouble of piecing it out over the city? The torso was meant to be found. It was meant to be found in mysterious circumstances. It was meant to pop out of nowhere with no tracks around it. If the killer wanted to get rid of it, why not just trot it out in the dead of night and kick it off a wagon and let it plop onto a dark road where it may? He is rid of it, after all. No trace. But no real mystery to baffle and terrify London either.

Pinhorn thought that anybody familiar with the area would not have dumped the body there because they would have known that those tunnels were often used at night by vagrants. But why should we agree? The leaving of the torso doesn't seem like a spontaneous affair. Nobody puts a stinking fraction of a gutted corpse in their carriage and trots it around aimlessly. They have a plan to get rid of it. The killer must have known the area. Seeing the coast clear, he deposited it there.

This now leaves us with more mystery. No coach was heard or observed. No person could have walked with it and not have been stopped. They would also have to walk back after dumping it with the very sack bundled under their arm. It would be reeking. No, this seemed like the job of a man in some sort of wagon or carriage. It seemed like a preconceived idea. It was executed well. He quietly came and went, and there was no trace. Like the Ripper, he knew the beats of the constables in the area. He squeezed between each one, a clockwork in crimson.

After the Pinchin Street torso affair, nothing much happened in London. In fact, nothing macabre, unusual or above and beyond the norm of crimes of the times happened. Neither Jack the Ripper nor The Torso Killer struck in all of 1890. Indeed, if we eliminate McKenzie from the list of the Ripper's victims, Mary Jane Kelly was his last known victim. He thus only terrorized for one brief autumn.

In contrast, the last killing in Whitechapel did not inspire even a tenth of the interest that Tabram's brutal murder had. Ironically, though, owing to the long hiatus between murders, it inspired far more than McKenzie's.

🏮

It was a bleak early morning, Friday February 13, 1891. Eeriness always accompanies locations of former habitation. Abandonment lends the feeling of trespassing on interrupted life and forsaken dreams. Vacant homes and rickety fences intermixed with blocks of brick cottages and quiet corner stores. The Tower of London was a black cut-away silhouette before the spired skyline of London. Cringing before it was a brick jungle of Victorian gables, tall chimneys and old Georgian brick warehouses chiseled by age from Fezziwig's time, now dilapidated buildings worthy of Fagan and his gang. It was a Dickensian world of old rooks leaning arthritically on long support beams. The wharfs reminded one they were nearby. Old tar and brine wafted from the ancient moorings where ships lounged on the indolent Thames.

The railroad yards were the newest architecture in the area. London had been rudely bisected in the industrial age by the iron horse of progress. In some areas, as off Pinchin Street, huge artificial hills were made for the trains to travel two stories over the city. Such was also the scene here off Chamber Street. Early Victorian buildings, some with Gothic facades, scowled on these ugly utilitarian brick bulwarks and old wood watch tower. In this section of the street three wide and tall arched tunnels ran underneath the artificial hill, connecting Whitechapel with St. George in the East, the area by the Thames.

One passage was known as Swallow Gardens, an apt name no doubt derived from all the swallows' nests clinging to the tall archway and long tunnel. The tunnel was about 40 yards long. Half was cut off by a tall wood fence that ran its entire length. There was room only for a cart at a time. One cottony orb stood at the entrance of Swallow Gardens on Chamber Street, and the other on Royal Mint. Together they cast a dim witching haze to the center of the deep tunnel.

Silence came as a tide. By 2:15 a.m. this area of London was like a tomb. It was a Poe landscape. The hubbub of daytime work— the cutting of rocks, the chiseling of tombstones, the forging of railroad steel— ebbed to the silence of a whisking leaf tumbling in the black trickle that was the gutter. Only the sound of the railroad workers was heard intermittently as they led their horses to stable. Hoofs echoed in the dark tunnel and then took on a crisp tone when emerging. In an area as silent and dark as this, one heard more than they saw. They judged by sounds more than by sight.

One sound was heard at this minute— footsteps casually receding away into the darkness.

Constable Ernest Thompson listened to them carefully. The steps were headed to Mansell Street. They faded away as he continued to walk his beat on Chamber Street. His shoes tapped along methodically. He walked along the archways of the railroad. He now turned down Swallow Gardens to walk through to Royal Mint Street. He stopped suddenly. In the center of the tunnel there was a lump— a body! He hurried. The light of his bull's eye danced about; his footsteps echoed back and forth. He concentrated the light on the spot. There in the bright halo it cast was a woman. Her throat was deeply cut and blood, glowing within the light, was flowing profusely from it. He now stood over her, gaping. Shocking but true, she opened one eye, then it shut. She was alive. He blew his whistle three times.

Within only minutes two other policemen came rushing from the Royal Mint side. One was Frederick Hart and the other George Elliot. After gaping at the scene, Hart immediately went for the local sawbones, Dr. John Oxley.

Soon the echoing clip clop of horse hoofs resounded through this hollow vault. More railway men were passing through, walking their horses. That was the note of mystery. One of their mates had just walked his horse through and there was no one here. How had all this happened so silently within seconds?

The details don't need to be repeated for the umpteenth time. But as with all the cases before, all here gathered gazed and were amazed. Hart had only been 250 yards from the tunnel when he heard Thompson's whistle. George Elliot basically could say the same. He was in plainclothes on Royal Mint Street and was never far from the tunnel, being stationed outside Baron Rothschild's refinery. He saw lots of people pass through the tunnel until 12:30 a.m., but after that he recollects seeing no one.

Taken together what this means is that the footsteps that Thompson heard must have been the killer's. Thompson passed through the tunnel every 15 to 20 minutes, so this suggests the killer knew the beats and knew the other bobbies were out the other end on Royal Mint. When asked by Wynne Baxter at the inquest "If there had been any cry for help from the archway would you have heard it?" Elliot replied: "I must have heard it; it was so quiet."

Elliot confirmed that due to the lights at both ends of the tunnel, the center of the tunnel is lighter at night than the day. Nevertheless, we know that the killer waited to get to the dimmest spot. This doesn't sound like a spontaneous attack, but one that took into account the police beats and knew their relative positions for 2:15 a.m., and the tunnel's darkest point.

In this pattern this Swallow Garden victim's murder was reminiscent of Jack the Ripper's careful, minute planning. In execution it is even more similar to the nearby Berner Street killing of Elizabeth Stride at Dutfield's Yard. This victim's death, too, was a slow death, like Stride's must have been. This victim was also found more to her left side, similar to Stride's death position. A dull knife was used here too, as in Stride's case.[7]

Bagster Phillips probably had forgotten the details of Stride's murder by this time. Therefore, although the same contradictory evidence exists here— dull knife, no mutilations, but skillful entrapment—he expressed his doubt the Ripper was involved. He was dutiful enough, however, to point out all the evidence at the autopsy, which he and Oxley jointly conducted the next day.

The knife had been passed over the throat "one from left to right, one from right to left, and the third from left to right"— very reminiscent of a butcher's style of cutting the neck. In Chapman's case, the Ripper's knife was sharp enough that he did not need to bring the knife back all the way on the second pass. In this case, however, the knife was too dull to even cut down to the vertebrae. It slit the windpipe twice but did not sever it. Its dullness is also seen in there was also an inch of skin at the beginning of the wound that was cut but not severed through to the tissue underneath. These dissimilarities were key in separating the case from the Ripper's hand.

But there were also a number of disturbing similarities. The greatest was in the strong hand that must have been involved. He noted the marks left by fingernails. "Below the wound there was an abrasion, as if caused by a finger nail. Above the wound there were four abrasions, possibly caused by finger nails. From the position of these marks I opine that the left hand was used. There were some contused wounds on the back of the head, which I am of opinion were caused by the head coming into violent contact with paving stones."

---

[7] Inspector James Flannagan searched about inside the tunnel and "behind an iron pipe I found a piece of newspaper in which were wrapped two separate shillings. I have no doubt that it had been purposely hidden there." Some sources erroneously say it was earrings and that they were found behind a gutter pipe at the end of the tunnel. Flannagan does not say if the pipe was prone or not. It may have nothing to do with the gutter but was extra pipe. From his wording, both shillings appear to have been individually wrapped. They probably had nothing to do with the murder.

The location of the abrasions explains the silence. The killer must have clutched her throat in a very strong hand and pushed her head back against the cement during the struggling. Obviously, the killer could not have run the knife along her throat with his hand in the way. After she was insensible, he shifted his fingers over her mouth, clutched tightly and pulled out his knife. A very strong hand was indeed involved.

Phillips supported the theory that the attack happened just before Thompson arrived. "I came to the conclusion that death had been almost instantaneous, occasioned by the severance of the carotid arteries and other vessels on the left side. In my opinion, the deceased was on the ground when her throat was cut. I think that her assailant used his right hand in making the incisions in the throat, and that he had used his left hand to hold her head back by the chin; that he was on the right side of the body when he made the cuts. The tilting of the body to the left was to prevent the perpetrator from being stained with blood. There was a complete absence of any struggle or even any movement from pain, but it may have arisen from the fact that the woman was insensible from concussion."

This was obviously a very premeditated attack, and the staging was too suggestive of Jack the Ripper to go unnoticed in the newspapers. The *East London Advertiser* declared (February 14 edition): ". . .the circumstances of the crime, the character of the victim, and the mysterious features by which the deed is environed, undoubtedly place it in the same category. The time chosen by the murderer, the locality, and the precautions taken to escape detection are in all respects similar to those followed on previous occasions." The *East London Observer*: "An impression prevails that she is the victim of the so-called 'Ripper,' who made Whitechapel a terror two years ago." The *Eastern Post and City Chronicle* headlines read: "THE RIPPER AGAIN. ANOTHER HORRIBLE TRAGEDY IN WHITECHAPEL."

The hiatus of killings throughout 1890 made this killing a little more interesting to London. Amidst this renewed hype, Wynne Baxter summoned a jury to begin the inquest on Saturday evening. He already had 11 inquests that day and didn't intend to do anything but establish the scene of the crime and the general chain of events of discovering the victim, so far only known as "Carrotty Nell."

The extent to which Whitechapel thought that Jack the Ripper had struck again, and that this might lead to another gruesome spree, can be found in the sad controversy which opened the inquest. When all the jurors that had been selected were not present, substitutes were sought. Albert Bachert, he who had reported the strange man with the black bag the night of the Double Event so long before, now stood up and offered himself as a viable substitute for Mr. Fielder, who had not come as expected. Baxter refused him.

"Why?" asked Bachert

"Because I decline," said Baxter.

Bachert became adamant. "You decline simply because I happen to be Chairman of the Vigilance Committee, and you think I shall fully investigate this matter. I have a right to be on the jury."

"I have decided you are not to serve on this jury," Baxter replied coolly.

"Yes," retorted Bachert, "because you know I shall inquire into the case."

"You have already been told I shall decline to accept you," officiously dismissed Baxter.

Bachert walked away to take his seat in the back of the room. "You will hear more of this," he grumbled.

Baxter shook his head and instructed the jury to be shown the body. While they were gone, the room was silent. . .

It was an odd thing for Bachert to say that to Baxter. If any coroner had been thought (and even accused) to have overstepped his authority to bring out too much at an inquest it was Baxter.

But much had changed in over two years since the fiasco over Kelly's inquest and the autumn of terror. This applied to the Vigilance Committee as well. By this time the Vigilance Committee was really nothing anymore, if it really even was an actual entity. Lusk was long gone and was in deep financial trouble. In only two months his name would appear on the bankruptcy lists. His business of using his wife's money to refurbish theatres hadn't panned out. The hiatus of killings, and the disagreement between everybody concerning the other ones (such as McKenzie's) made it a 2 year dearth of universally accepted Jack the Ripper activity. The purpose and authority behind the Vigilance Committee had faded commensurately. Indeed, when the Press reported the set-to between Baxter and Bachert they introduced Bachert as Chairman of the "so-called" Vigilance Committee.

After the jury returned, Bachert pursued it again. He spoke up. "It was only after you heard who I was that you would not allow me to serve on the jury," he complained.

Baxter essentially ignored him after: "If you do not keep quiet I will have you ejected from the room."

One wonders what caused Bachert to take such an attitude. Was he merely the fag end of a once respected committee? Or were there rumors of a cover-up? Knowing Baxter, that is hard to believe. Details would have assuaged the tensions, but Baxter would not be forthcoming with such as Bachert's ilk. Instead he compounded the worries of cover-up by not calling Phillips this day. In order to secure the jury's approval, he had promised to take his evidence "on the next occasion." Yet to compound matters again, he did not.

Rather, an astounding turn of events happened. The police finally thought they had the man, and that he might even be Jack the Ripper. It wasn't like before where many dotty suspects had been arrested. The police really thought they had their man dead to rights.

When Baxter reconvened the inquest on Tuesday the 17th, he knew this for certain. He didn't intend to shrink back. He announced, as the *Times* reported: "The coroner, in opening the proceedings, said that, in view of the turn events had taken, and considering the fact that a man was in custody charged with the crime, their inquiry would have to take a much larger range than he had at first deemed necessary." Baxter declared that the "interests of justice" compelled him to not only trace the movements of the victim, but those of the accused as well. It was indeed Baxter at his finest. Now more than ever he had a chance to turn this into a trial.

A sailor, James Sadler, had been arrested. Attention had been drawn to him when he supposedly sold a dull knife to a man in order to get money. He had a lousy story to tell. He was flat broke, had been robbed thrice that night and was beaten from several dock fights. . .but unfortunately for him the only known fact was that he was the last person identified with "Nell."

The road of Carrotty Nell to her ignominious and brutal fate is a familiar one. Her actual name was Frances Coles. She was at the time of her death only 31 years old. Her father had been a respectable boot maker. When young he had moved his family to the Bermondsey Leather District. By 21, Frances had a job in a wholesale chemist shop in the Minories, sealing the bottles properly with gauze and their stoppers. Since the chemist was a wholesaler who shipped all over London and probably Britain, this was a fulltime job. It soon got to Frances' knuckles, which were covered with hard skin due to the labeling process.

After quitting the chemist job things apparently had not gone well for her. She was beginning to drink. By 1891 it seems she had prostituted herself for some 8 years. When on Boxing Day 1890 she visited her sister, Mary Ann, she still concealed her actual level of poverty. She said she was still working at the chemist. She also said she was living on Richard Street with a widow. Mary Ann, however, noticed how poor she was. She could also smell the alcohol. Frances asked for some food and drink. Before she left, Mary Ann gave her a dress.

Frances also continued to put on quite a good appearance with her father. Now quite old, he was a permanent inmate of the Bermondsey Working House. Every Sunday she would go to church with him. She still maintained she lived at her old place, but she finally confessed she had quit her job.

All these years her father, James, had never suspected anything. At the inquest he couldn't even remember her actual age. Wynne Baxter graciously informed him that the "Common Lodginghouse Mission had written to him offering to bury his daughter and defray all expenses." James Coles was only too happy to accept.

It was a sad snapshot of poverty. Yet though many were poor, not all turned to the illegal vices. Frances may have turned to prostitution out of desperation, but having plied it for eight years is quite a long time. It is probably better to assume that drink was getting the best of her and she couldn't get or hold down a job.

This is made evident on February 11. Her path crossed with a former client, that boisterous seaman James Sadler. He was discharged from the *Fez*, with money to burn, and met up with her, probably by accident, at the Princess Alice Pub. After a few down the gullet, they decided to make a go together. They slept together at Spitalfields Chambers lodging house that night, and the next day made the rounds of the gay pubs, boozing away.

The young Frances Coles was quite a catch for him. He was by the standard of the times an old geezer. He was about 53, with a gray beard groomed to a point. Everything about him was that of a man who spent his life on a deck. Now on shore, he lived it up. Frances played along. At 7:30 p.m. that evening, Thursday the 12th, she went into Hawkes milliner's shop in Bethnal Green. Sadler remained outside and looks in the window a bit while she shops. She falls in love with a black crape hat. It was almost two shillings! She goes outside with Sadler, and after a bit she returns and buys it. According to Peter Hawkes she was "three sheets to the wind."

She returns to the lodging house at 11:30 p.m., still drunk. She sits in the kitchen and passes out at the table, with her head resting on her outstretched arms. Samuel Harris, another lodger, sees James Sadler come in, also stinko, look around and join her. He is bloodied. He had encountered hooligans, he says to her.

"I have been robbed, and if I knew who had done it I would do for them!" She sluggishly raises her head. He asks if she has the doss money. She says "No."

Sadler walks over to Harris. He thinks he is the lodging house deputy. He asks him if he could be allowed to sleep there tonight. He showed him a certificate of money due him worth 4 pounds. Harris tells him he only lodges there himself. Close by is Charles Gyver, the watchman. Sadler explains he was robbed of 3 shillings 6 ducats. He insists that he gave Frances a shilling for the beds. There is nothing they can do. She hadn't paid. But Harris helps him get washed up in the yard. He came back into the kitchen and remained there with Frances and Harris until 12:30 a.m. Then he started to cause a drunken row with the other lodgers in the kitchen, so Gyver had no choice but to oust him.

Moments later Frances gathers her wherewithal, tucks her new hat under her arm, and follows him. She obviously didn't have any money for her own doss. But she apparently didn't stick with him. She is next seen at 1:30 a.m. in Shuttleworth's eating house, where she buys 3 halfpenny's worth of mutton and bread. Instead of taking it elsewhere she eats it there, in the corner. This irks Joseph Haswell, one of the employees, who tells her three times to hop it.

"Mind your own business!" she snaps back finally.

At 1:45 a.m. she finally leaves and heads toward Brick Lane, stopping along Commercial Street. She is in the heart, of course, of Whitechapel's area of vice and the former stomping ground of the faded wraith, Jack the Ripper.

Here on Commercial Street she loiters a bit with Ellen Callana, another prostitute. They haven't parted long when an aggressive man "in a cheesecutter hat" solicits Callana. She tells him to pip-off and he punches her in the face. He now solicits Coles. Either she is too desperate or still too hung-over to care. She walks off with him down Commercial Street to the Minories, far from the center of vice.

The next time she would be seen would be in the dim center of the long Swallow Gardens tunnel, bleeding to death. Her crape hat was laying by her side; the other tucked in her dress.

As for Sadler's movements, he returned to the lodging house at 3 a.m. Gyver was sweeping it. Sadler came in the door. He asked to be allowed in the kitchen. His clothes were dirty as if he had been rolling on the ground again. Blood was running down his face. He said he was faint.

"I have no power," replied Gyver. "You must ask the deputy."

"I have been knocked about and robbed in the Highway," he declared.

"What, have you been at it again?" cried Gyver. "I thought you were robbed of three shillings six ducats in Thrawl Street, and that was all you had."

"Well, they thought I had some money about me, but I had none."

At that moment the deputy of the lodging house, Mrs. Sarah Fleming, just a stone short of a Hereford, slid open the office window and asked what the brouhaha was about.

Sadler asked her if she had seen Frances. She said no. "Let me go into the kitchen," pled Sadler. "I feel so faint."

Fleming growled no and slid shut the window. Sadler begged Gyver again. Gyver said he could not. He told him to go to the London Hospital. Gyver thought it was all said and done. He went into the kitchen to do some work. Yet not long after this, Mrs. Fleming called him to come give Sadler the chuck. When he approached him, Sadler left peacefully. The time was 3:30 a.m.

Sadler was next seen at a coffee house at 19 Whitechapel Road at 4:05 a.m. The manager, Joe Richards, noticed how banged up Sadler was. He had a cut over his right eye, a cut on the right side of his head, blood on his left cheek. His left hand had a cut and both his hands had dried blood on them. Sadler wanted a cup of coffee, but he had no money. He repeated here too that he had been robbed. He showed Richards a note for wages totaling 4 pounds. That didn't work. He had some tobacco. He wanted Richards to buy it. Richards threw him out.

Next he was treated by the night porter at the London Hospital, William Fewell. It was 4:45 a.m. "He had a small scalp wound on the right side of the head and another over the right eye. His face was covered with blood. I trimmed his hair from the wound and washed his face. I then noticed that his hands were cut on the back, front, and between the fingers. They were covered with blood and I allowed him to wash them. I asked him how it happened."

"I have been with a woman," he replied. "She is a very decent woman, but she did me."

Fewell asked him how much she had pinched from him. Sadler said seven or eight shillings and his watch. "He was trembling very much, but said it was only from cold. I asked him where it had happened, and he said, 'In a little street off the highway, at the bottom of Leman Street' [which is near Swallow Gardens]. After his wounds were dressed he sat on the sofa for a short time and then went away."

Sadler is next supposedly seen at the Sailor's Home.

Thomas Johnson, from the *Mandolar*, was standing by the fire with his friend Duncan Campbell. It was 10:30 a.m. A man left the building around this time. Johnson didn't pay much attention, but he noticed that he had a mark on his left cheek. He was wearing a hat with a shiny peak and possibly a striped coat. It was then that Campbell told Johnson that he had bought a knife from him for a shilling.

After the murder was announced it wasn't long before Ellen Callana went to the police and told them of her last encounter with Frances and the aggressive sailor. Johnson turned up and told his story. So did Samuel Harris.

It is no wonder that Sadler was arrested that Saturday evening. Everything pointed to a sailor, and it seems that Sadler, amazingly, had had three or more brawls that day. Many witnesses were brought forward to identify him, and apparently either Joseph Hyam Levy or Joseph Lawende was also brought to see if Sadler was the "sailor" they saw at Church Passage 2 years before with Catherine Eddowes.

On Sunday evening at 11:45 p.m. Inspector Henry Moore told Sadler clearly that he was preferring charges "of willfully causing the death of Frances Coles, at Swallow Gardens, Whitechapel, on the morning of the 13th instant."

Sadler was facetious. In an undertone, he replied: "Yes, yes."

Moore didn't care for it. He told him to "pay attention while the charge was being read."

"I don't see the reason; I know the charge, and I suppose I shall have to go through the routine."

Moore was searching him.

"The old man [Campbell] has made a mistake about the knife," said Sadler. "He never saw me before."

Moore found him to be quite healed financially. He found "a purse, £2 17s. 4d., 36 seamen's discharges, a wages account, and eight lottery tickets, a quantity of loose tobacco, and a postal order for £2."

Moore ordered the men to escort him off to his cell.

"Make it as light as you can, gentlemen," said Sadler winsomely.

Baxter was going to ferret this all out and put it together. Because there was a man in custody, Mr. Charles Mathews appeared on behalf for the Public Prosecutor. It was perhaps a wise choice on the Met's part. Baxter was going to conduct this as a trial anyway despite the fact the police had an actual suspect to investigate on their own. With Sadler in custody, the police, if he was indicted, would naturally have to set him to a real trial. So it was wise that they wanted to be kept abreast of what the snoopy Baxter was finding out.

Despite the large amount of news coverage, Charles Mathews presented a poor appearance, even obstructionary at times. He began to hog the lime, and asked more questions than Baxter did. On one instant he even tangled with Baxter. It had to deal with a witness' recollection of time. Mrs. Ann Shuttleworth said that Frances Coles and a man looking like a sailor ate together about 5:20 p.m. that Thursday evening. She described Sadler and then said they left around 5:45 p.m. Then William Steer, barman at the Bell on Middlesex Street, said Frances Coles came in with a sailor at 4:30 p.m. and stayed with him until 5:30 p.m. He described Sadler perfectly.

Baxter said: "There is a great discrepancy in the time of this witness and the last."

Mathews amazingly said: "You cannot expect the times to be exact. It is quite near enough for our purpose. If we are to go so minutely into the times, there is no end to the inquiry."

"Oh, no," replied Baxter. "I only wish to have the times exact."

Then several of the jurors spoke up and agreed. Mathews had to back off.

True, none of the times were actually relevant to the time of death around 2:15 a.m. Friday morning; but Baxter was going to assert himself. Mathews was already growing irked no doubt by the 20th February when that exchange took place. Baxter was dragging it out to prove or not prove Sadler guilty.

Such a prolongation was in Sadler's interest. On the 20th it was clear that the Sailor's Union would represent him. Mr. Lawless (great name for a lawyer), of Messrs. Wilson & Wallis, was now present and watching over Sadler's interest in the inquest. He started asking questions as well. He was, indeed, giving a good account of himself. Baxter continued to butt out because he was in essence a judge monitoring the match between a prosecutor and a defense attorney.

It was fortunate that Baxter was an immovable coroner in his ways. On this very day he would essentially clear Sadler of the crime. He called a number of police officers and dock workers who testified beyond doubt where Sadler was at the time of the crime.

Sadler had, in fact, tried to tumultuously go back aboard the *Fez* to sleep. Dock Constable Henry Sutton explained that Sadler had come to the gate and said he wanted aboard. Sutton let him in but then realized he was drunk, dirty and scratched up. Sadler said he had gotten in a row in Brick Lane. "I turned him out of the dock as I did not think he was in a fit state to be allowed to go to his ship." Dock Constable Fredrick Session explained that later the gate keeper called his attention to a sailor outside the gate. Session was checking laborers being let go for the night. Session told him to scat. Sadler was so drunk that one of the men offered to pay his lodging for the night.

"I don't want your money, you dock rats," Sadler grumbled in a drunken stupor.

After this he supposedly swung at them. They then went to work on him. One of them, John Dooley, cleaned it up at the inquest. "I was at the entrance to the London Docks with a friend, when a man who was very drunk began to abuse us and struck at my mate, who got out of the way. I struck the man in the side with my fist, and he fell down, striking his head against the dock gate. We walked away and left the man on the ground."

Police constables came across Sadler shortly thereafter. Constable Edwards testified: "On the early morning of Friday week I was on duty on the Mint pavement. Shortly before 2 o'clock a man, whom I have since identified as Sadler, came up to me and said he had been assaulted by some men at the dock gates. I walked with him about 30 yards in the direction of the Minories, and when opposite Lockhart's Coffee Rooms I examined his ribs, but could not say they were broken. I parted from him soon after the clock struck 2, and it would take him about three minutes to walk from there to the scene of the murder. It was not more than two or three minutes past 2."

Police Constable Bogan saw him before his skirmish and after. He saw him first at 1:15 a.m. He was lying in the gateway to the docks, drunk. He had a cut over his left eye already. Bogan took him by the scruff of the neck and pulled him up. The gate keeper explained it all to Bogan.

Sadler took off his hat and a paper fell out. Bogan picked it up for him.

"That is my account of wages— four pounds sixteen," slobbered Sadler.

Bogan told him to hop it.

"I'll be locked up first."

Bogan gave him a chance to walk away. He did a bit, but as Bogan continued on his beat Sadler still remained close to the gate.

Bogan next saw him around 2 a.m. He had a bloodier face and his hand was on his hip.

Baxter lit up. "This is very important," he said. "Can you be sure about the time?"

"Yes, the Tower clock had just struck 2."

Even Mathews licked his chops. "Were you in the company of Sergeant Edwards," he asked, "and did you notice any further injuries?"

Bogan explained that Sadler now said he had been whooped by men down at the London Docks. He had been kicked in the ribs.

Bogan left him with Sergeant Edwards, who then walked away with him. Bogan was certain it was around 2:12 a.m.

The simple truth is that Sadler in that condition, though close to Swallow Gardens, could not have made it in a few minutes time. He could not have gotten to the spot, which required first meeting Coles at the lucky moment she was alone, walking her there silently, and then in a very premeditated way killing her.

In fact, the inquest ended on mystery. On the 27th of February, the last day, Baxter called Jumbo Friday, a witness who had seen a couple nearby to the tunnel and was sure the woman must have been Stride. She had a crape hat. The couple couldn't have been his friends and neighbors, Kate McKarthy and her beau Thomas Fowles. After him, Baxter called McKarthy and Fowles. It was indeed them. They remembered seeing Jumbo. Solomon Guttridge, a shunter on the railway, had testified that that very morning at 2:12 a.m. he went down the tunnel with his horse from the Chamber Street side. Three minutes later another shunter confirmed he had been down the tunnel. (No direction is given.) No one was there.

Coles and her killer seem to have been remarkably ghostly. It was like all the other killings. One minute the body wasn't there. The next it was. No witnesses. No sound.

Baxter's summation was to the point. "The case, he said, had many characteristics in common with the murders which had preceded it; but it was for the jury to decide, taking well into consideration Sadler's drunken condition, the conflicting evidence as to times and the connected account given by him of his movements before and after the murder was committed, whether they could fairly charge him with the deed, or must attribute it to some person or persons unknown."

The jury returned a verdict of "willful murder against person or persons unknown."

On March 3, Sadler was brought before the Thames Police Court. He was placed in the dock. Mathews rose and addressed the judge. "Having had the advantage of a consultation with the learned Attorney-General, who has carefully considered the evidence given in the course of the inquiry before the coroner, as well as the most able summing up to the jury impanelled before him, and having regard to the verdict returned by that jury, after a patient and exhaustive inquiry, I do not propose, on the materials at present in our possession, to proceed further with this prosecution, and, Sir, if it should meet with your approval, it will have the sanction both of the learned Attorney-General and of the Treasury authorities, that no further evidence should now be offered against the accused."

"I need hardly say," said Mr. Lawless upon rising, "on behalf of the prisoner, that I have no objection to that course."

The learned Mr. Justice Mead declared: "Of course, I acquiesce in that course being taken. You are discharged."

The gaoler, Sergeant Baker, turned to Sadler. "Go away."

Sadler had the last word, though. The *East London Advertiser* reported: "Sadler then left the dock and went into the

gaoler's room, accompanied by his solicitor. He did not leave
the Court for some time after, in order to avoid any demonstration on the part of the crowd outside. Ultimately a cab
was drawn up in the yard adjoining the Court, into which
Sadler got with his solicitor. As the vehicle drove away, the
crowd cheered and ran after it. When in Charles Street Sadler
put his head out of the cab window and waved his hat."

And so it was. This was the end. There would be no more
murders of prostitutes in Whitechapel. There would be no
more torsos popping up out of nowhere. It was over. Nothing
of significance would be placed in the Scotland Yard files after this on the "Whitechapel Murders," as they were officially
known. Time— that glorious retrospect— would prove this
was another significant moment.

Jack the Ripper had inexplicably faded away. Like those
last pair of footsteps seguing into the night, the legend and
crimes of the Ripper transposed into the nightlife of Whitechapel, without crescendo, without explanation. The reason
he killed and the reason he stopped remained a mystery.

13

A Clockwork in Crimson

BEFORE WE DELVE into the many opinions, theories and suspects that have since been put forward, it might be best to do our own summing up here lest we lose sight of the threads that link all these cases together. The paramount thread, of course, is the mystery that surrounds each crime scene. It is not the brutality or the grisly nature of the scene. This only served to heighten the mystery, for it made all wonder even more how such heinous things could be done to a person in such narrow spans of time, in public, with such silence, and with no blood trail from the scene.

It all began with Martha Tabram's murder. Before that crime was still brutal, but murders were over brawls, theft or some other understandable motive of revenge, passion or greed. None of that seemed evident here. She was but a fat middle-aged drab. She was stabbed 39 times, once for each year of her life, and the only motive seems to be that she was an easy target: drunk, prostitute, a person for whom few if any would mourn.

Whether the killer knew her and sought violent revenge, we do not know. If so, the mystery surrounding her death scene might merely have been incidental and not intentional. Maybe she was even killed by more than one person— by a genuine "High Rip Gang." Thus they could keep her silent, and they made off quickly and no one heard or saw anything.

There certainly would be no stabbing like hers again. It stands alone in that regard.

But a mysterious death scene with a middle-age drunken harlot at its center ripped to pieces would repeat itself. It would only be a few weeks later that the Ripper would strike, but with a very different MO. Instead of simply stabbing a poor drab, the Ripper cut their throats and then began what appeared to be a very directed process of fetching their uterus.

Yet the sequence of murders, into which we must now probe, actually argues against this being the Ripper's original motive. This is evident in Polly Nichols' murder. She is universally acknowledged as the Ripper's victim, almost universally acknowledged as his first victim. Nevertheless, the wounds in her lower abdomen were simply mutilations. They were deep slices, both downward and across. There was no attempt to open the abdomen. The news reports of "disemboweling" were grisly exaggerations. The mutilations were only below the navel. Nichols' stays had not even been removed. They were only loosened.

This would not be the case with the next victim, Annie Chapman. The whole abdomen was laid open. There were no unnecessary cuts. Three distinct flaps of skin were created by the incisions, and the uterus was neatly taken.

This hardly reflects an expected step forward in skill. Rather, Chapman's evisceration reflects a massive stride that cannot be accounted for by any skill acquired from the random mutilations in Nichols. The great difference between the two murders can only be reconciled by accepting that the Ripper already had the skill but simply did not have any intention to take a uterus from Nichols. The theft of her blood rather appears to have been his motive. Therefore somewhere between Nichols' and Chapman's murders, the Ripper developed a sinister motive to secure a uterus.

Chapman's murder is considered the epitome, the apotheosis, of the Ripper's style. Here he supposedly was left uninterrupted to carry out his diabolical intentions to gruesome fruition. It is truly from her murder alone that the whole popular image of the mad doctor developed. There is a clear ulterior motive here other than just the desire to leave a harlot at the center of an unfathomable death scene.

Soon after the crime spree was believed to have ended, the debate began on whether Martha Tabram should actually have been considered a victim of Jack the Ripper. The arguments against her rely on the facts that her throat was not cut nor was there any indication that there was an attempt to take her uterus, thus making her murder a stark contrast to Polly Nichols' and Annie Chapman's murders. By contrast then, the image Chapman's sleek gutting created of the mad doctor or mortician makes Tabram's murderer look like the spontaneous work of some unskilled gutter maniac. This is not the image of the cool and careful and anatomically knowledgeable Jack the Ripper.

Bagster Phillips relied heavily on Chapman's murder to form this image. However, he never examined Polly Nichols. She was murdered in "J" Division, not "H" Division where he was the official police surgeon. As we've seen in the actual evidence, there was also no attempt to take her uterus. Evidence rather tells us her murderer was far more rehearsed and prepared than Tabram's murderer. But this does not negate that the Ripper was responsible for Tabram. Tabram fought back. This could have necessitated cutting the throats in the next victims in order to have instantly mobilized them. Nevertheless, it is true that nothing appears to have been taken from Tabram except her life. Her murder can therefore be promoted as a botched job. The maniacal vengeance, however, does not seem in keeping with the Ripper's known calm and coolness.

But although we can argue Tabram's case, we cannot argue the other two. There can be no doubt that Nichols was murdered by the same man who murdered Chapman. Both their throats were cut with skill, and those telltale bruises were on their face indicating an assailant with a very strong grip.

Acknowledging the dissimilarities in these first 3 victims actually draws our attention to something quite intriguing. It shows us that Nichols' death is as closely related to Tabram's as it is to Chapman's. Her murder does not represent the beginning of a killer's MO; it is a visual bridge between the first three murders. If we do not begin with Tabram as the first victim and work forward the incongruity that Polly Nichols' death presents is overlooked. Her murder is neither that of a random maniac's, nor is she the object of a sleek dissection.

This progression is a valuable clue which we must bring up later. But suffice it to say for now, whether or not the Ripper did or did not kill Martha Tabram, her death remains incredibly significant to understanding the Ripper crime spree.

In working forward, we should see the Ripper's style climb toward a plateau and either remain there or get more diabolical. This is, however, not the case. Elizabeth Stride is not mutilated at all. Catherine Eddowes is butchered clumsily. Nevertheless, both of these facts can be explained by the Ripper being interrupted in Stride's case and, as a result, he had to quickly find an impromptu victim in Catherine Eddowes. There is no question that her murderer operated and had to operate very quickly. Despite the rush, he still took the time to perform unnecessary mutilations, which is the antithesis of the signature seen in Chapman's murder.

Yet we cannot separate Eddowes' murder from the chat of the times. It was at this time more than any other that the Ripper was said to be a mad doctor or mortician. Was the skill shown in Chapman's gutting a mistake, and did the Ripper perform those hasty mutilations in an attempt to hide the training of a much more select class of people to which he belonged? If this is the case, we are somewhat better able to understand the many paradoxes in her murder scene— the sloppy taking of her uterus, for one example, but the neat retrieval of her kidney.

Both of these latter victims are also linked by the fact the same politics enter their killer's motive. Stride was killed in the shadow (literally) of a Jewish socialist club, and after Eddowes' murder the Ripper took the risk to come back out of hiding 45 minutes after-the-fact and throw down her soiled apron and over it write an assignation implicating the "Juwes." Investigation also showed that Stride had charred for Jews and might even have known Yiddish.

The murder and mutilations of Mary Jane Kelly would appear an undisputed progression of horror from that seen in Catherine Eddowes' murder. Here, like with Chapman, the Ripper reverted to major incisions that resulted in flaps of abdominal skin, something he did not waste his time with in

Eddowes' case. Kelly's murder carries the most pointless mutilations. None of them were necessary to extract her heart or cover up the skill of the killer. Her uterus was left behind, so this could not have been for 20 quid. Her face was hacked up; but, interestingly, Dr. Bond, due to slices in the sheets nearby, thought her face had been covered at the time the mutilations were performed. It would seem as if the Ripper did not want to see the effects himself. This seems at odds with the goriness of the other mutilations he performed. He simply may not have wanted to be bespeckled by flying flesh and blood. All the other evidence, as noted in Chapter 13, shows that the Ripper remained calm and cool despite the gory tokens of bloodlust.

A number of the victims are connected by various strands, both solid and subjective. The Ripper clearly had strong hands. Polly Nichols' and Annie Chapman's throats were slit with the force of a butcher. Each had those telltale finger bruise marks. The bruise marks were those of a single hand tightly holding the mouth, with thumb and fingerprint bruises on opposite *cheeks* and *jawline*. This had nothing to do with strangling them. Nichols showed no signs of that. These marks had nothing to do with them struggling. Annie Chapman wasn't even *compos mentis* after being strangled to insensibility. It seems the Ripper merely had that strong of a grasp. The same hand literally committed both crimes. For Catherine Eddowes, the bruises were not so telltale, but abrasions existed under her left ear, like with Chapman, that corresponded to the Ripper's fingernails. The victims were on their backs, and he seems to have grabbed their mouths, his long boney fingers curling into their jaws and under their ear, and then slit their throats.

From Mary Kelly to Alice McKenzie's murder we take an enormous step backward. There was no sign of a desire to take any organ or even to finish the second slit in the throat. However, her murder was carried out with unbelievable stealth and was close enough in macabre setting and style to convince even Monro that the Ripper was still afoot in the summer of 1889. She, too, had charred for Jews.

It also occurred during a rainy night. All but Chapman's murder occurred during rainy nights. This is a subtle link.

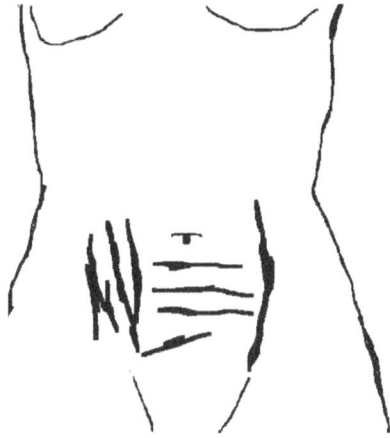

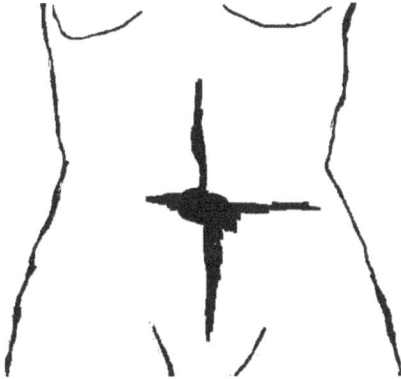

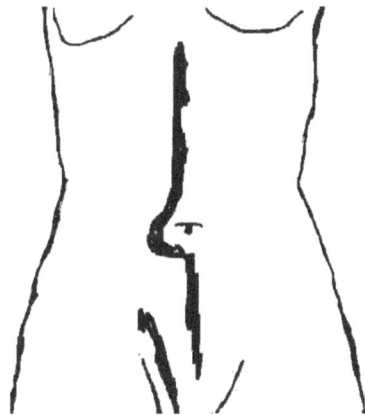

Top, left 1) the location of wounds in Tabram's torso. The major wounds alone were described at the inquest. These total 21. The other 18 are only alluded to in the Press as "too disgusting to mention" and involved the groin. 2) Nichols' wounds, according to Llewellyn. 3) Chapman's wounds, according to Bagster Phillips. Three flaps of skin were created by the incisions. 4) Eddowes.

The Ripper perhaps intended the weather to be an accomplice to wiping away his tracks, in case there should be a slip-up at the scene.

In signature, however, we may regard it as an eerie retrogression to Nichols' murder. But we must also wonder what new thing the Ripper could have done to a woman that would constitute some advance in mutilation over what was done to Mary Kelly. Seemingly, there is very little. Also, what was there to take? Mary Kelly's murder shows that uteri were no longer the object. The original object of Tabram's murder is satisfied: pointless murder of a middle-aged drab. . .and unbelievable mystery. Without a new thrill possible, perhaps this was enough.

Frances Coles' killing is also a throwback. It is remarkably like Stride's, and happened only a few blocks away.

Progression does not form a strong thread tying all these together. But the retrogressions make for an interesting pattern in themselves. They were not random. Each retrogression was a throwback to a different but distinct murder—McKenzie to Nichols, Coles to Stride. Either more than one murderer kept his style and took great breaks in killing or one murderer varied his MO over time. Only one thing does not vary: the ghostly stealth of the killer. One minute the body was not there. The next minute it was.

After Coles' murder the *East London Observer* adamantly took exception to the idea of mystery inherent in *any* of the killings. In commentary the *Observer* expressed its growing intolerance over how the "manner in which her destroyer has disappeared, silently and mysteriously, without leaving the shadow of a clue behind, is spoken of with awe bordering almost on the superstitious." It countered: "We must again insist, as we have consistently insisted throughout the whole of the previous murders, that there is nothing mysterious, or, still less, anything supernatural, in the perpetration of these crimes upon this particular class of victims. We will go further, and say that the murderer, whoever he may be, could perform a similar series of crimes among the same class of women, with almost equal impunity in any other district in London. That may be rather a startling assertion to make, but it is confirmed by the experience of all who have penetrated the depths of human misery and degradation.

"The class of women from whom the victims of the murderer, or murderers, have hitherto been recruited, are compelled by the exigencies of the degrading trade to know every secluded lot, and every unfrequented court, alley and bye-way in the district or part of in the district, where they ply that trade. They are as well acquainted— perhaps even better acquainted— with the extent and duration of the police 'beats' in their neighbourhood as the local sergeant or inspector. When the measured tread of the police constable on night duty has died away on their ears, they can tell to a minute, almost to a second, at what time to expect it again. Secrecy is essential to their calling, and in securing secrecy they are rendering comparatively easy the task of their would-be murderer. In other words, they are accessories to their own murders."

Was the *East London Observer* right? Do we make too much of the mystery? This is hard to believe for a number of reasons. The prostitutes' knowledge may lead them safely to a spot, but afterward the killer would not know from whence would come other bobbies going about their beats. Many crisscrossed and overlapped. Without the prostitute's knowledge how would the killer always get away without a bobby witnessing him? The *Observer*'s argument also wouldn't apply to Polly Nichols' killing, the first one attributed to Jack the Ripper. Buck's Row was far off the turf for prostitutes. She would have no particular knowledge of police beats here. It certainly doesn't apply to Catherine Eddowes. She didn't ply trade as a rule. It had been a long time and she was just that night desperate. How would she know Watkins' beat times in Mitre Square? How also to avoid casual laborers going about their business? They came and went without schedule. Only minutes, if not seconds, divide the time between railroad laborers walking through the long tunnel where Coles would soon be found. Yet none saw. Only Thompson heard casual footsteps walking away into the barren night.

Behind-the-scenes Scotland Yard knew this stealth, especially for that crowded district, was quite unusual. On October 23, 1888, Robert Anderson was firmly in place and briefed as head of C.I.D. He wrote to the Home Office "that a crime of this kind should have been committed without any clue being supplied by the criminal is unusual, but that five successive murders should have been committed without our having the slightest clue of any kind is extraordinary."

Examining the clues at each death scene reveals to what extent *the Ripper* was the planner and to what extent he planned as little mess as possible. No victim who had been slaughtered outside showed signs that their carotid or jugulars had spurted out blood when slit, and yet from a living person blood can spurt up to 3 feet away from the neck. Stride's blood hadn't even hit the wall 6 inches away.

The glaring exception was Mary Jane Kelly. Amongst many exceptions in her case is the fact she was the only indoors killing. Her throat was slit from the right side — also an exception — and the blood spurted out to the wood partition. Exceptions though these may be, they fit the pattern in the killer's desire to reduce any chance of personal mess (See Chapter 13). Outside it did matter if the blood spurted. In the darkness, the Ripper could soil himself or even step in it.

It must be injected here that all these victims were killed by somebody who had incredible night vision. Stride was placed so that her neck was over the rut in the gateway. The blood therefore would neatly flow away down the gutter toward the drain. The pitch darkness of the gateway is underscored by the fact that Morris Eagle had passed through and said it would not have been possible to even see a body in the way. Despite the fact that McKenzie was so close to a gaslight, Andrews had to shine his bull's eye to see the cut in her throat.

Somehow it is hard to avoid the fact that Jack the Ripper carefully chose his spots beforehand. Therefore if he is not responsible for all the "Mystery Murders" throughout those 2 and a half years, a number of killers either took the same precautions successfully (and only in Whitechapel) or were indeed on an instance or two assisted by the prostitute's knowledge of the police beats and the killers were just lucky no one else was meandering by.

It is a fact of human nature that practice makes perfect, even for crime. Nobody just starts out killing and gutting a person efficiently. Therefore both then and now all who have pondered the cases have had no choice but to defer to the idea that the Ripper had some medical knowledge, was a mortician, and/or had killed before somewhere else without receiving much attention.

This introduces the conundrum that is The Torso Killer. On October 2, a few days after the Double Event, a woman's torso appeared out of nowhere in the dark vaults that would one day be the basement of New Scotland Yard. Her head was never found. But her torso told us that her uterus had been taken. Putting some body pieces in the future central police headquarters basement was enormous grandstanding. Only workers knew their way there, and they needed artificial light to see anything. It was a tantalizing mystery. . .and it was meant to be that by the killer.

This and not how the nameless victim was killed set the stage for mystery. This would be seen in The Thames Mystery of June 1889 and in The Pinchin Street Torso of September 1889, found on the 10th but the victim suspected to have been killed on the 8th exactly one year after Chapman's murder (a coincidence which did not escape police notice), and found on a silky soft carpet of rock dust without footprints or carriage wheel marks.

These torso killings argue for the idea that the popularity of the Ripper's murders set a new vogue in prostitute murder: baffle. This can be better appreciated if looking at the torso killings as only an installment in a series of longstanding crimes.

The same evil person seems responsible for the Rainham Mystery in May 1887 when parts of a woman's body were found in the Thames throughout the month and finally reassembled (*sans* a head, of course). Prior to this there was a series of at least two murders in which body parts were also retrieved from the Thames. On September 5, 1873, a police boat at the Battersea area began to find the human flotsam. They were of an unidentified woman. Eventually even her head was found, though badly decomposed. Medical examination showed that the face had been mutilated: nose and chin had been cut off. The incident attracted some attention, especially from dealers in horror who wanted to sketch the body once it was sewn back together. Then in June 1874 the torso of a woman missing head and one leg was pulled out of the Thames near Putney. The torso had been cut along the spinal column area.

The most intriguing incident happened a decade later. In Tottenham Court Road, October 1884, we get a foretaste of The Torso Killer's style, and it proves disturbing. A decomposed skull with flesh still on it was found plus a piece of the thighbone and flesh. Then an arm wrapped in a parcel was found in Bedford Square. The arm had been thrown over the railing and it contained a tattoo, which pointed to the notion it belonged to a prostitute. Then the greatest part of the mystery turned up five days later. A large brown paper parcel appeared from nowhere before 33 Fitzroy Square, a military armory. Part of a woman's torso was therein. The *Pall Mall Gazette* reported why the mystery was equal to the horror. "The sidewalk in front of the house is constantly patrolled by police. . .it is believed that the parcel was deposited between ten o'clock and ten fifteen, when the police relief takes place."

This is the one instance before the Ripper killings where we get a remarkably pungent taste of a killer who knew police beat times intimately and was out to terrorize the public and baffle and challenge the constabulary. Was it simply chance? It seems unlikely. The mutilator of 1884 is seemingly the selfsame Torso Killer of 1888-1889. And in these later killings we know he took great pains to plant some of the body parts — in Whitehall, Sir Percy Shelley's yard, and under the railroad arch.

It is because of this that we must wonder whether the Press reports over the Ripper's clever murder scenes inspired The Torso Killer to rise up to the challenge or whether he simply came back into action to dovetail on the popularity of mystery murders. He didn't get as much attention in 1884, but now every time a body part was found the name of Jack the Ripper was brought up and the torso killings given great press. He rather insured this by tucking away the one body part in New Scotland Yard that would show the uterus had been taken, the very same object the Ripper was said to have desired at this time. The rub here is that the body was thought to have been dead for weeks, so that The Whitehall

Tottenham Court Road

Mystery victim could have died before either Nichols or Tabram or, more interestingly, between Nichols and Chapman's murders. This could therefore be the first time a uterus was lifted from any victim. If he is the Tottenham Court Road murderer of 1884, then he was long before the Ripper committing similar feats of daring and with the same motive to baffle.

There is no question, however, that the Ripper succeeded in taking his crimes to new levels of public ponder and political unrest. The Torso Killer's victims' body parts merely turned up in the most unlikely and suggestive places. The Ripper's victims were entirely murdered and mutilated in the most unbelievable places and circumstances. In this The Torso Killer never got near to the Ripper's audacity and skill, though he remained more of a formless phantom to and from the scene.

The modern image of Jack the Ripper — the silk hat gent — might be pure fancy, but one wonders if it does not more accurately fit The Torso Killer. He must have had a coach and therefore looked quite the gentleman. The women were enticed by something far more than a thrupence offer. They were taken someplace far more exclusive than a dirty yard. Their hands were far more refined. The West End where he began his killing had high end brothels and exclusive clubs. Amidst these higher end customers there may have been a devilish sadist gent who would not be suspected for carting off women in his coach. PM Gladstone was known to rescue them from the street and take them to rehab. A similar method may have been done by a gent who had no benevolence in his intent.

Despite contemporary police beliefs that The Torso Killer and the Ripper were not the same killer, there were attempts to draw parallels between them. Disturbingly, there really are great similarities. The most obvious is that both had anatomical knowledge. The Ripper was thought to have some medical knowledge, and The Torso Killer was thought to be a butcher or knackerer. Another similarity, apparently, is how the heads were removed from at least one of the torso victims and how the Ripper tried to "remove" Chapman and Kelly's heads. But this may merely have been Phillips' mistake.

But there is evidence that also shows that The Torso Killer was learning things the Ripper already knew, or was more fiendish than the Ripper ever hoped to be, indicating they were two different killers. In the Thames Mystery, one of the arms was found with a string tied around the cut end, acting as a tourniquet. When undone the blood came flowing out. This is a poor way to limit bleeding while cutting up the victim. One would think that a butcher would already know how to bleed a body. The tourniquet may therefore have a more sinister motive, such as The Torso Killer wanting to limit bleeding while dissecting his victims alive. In later killings he graduated to cutting their throats to bleed them.

There is no doubt, however, about how strong their hands were. Both left finger bruises on their victims. Both also had incredibly good night vision.

The actual Jack the Ripper was described as of foreign appearance, about 5 foot 6 or 7 inches, stout, dark hair, about 35 to 40 years old. He was shabby genteel and clerkly in appearance. He also engaged in a bit of blatant gaucherie — that deerstalker hat. (The man seen with Eddowes was only shabby looking. He was about 5 foot 3 to 5 inches, sandy hair and mustache. His hat was of single peak gray cloth.) This misplaced bit of rural gentlemanly fashion may be what gave the Ripper's clerkly appearance a "genteel" air.

The Torso Killer may indeed have been seen, too. According to the *Daily News* for October 5, 1888, in discussion on The Whitehall Mystery, on Saturday afternoon at 5:20 p.m. after work had ceased and the construction grounds of New Scotland Yard were vacant, "a respectably dressed man, about 35 years of age, was seen to get over from the hoarding in Cannon Row, and to walk quietly away, and that he was not followed, or the police informed of the matter, because no importance was attached to the matter at the time."

This description, of course, suggests the clerkly, calm Jack the Ripper. It obviously wasn't a thief. He had nothing in his hands. Could this have been The Torso Killer? Laborer Ernest Edge testified that he was in the vault at 4:40 p.m. before closing on Saturday and was in the very corner, with match struck, to look for a hammer. There was no parcel. After the weekend, workers noticed the parcel in the cellar/vault.

The greatest disturbing coincidence ties all these incidents together: they occurred over the same two bewildering years. There was no clue or evidence to link the Ripper and Torso Killer except a clockwork in crimson; a careful and daring planning. . .and most disturbing of all, they stopped at the same time.

Dividing bone and marrow suggests many things and many killers. Copycats may have been involved. Somebody may have been clever enough to cover their motive for killing Coles or McKenzie by imitating the notorious Ripper of 1888. If so, they were rather talented at it. They had more than luck in their timing. No witnesses. No clue. No trace. No motive. Rehearsed. Brutal. Cold. Casual. As casual as those last footsteps that signaled farewell to the most perplexing spree of mystery murders in history.

Given all this, it is not surprising that various police involved in the cases would hold radically different opinions. When these viewpoints first started becoming public in the early 20th century they underscored how none of them had agreed.

14

FOOLSCAP

A COMMON NOTEPAPER it was, foolscap, good for odd thoughts, rough drafts and all-in-all the jottings of thinking out loud. Understanding this is quite important. It rather contextualizes the ideas expressed in such papers when they are found. They cannot be taken as the final product or the jottings of careful and belabored thought. Interviews in magazine, reactionary replies to foolscap and other offhand and passing theories, are in the same category. The words of foolscap are the words of a starting point. They are clues that lead us on. They need not be denigrated, but they must be viewed with reserve.

It is in this context we must view the expressed opinions and theorizing of some of the most important detectives involved in the Jack the Ripper investigation, for certainly as time would go by their opinions became public, and much weight has been added to some whereas perhaps too little has been accorded to others.

The first glimpse of privileged information leaked out due to a rather benign article. In 1896 Major Arthur Griffiths commented on the Whitechapel Murders in *Unsolved Mysteries of Crime* (April issue) of the Cassell's Family Magazine. He was an exciting fiction writer and credible writer of crime history (having been a deputy governor and inspector of prisons). In this issue he had said that "No solution has ever been offered as of yet of the notorious Whitechapel murders, no reasonable surmise made of the identity of the most mysterious monster, 'Jack the Ripper.'" He went over various theories that ran the gamut of sailor or stoker who only visited London occasionally, or a man from the cattle boats, a mad Malay or Lascar or, most interesting, that it was a man of a double personality. Robert Louis Stevenson's *Dr. Jekyll and Mr. Hyde* was a popular play in London, and it is from that triumph that Griffiths took his inspiration.

Only two years later Griffiths surprisingly presented a 180 degree view about the identity issue in his new book *Mysteries of Police and Crime.* Without mentioning names he went into what appeared to be authoritative detail about three men, which in Griffiths' pen were promoted as having been regarded officially by Scotland Yard as the prime suspects.

The outside public may think that the identity of that later miscreant, "Jack the Ripper," was never revealed. So far as actual knowledge goes, this is undoubtedly true. But the police, after the last murder, had brought their investigations to the point of strongly suspecting several persons, all of them known to be homicidal lunatics, and against three of these they held very plausible and reasonable grounds of suspicion. Concerning two of them the case was weak, although it was based on certain colourable facts.

One was a Polish Jew, a known lunatic, who was at large in the district of Whitechapel at the time of the murders, and who, having afterwards developed homicidal tendencies, was confined to an asylum. This man was said to resemble the murderer by the one person who got a glimpse of him— the police-constable in Mitre Court. The second possible criminal was a Russian doctor, also insane, who had been a convict both in England and Siberia. This man was in the habit of carrying about surgical knives and instruments in his pockets; his antecedents were of the very worst, and at the time of the Whitechapel murders he was in hiding, or, at least, his whereabouts were never exactly known.

The third person was of the same type, but the suspicion in his case was stronger, and there was every reason to believe that his own friends entertained grave doubts about him. He was also a doctor in the prime of life, was believed to be insane or on the borderland of insanity, and he disappeared immediately after the last murder, that in Miller's Court, on the 9th November, 1888. On the last day of that year, seven weeks later, his body was found floating in the Thames, and was said to have been in the water a month.

The theory in this case was that after his last exploit, which was the most fiendish of all, his brain entirely gave way, and he became furiously insane and committed suicide. It is at least a strong presumption that "Jack the Ripper" died or was put under restraint after the Miller's Court affair, which ended this series of crimes. It would be interesting to know whether in this third case the man was left-handed or ambidextrous, both suggestions having been advanced by medical experts after viewing the victims. Certainly other doctors disagreed on this point, which may be said to add another to the many instances in which medical evidence has been conflicting, not to say confusing.

Griffiths' tome proved influential. It popularized the view, still with us today, that Mary Jane Kelly was the Ripper's last victim, and it also presented the Ripper as most likely being a doctor who drowned himself shortly thereafter. Although Griffiths' source at this point remained unidentified, the inference that coursed through his entire treatment was that it was a highly placed individual with inside knowledge.

Magazines, on the other hand, don't survive as long as books do in order to influence history. But meticulous research on the part of several "Ripperologists" has uncovered surviving examples of Edwardian issues of once popular rags wherein key investigators had been interviewed. This showed that for those who had been close to the case there was no such agreement with Griffiths' assertions.

One was Inspector Frederick Abberline. In 1903 a celebrated murder case came to trial: that of Severin Klosowski alias George Chapman. He had slow-poisoned 3 common law wives to death and was now the center of news. Press speculation eventually ran high that Chapman could have been the Ripper. Any fiend who could slow poison women, it was thought, was capable of those infamous crimes. Abberline agreed. He, too, was struck by the prosecuting attorney's opening remarks as published in various journals. By this time Abberline had largely been forgotten. He had taken early retirement and had traveled and engaged in other businesses. He and his wife had come to live in a nice house in Clapham, with a servant and two take-in lodgers. One of them turned out to be a *Pall Mall Gazette* reporter. With the rival *The Daily Chronicle* reintroducing the case of the Ripper, Abberline was interviewed for *Pall Mall*. He insisted that Scotland Yard never had the slightest idea who the Ripper was, but in seeing how Chapman was described and, furthermore, that he was around Whitechapel in 1888, he had a strong suspicion that the brute was finally on trial.

Crime reporter George Sims, a devotee of Griffiths, challenged Abberline's statement. In the *Referee* on March 29, 1903, he enlarged upon Griffiths' work with dogma. "It is perfectly well known at Scotland Yard who 'Jack' was, and the reasons for the police conclusions were given in a report to the Home Office, which was considered by the authorities to be final and conclusive."

Aside from the presumption of a crime reporter correcting the chief investigator's comments, Sims was pompously misrepresenting Griffiths' own caution. *Pall Mall Gazette* went back to Abberline. Sims' comments amazed him. "You can state most emphatically that Scotland Yard is none the wiser on the subject than it was fifteen years ago," declared Abberline. "It is simple nonsense to talk of the police having proof that the man is dead. I am, and always have been, in the closest touch with Scotland Yard, and it would have been next to impossible for me not to have known about it. Besides, the authorities would have only been too glad to make an end of such a mystery, if only for their own credit.

"I know that it has been stated in several quarters that Jack the Ripper was a man who died in a lunatic asylum a few years ago, but there is nothing of a tangible nature to support such a theory."

When asked by the *Pall Mall* reporter about the truth behind the stories that the Ripper committed suicide by drowning himself in the Thames, Abberline responded: "Yes, I know all about that story. But what does it amount to? Simply this. Soon after the last murder in Whitechapel the body of a young doctor was found in the Thames, but there is absolutely nothing beyond the fact that he was found at the time to incriminate him. A report was made to the Home Office on the matter, but that it was 'considered final and conclusive' is going altogether beyond the truth. Seeing that the same kind of murders began in America afterwards, there is much more reason to think the man emigrated. Then again, the fact that several months after December, 1888, when the [medical] student's body was found, the detectives were told still to hold themselves in readiness for further investigations seems to point to the conclusion that Scotland Yard did not in any way consider the evidence final."[8]

Inspector Edmund Reid now took a hand. The *Morning Advertiser* published two letters by him in response to all this. The first was on March 30th and the second on April 6. He stated his belief that the Ripper killed 9 prostitutes and the last one was Coles in 1891. This nixed the whole idea that the killer committed suicide after the Miller's Court murder of Mary Kelly. In this, Abberline disagreed with Reid apparently. As early as 1892 he believed that at Miller's Court "the murderer reached the culminating point of gratification of his morbid ideas" and therewith there was little reason to continue the spree. We must remember, however, that Abberline basically was no longer on the case after March 1889, having gone back to A Division and his cabinet post. Reid was still head of H Division and was directly overseeing the investigations.

Robert Anderson stayed out of the fray at this time, but when Abberline had mentioned the theory that the Ripper had died in an asylum he was obliquely referencing Anderson's own theory. As early as 1895, "Alfred Aylmer" (possibly the pseudonym of Griffiths himself as used in Wyndsor's Magazine for *Detectives in Real Life*), had written of Anderson: "Although he has achieved greater success than any detective of his time, there will always be undiscovered crimes, and just now the tale is pretty full. Much dissatisfaction was

---

[8] Possibly Dr. John Hewett, a veterinary student who was later committed to an asylum. Also, the very fact Monro thought the Ripper killed McKenzie in July 1889 testifies that nobody at Scotland Yard paid attention to the "Thames doctor" report.

vented upon Mr. Anderson at the utterly abortive efforts to discover the perpetrator of the Whitechapel murders. He has himself a perfectly plausible theory that Jack the Ripper was a homicidal maniac, temporarily at large, whose hideous career was cut short by committal to an asylum." Aside from Aylmer-Griffiths' comments, Anderson had himself penned in *The Nineteenth Century* (February 1901) that the Ripper "had been safely caged in an asylum." In a 1904 lecture at the London Institute he repeated it, apparently unaffected by the reports created by Abberline that Scotland Yard never knew and that Chapman fit the bill far better than anybody.

Anderson would finally stir the embers in detail. As a promo for his upcoming memoirs, *The Lighter Side of My Official Life*, some of it was serialized in *Blackwood's Magazine* for March 1910. The following excerpt is on his reminiscences on the Ripper case:

One did not need to be a Sherlock Holmes to discover that the criminal was a sexual maniac of a virulent type; that he was living in the immediate vicinity of the scenes of the murders; and that, if he was not living absolutely alone, his people knew of his guilt, and refused to give him up to justice. During my absence abroad the Police had made a house-to-house search for him, investigating the case of every man in the district whose circumstances were such that he could go and come and get rid of his bloodstains in secret. And the conclusion we came to was that he and his people were low-class Jews, for it is a remarkable fact that people of that class in the East End will not give up one of their number to Gentile justice.

And the result proved that our diagnosis was right on every point. For I may say at once that 'undiscovered murders' are rare in London, and the 'Jack-the-Ripper' crimes are not within that category. And if the Police here had powers such as the French Police possess, the murderer would have been brought to justice. Scotland Yard can boast that not even the subordinate officers of the department will tell tales out of school, and it would ill become me to violate the unwritten rule of the service. So I will only add here that the "Jack-the-Ripper" letter which is preserved in the Police Museum at New Scotland Yard is the creation of an enterprising London journalist.

In a post scriptum, he wrote: "Having regard to the interest attaching to this case, I should almost be tempted to disclose the identity of the murderer and of the pressman who wrote the letter [Dear Boss letter] above referred to, provided that the publishers would accept all responsibility in view of a possible libel action. But no public benefit would result from such a course, and the traditions of my old department would suffer. I will only add that when the individual whom we suspected was caged in an asylum, the only person who had ever had a good view of the murderer at once identified him, but when he learned that the suspect was a fellow-Jew he declined to swear to him."

Anderson lit London on fire with his steamy political comments, those regarding Jack the Ripper above being only one example. By April, Anderson was grinning at the furor the serialization of parts of his memoirs had caused. It reinvigorated him and he felt years younger.

In his book he defended the early excerpts by qualifying: "In saying that he was a Polish Jew I am merely stating a definitely ascertained fact. And my words are meant to specify race, not religion. For it would outrage all religious sentiment to talk of the religion of a loathsome creature whose utterly unmentionable vices reduced him to a lower level than that of the brute."

Winston Churchill commented on Anderson's recollections with dry sarcasm. Aside from calling his memoirs a work of "gross boastfulness," he said "they are written, if I may say so, in the style of 'How Bill Adams won the Battle of Waterloo.' The writer seems anxious to show how invariably he was right, and how much more he could tell if only his mouth was not, what he pleased to call, closed."

As Churchill derogatorily noted, Anderson dangles carrots but never elaborates to give us something reliable to go by. And time has shown that we cannot rely on his accuracy, as his memory frequently swims in geriatric moments. For example, he recalled that at the time of the Ripper murders the Home Secretary was Sir William Harcourt when it had been the disliked Henry Matthews. In addition to this, from Abberline's statement we know that Anderson's claim the house-to-house search led them to the low class Jew theory is nonsense, for Abberline was very much in charge of the case at that point and never heard of anything. Indeed, Anderson said as much in his letter, already quoted, to the Home Secretary, about how extraordinary it was that they had no clue.

After a Jew was fingered by another Jew, by whatever conduit this came about, Anderson must have put much of his theory together in his mind and simply used the "Royal we." His train of logic is so fluid it is hard to imagine his theory reflects the consensus of several investigators. In essence, he eventually believed that since they didn't find any evidence amongst those who lived alone in the squalor, the Ripper must not live alone but with people. These people must know of his crimes. This being said, the assumption is that they must be Jews because Gentiles would give up a bloody murderer. His attitude was most likely also reinforced by some comparatives, such as Sadler. He, a Gentile, was quickly turned in by all and sundry. But the stealthy Ripper's success just seemed beyond probability without an entire culture protecting him. Ultimately, though, Anderson's entire theory is only anchored by (and probably didn't even exist until) an actual eyewitness— another Jew no less— corroborated their "diagnosis."

Behind-the-scenes, others had not been as mum on their encounters with Anderson. Earlier in his career (1883), Edward Jenkinson, one of the chief administrator's looking into the actions of Irish revolutionaries, told the then Home Secretary Sir William Harcourt that Anderson was a "second-class detective." At the end of his career, upon his retirement, the *Police Review* said that, due to his religious fervor, he did not have the "requisite kind of knowledge of the world and of men" for the job, and as a result he was not the best choice for Assistant Commissioner and head of C.I.D.

Anderson's views on Jack the Ripper play into these negative assessments. We should stand amazed that he didn't seem to understand the obvious sequence of events during that horrid autumn of terror. Why would a low-class Polish Jew attempt to incite riot against his own people and do so only *after* the *Star* introduced the whole idea of a "crazy Jew" as the culprit? The Ripper clearly sought to cause upheaval *only* when he saw that he could, first against Jews then against the government on November 9.

The only ones dead-set on what *appeared to be* a Jew was the City of London C.I.D., and they were far outside of the Met's jurisdiction. The result was an investigation in which Anderson would have played no direct part. His knowledge of it would only be by briefing, and this may have been couched in very casual terms. . .and *this* may explain Anderson's unique and distinct conclusions from others on his own force.

We know that at one point during the autumn of terror the City C.I.D. was monitoring a man in Butcher's Row whom they believed to be the murderer. Significantly, Jewishness is *not* overtly mentioned in any City correspondence so far uncovered. Initially, even the name of the actual street was not mentioned in published accounts. Carefully worded details appeared first in print in *Thomson's Weekly News*. In 1906 a series of articles was published by retired City detective inspector Harry Cox. The most sensational was the December 1st issue "The Truth About the Whitechapel Mysteries."

In this article, Cox recalled that they maintained a protracted surveillance on a suspect's shop in an unidentified street, using a house across as their headquarters. The fact that it is a predominantly Jewish neighborhood comes by inference when Cox writes that the Jews went into a panic when they learned of their presence. In order to calm them, Cox and his fellow detectives passed themselves off as factory inspectors looking for tailor sweatshops to shut down. Having acquired their trust, Cox found that the Jews talked openly about the Jack the Ripper murders. From Cox's experience with the suspect, he was certain he had something to do with the crimes. He and his comrades took turns tailing him at night. During one of Cox's turns, he watched this man openly accost prostitutes. He was low class. He seemed insane and a woman hater. For Cox that seemed enough. Given what we know about the Ripper's subtleness, however, Cox's impression may seem the result of too much simple stereotype.

But it is a fact that suspicion must come before a stakeout. How did City C.I.D.'s upper echelons come to suspect this man to begin with in order to set Cox and his companions on his trail?

Butcher's Row, Algate High Street.

The top of the food chain would have been Robert Sagar, an impressive heavyweight not only in London's C.I.D. but in international crime sleuthing. He had even traveled on behalf of the police to assist in breaking up a plot against the King of Spain. Sagar's rise in the City C.I.D. is a unique and impressive one. He went from gifted amateur criminologist straight to police detective, and he was universally hailed as a "real life Sherlock Holmes."

Although Major Smith does not mention the name of the heavy inspector with him in the hansom ride, it was probably Sagar. We know for certain that he was Smith's liaison at the Leman Street Police Station that night. He would have heard Bagster Phillips agree that there was little of the Ripper's previous finesse in the Eddowes butchery. Sequeira and Gordon Brown would also later agree that it was the work of a butcher. Sagar no doubt took their observations to heart. Under his auspices, City C.I.D. started rooting about looking for a butcher and not a skilled medical man.

Upon his retirement in 1905, we get a glimpse of the final outcome of City C.I.D.'s search. The *City Press* reported:

His professional association with the terrible atrocities which were perpetuated some years ago in the East End by the so-styled "Jack-the Ripper" was a very close one. . .Much has been said and written— and even more conjectured— upon the subject of the "Jack-the-Ripper" murders. It has been asserted that the murderer fled to the Continent, where he perpetrated similar hideous crimes; but that is not the case. The police realised, as also did the public, that the crimes were those of a madman, and suspicion fell upon a man, who, without a doubt, was the murderer. Identification being impossible, he could not be charged. He was, however, placed in a lunatic asylum, and the series of atrocities came to an end.

When Sagar died in 1924, more details came out. In part, the *Brighton and Hove Herald* (December 6, 1924) reported: "It was Mr. Sagar's view that the murders were committed by an insane man employed at Butcher's Row, Aldgate, who was subsequently placed by his friends in a private asylum." From his unpublished memoirs (now lost) on 15 September 1946 *Reynold's News* would print personal extracts, confirming directly these were Sagar's own views: "We had good reason to suspect a man who worked in Butcher's Row, Aldgate. We watched him carefully. There was no doubt that this man was insane, and after a time his friends thought it advisable to have him removed to a private asylum. After he was removed there were no more Ripper atrocities."

We have in this scenario something close to Anderson's dogmatic insistence that the man was known completely and then locked up. As the body of foolscap grows, we can begin to suspect that it was from Sagar that Anderson was getting *some* of his information on the "low class Polish Jew" (although Sagar did not say he was Jewish) and from where Cox and his comrades ultimately got their marching orders.

Decades would go by before greater clarity and controversy would give form to this man in Aldgate. In the interim, Anderson's "low class Jew" theory would take the backseat if not altogether wait off stage as Jack the Ripper secured his place in world romance and horror folklore as a top-hatted gent in a cape who went about murdering East End strumpets. He was now definitely a doctor, a mad surgeon, or Simon Pure who had any number of bloodlust or pious motives to kill during fits of Jekyll and Hydery.

Along with the image of the mad doctor, there was always that rumor that he had committed suicide in the river Thames shortly after the Miller's Court savagery. After those involved in the case had long passed away there was also no one to challenge the increasingly popular point of view that Jack the Ripper killed only in the autumn of 1888 and killed only 5 prostitutes. These became the "Canonical 5"— Nichols, Chapman, Stride, Eddowes, Kelly. Everything was neat and tidy. The mystery remained to titillate the buffs, and the suicide added the self-retribution and made for a nice moral ending. It would not be until 71 years later and a journalist's stunt that the origins of these notions would be uncovered.

In 1959, foolscap notes were found in the documents of Lady Aberconway, the daughter of the late Melville Macnaghten. These notes contained Macnaghten's working draft on Jack the Ripper's murders, and thus despite the language contained in the notes they struck their finder, journalist Daniel Farson, as representing official inside knowledge. This was a great find, for the papers mentioned three suspects that Macnaghten had suspicions about. Thus his memorandum constituted a sneak peek at official files on the case (British law does not allow documents to be released until 100 years after the fact). Farson would break the story on his TV show *Farson's Guide to the British* in an episode that dealt with Jack the Ripper. He would mention no names, just initials. The prime suspect was MJD. He committed suicide in the Thames. The Ripper had finally been identified.

It needed no more. What a British journalist had begun set an American journalist upon the path, and in 1965 the first truly respected postwar book on Jack the Ripper would be published. The journalist was Tom Cullen. He was the first to use the memorandum to finger Macnaghten's lead suspect Montague John Druitt as Jack the Ripper.

Due to its early promotion as an official document, The Macnaghten Memorandum, as it has become known, has been elevated to a monumental position in Ripper studies. Unfortunately, those who make much out of Macnaghten's foolscap make too much. This document was far from official. It did not reflect a synthesis of Scotland Yard's actual investigation on the Whitechapel Murders. Nor was the information therein actually lifted from police files on the suspects. Macnaghten had a well-known obsession with Jack the Ripper. It was to such an extent that he considered not having been on the Force at the time of the murder spree to be one of his two great regrets in life. When the London newspaper *Sun* ran an article in 1894 questioning whether a certain Thomas Cutbush might have been the Ripper, Macnaghten seized the opportunity and took it upon himself to draft his memorandum to be used to brief the current Scotland Yard staff on the particulars of the case. Only in that he was Chief Constable was this "official." In everything else his accounts seem to be from his memory's synthesis of hearsay.

Thomas Cutbush had been arrested for going around and stabbing young women in their bustles (to put it politely). This was hardly Ripper material. In this memorandum, Macnaghten introduces Cutbush and then details some of the Ripper crimes. He then offers three suspects who were in his opinion more likely candidates than Cutbush to be Jack the Ripper.

His prime candidate was Montague John Druitt. Of him, he summarizes:

1) A Mr. M. J. Druitt, said to be a doctor & of good family — who disappeared at the time of the Miller's Court murder, & whose body (which was said to have been upwards of a month in the water) was found in the Thames on 31st December — or about 7 weeks after that murder. He was sexually insane and from private information I have little doubt but that his own family believed him to have been the murderer.[9]

The memorandum did not simply reflect his home jottings. Donald Rumbelow, curator of the City of London crime museum, found the Scotland Yard version in its files in 1975. It is dated February 23, 1894, and marked as confidential.

Despite this last category, Macnaghten had slipped some

---

[9] The extract above is taken from the Scotland Yard version because it reflects Macnaghten's finalized draft. His home version contained the error that Druitt was 41 years old.

of this information out to the public. Unquestionably, he was the source for Major Arthur Griffiths' about-face in his 1898 tome. Griffiths' general wording and his many mistakes essentially parrot the language and structure of Macnaghten's memorandum. It is likely that Macnaghten gave him a copy, perhaps redacted of names, after his inaccurate magazine article in 1896. Griffiths also makes it plain in his book that he had personal contact with Macnaghten. He describes him at work in his office: "Mr Macnaughten [sic] keeps by him, as a matter of business, some other and more gruesome pictures, always under lock and key; photographs, for instance, of the victims of Jack the Ripper, and of other brutal murders, taken immediately after discovery, and reproducing with horrible fidelity the mutilated remains of a human body, but which might belong to a charnel-house or abattoir. It is Mr. Macnaughten's duty, no less than his earnest desire, to be first on the scene of any such sinister catastrophe. He is therefore more intimately acquainted perhaps with the details of the most recent celebrated crimes than anyone in Scotland Yard."

Macnaghten's memorandum would prove otherwise. It is fraught with inaccuracies. So many that it cannot be explained as simply the result of a man who had nothing to do with the Force in 1888. He could not have been looking at *any* official documents. He seemed to have some shards of suspicions and from there glued together vases to hold inference. This is evident in his clause "said to be a doctor" — wording that does not reflect any real personal investigation. In fact, Druitt was a barrister.

And, quite frankly, Macnaghten was not a detective. He was an administrator, and it wasn't his duty to be first on any gruesome scene. His background did not even qualify him to be an active investigator on the Force. It was for more than lack of qualifications that Charles Warren resisted his appointment even as an administrator via Monro's chum system of old India hands. Macnaghten had, for unexplained reasons, been the only man beaten by his serving Hindus in India during an uprising. Given Macnaghten's inappropriate taste for the macabre, as subtly recorded by Griffiths, perhaps there was other information which made Warren recoil. Monro had thought him a man able to handle men "firmly," but could

Warren have discovered that Macnaghten had been excessively brutal, even sadistic?

Whether yea or nay, perhaps it is not relevant to the immediate question. What is relevant is to contextualize Macnaghten's memorandum. There is no "buff" or amateur detective interested in the Ripper case who does not know of the memorandum and its many mistakes and inaccuracies. We don't need to go over that here. However, it needs to be reintroduced chronologically into the foolscap again so it can be contextualized. When Farson found it much of the old magazines of the early 20th century containing varied opinions from those who had actually been on the case had been forgotten. The words of Anderson, Sagar, Cox, Abberline, Reid, had been lost. Unrivaled, it ignited interest, and because of this it has supplanted much more weighty information that tempers what Macnaghten presents.

For example, Inspector Abberline's clear rebuttal of the idea that a drowned doctor in the Thames had any official weight behind it causes Macnaghten's pet suspect to fall apart. And indeed Macnaghten offers no official evidence in the memorandum. He has "private" information. It must not have been very detailed. Macnaghten didn't even know Druitt's occupation.

Another point of fact contextualizes Macnaghten's memorandum even more: Tom Cullen found out much more about Druitt than Macnaghten ever knew, and yet even with this nothing actually points suspicion on him. Aside from being a barrister, Druitt was also a part time teacher at Blackheath. In November 1888 he had been sacked from the teaching job for undisclosed reasons, possibly for homosexual activity, wrote a note which was tantamount to a suicide note, and left it in his chambers. After December 1, 1888, he was not seen again until his body was pulled out of the Thames downstream. To this day, despite the work of many avid "Ripperologists," no one has come up with a shred of evidence to link Druitt to being Jack the Ripper at all. In fact, evidence has turned up indicating that Druitt was playing cricket (he was an avid competition cricket player) the mid-morning of two of the murders. He could not have been in Whitechapel and then hours later on the playing field. Nothing, in fact, contradicts

Abberline's words in 1903 that there was nothing more to it than a report about a man found drowned in the Thames.

Time and genuine research has rather shown how Macnaghten was grossly wrong. Not only has time proven nothing against Druitt, it has revealed some of the standards of Macnaghten's generation to be utterly unfounded. It seems Macnaghten's information on Druitt was that he was possibly homosexual. To Macnaghten this probably made him "sexually insane" and a woman hater. On top of this, Macnaghten had also formed his own ideas about what constituted "sexual insanity." He believed that any act of violence was sexually motivated.

Overlaying the psychological theories of today on Victorian Whitechapel also has its dangers. But one consistent thing 20th century profiling of serial killers has yielded is quite applicable. No known serial killer has ever committed suicide. This should not surprise us at all. The ability of a person to take life for pleasure or fancy betrays them as a presumptuously egotistic individual. Suicide would seem outside the realm of someone with that sort of self-indulgent arrogance. Suicide would be more expected in an average person who is carried away or accidently contributes to manslaughter. Guilt and the sense of retribution might urge them to take their own life. But someone like the Ripper who so carefully planned his murders is not suddenly going to feel remorse and do away with himself.

The most damning thing about Macnaghten's choice of Druitt is the mug shot of the Ripper. A study of the actual inquest proceedings reveals that Jack the Ripper was only around 5 foot 6 or 7 inches tall, and stout in body proportion. Druitt was 5 foot 10 inches and very lean, with an unusually long neck.

Tom Cullen's *Autumn of Terror* became a huge success in 1965 and ushered in modern Ripperology, making its author the father of serious postwar Ripper studies. Ironically, despite Cullen's greater level of fruitless investigation he still ended up fingering Druitt. Yet Druitt became guilty by suspicion. He fit the dramatic bill better— surgeon's son, gentle background, a melancholy, brooding appearance. Cullen also wanted to promote social reform as the motive. He rightly saw in the Ripper's evolving crime spree an ulterior motive to incite more. He believed that Druitt's unhinged but educated mind could have conceived of killing the drabs as a way to highlight the enormous squalor that was Whitechapel and the disparagingly inequality that a negligent British society had allowed to form. A low class, demented bully simply wasn't capable of this twisted moral goal.

The upshot was that the second name on the list was largely ignored.

2) Kosminski— a Polish Jew— & resident in Whitechapel. This man became insane owing to many years indulgence in solitary vices. He had a great hatred of women, specially of the prostitute class, & had strong homicidal tendencies: he was removed to a lunatic asylum about March 1889. There were many circs connected with this man which made him a strong 'suspect'.

There can be no doubt that this is the suspect behind Sir Robert Anderson's controversial and dogmatic "low class Polish Jew" theory. What is particularly interesting is that in 1894 already, when Macnaghten compiled his memorandum, he deemed the suspect worthy of only 2nd place. This is not surprising. The information must have been incredibly scant and inconclusive. Kosminski's elevated place on the list could not have been based on official files, for Macnaghten does not even know Kosminski's first name. He must simply have been told snippets privately, from the usual old boys' grapevine.

A remarkable discovery in 1987 would begin to unravel the mystery about this enigmatic suspect. The discovery would also reveal that the information on him had been so thin that Scotland Yard had *never* known Kosminski's first name. Until that time no one had suspected the role that Inspector Donald Swanson had played in the Ripper murders. He had been assigned by Anderson to sift and collate all the data that was coming in. This makes it likely that Anderson was getting most of his information directly from Swanson, not from Abberline or Reid or other inspectors on the ground floor. Anderson and Swanson actually became good friends and remained so the rest of their lives. Swanson was a fairly

close-lipped officer, and viewed his job as one of keeping secrets. This no doubt set well with Anderson. Despite Anderson tying many a knickers in a knot with his incendiary
comments in his memoirs, he valued secrecy since he himself
was a former secret service man.

Due to their friendship, Anderson gave Swanson a signed
copy of *The Lighter Side of My Official Life* in 1910. Swanson remained discreet but not mum. He read his old and beloved mentor's book carefully, and often left qualifying remarks, even initialing them to set them in stone for posterity.
He was indeed a discreet man. He knew his children and
grandchildren would inherit his books, and one day they
might even look into one and see he had written comments.

This came to pass when his grandson James Swanson came
into the book in 1981. He inherited it from his aunt, Alice,
Swanson's last surviving child. In going through the contents
of her library, he browsed through the book and noticed
marginalia. When he came to Anderson's dogmatic views that
they had known the Ripper was a low class Polish Jew, and
that he was confronted in police presence by a witness who
identified him but refused to give evidence, he saw that his
grandfather had elaborated in the margin—". . .because the
suspect was also a Jew and also because his evidence would
convict the suspect and witness would be the means of murderer being hanged which he did not wish to be left on his
mind. And after this identification which suspect knew no
other murder of this kind took place in London."

These comments have since become famous as the "Swanson Marginalia." They are famous for two reasons: Swanson
clarifies how they took the suspect to be identified by the
witness, that the man was identified and *knew* he had been
outed, and then Swanson names him.

The marginalia continued on the back of the next page:

Continuing from page 138, after the suspect had been identified at the Seaside Home where he had been sent by us with difficulty in order to subject him to identification, and he knew he
was identified. On suspect's return to his brother's house in
Whitechapel he was watched by police (City CID) by day &
night. In a very short time the suspect with his hands tied be-

hind his back, he was sent to Stepney Workhouse and then to Colney Hatch and died shortly afterwards— Kosminski was the suspect – DSS

Swanson's marginalia tells us many things outright, by omission and by reading between the lines. Only two Jews were witnesses— Joseph Lawende and Joseph Hyam Levy, the latter reported by the Press to be cagey and intimating he knew more; he was certainly the nervous one at the inquest. That the witness is either of the two above is attested to by the fact that Swanson says that City C.I.D. undertook the surveillance of the suspect. Only Eddowes' murder, to which these two were the witnesses to the suspect beforehand, took place within the City of London's jurisdiction. It was only here that the killer's face was seen. Therefore this would be the only murder for which the law could bring the Ripper to trial. Even though Whitechapel was outside their jurisdiction, it would be City C.I.D. who would have the biggest stake in this suspect. Not the Met. Notwithstanding, because the suspect lived in the Met's jurisdiction it was their responsibility to take him to the "Seaside Home" for identification.

It would seem it was over. Jack the Ripper had been found and identified. A short time later, after vigorous surveillance, he was carted off to the asylum where he soon died.

Unfortunately, that is not the case. True crime writers and Ripperologists wanted to find out more about Jack the Ripper. This naturally inspired a search through the civil and lunatic asylum records for a Kosminski, *any* Kosminski.

Martin Fido was the first (*The Crimes, Detection and Death of Jack the Ripper*). He was able to determine that "Kosminski" could only be Aaron Mordke (Mordecai) Kosminski. He was born in Poland on September 11, 1865. Fido was able to uncover an interesting trail that showed that in July 1890 Kosminski was ill enough to be admitted to Mile End Old Town Workhouse for care. He was living at that time with his sister and brother-in-law, Betsy and Woolf Abrahams, at 3 Sion Square, Whitechapel. He was discharged 3 days later back into their care.

By February 1891 Aaron Kosminski was clearly growing worse. He was having delusions. He wouldn't eat food if offered him. He ate only garbage from the streets. He wouldn't bathe. He was dirty and hadn't worked for years. He was at this time living with another sister, Matilda, and her husband, Morris Lubnowski. On February 4, 1891, he was taken to the Mile End Old Town Workhouse yet again. It was clear there was no help for him. He was declared insane. On 7 February he was admitted to Colney Hatch sanitarium. He was registered as a hair-dresser. The mental disorder: Mania. Cause for insanity: Self Abuse. Under "Facts indicating insanity observed by Medical Man" it is written:

> He declares that he is guided and his movements altogether controlled by an instinct that informs his mind, he says that he knows the movements of all mankind, he refuses food from others because he is told to do so, and he eats out of the gutter because he is told to do so.

A search of all the records finds only this Kosminski. There is no other. The description also clearly matches that of the man given by Anderson and Macnaghten and the cause of insanity— "solitary vices," etc.

It would seem Fido had found Jack the Ripper. The problem is that none of the above suggests the man who so adroitly planned and carried out such baffling murders in 1888. True, the crippling insanity is said to have come on in July 1890, but there is nothing that can possibly suggest that this poor demented Jewish hair-dresser was ever Jack the Ripper before his mental problems became unavoidable to his family.

There are other irreconcilable differences between Kosminski and Jack the Ripper. In 1888 when Nichols and Chapman were killed he was only 22. He would have turned 23 on September 11. This does in no wise match the 30 something to middle-age stocky, dark, shabby genteel Ripper. According to his family, Kosminski hadn't worked for years. Thus we know he was not in a position to have been able to afford a clerkly appearance. Nor did he have a place alone where he could bring his bodily trophies. He wasn't someone who could mutilate skillfully, not even at the level of a butcher. He certainly couldn't speak like an educated man. Moreover, he did not die soon after incarceration. He lived on until 1919, outliving even Robert Anderson who had passed away in November 1918. The closest he comes to any description is that of the man seen with Eddowes; and this is only in that both are described as being fair-haired. Nothing, in fact, about Kosminski matches the person and the style seen in the Jack the Ripper crimes. In short, he is simply too young, too poor, and too crazy. . .and, most significantly, too Jewish. He was a schlemiel who in October 1889 appeared in the Press for having been fined for walking a dog off a lead. It wasn't his dog he insisted. Nevertheless he was fined. He said he couldn't pay since it was the Jewish Sabbath. He was given till Monday or he would go to jail. Once again, with the known sequence of events, why would a Jew attempt to escalate the murder spree into race riots against his own people?

Despite Swanson writing that they (the Met) had a direct hand in taking Kosminski to his identification, there is reason to doubt Swanson had anything to do with it. Frustratingly, like Macnaghten, he doesn't seem to know a first name for Kosminski. He only knows that *after* the identification City C.I.D. now watches Kosminski in the Met's jurisdiction. His knowledge of the whole affair ceases after Kosminski is carted off by his family, perhaps in cuffs, with the assistance of the local constabulary or workhouse barmy brigade.

Initially, one would logically assume that Kosminski is Robert Sagar's suspect in Butcher's Row, who also got hauled off by his friends. But a little digging does not allow that interpretation. Harry Cox described him in *Thomson's Weekly* along the lines of the "original" profile of the Ripper. "The man we suspected was about 5 foot 6 inches in height, with short, black, curly hair, and he was in the habit of taking late walks abroad. He occupied several shops in the East End, but from time to time he became insane, and was forced to spend a portion of his time in an asylum in Surrey." This certainly isn't the fair-haired unemployed 23 year old Kosminski.

Cox admitted that during the course of the murder spree they had had several suspects under surveillance. City C.I.D. must, in fact, have *discounted* Kosminski as a viable suspect, left off the surveillance, and favored their longstanding suspect in Butcher's Row. Over sherry or something good ol' boy fashion, Sagar or Major Smith must have told Anderson that 'You know, that suspect who got hauled off, finally died' and Anderson took this to be Kosminski, the only suspect that they had a hand in with City C.I.D.

There are a number of coincidences that support this conjecture. Both suspects were carted off by their friends, only months apart. In fact, the 2 cases are remarkably similar, with significant variations that underscore they were mixed together in the official gossip pipe.

As it stands today, Sagar's and the City's slant on things suggests a local Jewish butcher who lived in Middlesex Street, the very street that forms the border between City of London and Whitechapel. This butcher was a native of Aldgate, born in 1856. He was therefore 33 years old in 1888. He was exactly 3 inches taller than Catherine Eddowes. It is interesting that Joseph Hyam Levy, the nervous little fellow whom the Press thought knew too much, whom the Press reported feared testifying, at whom for his fears the inquest audience laughed, said that the man with Eddowes was 3 inches taller than her. Not a few. Not a little. Exactly 3. "I should think he was three inches taller than the woman, who was, perhaps, 5 feet high. I cannot give any further description of them." Was his precise answer a mistake? For you see, the Jewish butcher in question was Jacob Levy.

Jacob Levy was a butcher at 111 Middlesex Street. He was living in Whitechapel with his family at 11 Fieldgate Street. Joseph Hyam Levy was also a butcher. His place of work was 1 Hutchinson Street, right at the crossroads of Middlesex Street. He was about 60 yards from where Jacob worked. Joseph Hyam Levy grew up at 36 Middlesex Street. Were they related? Both were natives of Aldgate, but Joseph was much older at 47 years of age.

Jacob lived with his wife Sarah and two children in 1881, but the family might have grown more by 1888. In 1886 Jacob was sentenced to jail, supposedly for a petty theft of beef from a butcher he worked at in Goulston Street. Instead of prison, however, he was sent to the Essex County lunatic asylum in Kent (not Surrey). He wasn't, however, just a simple butcher gone barmy. His wife's statement was on some of the committal paperwork. The background she gave on her husband was that he had been a shrewd businessman at one point, but now his mental problems were ruining their business. "He also feels that if he is not restrained he will do some violence to someone; he complains about hearing strange noises; cries for no reason; feels compelled to do acts that his conscience cannot stand; and has a conscience of a feeling of exaltation. . .He does not sleep at nights and wanders around aimlessly for hours."

During the Whitechapel murders Jacob Levy was out and about and presumably holding down butcher jobs around Aldgate. He was, however, suffering from syphilis, which means during his earlier night prowls he probably had had contact with some of the Whitechapel drabs. Syphilis may explain the onset of his mental problems, as it can affect the brain and lead to complete mental breakdown.

. . .And this was the fate for Levy. On August 15, 1890, he was declared insane and was committed to the City of London's asylum in Stone, Kent. He would never leave. Less than a year later, on July 26, 1891, he died of the complications (General Paralysis of the Insane) brought about by syphilis.

In separating the two cases of Kosminski and Levy, one can begin to see where the Met was making their mistakes. This date of death underscores the idea that Kosminski and Levy together form a composite. Kosminski was hauled off in February 1891. Levy's death date is only 5 months after Kosminski was committed. Both Anderson and Swanson recall the Ripper died shortly after committal. Macnaghten's date of March 1889 is simply another one of his mistakes. He interpreted the withdrawal of the plainclothes detectives from the streets as indicating the suspect was carted off. Cox made the same mistake too. He believed that the Butcher's Row suspect "left off his usual haunts" after being tailed. Cox had merely been pulled from the beat in March 1889.

There are more corollaries. Kosminski was committed to an asylum only once, at the very last. But Cox had said that his suspect had been committed in Surrey before the crimes. Anderson, too, seems to have heard this. In the 1895 Alfred Aylmer article for Wyndsor Magazine, he speaks of Anderson's theory and says that the Ripper was a homicidal maniac "temporarily at large." Lady Anderson later recalled hearing that the Ripper had been committed to an asylum, not erroneously in Surrey as Cox remembered but at the actual asylum to which Levy had been committed at *Stone, Kent.*

According to Macnaghten's memorandum, Kosminski had a great hatred for prostitutes. Yet there is no evidence for this at all. Rather, this is the suspect that Cox watched. While shadowing him one night, he saw him openly revile one drunken prostitute and then hook up with another. "Just as I was beginning to prepare myself for a terrible ordeal, however, he pushed her away from him and set off at a rapid pace."

There isn't much known about Jacob Levy to help Ripperologists build a profile. But one can make some solid deductions. One, being a native of Aldgate he knew the area well. He could have many potential places at his disposal for night use. He seems to have had contact with Whitechapel's prostitutes. He would know the hot spots. He would probably even know offbeat places like Buck's Row and Winthrop Street due to the slaughterhouses.

Cox writes something to intrigue our curiosity about Hyam Levy. "We had many people under observation while the murders were being perpetrated, but it was not until the discovery of the body of Mary Kelly had been made that we seemed to get upon the trail." This is an interesting statement. Could one of the Mitre Square witnesses have been pushed over the edge by this and come forward to inform the police of whom he had actually seen?

Joseph Lawende was cool and closed-lipped at the inquest. He didn't think he could recognize the man he saw at Church Passage with Eddowes again. In contrast, Joseph Hyam Levy was nervous, and the papers had prepared London that he was nervous. Could Hyam Levy have been wrestling with his conscience? Had he been trying to convince himself it had not been Jacob Levy? Was he in a quandary as what to do if asked outright at the inquest? If this supposition, and highly speculative supposition at that, is true then one thing may have sent Joseph over the edge— the ghastly murder in Miller's Court. He would realize that Jacob isn't going to stop. He can't turn him in with any dogma. He's then convicted for not turning evidence earlier at Eddowes' inquest. He must suggest that they look into Jacob Levy. They now have their prime suspect, which Cox is assigned to follow.

Questions are a mandatory step of science; but the answers may never be forthcoming in this instance. Even Cox and Sagar caution us that there was no evidence against their suspect whatsoever. How can it be found today? Moreover, we simply don't know how all the City suspects fit in. Cox said there was more than one. By his own admission most of the detectives believed that their particular Butcher's Row suspect had something to do with the crimes. But who indeed had any facts? They were looking for madmen. Their suspect appeared crazy and he hated women. That may have been enough.

Personally, I believe that Jacob Levy is Sagar's suspect. But is he the Ripper? In truth, there are things in the Jacob Levy angle that contradict the mug shot of the Ripper. Clearly, the first is that the Ripper was a smooth character. He did not openly accost harlots (as the Butcher's Row suspect did). As a Jew, Levy would hardly want to escalate the murders into anti-Jewish riots viz. the Goulston Street graffito. The Ripper and the Butcher's Row suspect were also taller. The 5 foot 3 estimate for Levy, of course, could be wrong. It may be, however, that in boots and a bonnet Eddowes appeared much taller than her 5 feet. In like manner, Levy may have appeared taller than his 5 foot 3 inches in shoes and a hat but still a few inches taller than Eddowes. Confusingly, though, the man with Eddowes— light mustache, hair— doesn't match Cox's description of the Butcher's Row suspect or the Ripper. We have no detailed description of Levy.

Was that poor schlemiel Kosminski trying his hand with Eddowes and she politely rebuffed the penniless twerp? Did the actual smooth Ripper then come out of the shadows moments later and lead her into the dark Church Passage? Considering the mistakes that Met officers made in reciting the Kosminski case, we can't even be sure that it was Kosminski who was taken all the way to the Seaside Home to be identified, presumably by Joseph Levy (there were seaside homes for workers). All we know is that that poor Kosminski is identified by name by someone. The identification impressed the Met, but obviously not City C.I.D.

We cannot rely word-for-word on memories and then reconcile them with known facts. Even substituting Levy in

Kosminski's place, there would be terrible problems in the scenario above. Anderson's wording is that the witness didn't know the suspect was Jewish ". . .but when he learned that the suspect was a fellow-Jew he declined to swear to him." The wording of Swanson's marginalia does not carry that, but it carries some indication of the suspect showing this guilt. Could it have been the suspect identifying himself as Jewish? 'You wouldn't turn in a fellow Jew, would you?' This would negate Jacob and Joseph Levy as the antagonist and protagonist. Alas, Joseph would already have known that Jacob was Jewish. He probably also would have known that Aaron Kosminski was Jewish. He might have known the family. When a furrier, Martin Kosminski, applied for citizenship, Joseph Levy vouched for him.

"Theories!" cried Abberline in an 1892 *Cassell's Saturday Journal* article. "We were almost lost in theories: there were so many of them."

Indeed.

The third name on the Macnaghten Memorandum reveals the liquid nature of Macnaghten's source information.

3) Michael Ostrog, a Russian doctor, and a convict, who was subsequently detained in a lunatic asylum as a homicidal maniac. This man's antecedents were of the worst possible type, and his whereabouts at the time of the murders could never be ascertained.

The last sentence sums up the evidence Macnaghten had — none. Ostrog was merely unaccounted for during the time but was a suspicious fellow.

Ostrog fits the Ripper in only one way. He alone fits the description of shabby genteel. He could pass himself off as a Polish count. He was accomplished in many languages and could even impress English gentry that he himself was gentrified. He was also foreign— Polish or Russian (or even Polish Jew). He had dark hair. . .and there the similarity ends. He was far too tall at 5 feet 11 inches. He had never been a doctor. He was also about 53 years old, though he looked younger. He wasn't a homicidal maniac. He was but a mountebank and a charlatan and petty thief for which he always got caught, very often around Eton or Oxford— perhaps why an old Etonian like Macnaghten knew of him. Ostrog was perhaps the biggest stranger to good luck since Honest John Brody tried to steal the Brooklyn Bridge.

As with everything, even with famous crime, there is a period in which interest in it vanishes before there comes renaissance. This began in the early 20th century when the Ripper crimes began to enter their own public legend. As with all legends, it is the most sensational elements that linger in the ether and then take form when the renaissance comes. Mitigating clues and evidence are lost. Hype and hyperbole take their place. Theorizing sprouts from half facts and clouded memories. For example, Arthur Conan-Doyle had popularized that a woman, euphemistically labeled by him as Jill the Ripper, might have been responsible. Through the dim haze of popular rendition it was recalled that two hats were found with Frances Coles. Could the other hat have been the killer's? (Even at the time of Sadler's arrest, the two hats inspired the newspapers to wonder if a woman and not Sadler was responsible.) There was, of course, nothing to it. Both hats belonged to Coles.

In 1905, interest in Jack the Ripper had inspired a tour conducted by Dr. Gordon Brown. He led a number of luminaries, included Conan-Doyle, around the murder scenes. He insisted there was anatomical knowledge, but it was that of a butcher, not a doctor. In itself this showed how City C.I.D. still clung to its own theory of a maniac in Butcher's Row.

When journalistic interest revived, it was the penny vibe of a fiendish Simon Pure or mad doctor, an image helped no little by Griffiths via Macnaghten's confidential memorandum. Marie Belloc Lowndes encrypted this image for us in *The Lodger*, her bestseller in 1913, a book which has inspired several film adaptations since then. In 1926, the first— *The Lodger: a Story of the London Fog*— was a silent-era screamer by no less than Alfred Hitchcock. As its title suggests, it gave us all the props and the moody backdrop. Thereafter this image had little to contend with. The Ripper became the embodiment of sophisticated or pious evil— the top hat, heavy overcoat, doctor's bag concealing his fiendish instruments and trophies. Many writers have rightly lamented that Jack the Ripper became one of the most romanticized figures in literature.

In 1965 the two first weighty studies were published, and we were given two extremely different (but not so original) images of the Ripper. Tom Cullen (*Autumn of Terror*) gave us the brooding Montague Druitt, a middle class, educated man fighting hereditary insanity. His twisted goal was social reform. Robin Odell gave us a low-class Jewish (even Hasidic!) butcher in *Jack the Ripper in Fact and Fiction.*

Since then the theories have reached out to include Royal conspiracies and numerous subplots. Amateur and professional sleuths alike have sought the most elusive serial killer. Jack the Ripper became real again. Someone had to have been the Ripper. Writers thereafter broke the mold of toff and lout. They have proposed candidates and they have molded them. From a patchwork of clues, they have given us an array of suspects.

15

ℌYPOTHESIS NON ℱINGO

GEORGE SIMS PERHAPS never forgot his 1903 broadsides with Abberline through the gun ports of popular gazettes. The Jack the Ripper case would remain on his mind, but he was no doubt satisfied enough with Griffiths' unknown but authoritative source to refrain probing too deeply into verifying his theory. Then Anderson stirred up so much in 1910. This must have affected Sims greatly and caused him to question Macnaghten's theory. He had never been given much information in the way of a name to actually verify the accuracy of the "drowned doctor in Thames" theory. He had only an initial, and this may have been given to him (probably by Griffiths) only verbally. This we know, for when he later tried to verify the "drown doctor theory" he only had "Dr. D" whereby to stimulate the memory of other inspectors.

One of his retired correspondents was Inspector John Littlechild. In 1913 an exchange of letters occurred between them. Not only was Littlechild not reticent to recall that most at Scotland Yard believed that "Tom Bullen [Bulling] of the Central News" was responsible for the Dear Boss letters, he frankly admitted "I never heard of a Dr. D. in connection with the Whitechapel murders but among the suspects, and to my mind a very likely one, was a Dr. T. (which sounds very much like D). He was an American quack named Tumblety and was at one time a frequent visitor of London and on these occasions constantly brought under the notice of police, there being a large dossier on him at Scotland Yard."

Tumblety was nothing in "Ripperana" until Stewart Evans and Paul Gainey introduced him in detail with their joint 1995 book *The Lodger: the arrest and escape of Jack the Ripper*, which was then reprinted as *Jack the Ripper: first American serial killer*. However, promoting Tumblety as a genuine suspect is the best example of violating *hypothesis non fingo*. Sir Isaac Newton was always so considerate to give us erudite expressions that conveyed basic concepts. All it means in Latin is "I feign no hypothesis." In other words, he would not dress up some idea that is possible but highly improbable with the language reserved for genuine and plausible theory. To do so is to mask excessive speculation for something that simply does not have enough credible evidence.

Francis Tumblety was an American of Irish birth who was a garish, flamboyant quack and fop. He touted a signature huge handlebar mustache. He was a high-end snake oil peddler who led an almost itinerant life of one jump ahead of the local sheriff. He advertised himself as a great healer and doctor wherever he went, and had a knack to ingratiate himself into the upper stratum of most any town in which he resided. Despite his lifestyle and various charges of malpractice brought against him he got rich, dying worth close to $150,000 greenbacks in 1903, which makes him sound more like he had been a high-end blackmailer than herbalist.

He was, however, in London at the time of the autumn of terror, and appears to be the man with the "American hat," as the newspapers reported the suspect, at Albert Chambers, who was the first American whisked off after the Double Event. Back in America, Tumblety later wrote a pamphlet capitalizing on his involvement with the now-famous Ripper killings. In this he said that "Someone had said that Jack the Ripper was an American, and everybody believed that statement. Then it is the universal belief among the lower classes that all Americans wear slouch hats; therefore Jack the Ripper must wear a slouch hat. Now I happened to have on a slouch hat, and this, together with the fact that I was an American, was enough for the police. It established my guilt beyond any question."

Truth is, Tumblety spun events for himself as best he

could. As Littlechild made clear later, he had quite a record. While in London he apparently had courted male prostitutes and perhaps even engaged in public sex. His apparent homosexual tendencies might have confirmed to the police that he was indeed a woman hater. Not only did he not care for women, he apparently beat his men. He had been arrested on several counts for gross indecency and assault on 4 men on four different dates. Two of the dates given are October 14 and again on November 2. Arrested yet again, he was given a date to appear before the Magistrate, and was released on bail, which two male friends put up for him. Tumblety, however, skipped town to France and from there back to America, leaving his "friends" in London to lose their bail money.

There is no question that Tumblety was a woman hater and was considered a "brute" by those who knew him. William Pinkerton himself, founder of the famous detective agency, so stated in the *Daily Picayune* in November 1888. Coupled with the assertion he was a doctor, this probably made him a likely suspect in the C.I.D.'s mind. As late as November 19, it seems certain that Tumblety was still suspect of something far more than accosting young men. On this date Robert Anderson had cabled San Francisco Police inquiring about samples of Tumblety's handwriting.

Nevertheless, as we know from Anderson's own views on the Ripper, Tumblety was not considered a suspect for very long. He simply doesn't fit the Ripper description. Not only was he 55 years old, in 1890 we get a clear physical description of him from the Washington DC police. They arrested him for lurking in the shadows with intent to do what they didn't know what. On his person they found the testimonial pamphlets about what a great doctor he is, his reply to charges that he was the Ripper, and several thousand dollars in diamonds and other articles. He was described by the police succinctly, including his famous mustache: He was "an enormous man, over 6 feet in height, with broad shoulders. His hair is black, tinged with gray, and his skin is red and coarse. His mustache is a rather large affair, evidently dyed black, and extends around the corners of his mouth. His eyes are steely blue, and he gazed steadily at nothing, as he spoke in a weak, effeminate voice. He was dressed in a big black overcoat and wore a German cap, and he had on rubber boots."

This is simply not Jack the Ripper. This description does not even bear a semblance to the man seen with any of the women before they were killed. And no one like this could have blended into Whitechapel.

A better case can probably be made for Tumblety being the American who offered 20 quid per uterus. . .but it can't really go beyond speculation. He was indeed a woman hater and would have associated with men of that ilk in London. But he wasn't a genuine doctor, only a quack, and there was little reason he would have needed a uterus for anything. And as we've seen in the actual evidence, the Ripper seems to have desired a uterus only once. From other victims he took Kidney, blood, heart.

Perhaps the most feigned hypothesis is the "Royal Conspiracy" in all its various incarnations. Its first incarnation has Prince Albert Victor, the heir presumptive to the British Empire, as Jack the Ripper. The reason he became Jack the Ripper is essentially because he went barmy from having syphilis. In his warped mind he decided to kill harlots, the very symbols of where he had gotten the fatal disease. His rampage was finally stopped because of the Royal Family physician, the ever-loyal and renowned Baronet William Gull. In the hands of this illustrious Royal Surgeon, Albert Victor was finally incarcerated and treated. Yet the disease and its damage was irreversible. Historically, Albert Victor died in 1892 of influenza. But according to the dark shadows of the Royal Conspiracy Theory he actually died of the immoral disease he contracted from too much indiscriminate contact with East End brothels.

Albert Victor was no snob, this is true. He was affectionately known as "Eddy." All and sundry remarked how both he and his brother George never put on any airs. This was a trait very desirable in the future King of England. His father, the Prince of Wales, was also known for his affability. It was his grandmother, Queen Victoria, who had lived largely reclusively after her husband, Prince Albert, had died unexpectedly. Thus London's greatest contact with Royalty was with two future kings: the Prince of Wales who would indeed later become Edward VII and his son, Eddy, who then would have succeeded him to be Edward VIII. Eddy's death would prove quite a shock to Britain. It deprived them of current Royal contact and a future popular king.

However, in contrast to the Royal Conspiracy Theory's slant on things, Eddy's known "common touch" was more like his father's. It didn't imply a street wandering prince. He may have been involved in some Cleveland Street scandal, where many of the gentry's future generation were enjoying illicit carnality at a "house," but he was not some lone stalker in the night interested in fairly ugly and stinky drabs. Catherine Eddowes' apron, to provide one graphic visual, was thought to be black until the police realized it was a white one that was merely that filthy. Can you imagine what she must have smelled like?

Anyway, the first wisps we hear of this diabolical connection is in 1962 from a seemingly respectable publication *Edouard VII*, the biography by Phillipe Jullien of Eddy's father, King Edward VII. Therein he stated in passing that Albert Victor, with the assistance of the Duke of Bedford, was *rumored* to have committed the murders. Had Jullien checked any original sources for the comment, he would have realized there was no contemporary rumor of the kind.

Rather, Jullien seems to have gotten his information from a doctor named Thomas Stowell. In 1970, Stowell finally went public and gives us his own intriguing slant on all this. The conduit was the niche magazine, the *Criminologist*. Supposedly, based on the papers of the late Sir Gull, Stowell made a case for Jack the Ripper's identity having been known by a few elite in the medical circle around the Royal Family. Stowell only referred to him as "S," but from his descriptions it seemed obvious to many crime readers that he was referring to Eddy. The illusion of trying to conceal the actual identity made his suspect even more exciting. The truth is no more salacious than when there is an attempt to mask it, no matter how poorly done.

It got even better. Stowell pioneered the syphilis angle as the motive for Eddy committing the murders. The Royal Family was cognizant of this, of course, and hushed it up. Immediately after Eddowes' murder, Eddy was captured and hauled off to a private sanitarium. He escaped, however, in time to stalk Whitechapel and kill Mary Jane Kelly. He was then recaptured and put permanently in a private ward in Sandringham, the family's personal country estate.

Stowell enlarged on the part played by psychic Robert Lees, saying that his psychic vibes led police on a chase to Sir Gull's home, whose wife, upon questioning, though miffed, confirmed her husband was absent during the times of which they enquired (the murder times). Stowell's source for this appears to have been Gull's daughter, Caroline Acland. Her husband, Theodore Acland, was once Stowell's superior and close friend. According to Stowell, Acland had said that her father had eventually come downstairs and confirmed that he had lapses of memory on account of a stroke. On one occasion, he said he even discovered blood on his shirt. From there, of course, Stowell's inference took over.

Stowell draws parallels between Albert Victor's resemblance to the Ripper— dark hair, height, etc. Aside from this, however, there really isn't anything else. In fact, it is not certain if Stowell truly meant Eddy by "S." His article caused such a furor that he made a statement denying the implication. Yet if Collin Wilson, an early Ripperologist, is right Stowell could not have meant anybody but Eddy. In 1962 Wilson and Stowell had had lunch after Wilson had written a series on the Ripper. Stowell overtly revealed his belief that Eddy was the Ripper. Another Ripperologist, Stewart Evans, who would later promote Tumblety, believed that Jullien actually got the information from Stowell via Wilson. However it's baked, it seems the leaven was Stowell.

In the interim, however, did Stowell refine his theory and shift suspects? That seems unlikely, since in his 1970 article he still referred to "S" as the heir of "power and wealth." Stowell would never be able to clarify. After the uproar, he had little time to prepare the thesis he proclaimed would expose all. Four days after the article's release he died of natural causes. He did not leave any sources.

Stowell's death was, however, a sensational climax to an already sensational scoop. Naturally, this inspired others to try and uncover the details of his implications. The first one to put this forward in serious print was Frank Spiering in his book *Prince Jack*. Spiering kept some of the original cast and even brings Gull deeper into the conspiracy. He claimed he found some of his notes in the New York Academy of Medicine. In these Sir Gull noted that he hypnotized Eddy. To his horror, Eddy reenacted killing the drabs in front of him. Spiering ponders whether Eddy's father did not conspire with Lord Salisbury, the PM, to have Eddy killed by morphine injection, thereby removing an unfit heir to the throne, and then merely claimed he died of influenza.

Spiering does not rank amongst the true Ripperologists, for his book clearly had no facts behind it. The New York Academy confirmed it had no such documents. No Ripperologist has ever found any. Spiering is next heard in 1978 when he demanded that Queen Elizabeth II come clean about Royal knowledge and release the Royal archives dealing with the period. Such were already open to view, but Spiering must have believed vital material was being kept back.

Perhaps Spiering made such a ta-do in 1978 in order to dovetail on the ultimate Royal Conspiracy adaptation to that date. In 1976, Stephen Knight had published *Jack the Ripper: the final solution*, and it had ignited the spreadsheets. In 1978 it was adapted to a Sherlock Holmes format, *Murder By Decree*, starring Christopher Plumber as the indomitable sleuth and James Mason as his trusty companion, Dr. Watson. The build up to its February 1979 release inspired much Ripper press and reinvigorated sales in Knight's unexpected triumph.

In his book, Knight removed some of the more obvious ludicrous elements from Stowell and Spiering's ideas, creating an interesting hybrid. Obviously, Prince Albert Victor could not have been Jack the Ripper. His whereabouts could easily be accounted for at that time (on one occasion, he was even having tea with his grandmother Queen Victoria in Scotland). But what about a conspiracy? What if others had conspired to save the young prince and future king's reputation? This would prove far more sales worthy and believable.

Britain had already gotten a foretaste of this scenario in 1973 when the BBC did a spectacular broadcast in which the fictional detectives were Barlow and Watt instead of the brand names of Holmes and Watson. The producers knew well of Stowell and Spiering's ideas, of course. But they also learned that a man named Joseph Sickert could provide sensational information on a motive for a conspiracy. It was an amazing claim: Albert Victor had been illegally married to a Catholic commoner. By British law, no member of the Royal Family can marry a Catholic without forfeiting their right to the throne. No Catholic may ever come to the throne. Period.

The producers were enthralled with Joseph Sickert's eccentric and controversial story. He was the son of a very famous painter, Walter Sickert, who, according to Joe Sickert, had married the girl, Alice Crook, born to Albert Victor and this Catholic commoner named Annie Elizabeth Crook. Thus Joe was actually Albert Victor's grandson.

According to Joe Sickert, he got the story from his famous father. The conspiracy took many forms. It involved Lord Salisbury, his father, Sir Gull, and Queen Victoria. . .and eventually the Masonic Brotherhood. The purpose was to get Eddy and Annie separated, and then get Annie to a private sanitarium where she could never divulge the existence of the marriage and the daughter. Gull supposedly performed experiments on Annie, framed in the deep irreligious lights of late Victorian austerity, that drove her insane. Some years after Albert Victor's death, Alice, despite the enormous age difference between her and Walter Sickert, married him. The result was the birth of Joseph.

This present author is no stranger to Royal pretenders. On one occasion I have been threatened with international lawsuit by one who insisted I had documents which would reveal her true family connections. According to her, even the Scottish parliament was awaiting the information, being very interested in her claims of being the long lost Royal Stuart heir. One does not have to be around this sort for long to develop a keen sense about them. No one pretends to be second best. To believe that is the result of absolute psychological naiveté. No one pretends to be an obscure princeling's decedent who is 100th in line from the throne. Every pretender is sole and primogeniture heir, either of a throne, title or fortune. It's a way for unaccomplished people to feel prestige or privilege without having the necessary accomplishments to merit that distinction. Pretenders are a little more practical than the reincarnation crowd, but that's about it. No one is a 17th century tinker with the crabs reincarnated. No one pretends to be the mule herder's grandson. Everybody is Rudolf Valentino.

Sickert's story follows along these lines. He invented a bizarre tale in which the heir presumptive of a vast empire sired his mother, and in turn he is the direct and bodily heir of Albert Victor and hence Queen Victoria, Catholicism aside. Whatever the motive was, he cashed in on Royal ancestry and the hottest mystery London ever knew. He meshed them together and Stephen Knight ran with it.

According to Joe Sickert, Mary Kelly was the nanny to his mother, Alice, when Alice was young. The reason Kelly and the other drabs were killed was because Kelly had told her whore friends the truth of it all. The scandal had to be silenced, which meant everyone who knew had to be greased.

Due to such infidelity's threat to the monarchy, a group of loyal Masons set about to do them in according to Masonic ritual, encrypting into the killings their code of vengeance. Sir Gull was, of course, central to killing them. His loyal henchman, John Netley, drove the stalking brougham and helped whisk them away. This was accomplished by drugging the harlots with doctored grapes. This featured prominently in Stephen Knight's book and in *Murder by Decree*.

Of this particularly fanciful episode, Wolf Vanderlinden (*Ripperana* No. 39, 2003) writes: "Knight's claim that Sir William Gull used poisoned grapes as a method of subduing the Whitechapel victims inside the coach driven by John Netley is key to the Sickert story. This claim shrivels to so many dried raisins when it is revealed that none of the Jack the Ripper victims had eaten grapes just before their deaths, a fact based on the post-mortem findings. Grapes were specifically mentioned as not being present during the Elizabeth Stride inquest while Dr. Sedgwick Saunders, who had been looking for drugs or poisons in Catherine Eddowes' stomach contents, found nothing. What can one say about this false clue? Just that it becomes another revealing piece of illuminating evidence of the total untrustworthiness of the entire Sickert fable."

Researchers uncovered more untrustworthiness. It was easily discovered that Joe Sickert's obscure grandmother, Annie Crook, was verified to have been in and out of workhouses and asylums in the 1890s. On top of this, Joe Sickert changed his story sometimes. When Knight was cashing in on it, Sickert claimed that the Masonic conspiracy angle was something he had just made up. After Knight's death, he retracted this retraction and perhaps saw his chance to cash in on it again.

On top of all this, it seems that Joe Sickert isn't even Walter Sickert's son, but the son of a man named William Gorman, a former professional boxer, and the Alice Crook in question. Yet his pretensions have been long in the making. In 1969 he presented himself to Helen Lassore, of Beaux Arts Galleries, as the *grandson* of Walter Sickert. A cousin of his also confirmed to Paul Begg and Mervyn Fairclough, high-profiled Ripperologists, that Walter Sickert was the "putative" father of Alice Crook. She also confirmed that certain stories had been in circulation since his childhood. Thus Joe may have elaborated on them, cut in Royal parentage and a Masonic conspiracy.

Amongst other absurdities, he claimed that Albert Victor was still alive until 1930, being kept by the Bowes-Lyon family. Their reward was that their daughter, Elizabeth (later Queen Elizabeth the Queen Mother), was allowed to marry the future king, George VI.

Walter Sickert himself has later been turned ignobly into Jack the Ripper. This is based on the notion that his paintings reflect knowledge of the murder scenes which only the killer could have known. Sickert, impressionist painter and eccentric, was known to only paint from life, from sketches he had made or from photographs. It did not simply invent scenes in his mind and put them on canvas. From what we have seen in the timing of the Ripper's strikes, wherein he killed and mutilated in only minutes, there was really no time (or light) for him to stand over the body and sketch the gruesome scene for his paintings. Also, like a surgeon, no painter compromises the delicacy of his hands. Two of the victims show that an incredibly strong hand clutched their faces, and it is highly unlikely, if it need even be elaborated, that a painter isn't going to possess surgical ability.

However, the idea that there was a relationship between a member of the Royal Family and Annie Crook was something that Walter Sickert had mentioned, perhaps as early as 1892. Even when Joe Gorman-Sickert retracted his Masonic conspiracy theory he maintained that his mother/grandmother was the product of this relationship.

If Gorman-Sickert's mother/grandmother Alice Crook was the product of a liaison with Albert Victor, it was never provable, perhaps even to the Royal Family, for even a Guelf and a Wettin would have taken better care of such a girl than was apparently her and her mother's fate. Researchers clearly proved that Alice's mother, Annie, was in workhouses and later sanitariums. If the liaison was invented by Annie, she may have done so to give her daughter some pedigree. Walter Sickert may have repeated this. But to extrapolate this to justify a Masonic/Royal conspiracy associated with Jack the Ripper is nonsense.

In the final analysis, the liaison was unlikely and the reason for a conspiracy is unlikely. To have illegally married a Catholic meant nothing. It would be annulled. George IV is said to have married the Catholic Mrs. Fitzherbert and kept it secret. Scandalous perhaps. But nothing throne shattering.

But you can't keep a good angle down. Royal Conspiracy sells. Prince Albert Victor is yet again associated with the Ripper killings in an indirect way. Supposedly, he had a homosexual love affair with his tutor at Cambridge, James Kenneth Stephen. When Stephen was jilted, he took up the murder of prostitutes, killing them on significant days in relation to Royal Family birthdays or, at the other end of an unconnected theoretical spectrum, on pre-Christian holidays. This was proposed by author Michael Harrison in his 1972 book *Clarence*. He took Stowell's theory yet again and ran with it sans the ludicrous Sickert fabalizing. He could also argue that Stowell meant (S)tephen when he used the initial "S" for the killer.

The above motive would be lacking in a sane man, but Stephen was known to have had his wits bashed from him in a terrible accident in 1886. He increasingly got worse, though denying that there was anything wrong with himself, and eventually died young in 1892.

Getting into more interesting and genuinely diabolical figures, we come to Dr. Thomas Neill Cream. He was a notorious American poisoner, a cross-eyed philanderer who finally got caught after one of his client's husbands got wind of the extramarital treatment she was receiving at his office. He then poisoned said husband, Daniel Stott, with strychnine in his medicine. Cream would have escaped detection except for his own stupidity. The death had been registered as due to epilepsy, thus there was no police investigation or suspicion. However, Cream wrote a letter to the coroner blaming the pharmacist. Although the coroner dismissed the letter, the District Attorney did not. After the exhumation, strychnine was discovered and it was traced to Cream. He was tried and found guilty and then sentenced to life in prison at Joliet near Chicago, Illinois. There he remained until 1891 when he was released for good behavior.

He immediately went to Canada to collect a sizable inheritance and thence to London, where he arrived and started practicing in the south of London. Two more women died by his poisoning hand, and in each case he would have escaped detection except for his stupid bragging that he knew a lot about the deaths. He even took a couple of people on tours of the death location. This had alerted Scotland Yard, and eventually they determined he was the murderer. He was tried for only one of the deaths and was found guilty and sentenced to be hanged.

As the trap was about to fall, he uttered the words "I am Jack—" and alas the trap door opened and the cross-eyed poisoner of women fell through. The hangman insisted that these were his last words. Thus despite the fact that he was in prison in Illinois at the time of the Ripper murders, some have tried to associate him with being the Ripper. He was a brutal, wicked looking man, who was a doctor. But nothing else fits. Attempts to seriously propose that he had a double in Jolliet to cover for his real movements have been met with collective laughter.

There should be little reason to doubt that Cream tried to claim to be Jack the Ripper. He was demented enough that he thought the murder of women was worth bragging over, in his "innocent" way, and even taking people to the crime scenes. Claiming to be Jack the Ripper was just another way of grandstanding. There is no DA who is not aware of the demented minds that confess to famous and publicized killings after they are reported. Scotland Yard was already aware of it during the autumn of terror. There was more than a few who confessed but who were dismissed as insane or drunk. Sadly, more than even this number boasted at pubs that they were impressed with the Ripper's style.

One of these even became another suspect momentarily. Alfred Napier Blanchard was a salesman of sorts; a canvasser, as they were called then. He had been drinking all day, October 5, 1888, in the Birmingham pub Fox and Goose. By eventide (and after 5 or more pints in him), he decided to sound off.

"I am the Whitechapel murderer," the fool declared. He then turned to an elderly patron and said: "Look here, old gentleman; perhaps you would not think there was a murderer in the house."

"I don't know about that," replied the old gent. "You might not look unlike one."

"I am one, then," declared Blanchard.

He excited only perfunctory curiosity. The old man asked him if he had the knife on him. But Blanchard said he had left it behind. Then another asked how he kept them quiet and from screaming. "Simply by placing the thumb and finger on the windpipe and cutting the throat with the right hand." He then told them they were fools if they didn't arrest him and claim the large reward. To his later regret, they carted him off.

When finally sober, he stood before the magistrate. Mr. Barradale asked Blanchard: "Were you suffering from the drink?"

Sheepishly, Blanchard admitted to this; and partly from "nervousness," he added. Naturally, they had to check into him. As he was being led to his cell, he stopped and supplicated a favor of Mr. Barradale. He asked that the Press be "kind enough not to mention this case." This was a very serious thing that he did, and he didn't want to get the sack.

"The magistrates have no power over the Press," replied Mr. Barradale.

Alas, this was true. The above exchange was reported in many papers on October 6, including the *Star* and the *Times*.

Mary Kelly's former light of love has even entered the world that treads upon *hypothesis non fingo*. Joe Barnett was sufficiently cleared at the time by the police who were able to show he was at the boarding house. His inquest testimony therefore was upheld. Thus there seems little reason to speculate further. However, it has been done. Starting in the 1970s, Bruce Paley championed Barnett as Jack the Ripper. Until the publication of his book *Jack the Ripper: The Simple Truth* in 1995, only one fictionalized novel had made Barnett the Ripper. Paul Harrison's 1991 attempt (*Jack the Ripper: The Mystery Solved*) also failed because it was exposed for its many errors in research.

Nevertheless, Paley's selection of Barnett does not fit the Ripper. He speculates that Barnett was increasingly agitated by Kelly plying trade. Barnett killed the old drabs in order to scare Kelly from walking the streets. In a nutshell his plan failed. When they had their final falling out, he killed Kelly in a rage of passion.

The "logic" of this rather reminds me of Level 1 philosophy students who ignore the warning from their tutor that their conclusions must be supported by the reasons they give in order for their comments to even be regarded as subject to logical discussion. Paley's scenario overlooks that to have effectively scared Kelly, Barnett would have to know that his killings would get sufficient Press, something he could not have foreseen. He could only expect this after Tabram's death. He would thus have to dovetail on that killing. It also assumes the Ripper only killed the "canonical 5," a canon which stems largely from Macnaghten. It overlooks that more than one killer might have been involved. There is, in fact, no reason to suspect Barnett. He would have no anatomical knowledge. Kelly was the first young prostitute targeted. How would killing middle-aged harlots cause her sufficient worry to stop? How is stealing organs and mutilation a necessity toward these proposed ends? How is trying to incite the East End into riots against Jews relevant?

Other corollaries pointing to Barnett as the Ripper have been proposed. He was 5'7" and age 30. However, this overlooks that he was not "shabby genteel" by any means. His age, mustache and build could point to thousands of men. It was the foreign appearance and shabby gentility of the Ripper that made him stand out. Nothing else. Barnett did not own a variety of deerstalkers and long coats, with which the Ripper was identified. Ginger beer bottles were found in 13 Miller's Court, and on one of the Dear Boss letters a Ginger beer bottle was mentioned. By the 1990s, however, it was fairly certain that those letters were hoaxes cooked up by either or both Tom Bulling and Fred Best. By Kelly's killing, Scotland Yard was already suspicious of them. Ginger beer bottles were not rarities. The mystery of the locked door also comes into play. This could indicate that the killer possessed the key that had mysteriously gone missing. Would this not finger Barnett? However, this overlooks the inquest testimony. The lock was a spring bolt and closed into place on its own when the door slammed. The killer would never have needed a key. He would have seen Kelly unlock the door by reaching through. He would know from this, without needing any pre-knowledge of the room, how to re-secure the bolt.

Legend and folklore have allowed another suspect to attain a high profile. James Maybrick was a successful top hat wearing Liverpool cotton merchant. He died of the effects of arsenic toxicity in May 1889. His wife, Florence, was tried and found guilty. Fifteen years later she was reprieved when too much evidence surfaced that her husband had been a longtime abuser of arsenic.

James Maybrick became a Ripper suspect in the 1990s due to the discovery of a journal purporting to be his diary. This journal was conveniently signed "Jack the Ripper." In this diary the writer details his movements between April 1888 and May 1889, a time that encompasses some of the period of the Whitechapel Murders. The writer speaks about taking lodgings in Whitechapel and his vengeance upon "whores," mentioning enough details, though obliquely, that he is responsible for the death of 5 harlots. When the journal finally saw the light of day, it caused quite a furor. The man to whom it had been given, Michael Barrett, had taken it to a literary agent in April 1992. She in turn had it investigated. Enough people were impressed to warrant the agent commissioning Shirley Harrison to research and write a book.

Even before publication, the book promised to be controversial. Its prelude had been a long one, fraught with scientific tests of the paper and ink and complete with contradictory findings and strong disagreements about its age and authenticity. Ripperologist Martin Fido also read it and noted 20 misspellings and anachronisms inconsistent with Victorian England. When it came time for the American rights, Warner Books expressed interest. They hired an impressive array of experts to reexamine the journal. Based on the slant of the calligraphy, it seemed conclusive this was not a daily journal. Several entries had been written at one time rather than as daily entries as is typical in a diary. Furthermore, handwriting analysis showed that the same hand that had written and signed Maybrick's will had not written the journal. Altogether Warner's experts declared it to be a fake. Warner backed out. Hyperion instead published Harrison's book.

Aside from the findings of these investigations, there are other problems with the journal's contents. Most damning is that the writer merely reflects the folklore and urban legend that developed after the Ripper killings. The mistakes traceable to this are numerous. The most obvious is that the writer implies there were only 5 victims. The writer's understanding of certain crime scenes is also horribly in error and stems only from later embellishments. For example, the writer claims that he had the key to No. 13 Miller's Court and that is how he left a locked door behind him. This was a garish mistake. He even uses it to inspire a grisly rhyme. The writer also says he left Kelly's breasts on the table when that was not the case.

Of Annie Chapman's death scene, the writer believed the erroneous legend that she was only wearing two rings. He added the two pills found by her head to help another gibberish rhyme. "One ring, two rings," reads the diary entry. "A farthing one and two Along with M ha ha Will catch clever Jim, Its true No'pill, left but two." Annie Chapman's *three* rings probably symbolized her 3 children. The writer also makes another mistake: he adds the legend that 2 farthings were also found by Chapman. In actuality, this is never mentioned at the Chapman Inquest. The only place that 2 farthings can be found mentioned in official papers is at the McKenzie Inquest, in which Edmund Reid said that the only other place farthings had been found was at Chapman's scene.

This may actually have been Reid's own mistake.

The writer's repeat usage of "ha ha" in his entries also reflects the usage in the Dear Boss Letters, an indication that the journal was inspired only by popular legend before the probable origin of their forgery became commonly known outside of Scotland Yard circles.

The errors continue. Of Polly Nichols' death, the diary inaccurately recalls:

> The whore was only too willing to do her business. I recall all and it thrills me. There was no scream when I cut. I was more than vexed when the head would not come off. I believe I will need more strength next time. I struck deep into her. I regret I never had the cane, it would have been a delight to have rammed it hard into her. The bitch opened like a ripe peach. I have decided next time I will rip all out. My medicine will give me strength and the thought of the whore and her whoring master will spur me on no end.

This reveals an incredibly sparse knowledge of Polly Nichols' death scene. The writer has no knowledge of the frustrating absence of blood nor the bruises that indicate her mouth was clutched from behind and she was laid down forcibly, not willingly.

Liz Stride is included as a victim and an interesting bit inspired by popular folklore follows: "I would have dearly loved to have cut the head of the damned horse off and stuff it as far as it would go down the whores [sic] throat. I had no time to rip the bitch wide, I curse my bad luck. I believe the thrill of being caught thrilled me more than cutting the whore herself. As I write I find it impossible to believe he [Diemshutz] did not see me, in my estimation I was less than a few feet from him. The fool panicked, it is what saved me. My satisfaction was far from complete, damn the bastard, I cursed him and cursed him, but I was clever, they could not out do me. No one ever will. Within the quarter of the hour I found another dirty bitch willing to sell her wares [Eddowes]. The whore like all the rest was only too willing."

Only popular folklore had Diemshutz interrupting the Ripper at Dutfield's Yard. From the flow of blood this is impossible. Yet "Maybrick the Ripper," if the diary is to be believed, is inspired by such an idea and even wants to shove Diemshutz's horse's head down Stride's throat.

An even worse mistake is that the writer of the journal believes the Ripper wrote the letters to the Central News, a belief widely held until the 1970s when research started turning up the evidence that Scotland Yard believed Bulling had done it. "That should give the fools a laugh," the writer of the journal says, "it has done so for me, wonder if they have enjoyed the name I have given? I said it would be on the lips of all, and indeed it is. Believe I will send another. Include my funny little rhyme. That will convince them that it is the truth I tell."

In short, the Maybrick Journal exposes itself as being written by an uninformed hand molded only by popular renditions.

On June 27, 1994, Barrett confessed to having made the forgery. The next day his attorneys withdrew his confession, saying he was not in possession of his faculties at the time he made it. Since that time, Barrett has confessed and retracted again.

But how old is the journal's writing? There is some question whether the journal was forged decades before. The diary had actually belonged to Bill Graham. His daughter, Anne Graham, admits seeing it in 1968, but did not express much interest in it. Bill Graham says he first saw it on leave during WWII in 1943. The diary had been left to him by his grandmother. But was it already annotated then? The first 48 pages of the old journal are cut away. The pages on which "Maybrick" wrote his compromising entries show signs of gum and glue as if pictures had once been attached.

The forgery itself could be quite old. Some of the entries, in fact, reflect Marie Belloc Lowndes' *The Lodger*, the first bestseller to capitalize on the Ripper killings (and has been made into at least 4 films thereafter). It is perhaps the first to truly cash-in on the Ripper mystique as a Simon Pure who went around killing whores. He stayed in a flat and nightly went out to roam the streets. The entire plot of the journal reflects this scenario. In the journal, "Maybrick" notes how he took a room on Middlesex Street and went about each night until Whitechapel was familiar to him.

How old then is the journal? Could it be a sick hoax from the 1920s? Did the hoaxer have to cut the first 48 pages out, as those identified the journal ownership with someone who could not possibly have been the Ripper? In order to perpetuate a hoax, a clever hoaxer would need an old journal and paper.

Soon after the Press furor about the journal's discovery, a watch also conveniently emerged. This watch supposedly had belonged to Maybrick. Behind the inner works on the inside casing was the signature *J. Maybrick* and "I am Jack." There then follow the initials of the five "canonical" victims. This in itself should have raised eyebrows, as the "canon" comes with no justification whatsoever.

No one seems able to agree about the watch either. Various tests have disputed the authenticity of the initials based on age residue. But the gross errors, indeed traceable errors, in the journal plainly tell us that Maybrick had nothing to do with being Jack the Ripper. Nor did the person who wrote the journal.

After "Ripper fever" in 1988— the centenary— many writers came forward with suspects. Melvin Harris would prove to be a prolific theorist. He was certain that Robert D'Onston Stephenson, a dissipated Bohemian who claimed many dubious distinctions, was the ultimate candidate. He was supposedly educated in medicine in Germany, New York and Paris. It is provable that he was in Whitechapel at the times of the murders. However, he was in the London Hospital trying to recoup from neurasthenia (or perhaps alcoholism). Harris posits that Stephenson could have gotten out at nights to roam Whitechapel, knowing that being an inmate of the hospital was the perfect cover. He could even have faked his illness so as to be in the hospital and be above suspicion. He was then free to roam Whitechapel and kill drabs according to black magic ritual. Stephenson was known to have associated with occultists and believed in black magic. Harris developed a fairly complex theory about the position of the murder sites (once again, of only the canonical 5). Supposedly they formed a cross, and therewith the murderer, engaging in black magic, desecrated the most hallowed Christian symbol.

In essence, with this knowledge it could only have been someone like Stephenson.

Problems with Harris' theory were immediately present. For instance, Stephenson was 47 years old, a bit too old to be the Ripper. Stephenson really wasn't sober enough to lift a dog's tail let alone a knife. Inspector Roots, who knew him personally, said he had been a heavy drinker and carried drugs to sober himself up and "stave off delirium tremens." Stephenson's mental processes at the time can be appreciated by his own attempt at amateur sleuthing. He not only wrote to the City Police offering the theory that "Juwes" could be "juives" (French for Jewesses), he proposed the same theory in December's *Pall Mall Gazette*. The logic of "the Jewesses are the *men* that will not be blamed for nothing" was no doubt something that didn't strike most as very clever.

Stephenson began to suspect one of the doctors at the hospital, Dr. Morgan Davies. Each night he visited Stephenson's ward-mate, Dr. Evans, who was also recuperating. On one occasion Davies reenacted what he believed to be the Ripper's MO in the Kelly case. Apparently, he believed that the Ripper sodomized Mary Kelly and cut her throat while behind her. When W.T. Stead, editor at the *Pall Mall*, informed Stephenson that the Ripper did just that with Mary Kelly, Stephenson was sure Davies was the killer. From the actual data, even the minimal amount of information that came out at Macdonald's inquest, Stead's scenario is patently impossible. Obviously Davies and Stephenson had no firsthand knowledge of the crime scenes. The whole notion probably stemmed from Stead to begin with.

What is worse for Harris' theory is that Stephenson can be confirmed as having been a member of the Currie Ward at the hospital. Jonathan Evans, the curator of the London Hospital Museum, confirmed in 2007 (to Mike Covell) that such patients were not allowed to leave the hospital at night. Although this was good for putting the final nail in the coffin of an absurd theory and suspect, it should not have been necessary for anyone who had studied the crime scenes and knew of Stephenson's genuine ignorance of the actual layouts. Jewesses as the *men* is another clue to his poor deductive methods. Modern detectives would probably recognize the typical nutty theorizer they have to deal with after a crime spree finally comes to the news. Scotland Yard eventually probably thought the same.

Murderer Frederick Deeming is a classic case of how quickly facts can be forgotten and replaced with hype and hyperbole. Visitors to Scotland Yard for long were shown his death mask (taken after hanging in 1892) as the face of Jack the Ripper. Deeming was indeed an insane fellow, probably driven that way from syphilis. He murdered his first wife and 4 children by cutting their throats, and then he did the same to his second wife. But during the time of the Whitechapel Murders in 1888 Deeming was most definitely in South Africa. He perhaps had helped to confuse the issue. While in prison he added himself to the list of twisted boasters by telling fellow inmates he was indeed the Ripper. They no doubt told the guards at one point. He had, truly, a sick mind.

Seemingly one of the most outlandish but curious suspects is the infamous Dr. Pedachenko. He burst upon the suspect list in 1928 in the book *Things I Know* by true crime and international spy/gossip writer William La Queux. The scurrilous Pedachenko is said by Le Queux to have been assigned by the Czar's secret police organizations, Okhrana, to infiltrate London and discredit the Metropolitan Police by causing unfathomable crimes. Supposedly, Russian secret police felt that the British government in general was too tolerant of radical anti-Czarist Russian immigrants. This only allowed London to become a hive of anti-Czarist plotters and revolutionaries. Pedachenko, a galloping loony, with medical education to some extent, was the perfect man for the plot. He had with him an assistant, known only by the sinister sobriquet of "Levitski," and a tailoress Jewess known only as Wineberg.

With their help Pedachenko was the scourge of London and the truth behind Jack the Ripper. After his success, he fled to France and thence to Russia. He was supposedly so crazy that he tried to kill a Russian woman. The Russian police caught him and hustled him off to Siberia for life.

Le Queux, of course, was known for tall tales, and this appears to be one of them. He has made Pedachenko the most wonderful anachronistic criminal. The entire plot that Le Queux dreamed up or embellished is possible only in a tumultuous world post the 1917 bolshy revolution. It would have little merit in 1888 (although Okhrana did stalk and break up anti-Czarist groups abroad). Le Queux even cuts in some of the darker figures of the late Russian empire, citing Rasputin as one of the sources for the information.

In the hands of Donald McCormick the plot grew more intricate. His book, *The Identity of Jack the Ripper* (1959), was the first to ride to more success than it deserved due to Farson's broadcast. He fingers Pedachenko and his comrades and goes into greater detail. Supposedly, "Pedachenko" was the alias of none other than Severin Klosowski AKA George Chapman, the man who poisoned a number of wives to death, the very same man whom Abberline believed fit the profile required to be the Ripper. McCormick even goes beyond this and gives Pedachenko another alias. He supposedly was one and the same with Vassily Konovalov, the notorious murderer of Parisian women in 1886.

Although McCormick cites certain sources, including Dr. Dutton's *Chronicles of Crime*, there really is no credible source for the elaborate criminal pedigree he gives Pedachenko. More than one Ripperologist has tried to backtrack his work and failed or ended up exposing much of his work as fabrication.

The penchant to fib must explain his unusual vignette about Albert Bachert. McCormick claimed that Backert had been told by Scotland Yard in March 1889 that they believed the Ripper was dead, having drowned in the Thames. Backert could never divulge this to anybody because in order to be given this exclusive bit of chat he had to swear an oath and never betray it. There is no seasoned Ripperologist who could possibly ever believe this. It contradicts many known facts. It contradicts Macnaghten's own words that the information suggesting Druitt came some years later; it contradicts the major investigators who still thought that McKenzie and later Coles were Ripper victims; and it overlooks that Backert himself made a big ta-do at the Coles Inquest, a sorry show that was unnecessary if he was sure the Ripper was dead in the Thames almost two years before.

In *The Medical Murderer* (1957), Robert Furneaux writes of a St. Petersburg doctor named Dmitri Panchenko who was involved in several poisonings. When this came to Ripperologists' attention, there was some wonder if this could be the thin origin of Dr. Pedachenko. The problem with this is that in 1995 Ripperologist John Pope de Locksley discovered in the *Almanac de Gotha* the names Le Major-Generals Levitski and Pedachenko listed consecutively. *Almanac de Gotha* was the definitive and respected directory of Europe's royalty, leading aristocracy and citizens. So it seems indisputable that two such men with those names existed. But being from some grand backgrounds, it seems unlikely they themselves were involved in hands-on murder in the ghetto of London. But are these names the inspiration for Le Queux's embellishments and McCormick's fabrication?

Neither authors' claims have any foundation. Murdering a few harlots is not going to bring down the British government. Also, like with the other theories that hinge on the murders creating an uproar, it presupposes that the murders will get the appropriate Press coverage, which no one could guarantee beforehand.

The closest suggestion that Le Queux's plot has any support can be found only if believing Israel Schwartz's story. According to him, two men were involved in molesting Stride before she was found murdered. One of the men was referred to as "Lipski," the name of a notorious killer in the area who had already been hung after a celebrated trial. Since Schwartz had a heavy accent, and that "p," "v," and "b" are often confused as sounds, the name called out could have been "Levitski." Thus it could have been Pedachenko calling to Levitski.

Hypothesis non fingo should probably also apply to such famous culprits as Severin Klosowksi AKA George Chapman. What evidence is there for this famous poisoner of women except that he lived in the area of Cable Street in Whitechapel at the time of the canonical murders? Others have proposed an Hungarian named Alois Szemeredy who supposedly killed women in Argentina in the same way. Yet he was clearly described by local authorities as tall and corpulent, which eliminates him as the 5' 7" shabby genteel Ripper. A dark Russian named Nicholas Vassily was suspected at the time and even fingered in *The Horrors of Whitechapel* by Samuel Hudson in 1888, but there is little proof he even existed.

The evidence in the Jack the Ripper case is not a tangled web. It is consistent and often impressively suggests a ruthless, premeditated killer with other motives and ulterior goals than merely eliminating old hags. It gets convoluted only when introducing suspects.

After browsing the words of those who were closest to it all, then the words of those who theorized over the century since, we know only one thing. None of the prime suspects fit the evidence. Despite flouting patterns and revealing clumsy opportunism, Jack the Ripper was clever enough so that he slipped away cleanly.

Quite obviously there has never been enough information, even contemporarily in 1888, to ever bring any individual to arrest let alone to trial. The failure of 125 years of attempting to find a solution underscores for us the words of Inspector Abberline: that Scotland Yard hadn't a clue. We have to be honest with ourselves and admit this applies to all who have followed. We must accept that we do not have a viable suspect, nor have we ever.

Failure should not deter us, however; it should redirect us. There is no onus in any theorist having been wrong. But we must put from our mind any bias, urban legends and folklore. Going back and restarting with the actual facts and sequence of events will collectively give us the sense of how to continue the search for the true identity of the most famous villain in history.

16

THE IDENTITY GAME

THE IDENTITY OF Jack the Ripper can only be approached along one pathway. He left 2 signatures — the intentional one and that which was the result of his mistakes and his actions in trying to cover those mistakes. Along with the context of the crimes, his signature and his eraser give us the one contemporary window into his motive and into the character responsible.

One of the key chronological events is the first. I'm not attempting to be droll. The murder of Martha Tabram can be interpreted only 2 different ways, and both form different foundations to build upon. Either she *was* or she was *not* the victim of the Ripper. Those in favor of throwing her off the list note that her throat was not cut nor her uterus taken whereas those who believe she represents the actual first victim note the unusual stealth of the killer and the fact there simply was no motive other than murder and mystery. If she was the first, then the Ripper sought to kill drunken middle-aged drabs and create mystery for his own thrill. If she wasn't, then the Ripper dovetailed on the phenomenal popularity her mystery murder created. He had then an ulterior motive for the murders.

The first gives us the simple scenario. Without any frills or fancies, Harry Cox's profile basically sums it up, and it tends to reflect the general opinion of the London police. "The

murderer was a misogynist, who at some time or another had
been wronged by a woman. And the fact that his victims were
of the lowest class proves, I think, that he was not, as has
been stated, an educated man who had suddenly gone mad.
He belonged to their own class."

In the simple scenario, this woman-hater begins with
Tabram and from there, intoxicated with the bloodlust of revenge, perfects his *modus operandi.*

A few of the obvious nuances in the Ripper crime spree
can also be incorporated into the simple scenario, with only
minor explanations needed. For instance, evolving events that
tumultuous autumn confirm for us the Ripper's undeniable
opportunistic nature. He capitalized on anti-Semitism when
he saw he could; then a national upheaval when that was suggested. In short, he really confused his identity and his motive. Ultimately, he was able to do what he wanted: kill
strumpets and get his thrill, and by changing diabolical goals
he merely covered his trail and misled police as to what type
of man he truly was.

This is the simple scenario. It gives us a demented thrill
killer. This is how a district attorney would clean it up. A district attorney doesn't want a tangled case. A DA knows that
in trying to throw a rope around too many and too much you
basically end up with a cross-eyed judge and jury; the result
is you may even fail to convict the suspect on trial.

Wisdom says go with the simplest scenario. But simple is
not always the truth. Life is not dictated by the courtroom
necessities of a prosecutor. There are grays and shadows and
levels of moral culpability. There are aspects and nuances of
the Ripper's crime spree that don't add up. The actual crime
scene evidence, and the evolving crime spree, in fact, indicates
a murderer who did not kill Martha Tabram but was rather
inspired by the phenomenal press accorded to the murder because of the unfathomable mystery of its setting.

This is the complex scenario: Although Martha Tabram's
murder can suggest a sexual killer getting revenge or a thrill,
there is nothing in the Ripper's actual crime spree—the "canonical 5"— that indicates a sexual killer motivated by some
thrill. The lower abdominal mutilations in Nichols can, in
fact, be viewed as only a feint to draw a parallel to Tabram's

pointless and brutal slaying and in doing so draw attention away from the actual motive for Nichols' murder: the fact that Nichols was actually missing something— blood. Nichols had a separate 4 inch slice in her neck, and there was only a little puddle of blood by her neck.

Not only does the above indicate that Jack the Ripper started out with an ulterior motive, his entire modus operandi that Fall displays how killing the harlots was only a means to an end. He was, to put it mildly, hasty to get the killings over. It is very well-established that Jack the Ripper never sexually accosted any of his victims. He killed like a humane butcher. Most of his victims didn't even know what happened to them. It's only with Annie Chapman that something must have gone wrong. For whatever reason, she must have suddenly refused him. He choked her insensible. Then like the others a quick deep slit sent her away instantly. The others weren't choked. The bruise marks were those of a single hand tightly holding the mouth shut and jaw steady. There was no torture. There was no time for it. There was too much risk in a public place. In short, the Ripper was brisk to do business. This helped inspire Wynne Baxter to speculate that the Ripper was indeed really doing business— intent on garnering 20 quid a pop from a rich American benefactor.

Baxter's theory is an improbable explanation, but his classification of the Ripper as a postmortem man may have been accurate. In fact, Baxter might have been too close. Was the skilled evisceration in Chapman's case a mistake on the Ripper's part? In the next victim (Eddowes), the lack of skill is simply too noticeable. Pointless and hurried mutilations now become a part of the gory murder scene. The uterus is not so neatly taken, but the kidney is. Were the mutilations designed by the murderer as a feint to cover his skill? Was the uterus taken needlessly in order to draw the scent to Baxter's theory? If so, then the object was the kidney.

The skill in Chapman's murder, that undeniable apotheosis, was a mistake. The Ripper's taking of petty rings and emptying the purse was a vain gesture to cover his skill. The slices in Nichols' lower abdomen were a far better cover. There it worked. But the petty thieving with Chapman didn't.

Yet all cases are linked by a complex series of contrasts

with one overriding theme: the desire to display his murders but paradoxically to cover any deeper motive. It was only when his level of skill was publically broached that he went out of his way to graphically mutilate.

While the Ripper disguised his surgical skill in the later murders, his careful pre-planning remained the same. He prevented blood from spurting. He made sure the victims were in positions so as to prevent any chance he might soil himself and leave a trail. Despite all the social and political opportunism by which the Ripper embossed his later killings, these two points of his signature remain consistent in all the victims except Kelly's, where it was not necessary to prevent spurting in the indoors environment.

The portrait this gives us is of someone who is remarkably careful to leave no trace whatsoever. This means he intended to kill in public, in darkness, and he intended to fetch certain organs. He had anatomical knowledge and surgical skill. It is overtly displayed in Chapman's and Eddowes' guttings, but more subtly displayed in his knowledge of the carotid artery— he cut Stride's throat in pitch darkness— and in how he bled Nichols. His latter killings also show us a man who is repeatedly trying to cover the horrible mistake he made in dissecting Chapman so neatly.

From the collective evidence, we have a profile of Jack the Ripper:

Psychologically, we know he was careful, cool, and cold-blooded. He was rightfully condemned in the papers as a "monomaniac," someone who obsesses on one thing. In his case, it was perfecting the clueless, supernatural appearance of his murder scenes. However helter-skelter he made the butchery of his later victims look, his careful planning and staging never altered.

Physically, he was clerkly, soft spoken, didn't give the appearance he did manual labor, and seemed educated to some extent. He was foreign looking, dark, about 5 foot 7 inches. He had a few peculiarities. He never cut clothes. He carefully unbuttoned them or pulled them apart. He was "shabby genteel" and had the unusual habit of wearing a deerstalker hat.

This last fact is an enormous clue. In an urban environment, this is an attention-grabbing hat. Yet he walked away cleanly, not only from the gruesome scene, but ghostly from the entire neighborhood. No one reported any bloke strolling along any of the streets wearing a deerstalker hat. Did he wear this uncouth bit of headgear only when stalking his game? If this is so, it certainly symbolized his attitude toward his victims; they were mere animals to be shrewdly hunted.

More tangibly, however, it would mean that after he killed them he tucked the deerstalker into his jacket or coat and pulled out another, less conspicuous hat. It would have to be some pliable hat like a cheesecutter or single peak cloth cap. If his hands were covered with blood and guts, he could not avoid soiling his deerstalker. That would make the hat worthless after each killing. He would have to wear a different one next time. It is interesting to note that two victims were seen just before they were killed talking to a man wearing a deerstalker. On each occasion it appears to be the same man, but the deerstalkers are different. The first was brown; the second was dark felt.

Unless he wiped his hands on the deerstalker to clean them, the soiling of the deerstalker when taking it off might also apply to any other hat he might put on. Therefore he might not have worn a hat at all while strolling away down the streets. This, too, would be unusual. Reports of a man seen in the vicinity *not* wearing a hat would have proven a valuable lead.

However, one must consider all angles. The description of the brown deerstalker could be a mistake on Wynne Baxter's part when he summed up the Chapman case. In actual testimony, Elizabeth Long described the hat as dark felt, just as Constable Smith would describe the deerstalker on the man seen with Stride. The Ripper therefore might consistently have worn the same deerstalker. It is hard to imagine that the Ripper did not use gloves when butchering Chapman. He then could have removed the gloves and removed the deerstalker without soiling it, and then walked away without a hat or with a different one on his head. One thing is certain. He did not wear this style of hat at any other time.

In whichever scenario, put the above together and the Ripper seems a far more complex character than merely a low class man trying to get even with prostitutes because he had been wronged or because he had contracted syphilis from one. We must also remember that poor but honest women walked along the streets at vulnerable hours—Elizabeth Long, for instance— and were never attacked. The Ripper killed only the dregs. He was not a poor man getting even with poor women. He killed what he considered the expendable. He killed the only type of woman he could get in a vulnerable position so he could quickly dispatch them.

But what could have been his ultimate motive? If he did not kill Tabram, then the ulterior motive must be encrypted into his first 2 victims, Nichols and Chapman. Mystery, yes, was both a requirement and a cover, but what did the taking of blood, a uterus with navel attached, then with the later victims, kidney, and heart signify?

A few points above raise a topic I personally do not care for but cannot avoid— conspiracy. Stride's murder, despite being most at odds with the Ripper's style, was preceded by her being seen with a man who roughly fit the description Elizabeth Long gave for the "shabby genteel" man talking with Chapman. Eddowes, on the other hand, though butchered similarly to the earlier victims, was seen with a man described radically different. If two murders were not preplanned that night by two men in concert then it indicates that Eddowes' was an impromptu stand-in to make up for failing with Stride. This would also mean that more than one man was involved and that it was necessary that a murder was committed, and an organ taken, on this *particular* date. This conjures up the occult, rituals, and so many other things that, although Victorians were certainly into the black arts, is far beyond the scope of this work to go into in detail.

Nevertheless, a few points deserve to be raised here. I don't need to itemize the number of Ripperologists who have expressed suspicion about George Hutchinson's actions on the night of Mary Kelly's murder. But his own account strikes a fishy chord. According to him, he watched outside Miller's Court to see what would happen. This doesn't make a lot of sense, since he couldn't see anything from where he stood and he didn't even bother to remain the whole time. What's the point of the half effort? Tangibly, all we know for sure is that he knew he had been observed (by Sarah Lewis).

Was his statement to the police a cover for being at Miller's Court? Was he, in fact, covering for the murderer? His description of the "Gaudy Jew" is that of a burlesque villain, not a real life person. It also capitalizes on the latest attempts to promote the Ripper as a Jew.

It is also interesting to note that if Polly Nichols was killed on the spot and bled, it would have taken more than one man to do it. It is impossible to hold a woman's mouth shut and jab a knife in her neck and direct the blood into a receptacle. It would take a third hand to hold the latter. Either she was indeed killed elsewhere and her body dumped on Buck's Row, or it seems a third hand was involved.

This second scenario, as we can see, is much more complex, with many potential layers that can make it very convoluted. Some of the evidence bears it out. A warped but complex individual could have taken advantage of Tabram's sensational murder to gain national attention for one or more ulterior motives. . .or to even cover his own trail and occult motives for which the murders of expendable dregs was deemed necessary.

However provocative an occult conspiracy might be, or an individual with a warped ulterior motive, this second scenario cannot wholly explain the murders that took place after the "autumn of terror." By the time McKenzie was murdered, in disturbing similarity to the Ripper's style, 8 months had gone by. Nothing was taken from her, so that some underlying ritual is not evident. Evidence doesn't suggest the killer was interrupted. Nor did another victim fall prey that same night to make up for the lack of retrieving an organ from McKenzie. There was no social wave the killing could ride. Even though the upper echelons of Scotland Yard seemed to have believed that Jack the Ripper was responsible, a mystery murder no longer interested the public and the Press as much.

The first scenario can explain all the killings. The first scenario gives us a deranged but clever killer who starts with Tabram and grows intoxicated over the publicity and his success at outwitting an entire empire. Over the spree he adds more motives to stir up more mayhem. After Kelly he took a long break, and tried again with McKenzie and maybe even Coles. He might then have been committed, died, or simply quit when the murders no longer presented any great public ponder.

The second and more complex scenario can only explain the autumn of terror. When Mary Kelly's murder truly fails to unsettle the government (beyond the public's perceived ousting of Warren), the crimes cease. Or, the occult ritual is complete with the taking of a heart. The other murders are committed by very clever imitators, and in the case of Coles by a very calm one who simply walked away into the night.

Is the reality the anticlimax provided by Sir Robert Anderson? Not Kosminski. Not the poor, demented hairdresser. But is Jacob Levy the reality behind this? He had feelings of being exalted. This might have prompted the vain attempt at gentility with the deerstalker. But how could he have gone unnoticed by those who knew him? Or is even he a mistake? Was Robert Sagar's actual suspect even Jewish? Was there a Gentile butcher who lived on Butcher's Row who was a part of a greater occult conspiracy? Or, even more possible, were they all wrong?

We must remember that eponymous is indeed the fact of the moniker. We do not know who Jack the Ripper was. He must be allowed to devolve from the theories that have come forward. We must let him return to the image of the shadowy man in the dark coat and deerstalker hat. We must let him speak only through his crimes, the clues, the context.

It seems certain that this shadow never made contact with the public, Press or police, except through his crimes. He was not a grandstander swinging carrots before the police via literary means. He left his motive(s) up to inference. With this, naturally, came more terror. No one knew why he did what he did. But they knew where. He limited himself to a confined area of Spitalfields and Whitechapel. This argues for the correctness of the City C.I.D. view that the killer had the use of several establishments in the area, be they butcher or tailor or candlestick maker shops.

But this does not mean he was one of the dregs himself. If he was, would he not then be recognizable to the local streetwalkers? How could he put on the airs of "shabby genteel" and not be laughed at by those who recognized him? Would not many, whether streetwalkers or honest merchants, recognize him walking about wearing a deerstalker on the nights in question? Shouldn't the Ripper's anonymity indicate some kind of cover, assistant, or, if not the hideaway of various shops, even a coach nearby?

It is more difficult today to appreciate the East End of 1888 and with this the true context of the crimes. The earliest serious "Ripperologists" in the 1960s could still walk on the same sets (cobblestones) as the Ripper and appreciate the narrow streets and hear the same reverberations off the old weathered brick buildings. Old East Enders could still recall firsthand accounts of the Ripper. A few could still remember the crimes. The body of the East End dictated the mystery. Shoulder to shoulder buildings stood. Alleys make wonderful, moody backdrops in movies, but in reality they were few and far between. If one didn't follow the narrow streets, they had to move through buildings.

It was impossible not to be impressed by the Ripper's stealth and knowledge of Whitechapel. The original environment impressed all who partook of it. The crime spree simply could not have been spontaneous nor the work of an impulsive fiend. The Ripper, if he did live in Whitechapel, could have walked easily through the City of London and killed elsewhere. He could have murdered all victims indoors. But he didn't. He limited himself to more dangerous ground, to narrow streets, reverberating courtyards and backyards, dark nights and the dregs of the streets. Standing in the narrow confines of the streets or the boxlike Mitre Square imposes upon one how preplanned and rehearsed the killing locations and the escape route were. The murders were designed to take place in the streets, not in parks, the West End, or the Thames. They were meant for Whitechapel and Spitalfields. They were meant to be mysteries and they were carefully preplanned.

Although the spirit of the Ripper survives, it survives in cinema and in books. It is growing thin in the East End. Now 125 years the dust of time has blown over Whitechapel. It has covered or swept away all the evidence. Urban renewal has done more than the Blitz. All the buildings at the crime scenes have come down; the cottages at Buck's Row (Durward Street) in the 1980s; Essex Wharf, gutted and forlorn, was the last to go in the 1990s. The wrecking ball did for 29 Hanbury and all the buildings along that side, though the opposite side remains intact and updated for modern business. Mitre Square retains its name and the cobblestones trace its original space, but all the buildings are gone, and the boxlike cubicle is more a purposeless space. Dorset Street is long gone, plus other haunts like Flower and Dean Street. Streets today are packed with parked cars and cut with deep shadows of glass high rises that obscure small groves of remaining Victorian buildings turned into something chic. The orderliness of Victorian streets is gone. Incongruity and ruined spaces result. Amidst this, the setting of the crimes and the ingenuity of the perpetrator is hard to fathom. But the name of Jack the Ripper remains. To go over his crimes in detail is to give body to that spirit again. It is to show how genuinely diabolical and enigmatic he was.

Police in the 20th century were not naïve about the lengths to which human ingenuity would go to commit mystery crimes. Documentation has given the criminologist a vast storehouse of precedence. But in the Ripper's day it was unique. He was the first. It would be as fascinating to learn of his original motive as it would be to learn his identity. Ingenuity was praised by the Victorians. It was the Age of Progress. The greatest mystery about the Whitechapel Murders is why they were the first. They came out of nowhere and stopped with equal mystery. The profile of the man who did them is merely assumption. Despite theories and pet suspects, the ultimate outcome of his work is the only remaining fact. With this he succeeded in creating an open verdict.

BIBLIOGRAPHY

Among the sources consulted to write this work, the author would like to list *inter alia* for recommended reading:

Begg, Paul,
Fido, Martin, &
 Skinner, Keith: *The Complete Jack the Ripper A to Z,*
                                John Blake, 2010.

Cornwall, Patricia,   *Portrait Of A Killer: Jack The Ripper — Case
                   Closed,*   Berkley, 2003.

Cullen, Tom,   *Autumn of Terror,*   The Bodley Head, London,
                                                    1965.

Evans, S. P. and Skinner, K.   *The Ultimate Jack the Ripper
                   Sourcebook,*
                   Constable and Robinson, London, 2001.

Evans, Stewart & Gainey, Paul: *Jack the Ripper: First American
                   Serial Killer,*
                   Kodansha American, Inc., 1996.

Fido, Martin,   *The Crimes, Detection and Death of Jack
                   the Ripper,*   Barnes & Noble, 1993.

Harris, Melvin.   *Jack the Ripper The Bloody Truth,* Columbus,
                                          London, 1987.
 "   "   *The True Face of Jack the Ripper,*
                   Michael O' Mara, London, 1997.

House, Robert,   *Jack the Ripper and the Case for Scotland
                   Yard's Number One Suspect,* John Wiley &
                   Sons, Hoboken, New Jersey, 2011.

Hudson, Sam'l E.   *Leather Apron: The Horrors of Whitechapel,*
                   Town Printing House, Philadelphia, 1888.

Knight, Stephen,   *Jack the Ripper: The Final Solution,* Academy
                              Chicago Publishers, 1986.

Macnaghten, Sir Melville Leslie,   *Days of My Years,* Longman,
                              Green & Co., New York,
                              Edward Arnold, London, 1914.

Paley, Bruce,   *Jack the Ripper: The Simple Truth,* Trafal-
                              gar Square Publishing, 1997.

Odell, Robin,   *Jack the Ripper in Fact and Fiction,* George
                              Harrap & Co. LTD., London, 1965.

Rumbelow, Donald,   *The Complete Jack the Ripper*, New
                              York Graphic Society, Boston,
                              Mass., 1975.

"   "   *Jack the Ripper: The Complete Casebook,*
                              Berkeley, 1990.

South Eastern Middlesex, Division of: Inquest into the death of
Martha Tabram on August 7, 1888, George Collier, assistant coroner, presiding.

South Eastern Middlesex, Division of: Inquest into the death of
Mary Ann Nichols aka Polly Nichols on August 31, 1888, coroner
Wynne E. Baxter presiding.

South Eastern Middlesex, Division of for Whitechapel and Spitalfields: Inquest into the death of Anne Chapman on September 8,
1888; Wynne E. Baxter, presiding.

South Eastern Middlesex, Division of: Inquest into the death of
Elizabeth Stride on September 30, 1888, Wynne E Baxter, coroner,
presiding.

London, City and Corporation of: Inquest into the death of Catherine Eddowes on September 30, 1888, Samuel Langham, coroner,
presiding.

Westminster, Division of: Inquest into unidentified remains of a woman found on October 2, 1888; John Troutbeck, coroner, presiding.

Northeastern Middlesex, Division of, for Hoxton and Hackney, Inquest into the death of Mary Jane Kelly on November 9 or thereabouts, 1888, Dr. Roderick Macdonald, coroner, presiding.

South Eastern Middlesex, Division of, Inquest into the death of Catherine Mylett on December 20, 1888; Wynne E. Baxter, coroner, presiding.

South Eastern Middlesex, Division of: Inquest into the death of Alice McKenzie on July 17, 1889, Wynne Baxter, coroner, presiding.

South Eastern Middlesex, Division of: Inquest into remains of an unidentified woman found on September 10, 1889; presiding: Wynne Baxter, corner.

South Eastern Middlesex, Division of: Inquest into the death of Frances Coles on February 13, 1891; presiding Wynne E. Baxter, coroner.

Various inquests for the remains of an unidentified woman found between June 4 and June 12, 1889, in Battersea, Wapping, Westminster, Greater London; A. Braxton Hicks, coroner for Mid-Surrey; John Troutbeck, coroner of Westminster, and Wynne Baxter, coroner for South Eastern Middlesex, presiding (collectively known as The Thames Mystery).

Press Reports:

Daily News: 1888, 8 August; 10 August; 15 August; 24 August; 1 September; 18 September; 24 September; 3 September; 4 September; 5 September; 7 September; 10 September; 11 September; 12 September; 13 September; 14 September; 15 September; 17 September; 20 September; 22 September; 26 September; 27 September; 1 October; 2 October; 3 October; 4 October; 6 October; 8 October; 9 October; 12 October; 16 October; 23 October; 24 October; 10 November; 12 November; 13 November; 14 November;

15 November; 16 November; 19 November; 20 November; 22 December; 24 December; 25 December; 26 December; 28 December.

Daily Telegraph: 1888, 1 September; 10 September; 18 September; 19 September; 24 September; 3 September; 4 September; 10 September; 11 September; 13 September; 14 September; 19 September; 20 September; 22 September; 27 September; 2 October; 24 October; 3 October; 4 October; 5 October; 6 October; 9 October; 12 October; 18 October; 19 October; 10 November; 12 November; 13 November; 16 November; 20 July.

East London Advertiser, 1888: 11 August; 18 August; 25 August; 1 September; 22 September; 29 September; 8 September; 15 September; 22 September; 29 September; 6 October; 13 October; 27 October; 17 November; 24 November; 29 December; 1889: 17 August; 14 September; 21 September; 28 September; 1891: 14 February; 21 February; 28 February; 7 March.

East London Observer, 1888: 11 August; 18 August; 25 August; 1 September; 22 September; 8 September; 15 September; 22 September; 6 October; 13 October; 10 November; 17 November; 1889: 12 January; 14 September; 28 September; 1891: 14 February; 21 February; 28 February; 28 March.

Echo, 1888: 10 August; 13 August; 15 August; 17 August; 23 August; 7 August; 9 August; 1 September; 17 September; 3 September; 31 August; 4 September; 5 September; 6 September; 10 September; 11 September; 12 September; 13 September; 14 September; 19 September; 26 September; 8 September; 1 October; 2 October; 3 October; 5 October; 4 October; 10 October; 15 October; 16 October; 17 October; 18 October; 19 October; 20 October; 22 October; 23 October; 9 November; 10 November; 12 November; 13 November.

London Times, 1888: 1 September; 3 September; 4 September; 18 September; 24 September; 10 September; 11 September; 12 September; 13 September; 14 September; 15 September; 18 September; 20 September; 27 September; 1 October; 2 October; 3 October; 4 October; 6 October; 9 October; 18 October; 19 October; 23 October; 24 October; 10 November; 12 November; 13 November; 14 November; 19 November; 20 November; 22 December; 24 December; 26 December; 29 December; 1889: 3 January; 10 January; 2 July; 26 July; 26 June; 4 July; 5 July; 9 July; 17 July; 18 July; 19 July; 20 July; 22 July; 29 July; 13 August; 12 September; 13 September; 14 September; 25 September; 22 December; 24 December; 25 December; 26 December; 28 December; 29 December; 1889: 10 January; 1891 14 February; 16 February; 18 February; 21 February; 24 February; 27 February; 28 February.

Star, 1888: 31 August; 1 September; 3 September; 4 September; 6 September; 8 September; 10 September; 11 September; 13 September; 14 September; 15 September; 26 September; 27 September; 1 October; 6 October; 9 November; 10 November; 12 November; 13 November; 14 November; 19 November; 24 December.

Morning Advertiser, 1888: 1 October; 2 October; 3 October; 4 October; 5 October; 6 October; 8 October; 9 October; 10 October; 17 October; 18 October; 19 October; 22 October; 23 October; 31 October; 24 October; 10 November; 12 November; 13 November; 15 November; 16 November.

New York Times, 1888: 5 September; 1891: 14 February; 15 February.

Special praise must go to the compilers of the number one online source of official documentation on Jack the Ripper:
www.casebook.org.

www.ingramcontent.com/pod-product-compliance
Lightning Source LLC
Chambersburg PA
CBHW020523270326
41927CB00006B/425